Communications
in Computer and Information Science

T0238945

Editorial Board

Simone Diniz Junqueira Barbosa
  Pontifical Catholic University of Rio de Janeiro (PUC-Rio),
  Rio de Janeiro, Brazil
Phoebe Chen
  La Trobe University, Melbourne, Australia
Alfredo Cuzzocrea
  ICAR-CNR and University of Calabria, Cosenza, Italy
Xiaoyong Du
  Renmin University of China, Beijing, China
Joaquim Filipe
  Polytechnic Institute of Setúbal, Setúbal, Portugal
Orhun Kara
  TÜBİTAK BİLGEM and Middle East Technical University, Ankara, Turkey
Igor Kotenko
  St. Petersburg Institute for Informatics and Automation of the Russian
  Academy of Sciences, St. Petersburg, Russia
Krishna M. Sivalingam
  Indian Institute of Technology Madras, Chennai, India
Dominik Ślęzak
  University of Warsaw and Infobright, Warsaw, Poland
Takashi Washio
  Osaka University, Osaka, Japan
Xiaokang Yang
  Shanghai Jiao Tong University, Shangai, China

More information about this series at http://www.springer.com/series/7899

Mohammad S. Obaidat · Joaquim Filipe (Eds.)

E-Business
and Telecommunications

International Joint Conference, ICETE 2012
Rome, Italy, July 24–27, 2012
Revised Selected Papers

Springer

Editors
Mohammad S. Obaidat
Monmouth University
West Long Branch, NJ
USA

Joaquim Filipe
Polytechnic Institute of Setúbal, INSTICC
Setúbal
Portugal

ISSN 1865-0929   ISSN 1865-0937 (electronic)
ISBN 978-3-662-44790-1   ISBN 978-3-662-44791-8 (eBook)
DOI 10.1007/978-3-662-44791-8

Library of Congress Control Number: 2014948790

Springer Heidelberg New York Dordrecht London

© Springer-Verlag Berlin Heidelberg 2014
This work is subject to copyright. All rights are reserved by the Publisher, whether the whole or part of the material is concerned, specifically the rights of translation, reprinting, reuse of illustrations, recitation, broadcasting, reproduction on microfilms or in any other physical way, and transmission or information storage and retrieval, electronic adaptation, computer software, or by similar or dissimilar methodology now known or hereafter developed. Exempted from this legal reservation are brief excerpts in connection with reviews or scholarly analysis or material supplied specifically for the purpose of being entered and executed on a computer system, for exclusive use by the purchaser of the work. Duplication of this publication or parts thereof is permitted only under the provisions of the Copyright Law of the Publisher's location, in its current version, and permission for use must always be obtained from Springer. Permissions for use may be obtained through RightsLink at the Copyright Clearance Center. Violations are liable to prosecution under the respective Copyright Law.
The use of general descriptive names, registered names, trademarks, service marks, etc. in this publication does not imply, even in the absence of a specific statement, that such names are exempt from the relevant protective laws and regulations and therefore free for general use.
While the advice and information in this book are believed to be true and accurate at the date of publication, neither the authors nor the editors nor the publisher can accept any legal responsibility for any errors or omissions that may be made. The publisher makes no warranty, express or implied, with respect to the material contained herein.

Printed on acid-free paper

Springer is part of Springer Science+Business Media (www.springer.com)

Preface

The present book includes extended and revised versions of a set of selected best papers from the 9th International Joint Conference on e-Business and Telecommunications (ICETE), which was held in July 2012, in Rome, Italy. This conference reflects a continuing effort to increase the dissemination of recent research results among professionals who work in the areas of e-business and telecommunications. ICETE is a joint international conference integrating four major areas of knowledge that are divided into six corresponding conferences: DCNET (Int'l Conf. on Data Communication Networking), ICE-B (Int'l Conf. on e-Business), OPTICS (Int'l Conf. on Optical Communication Systems), SECRYPT (Int'l Conf. on Security and Cryptography), WINSYS (Int'l Conf. on Wireless Information Systems) and SIGMAP (Int'l Conf. on Signal Processing and Multimedia).

The program of this joint conference included several outstanding keynote lectures presented by internationally renowned distinguished researchers who are experts in the various ICETE areas. Their keynote speeches have contributed to heighten the overall quality of the program and significance of the theme of the conference.

The conference topic areas define a broad spectrum in the key areas of e-business and telecommunications. This wide view reporting made ICETE appealing to a global audience of engineers, scientists, business practitioners, ICT managers, and policy experts. The papers accepted and presented at the conference demonstrated a number of new and innovative solutions for e-business and telecommunication networks and systems, showing that the technical problems in these closely related fields are challenging and worthwhile approaching in an interdisciplinary perspective such as that promoted by ICETE.

ICETE 2012 received 403 papers in total, with contributions from 56 different countries, on all continents, which demonstrate its success and global dimension. To evaluate each submission, a double-blind paper evaluation method was used: each paper was blindly reviewed by at least two experts from the International Program Committee. In fact, most papers had 3 reviews or more. The selection process followed strict criteria in all tracks so only 45 papers were accepted and orally presented at ICETE as full papers (11 % of submissions) and 77 as short papers (19 % of submissions). Additionally, 50 papers were accepted for poster presentation.

We hope that you will find this collection of the best ICETE 2012 papers an excellent source of inspiration as well as a helpful reference for research in the aforementioned areas.

December 2013

Mohammad S. Obaidat
Joaquim Filipe

Organization

Conference Chair

Mohammad S. Obaidat   Monmouth University, USA

Program Co-chairs

DCNET

Mohammad S. Obaidat   Monmouth University, USA
José Luis Sevillano   University of Seville, Spain
Zhaoyang Zhang   Zhejiang University, China

ICE-B

David Marca   University of Phoenix, USA
Marten van Sinderen   University of Twente, The Netherlands

OPTICS

Jose L. Marzo   University of Girona, Spain
Petros Nicopolitidis   Aristotle University, Greece

SECRYPT

Pierangela Samarati   Università degli Studi di Milano, Italy
Wenjing Lou   Virginia Polytechnic Institute and State University,
                                    USA
Jianying Zhou   Institute for Infocomm Research, Singapore

SIGMAP

Enrique Cabello   Universidad Rey Juan Carlos, Spain
Maria Virvou   University of Piraeus, Greece

WINSYS

Mohammad S. Obaidat	Monmouth University, USA
Rafael Caldeirinha	Polytechnic Institute of Leiria, Portugal
Hong Ji	Beijing University of Post and Telecommunications (BUPT), China
Dimitrios D. Vergados	University of Piraeus, Greece

Organizing Committee

Marina Carvalho	INSTICC, Portugal
Helder Coelhas	INSTICC, Portugal
Bruno Encarnação	INSTICC, Portugal
Andreia Moita	INSTICC, Portugal
Raquel Pedrosa	INSTICC, Portugal
Vitor Pedrosa	INSTICC, Portugal
Cláudia Pinto	INSTICC, Portugal
Susana Ribeiro	INSTICC, Portugal
José Varela	INSTICC, Portugal
Pedro Varela	INSTICC, Portugal

DCNET Program Committee

Julio Barbancho, Spain
Alejandro Linares Barranco, Spain
Fernando Beltrán, New Zealand
Christos Bouras, Greece
Roberto Bruschi, Italy
Christian Callegari, Italy
Periklis Chatzimisios, Greece
Hala ElAarag, USA
Sebastià Galmés, Spain
Katja Gilly, Spain
Abdelhakim Hafid, Canada
Aun Haider, Pakistan
Zbigniew Kalbarczyk, USA
Dimitris Kanellopoulos, Greece
Randi Karlsen, Norway
Abdallah Khreishah, USA
Michael Kounavis, USA
Andy (Zhenjiang) Li, USA
Pascal Lorenz, France
S. Kami Makki, USA

Carlos León de Mora, Spain
Petros Nicopolitidis, Greece
Ibrahim Onyuksel, USA
Elena Pagani, Italy
José Pelegri-Sebastia, Spain
Juan-Carlos Ruiz-Garcia, Spain
José Luis Sevillano, Spain
Hangguan Shan, China
Kenji Suzuki, USA
Vicente Traver, Spain
Pere Vilà, Spain
Luis Javier Garcia Villalba, Spain
Manuel Villen-Altamirano, Spain
Wei Wang, China
Bernd E. Wolfinger, Germany
Hirozumi Yamaguchi, Japan
Zhaoyang Zhang, China
Caijun Zhong, China
Cliff C. Zou, USA

DCNET Auxiliary Reviewer

Nader Chaabouni, Canada

ICE-B Program Committee

Anteneh Ayanso, Canada
Ladjel Belllatreche, France
Morad Benyoucef, Canada
Indranil Bose, India
Rebecca Bulander, Germany
Wojciech Cellary, Poland
Dickson Chiu, China
Soon Chun, USA
Michele Colajanni, Italy
Rafael Corchuelo, Spain
Peter Dolog, Denmark
Yanqing Duan, UK
Erwin Fielt, Australia
José María García, Spain
Andreas Holzinger, Austria
Ela Hunt, Switzerland
Arun Iyengar, USA
Yung-Ming Li, Taiwan
Liping Liu, USA
David Marca, USA

Tokuro Matsuo, Japan
Brian Mennecke, USA
Adrian Mocan, Germany
Ali Reza Montazemi, Canada
Maurice Mulvenna, UK
Daniel O'Leary, USA
Krassie Petrova, New Zealand
Pak-Lok Poon, China
Philippos Pouyioutas, Cyprus
Bijan Raahemi, Canada
Sofia Reino, Spain
Ana Paula Rocha, Portugal
Gustavo Rossi, Argentina
Jarogniew Rykowski, Poland
Marten van Sinderen, The Netherlands
Thompson Teo, Singapore
Michael Weiss, Canada
Qi Yu, USA
Lina Zhou, USA

OPTICS Program Committee

Anjali Agarwal, USA
Víctor López Álvarez, Spain
Adolfo Cartaxo, Portugal
Walter Cerroni, Italy
Jitender Deogun, USA
Marco Genoves, Italy
Masahiko Jinno, Japan
Miroslaw Klinkowski, Poland
Franko Küppers, USA
David Q. Liu, USA
Anna Manolova, Denmark
Jose L. Marzo, Spain

Amalia Miliou, Greece
Petros Nicopolitidis, Greece
Jordi Perelló, Spain
João Rebola, Portugal
Enrique Rodriguez-Colina, Mexico
Sarah Ruepp, Denmark
Mehdi Shadaram, USA
Surinder Singh, India
Wolfgang Sohler, Germany
Salvatore Spadaro, Spain
Naoya Wada, Japan
Changyuan Yu, Singapore

SECRYPT Program Committee

Claudio Ardagna, Italy
Ken Barker, Canada
Carlo Blundo, Italy
David Chadwick, UK
Aldar Chan, Singapore
Ee-chien Chang, Singapore
Yingying Chen, USA
Cheng-Kang Chu, Singapore
Marco Cova, UK
Jorge Cuellar, Germany
Frederic Cuppens, France
Reza Curtmola, USA
Tassos Dimitriou, Greece
Josep Domingo-ferrer, Spain
Eduardo B. Fernandez, USA
Eduardo Fernández-medina, Spain
Alberto Ferrante, Switzerland
Josep-Lluis Ferrer-Gomila, Spain
Simone Fischer-Hübner, Sweden
Sara Foresti, Italy
Keith Frikken, USA
Steven Furnell, UK
Mark Gondree, USA
Dimitris Gritzalis, Greece
Yong Guan, USA
Xinyi Huang, China
Michael Huth, UK
Cynthia Irvine, USA
Sokratis Katsikas, Greece
Stefan Katzenbeisser, Germany
Shinsaku Kiyomoto, Japan
Costas Lambrinoudakis, Greece
Bo Lang, China
Loukas Lazos, USA
Adam J. Lee, USA
Patrick P.C. Lee, Hong Kong
Albert Levi, Turkey
Jiguo Li, China
Ming Li, USA
Giovanni Livraga, Italy
Javier Lopez, Spain
Emil Lupu, UK

Luigi Mancini, Italy
Olivier Markowitch, Belgium
Vashek Matyas, Czech Republic
Carlos Maziero, Brazil
Chris Mitchell, UK
Atsuko Miyaji, Japan
Marco Casassa Mont, UK
David Naccache, France
Guevara Noubir, USA
Eiji Okamoto, Japan
Rolf Oppliger, Switzerland
Stefano Paraboschi, Italy
Gerardo Pelosi, Italy
Günther Pernul, Germany
Raphael C.-w. Phan, UK
Roberto Di Pietro, Italy
Joachim Posegga, Germany
Jian Ren, USA
Kui Ren, USA
Sushmita Ruj, Canada
Gokay Saldamli, Turkey
Pierangela Samarati, Italy
Martin Schläffer, Austria
Miguel Soriano, Spain
Cosimo Stallo, Italy
Neeraj Suri, Germany
Willy Susilo, Australia
Chiu Tan, USA
Juan Tapiador, Spain
Sabrina De Capitani di Vimercati, Italy
Guilin Wang, Australia
Haining Wang, USA
Lingyu Wang, Canada
Xinyuan (Frank) Wang, USA
Osman Yagan, USA
Danfeng Yao, USA
Alec Yasinsac, USA
Shucheng Yu, USA
Futai Zhang, China
Wensheng Zhang, USA
Wen Tao Zhu, China

SECRYPT Auxiliary Reviewers

Onur Aciicmez, USA
Cristina Alcaraz, USA
Andrew Blaich, USA
Abian Blome, Germany
Ning Cao, USA
Richard Chow, USA
Prokopios Drogkaris, Greece
Dimitris Geneiatakis, Greece
Mario Kirschbaum, Austria

Thomas Korak, Austria
David Nuñez, Spain
Martin Ochoa, Germany
Evangelos Reklitis, Greece
Lu Shi, USA
Nikos Vrakas, Greece
Boyang Wang, Canada
Mu-En Wu, Taiwan
Jiawei Yuan, USA

SIGMAP Program Committee

João Ascenso, Portugal
Arvind Bansal, USA
Alejandro Linares Barranco, Spain
Adrian Bors, UK
Enrique Cabello, Spain
Wai-Kuen Cham, China
Chin-Chen Chang, Taiwan
Shu-Ching Chen, USA
Wei Cheng, Singapore
Ryszard S. Choras, Poland
Cristina Conde, Spain
Isaac Martín De Diego, Spain
Rob Evans, Australia
Jianping Fan, USA
Quanfu Fan, USA
Wu-Chi Feng, USA
William Grosky, USA
Malka Halgamuge, Australia
Hermann Hellwagner, Austria
Wolfgang Hürst, The Netherlands
Razib Iqbal, Canada
Mohan Kankanhalli, Singapore
Sokratis Katsikas, Greece
Brigitte Kerherve, Canada
Constantine Kotropoulos, Greece
Tayeb Lemlouma, France
Jing Li, UK

Zhu Liu, USA
Hong Man, USA
Daniela Moctezuma, Spain
Arturo Morgado-Estevez, Spain
Chamin Morikawa, Japan
Alejandro Murua, Canada
Mokhtar Nibouche, UK
Ioannis Paliokas, Greece
Maria Paula Queluz, Portugal
Rudolf Rabenstein, Germany
Matthias Rauterberg, The Netherlands
Pedro Real, Spain
Luis Alberto Morales Rosales, Mexico
Javier Del Ser, Spain
Mei-Ling Shyu, USA
Oscar S. Siordia, Spain
George Tsihrintzis, Greece
Andreas Uhl, Austria
Steve Uhlig, Germany
Maria Virvou, Greece
Michael Weber, Germany
Xiao-Yong Wei, China
Lei Wu, USA
Kim-hui Yap, Singapore
Chengcui Zhang, USA
Tianhao Zhang, USA
Yongxin Zhang, USA

SIGMAP Auxiliary Reviewers

Mariana Lobato Baez, Mexico   Elisavet Konstantinou, Greece
Eduardo López Domínguez, Mexico

WINSYS Program Committee

Ali Abedi, USA   Jehn-Ruey Jiang, Taiwan
Dharma Agrawal, USA   Abdelmajid Khelil, Germany
Vicente Alarcon-Aquino, Mexico   Hsi-pin Ma, Taiwan
Josephine Antoniou, Cyprus   Imad Mahgoub, USA
Francisco Barcelo Arroyo, Spain   S. Kami Makki, USA
Novella Bartolini, Italy   Maja Matijasevic, Croatia
Bert-Jan van Beijnum, The Netherlands   Luis Mendes, Portugal
Luis Bernardo, Portugal   Paul Patras, Ireland
Matthias R. Brust, USA   Symon Podvalny, Russia
Periklis Chatzimisios, Greece   António Rodrigues, Portugal
Cheng-Fu Chou, Taiwan   Jörg Roth, Germany
Iñigo Cuiñas, Spain   Manuel García Sánchez, Spain
Christos Douligeris, Greece   Christian Schindelhauer, Germany
Amit Dvir, Hungary   Kuei-Ping Shih, Taiwan
Val Dyadyuk, Australia   Shensheng Tang, USA
Marco Di Felice, Italy   George Tombras, Greece
David Ferreira, Portugal   Cesar Vargas-Rosales, Mexico
Mohammad Ghavami, UK   Dimitrios D. Vergados, Greece
Hong Ji, China   Natalija Vlajic, Canada

WINSYS Auxiliary Reviewers

Luca Bedogni, Italy   Stefanos Nikolidakis, Greece
Xiaojing Huang, Australia   Pravin Amrut Pawar, The Netherlands
Nikos Miridakis, Greece

Invited Speakers

Venu Govindaraju   University at Buffalo, USA
Sushil Jajodia   George Mason University Fairfax, USA
Andreas Holzinger   Medical University Graz, Austria
Geoffrey Charles Fox   Indiana University, USA
Luis M. Correia   IST/IT-Technical University of Lisbon, Portugal

Contents

Security and Cryptography

Signal Processing and Multimedia Applications

Wireless Information Networks and Systems

Invited Speaker

Big Complex Biomedical Data: Towards a Taxonomy of Data

Andreas Holzinger[1]([✉]), Christof Stocker[1], and Matthias Dehmer[2]

[1] Research Unit Human-Computer Interaction, Institute for Medical Informatics,
Statistics and Documentation, Medical University Graz, 8036 Graz, Austria
{a.holzinger,c.stocker}@hci4all.at
[2] Institute for Bioinformatics and Translational Research,
UMIT Tyrol, Hall in Tirol, Austria
matthias.dehmer@umit.at

Abstract. Professionals in the Life Sciences are faced with increasing masses of complex data sets. Very few data is structured, where traditional information retrieval methods work perfectly. A large portion of data is weakly structured; however, the majority falls into the category of unstructured data. To discover previously unknown knowledge from this data, we need advanced and novel methods to deal with the data from two aspects: time (e.g. information entropy) and space (e.g. computational topology). In this paper we show some examples of biomedical data and discuss a taxonomy of data with the specifics on medical data sets.

Keywords: Complex data · Biomedical data · Weakly-structured data · Information · Knowledge · Human-Computer Interaction · Data visualization · Biomedical informatics · Life sciences

1 Introduction

Data exploration has recently been hailed as the *fourth paradigm* in the investigation of nature, after empiricism, theory and computation [1]. Whether in astronomy or the life sciences, the flood of data requires sophisticated methods of handling. For example, researchers in bioinformatics collect, process and analyze masses of data, or in computational biology, they simulate biological systems, metabolic pathways, the behavior of a cell or how a protein is built [2]. In clinical medicine, the end users are confronted with increased volumes of highly complex, noisy, high-dimensional, multivariate and often weakly-structured data [3]. The field of biomedical informatics concerns the information processing by both humans and computers, dealing with biomedical complexity [4] to support decision making which is still a central topic in biomedical informatics [5].

Whereas Human-Computer Interaction (HCI) concentrates on human intelligence, and Knowledge Discovery in Data Mining (KDD) concentrates on machine intelligence, the grand challenge is to combine these diverse fields to support

© Springer-Verlag Berlin Heidelberg 2014
M.S. Obaidat and J. Filipe (Eds.): ICETE 2012, CCIS 455, pp. 3–18, 2014.
DOI: 10.1007/978-3-662-44791-8_1

the expert end users in learning to interactively analyze information properties thus enabling them to visualize the relevant parts of their data. In other words, to enable effective human control over powerful machine intelligence and to integrate statistical methods with information visualization, to support human insight and decision making [6]. The broad application of business enterprise hospital information systems amasses large amounts of medical documents, which must be reviewed, observed, and analyzed by human experts [7]. All essential documents of the patient records contain a certain portion of data which has been entered in non-standardized format (aka *free text*). Although text can easily be *created* by the end users, the support of automatic analysis is extremely difficult [8–10].

2   Look at Your Data

Each observation can be seen as a data point in an n-dimensional Euclidian vector space $\mathbb{R}^n$. An n-dimensional vector is given by

$$\boldsymbol{x}_i = [x_{i_1}, \ldots, x_{i_n}], \, i_1, \ldots, i_n \in \mathcal{I}, \tag{1}$$

where $\mathcal{I}$ is an index set.

In an arbitrarily high dimensional space, methods from algebraic topology have proved to be compelling, because topological data abstractions let us investigate structures in a semantic context [11]; this can be seen as one step towards sensemaking [12]. The *global character* of the data requires that the domain expert is able to extract information about the phenomena represented by the data (Fig. 1). This expert asks a question, forms a hypothesis and transforms data into knowledge; which can be seen as a transfer from the *computational space* into the *cognitive space* [13] of 2D or 3D representations developing in time:

$$\mathbb{R}^n + t \rightarrow \mathbb{R}^2 + t \text{ or } \mathbb{R}^3 + t \tag{2}$$

The time t is an important, yet often neglected dimension in medicine [14]. The expert in Fig. 1 looks for interesting data. Interest is a human construct, a perspective on relationships between data, and is influenced by emotion, personal likings and previous experience. Interest is similar to beauty, which is in the eye of the beholder [15]. It is difficult to make knowledge discovery automatic, we need human intelligence for sensemaking. For example, fitness functionality cannot be formulated generally; hence automatic algorithms may not find a solution alone.

3   Seeing the World in Data

Current technological developments offer the opportunity to collect, store and process all kinds of data in an unprecedented way, in great detail and very large scale [16]. Although, we are aware that data is not information and information is not knowledge, we are able to perceive the fascinating perspectives of our world

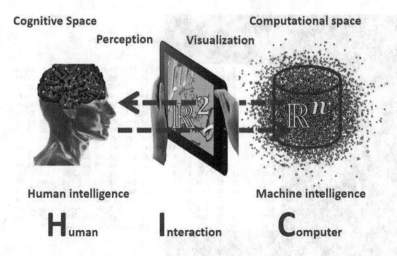

Fig. 1. Human-Computer Interaction bridging the cognitive space with the computational space.

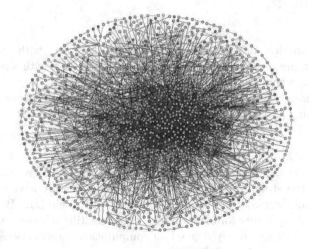

Fig. 2. First visualization of a human PPI structure; Experts gain knowledge of it, e.g. to understand complex processes, thereby understand illnesses [20].

in data. Let us look into the microscopic dimension (Fig. 2): Protein-protein interaction (PPI) [17,18] plays a fundamental role in all biological processes. A systematic analysis of PPI networks enables us to understand cellular organization, processes and function. This is big, complex, noisy data, consequently it is a great challenge to effectively analyse these massive data sets for biologically meaningful protein complex detection [19]. Moreover, this calls for novel techniques to infer biological networks as those are erroneous (measurement errors) and, hence, deterministic techniques can not be applied, see [18].

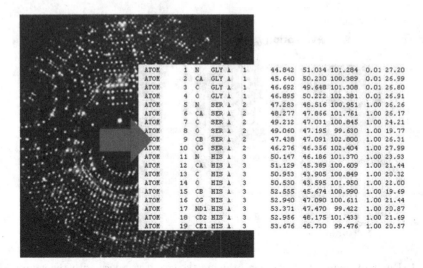

ATOM	1	N	GLY	A	1	44.842	51.034	101.284	0.01	27.20
ATOM	2	CA	GLY	A	1	45.640	50.230	100.389	0.01	26.99
ATOM	3	C	GLY	A	1	46.692	49.648	101.308	0.01	26.80
ATOM	4	O	GLY	A	1	46.895	50.222	102.381	0.01	26.91
ATOM	5	N	SER	A	2	47.283	48.516	100.951	1.00	26.26
ATOM	6	CA	SER	A	2	48.277	47.866	101.761	1.00	26.17
ATOM	7	C	SER	A	2	49.212	47.031	100.845	1.00	24.21
ATOM	8	O	SER	A	2	49.060	47.195	99.630	1.00	19.77
ATOM	9	CB	SER	A	2	47.438	47.091	102.800	1.00	26.31
ATOM	10	OG	SER	A	2	46.276	46.356	102.404	1.00	27.99
ATOM	11	N	HIS	A	3	50.147	46.186	101.370	1.00	23.93
ATOM	12	CA	HIS	A	3	51.129	45.389	100.609	1.00	21.44
ATOM	13	C	HIS	A	3	50.953	43.905	100.849	1.00	20.32
ATOM	14	O	HIS	A	3	50.530	43.595	101.950	1.00	22.00
ATOM	15	CB	HIS	A	3	52.555	45.674	100.990	1.00	19.69
ATOM	16	CG	HIS	A	3	52.940	47.090	100.611	1.00	21.44
ATOM	17	ND1	HIS	A	3	53.371	47.470	99.422	1.00	20.87
ATOM	18	CD2	HIS	A	3	52.956	48.175	101.433	1.00	21.69
ATOM	19	CE1	HIS	A	3	53.676	48.730	99.476	1.00	20.57

Fig. 3. Structures of protein complexes, determined by X-ray crystallography, and stored in the PDB [23].

The mathematical investigation of PPI networks starts with the inferred relational structure represented by a finite graph $G = (V, E)$, with a set of nodes V and edges E, where $E \subseteq V \times V$.

Proteins interact with each other to perform cellular functions or processes. These interacting patterns form the PPI network [21]

$$V \times V = \{(v_i, v_j) \mid v_i \in V, v_j \in V, i \neq j\} \tag{3}$$

Protein structures are studied for example with crystallographic methods (Fig. 3). Once the atomic coordinates of the protein structure have been determined, a table of these coordinates is deposited into a Protein Data Base (PDB), an international repository for 3D structure files. Scientific achievements coming from molecular biology greatly depend on computational applications and data management to explore lab results [22].

In Fig. 3, we see the structure and the data, representing the mean positions of the entities within the substance and their chemical relationships.

The structural information, stored in the PDB contains: a running number, atom type, residue name, the chain identification, the number of the residue in the chain, the triplet of coordinates. The PDB data files are downloaded from the database as input files for protein analysis and visualization.

Our quest is that an expert can gain knowledge from this data; for example by providing an interactive visualization of this data (Fig. 4): The Tumor Necrosis Factor (TNF - upper part) is interacting with the extra cellular domain of its receptor (lower part). The residues at the macromolecular interface are visualized in a "balland-stick" representation. The covalent bonds are represented as sticks between atoms, which are represented as balls. The rest of the two chains is

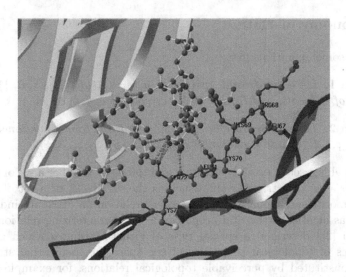

Fig. 4. Gaining knowledge from the data by interactive visualization [24].

represented as ribbons. Residue names and numbers of the TNF receptor are labelled, hydrogen bonds are represented by dotted lines (circled in Fig. 4).

Such complex network theory can be traced back to the first work on graph theory, developed by Leonhard Euler in 1736. However, stimulated by works as from Barabási, Albert and Jeong [25], research on complex networks has only recently been applied to biomedical informatics. As an extension of classical graph theory, complex network research focuses on the characterization, analysis, modeling and simulation of complex systems involving many elements and connections, examples including the internet, gene regulatory networks, PPI-networks, social relationships, the Web, and many more. Attention is given not only to the identification of special patterns of connectivity, such as the shortest average path between pairs of nodes [26], but also to the evolution of connectivity and the growth of networks, an example from biology being the evolution of PPI networks in different species (as shown in Fig. 2).

In order to understand complex biological systems, the three following key concepts have to be considered:

(i) emergence: the discovery of links between elements of a system as the study of individual elements (genes, proteins, metabolites) to explain the whole systems behavior;
(ii) robustness: biological systems maintain their main functions even under perturbations imposed by the environment; and
(iii) modularity: vertices sharing similar functions are highly connected.

Due to the ready availability of various network visualization tools [27], network theories can be applied to biomedical informatics.

4 Taxonomy of Data

Let us list some definitions first:

Definition 1. *Let a **relational system** be a pair* $(A, \{R_1, R_2, ..., R_n\})$, *where* A *is a set of elements, and* $R_1, R_2, ..., R_n$ *are relations defined on* A.

Definition 2. *Let an **attribute** be a homomorphism* $\mathcal{H}$ *from a relational system* $(A, \{R_1, R_2, ..., R_n\})$ *into a relational system* $(B, \{S_1, S_2, ..., S_n\})$.

The set A is a set of (visual) elements and the set B is either a set of (visual) elements or a set of attribute values such as the set $\mathbb{R}$, $\mathbb{Z}$ or a set of strings. The homomorphism $\mathcal{H}$ guarantees that every relation an attribute induces on elements has identical structural properties as its characterizing relations.

Dastani [28] described a special type of visual attributes which concerns various uses of topological properties of the space, i.e. perceptual structures that are constituted by perceivable topological relations, for example used in network visualizations (inside, outside, overlap, ...). This goes back to Egenhofer [29], who distinguished between spatial/nonspatial perceptual structures that are constituted by characterizing the relations of spatial and non-spatial attributes, and topological structures that are based on two or more topological attributes (Fig. 5). He used the nine-intersection model [30], which provides a framework and a relation algebra, for the description of topological relations between objects of area type, line, and point. This is based on the principles of algebraic topology, a branch of mathematics which deals with the manipulation of symbols that represent geometric configurations and their relationships to each other [31]. The data model is based on primitive objects, called cells, defined for different spatial dimensions: A 0-cell is a node (0-dimensional object); a 1-cell is the link between two 0-cells; a 2-cell is an area described by a closed sequence of three non-intersecting 1-cells and a face f is any cell that is contained in A. The relevant topological primitives include interior $A°$, boundary ∂A and exterior

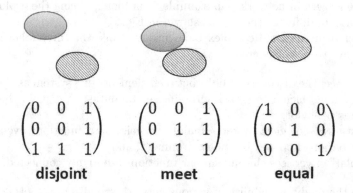

$$\begin{pmatrix} 0 & 0 & 1 \\ 0 & 0 & 1 \\ 1 & 1 & 1 \end{pmatrix} \qquad \begin{pmatrix} 0 & 0 & 1 \\ 0 & 1 & 1 \\ 1 & 1 & 1 \end{pmatrix} \qquad \begin{pmatrix} 1 & 0 & 0 \\ 0 & 1 & 0 \\ 0 & 0 & 1 \end{pmatrix}$$

disjoint   **meet**   **equal**

Fig. 5. Selected topological relations.

A^- of a cell; e.g., the boundary denoted by ∂A is the union of all r-faces $r - f$ where $0 \leq r \leq n$, i.e.

$$\partial A = \bigcup_{r=0}^{n-1} r - f \in A \tag{4}$$

The topological relation between two such geometric objects, A and B, is characterized by the binary values (empty, non-empty) of the 9-intersection, represented as a 3×3 matrix:

$$R(A, B) = \begin{pmatrix} A^\circ \cap B^\circ & A^\circ \cap \partial B & A^\circ \cap B^- \\ \partial A \cap B^\circ & \partial A \cap \partial B & \partial A \cap B^- \\ A^- \cap B^\circ & A^- \cap \partial B & A^- \cap B^- \end{pmatrix} \tag{5}$$

An important invariant is the number of components. Following the definition of Egenhofer and Franzosa [32] a component is based on the topological concepts separation and connectedness, i.e., for a set Y, a component is the largest connected (non-empty) subset of Y. Whenever any of the 9-set intersections is separated into disconnected subsets, these subsets are the components of this set intersection. Hence, any non-empty intersection may have several distinct components, each of which may be characterized by its own topological properties. This leads us to the definition of:

Weakly-structured Data. This must not be confused with weakly-structured information (e.g. [33], instead we follow the notions of topological relations (Fig. 5): Let $Y(t)$ be an ordered sequence of observed data, e.g., of individual patient data sampled at different points $t \in T$ over a time sequence. We call the observed data $Y(t)$ weakly structured, if and only if the trajectory of $Y(t)$ resembles a random walk [34,35].

Well-structured data has been seen to be the minority of data and an idealistic case when each data element has an associated defined structure, e.g., relational tables.

Ill-structured is a term often used for the opposite of well-structured, although this term originally was used in a different context of problem solving [36].

Semi-structured is a form of structured data that does not conform with the strict formal structure of tables and data models associated with relational databases, but contains tags or markers to separate both structure and content, i.e. these data are schema-less or self-describing; a typical example is a markup-language such as XML.

Non-structured data or unstructured data is an imprecise definition often used for data expressed in natural language, when no specific structure has been defined. Yet, this is not true: Text has also some structure: words, sentences, paragraphs. To be precise, unstructured data would mean completely randomized data which is usually called noise. Duda, Hart and Stork [37] define it as any property of data which is not due to the underlying model but instead to randomness (either in the real world, from the sensors or the measurement procedure). In Informatics, particularly, it can be considered as unwanted non-relevant data without meaning, or, even worse: with a not detected wrong meaning typical artifacts.

In addition to the above described structurization, data can also be standardized (e.g. numerical entries in laboratory reports) and nonstandardized (e.g. nonstandardized text often maybe inappropriately called "free text" in an electronic patient record, see e.g. [38].

Standardized data is a basis for accurate communication. In the medical domain, many different people work at different times in various locations. Data standards can ensure that information is presented in a form that facilitates interoperability of systems and a comparability of data for a common end user interpretation. It supports the reusability of the data, improves the efficiency of healthcare services and avoids errors by reducing duplicated efforts in data entry. Data standardization refers to (a) the data content; (b) terminologies used to represent the data; (c) how data is exchanged; and (d) how knowledge is applied; The last entry *"knowledge"* means e.g. clinical guidelines, protocols, decision support rules, checklists, standard operating procedures, etc. Technical elements for data sharing require standardization of identification, record structure, terminology, messaging, privacy etc. The most used standardized data set to date is the international Classification of Diseases (ICD), which was first adopted in 1900 for collecting statistics [39].

Non-standardized data as the majority of all data impedes data quality, data exchange and interoperability [40].

Uncertain data is a challenge in the medical domain, since the aim is to identify which covariates out of millions are associated with a specific outcome such as a disease state. Often, the number of covariates is orders of magnitude larger than the number of observations, involving the risks of false knowledge discovery and overfitting. The possibility that important information may be contained in the complex interactions, along with the huge number of potential covariates that may be missed by simple methods, can be addressed by new and improved models and algorithms for classification and prediction [41].

5   Specifics of Medical Data

Biomedical data covers various structural dimensions, ranging from microscopic structures (e.g. DNA) to whole human populations (disease spreading). Clinical-medical data are defined and collected with a remarkable degree of uncertainty, variability and inaccuracy. Komaroff [42] stated that *"medical data is disturbingly soft"*. Three decades later, the data still falls far short of the exactness that engineers prefer.

What did Komaroff mean with *soft*? The way patients define their sickness, questions and answers between clinicians and patients, physical examinations, diagnostic laboratory tests etc. Even the definitions of the diseases themselves are often ambiguous; some diseases cannot be defined by any available objective standard; other diseases do have an objective standard, but are variably interpreted.

Another complication inherent in the data is that most medical information is incomplete, with wide variation in the degree and type of missing information. In both the development and the application of statistical techniques, analysis of data with incomplete or missing information can be much more difficult than analysis of corresponding data with all the information available - interestingly this was known before the term medical informatics was defined [43].

Let us give a last example for the size aspect of medical data: In 1986, the INTERNIST-1 knowledge base (for diagnosis in internal medicine) contained 572 disorders, approx. 4,000 possible patient findings and links detailing the causal, temporal and probable interrelationships between the disorders [44]. Ten years ago, in 2002, a typical primary care doctor was kept informed of approximately 10,000 diseases and syndromes, 3,000 medications, and 1,100 laboratory tests [45]. In 2008, there were 18 million articles catalogued in the biomedical literature.

Working with big data requires certain issues to be addressed, such as data security, intellectual property and, particularly in the case of medical data, privacy issues [46].

6   Visualization of Data

How can visual representations of abstract data be used to amplify the acquisition of knowledge? [47].

Unfortunately, the creation of visualizations for complex data still remains more of a personal effort than a commercial enterprise. So many sophisticated visualization concepts have been developed, e.g. Parallel Coordinates [48], RadViz [49], or Glyphs [50], to mention only a few, but in business enterprise hospital information systems they are still not in use.

An interesting example is from the publication by Hey et al. [2] from the introduction to this paper, wherein from 30 essays on the emerging area of data-intensive science, all including visualizations of scientific results, only one is on visualization needs [51].

As a practical example, interactive computer simulations to teach complex concepts have become very popular [52]. The nature of such simulations ranges from compelling visualizations [53,54] to educational computer games [55,56]. A recent example is Foldit [57], where gamers can play cellular architect and build proteins. Scientists can crowdsource the data and design brand-new molecules in the lab. Such exploratory learning with interactive simulations is highly demanding from the perspective of *limited cognitive processing capabilities* and the research on interactive simulations [58,59] has revealed that learners *need further support and guidance.*

Learning in the area of physiology is difficult for medical students, because mostly they are lacking the mathematics necessary to understand the dynamics of complex mathematical rules related to physiological models.

In our application HAEMOSIM, we make complicated physiological data [60] interactively visible to medical learners (Fig. 6), so that they gain insight into the

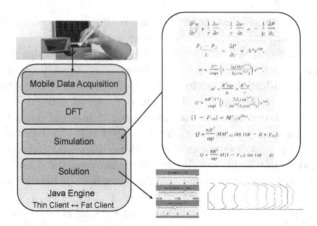

Fig. 6. Real data are used for the simulation of certain clinical relevant solutions and can be interactively displayed by a learner [68].

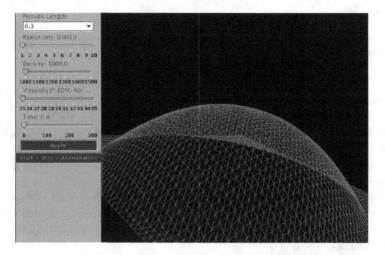

Fig. 7. The visualized data allows insights into medical contexts and sensemaking [68].

behavior of blood circulation dynamics, and to simulate certain defects (Fig. 7) and the dangers of diseases. The application simulates mathematical models [61–64] and presents these models in form of dynamic 2D and 3D visualizations. Special focus during the development was directed on usercentered design [65–67], for example, to understand the context and to adapt the various applets to the previous knowledge of the end users.

7   Conclusions and Future Outlook

Life sciences and human health are fundamentally biological, and biology is often described as *the* information science [69].

Consequently, research in computational biology may yield many beneficial results for medicine and health. A very intriguing question is to what extent randomness and stochasticity play a role. By adopting the computational thinking approach [70] to studying biological processes, we can improve our understanding and at the same time improve the design of algorithms [71].

The ability to define details of the interactions between small molecules and proteins promises unprecedented advances in the exploration of rational therapeutic strategies, for example, to combat infectious diseases and cancer. The opportunity to probe large macromolecular systems offers exciting opportunities for exploring the nature of PPIs and the mechanisms of trafficking of molecules to different regions of a cell, a process involving transport through membranes and diffusion over significant distances in the cytoplasm [72].

Following the quest "Science is to test ideas, engineering is to put these ideas into practice" [73], not only the scientific aspects will be challenging, but also the engineering ones, to support human intelligence with computational intelligence in the clinical domain. One challenge is in contextual computing; i.e. a medical professional may ask the business enterprise hospital information system: "Show me the similarities between patients with symptoms X and patients with symptoms Y". This brings us immediately back to the deep questions in computing [74], including: What is information? What is computable? What is intelligence? And most of all: (How) can we build complex systems in a simply?

Decision making is the key topic in medical informatics. For this we need to follow the three column approach: data - information - knowledge, with emphasis on the latter. Successful knowledge discovery and information retrieval systems will be those that bring the designer's model into harmony with the end user's mental model. We can conclude that combining HCI together with KDD will provide benefits to the medical domain. For this purpose, we must bridge Science and Engineering in order to answer fundamental questions on information quality [75] and to implement the findings on building information systems simply at the engineering level. A few important examples of future research aspects include:

1. Research on the physics of (time-oriented) information to contribute to fundamental research;
2. Considering temporal and spatial information; in networks, spatially distributed components raise fundamental issues on information exchange since available resources must be shared, allocated and reused. Information is exchanged in both space and time for decision making, therefore timeliness along with reliability and complexity constitute the main issues and are most often ignored;
3. We still lack measures and meters to define and appraise the amount of information embodied in structure and organization for example the entropy of a structure;
4. Considering information transfer: how we can assess, for example, the transfer of biological information;
5. Information and knowledge: In many scientific contexts we are dealing only with data without knowing precisely what these data are representing;
6. and most of all, we must gain value out of data making data valuable.

Concluding, we can say that the future in the life sciences will be definitely data-centric. This will apply equally to the medical clinical domain and health care. Mobile, ubiquitous computing, sensors everywhere, computational power and storage at very low cost will definitely produce an increasing avalanche of data and there definitely will be the danger of drowning in data, but starving for knowledge. Herbert Simon pointed out 40 years ago, when medical informatics was in its infancy: "A wealth of information creates a poverty of attention and a need to allocate that attention efficiently among the overabundance of information sources that might consume it" [76].

Consequently, Human-Computer Interaction and Knowledge Discovery along with Biomedical Informatics are of increasing importance to effectively gain knowledge, to make sense out of the big data. This is our central quest the holy grail for the future. Let us put together all efforts to jointly make advances in this interesting, challenging and important area to benefit medicine, to benefit humans, to benefit us all.

However, even the best team is ineffective if there is no funding. A substantial budget is required to cover staff costs, premises and basic equipment, travel, computers and software, a scientific software portfolio, hosting, special equipment, literature, workshop organization, visiting researcher invitations, etc. In an environment of decreasing public budgets, external funding becomes increasingly important in order to sustain international competitiveness, quality and to maintain excellence [77].

References

1. Bell, G., Hey, T., Szalay, A.: Beyond the data deluge. Science **323**(5919), 1297–1298 (2009)
2. Hey, T., Tansley, S., Tolle, K.: The Fourth Paradigm: Data-Intensive Scientific Discovery. Microsoft Research, Redmond (2009)
3. Holzinger, A.: Weakly structured data in health-informatics: the challenge for human-computer interaction (2011)
4. Patel, V.L., Kahol, K., Buchman, T.: Biomedical complexity and error. J. Biomed. Inform. **44**(3), 387–389 (2011)
5. Holzinger, A.: Biomedical Informatics: Discovering Knowledge in Big Data. Springer, New York (2014)
6. Holzinger, A., Jurisica, I.: Knowledge discovery and data mining in biomedical informatics: the future is in integrative, interactive machine learning solutions. In: Holzinger, A., Jurisica, I. (eds.) Interactive Knowledge Discovery and Data Mining in Biomedical Informatics. LNCS, vol. 8401, pp. 1–18. Springer, Heidelberg (2014)
7. Holzinger, A., Geierhofer, R., Modritscher, F., Tatzl, R.: Semantic information in medical information systems: utilization of text mining techniques to analyze medical diagnoses. J. Univ. Comput. Sci. **14**(22), 3781–3795 (2008)
8. Gregory, J., Mattison, J.E., Linde, C.: Naming notes - transitions from free-text to structured entry. Meth. Inf. Med. **34**(1–2), 57–67 (1995)

9. Holzinger, A., Kainz, A., Gell, G., Brunold, M., Maurer, H.: Interactive computer assisted formulation of retrieval requests for a medical information system using an intelligent tutoring system. World Conference on Educational Multimedia, Hypermedia and Telecommunications ED-MEDIA 2000, pp. 431–436. AACE, Charlottesville (2000)
10. Lovis, C., Baud, R.H., Planche, P.: Power of expression in the electronic patient record: structured data or narrative text? Int. J. Med. Inf. **58**, 101–110 (2000)
11. Pascucci, V., Tricoche, X., Hagen, H., Tierny, J.: Topological Methods in Data Analysis and Visualization: Theory, Algorithms, and Applications. Springer, Heidelberg (2011)
12. Blandford, A., Attfield, S.: Interacting with information. Synth. Lect. Hum. Centered Inf. **3**(1), 1–99 (2010)
13. Kaski, S., Peltonen, J.: Dimensionality reduction for data visualization (applications corner). IEEE Signal Process. Mag. **28**(2), 100–104 (2011)
14. Holzinger, A., Hörtenhuber, M., Mayer, C., Bachler, M., Wassertheurer, S., Pinho, A.J., Koslicki, D.: On entropy-based data mining. In: Holzinger, A., Jurisica, I. (eds.) Interactive Knowledge Discovery and Data Mining in Biomedical Informatics. LNCS, vol. 8401, pp. 209–226. Springer, Heidelberg (2014)
15. Beale, R.: Supporting serendipity: using ambient intelligence to augment user exploration for data mining and web browsing. Int. J. Hum. Comput. Stud. **65**(5), 421–433 (2007)
16. Yau, N.: Seeing the World in Data, pp. 246–248. Princeton Architectural Press, New York (2011)
17. Pržulj, N., Higham, D.J.: Modelling protein-protein interaction networks via a stickiness index. J. Roy. Soc. Interface **3**(10), 711–716 (2006)
18. Emmert-Streib, F., Dehmer, M. (eds.): Analysis of Microarray Data: A Network-Based Approach. Wiley VCH Publishing, Chichester (2010)
19. Shi, L., Lei, X., Zhang, A.: Protein complex detection with semi-supervised learning in protein interaction networks. Proteome Sci. **9**(Suppl. 1), S5 (2011)
20. Stelzl, U., Worm, U., Lalowski, M., Haenig, C., Brembeck, F.H., Goehler, H., Stroedicke, M., Zenkner, M., Schoenherr, A., Koeppen, S., Timm, J., Mintzlaff, S., Abraham, C., Bock, N., Kietzmann, S., Goedde, A., Toksz, E., Droege, A., Krobitsch, S., Korn, B., Birchmeier, W., Lehrach, H., Wanker, E.E.: A human protein-protein interaction network: a resource for annotating the proteome. Cell **122**(6), 957–968 (2005)
21. Zhang, A.: Protein Interaction Networks: Computational Analysis. Cambridge University Press, Cambridge (2009)
22. Arrais, J.P., Lopes, P., Oliveira, J.L.: Challenges storing and representing biomedical data. In: Holzinger, A., Simonic, K.-M. (eds.) USAB 2011. LNCS, vol. 7058, pp. 53–62. Springer, Heidelberg (2011)
23. Wiltgen, M., Holzinger, A.: Visualization in Bioinformatics: Protein Structures with Physicochemical and Biological Annotations, pp. 69–74. Czech Technical University (CTU), Prague (2005)
24. Wiltgen, M., Holzinger, A., Tilz, G.P.: Interactive analysis and visualization of macromolecular interfaces between proteins. In: Holzinger, A. (ed.) USAB 2007. LNCS, vol. 4799, pp. 199–212. Springer, Heidelberg (2007)
25. Barabási, A.L., Albert, R., Jeong, H.: Mean-field theory for scale-free random networks. Physica A: Stat. Mech. Appl. **272**(1–2), 173–187 (1999)
26. Newman, M.: The structure and function of complex networks. SIAM Rev. **45**, 167–256 (2003)

27. Costa, L., Rodrigues, F., Cristino, A.: Complex networks: the key to systems biology. Genet. Mol. Biol. **31**(3), 591–601 (2008)
28. Dastani, M.: The role of visual perception in data visualization. J. Vis. Lang. Comput. **13**, 601–622 (2002)
29. Egenhofer, M.: Reasoning about binary topological relations. In: Günther, O., Schek, H.-J. (eds.) SSD 1991. LNCS, vol. 525, pp. 141–160. Springer, Heidelberg (1991)
30. Egenhofer, M., Herring, J.: Categorizing binary topological relations between regions, lines, and points in geographic databases. Technical Report, Department of Surveying Engineering, University of Maine (1990)
31. Aleksandrov, P.: Elementary Concepts of Topology. Dover Publications, New York (1961)
32. Egenhofer, M., Franzosa, R.: On the equivalence of topological relations. Int. J. Geogr. Inf. Syst. **9**(2), 133–152 (1995)
33. Stuckenschmidt, H., van Harmelen, F.: Information Sharing on the Semantic Web. Advanced Information and Knowledge Processing. Springer, Heidelberg (2005)
34. Kapovich, I., Myasnikov, A., Schupp, P., Shpilrain, V.: Generic-case complexity, decision problems in group theory, and random walks. J. Algebra **264**(2), 665–694 (2003)
35. de Silva, V., Carlsson, G.: Topological estimation using witness complexes. In: Proceedings of Eurographics Symposium on Point-Based Graphics, pp. 157–166 (2004)
36. Simon, H.A.: The structure of ill structured problems. Artif. Intell. **4**(3–4), 181–201 (1973)
37. Duda, R.O., Hart, P.E., Stork, D.G.: Pattern Classification, 2nd edn. Wiley, New York (2000)
38. Kreuzthaler, M., Bloice, M., Faulstich, L., Simonic, K., Holzinger, A.: A comparison of different retrieval strategies working on medical free texts. J. Univ. Comput. Sci. **17**(7), 1109–1133 (2011)
39. Ahmadian, L., van Engen-Verheul, M., Bakhshi-Raiez, F., Peek, N., Cornet, R., de Keizer, N.F.: The role of standardized data and terminological systems in computerized clinical decision support systems: Literature review and survey. Int. J. Med. Inf. **80**(2), 81–93 (2011)
40. Batini, C., Scannapieco, M.: Data Quality: Concepts, Methodologies and Techniques. Springer, Heidelberg (2006)
41. Richman, J.S.: Multivariate Neighborhood Sample Entropy: A Method for Data Reduction and Prediction of Complex Data, pp. 297–408. Elsevier, Amsterdam (2011)
42. Komaroff, A.L.: The variability and inaccuracy of medical data. Proc. IEEE **67**(9), 1196–1207 (1979)
43. Walsh, J.E.: Analyzing medical data: some statistical considerations. IRE Trans. Med. Electron. **ME–7**(4), 362–366 (1960)
44. Miller, R., McNeil, M., Challinor, S., Masarie Jr, F., Myers, J.: The internist-1/quick medical reference project-status report. West. J. Med. **145**(6), 816 (1986)
45. Davenport, T., Glaser, J.: Just-in-time delivery comes to knowledge management. Harvard Bus. Rev. **80**(7), 107–111 (2002)
46. Manyika, J., Chui, M., Brown, B., Bughin, J., Dobbs, R., Roxburgh, C., Byers, A.H.: Big Data: The Next Frontier for Innovation, Competition, and Productivity. McKinsey Global Institute, Washington (DC) (2011)
47. Card, S.K., Mackinlay, J.D., Shneiderman, B.: Information Visualization: Using Vision to Think, pp. 1–34. Morgan Kaufmann, San Francisco (1999).

48. Inselberg, A.: Parallel Coordinates: Visual Multidimensional Geometry and Its Applications (foreword by Ben Shneiderman). Springer, Heidelberg (2009)
49. Novakova, L., Stepankova, O.: Radviz and identification of clusters in multidimensional data. In: 13th International Conference on Information Visualisation, pp. 104–109 (2009)
50. Meyer-Spradow, J., Stegger, L., Doering, C., Ropinski, T., Hinirchs, K.: Glyph-based spect visualization for the diagnosis of coronary artery disease. IEEE Trans. Visual Comput. Graphics **14**(6), 1499–1506 (2008)
51. Fox, P., Hendler, J.: Changing the equation on scientific data visualization. Science **331**(6018), 705–708 (2011)
52. de Jong, T.: Computer simulations - technological advances in inquiry learning. Science **312**(5773), 532–533 (2006)
53. Chittaro, L.: Information visualization and its application to medicine. Artif. Intell. Med. **22**(2), 81–88 (2001)
54. Johnson, C.R., MacLeod, R., Parker, S.G., Weinstein, D.: Biomedical computing and visualization software environments. Commun. ACM **47**(11), 64–71 (2004)
55. Ebner, M., Holzinger, A.: Successful implementation of user-centered game based learning in higher education an example from civil engineering. Comput. Educ. **49**(3), 873–890 (2007)
56. Kickmeier-Rust, M.D., Peirce, N., Conlan, O., Schwarz, D., Verpoorten, D., Albert, D.: Immersive Digital Games: The Interfaces for Next-Generation E-Learning?, pp. 647–656. Springer, Heidelberg (2007)
57. Cooper, S., Khatib, F., Treuille, A., Barbero, J., Lee, J., Beenen, M., Leaver-Fay, A., Baker, D., Popovic, Z., Players, F.: Predicting protein structures with a multiplayer online game. Nature **466**(7307), 756–760 (2010)
58. Mayer, R.E., Hegarty, M., Mayer, S., Campbell, J.: When static media promote active learning: annotated illustrations versus narrated animations in multimedia instruction. J. Exp. Psychol. Appl. **11**(4), 256–265 (2005)
59. Holzinger, A., Kickmeier-Rust, M., Albert, D.: Dynamic media in computer science education; content complexity and learning performance: is less more? Educ. Technol. Soc. **11**(1), 279–290 (2008)
60. Hessinger, M., Holzinger, A., Leitner, D., Wassertheurer, S.: Haemodynamic models for education in physiology. Math. Comput. Simul. Simul. News Eur. **16**(2), 64–68 (2006)
61. McDonald, D.: The relation of pulsatile pressure to flow in arteries. J. Physiol. **127**, 533–552 (1955)
62. Womersley, J.R.: Method for the calculation of velocity, rate of flow and viscous drag in arteries when the pressure gradient is known. J. Physiol. **127**(3), 553–563 (1955)
63. Pedley, T.: The Fluid Mechanics of Large Blood Vessels. Cambridge University Press, Cambridge (1980)
64. Leitner, D., Wassertheurer, S., Hessinger, M., Holzinger, A.: A lattice boltzmann model for pulsative blood flow in elastic vessels. New Comput. Med. Inf. Health Care **123**(4), 64–68 (2006). Special Edition of Springer e&i
65. Holzinger, A., Ebner, M.: Interaction and Usability of Simulations & Animations: A Case Study of the Flash Technology, pp. 777–780. IOS Press, Zurich (2003)
66. Holzinger, A.: Application of rapid prototyping to the user interface development for a virtual medical campus. IEEE Softw. **21**(1), 92–99 (2004)
67. Holzinger, A.: Usability engineering for software developers. Commun. ACM **48**(1), 71–74 (2005)

68. Holzinger, A., Kickmeier-Rust, M.D., Wassertheurer, S., Hessinger, M.: Learning performance with interactive simulations in medical education: lessons learned from results of learning complex physiological models with the haemodynamics simulator. Comput. Educ. **52**(2), 292–301 (2009)
69. Schrödinger, E.: What Is Life? The Physical Aspect of the Living Cell. Dublin Institute for Advanced Studies at Trinity College, Dublin (1944)
70. Wing, J.M.: Computational thinking. Commun. ACM **49**(3), 33–35 (2006)
71. Fisher, J., Harel, D., Henzinger, T.: Biology as reactivity. Commun. ACM **54**(10), 72–82 (2011)
72. Vendruscolo, M., Dobson, C.M.: Protein dynamics: moore's law in molecular biology. Curr. Biol. **21**(2), R68–R70 (2011)
73. Holzinger, A.: Process Guide for Students for Interdisciplinary Work in Computer Science/Informatics, 2nd edn. BoD, Norderstedt (2010)
74. Wing, J.M.: Computational thinking and thinking about computing. Philos. Trans. Roy. Soc. A: Math. Phys. Eng. Sci. **366**(1881), 3717–3725 (2008)
75. Holzinger, A., Dehmer, M., Jurisica, I.: Knowledge discovery and interactive data mining in bioinformatics - state-of-the-art, future challenges and research directions. BMC Bioinform. **15**(Suppl 6), I1 (2014)
76. Simon, H.: Designing Organizations for an Information-Rich World, pp. 37–72. The Johns Hopkins Press, Baltimore (1971)
77. Holzinger, A.: Human-computer interaction and knowledge discovery (HCI-KDD): what is the benefit of bringing those two fields to work together? In: Cuzzocrea, A., Kittl, C., Simos, D.E., Weippl, E., Xu, L. (eds.) CD-ARES 2013. LNCS, vol. 8127, pp. 319–328. Springer, Heidelberg (2013)

Data Communication Networking

Study on a Fast OSPF Route Reconstruction Method Under Network Failures

Hiroki Doi[✉]

System Engineering Research Laboratory,
Central Research Institute of Electric Power Industry,
Iwado kita 2-11-1, Komae-shi, Tokyo, Japan
doi@criepi.denken.or.jp

Abstract. OSPF (Open Shortest Path First), which is used widely on networks, has a *Router Dead Interval* problem. If a (backup) designated router has stopped operation due to failure, the OSPF routers await a hello packet acknowledgment for the router dead interval to recognize that the designated router has ceased the operation. The Router Dead Interval is 40 sec This interval time is not only long for many real-time applications but also involves huge buffering of data and a burst of traffic after the router reconstruction. To avoid the Router Dead Interval, we propose a fast method of designated router detection by enhanced OSPF. In this report, we show how our method reduces the route reconstruction time from 45 sec to 10 or less on OSPF networks.

Keywords: OSPF · Router dead interval · Delay time · Route · Designated router

1 Introduction

In Japan, many Japanese people and Japanese companies were damaged by the Great East Japan Earthquake. Following this disaster, Japanese commercial ISPs and the government reexamined the plan for disaster estimation and protection against disasters. According to this protection plan, commercial ISPs must reconstruct robust networks against disasters. Networks require high reliability and fast recovery. One of the important problems for these requirements is that of routing, since considerable time is required to reroute paths on IP networks, when multiple routers have ceased operation due to failures. To study this problem, we focus on OSPF (Open Shortest Past First) [1,2] behavior, which is one of the major routing protocols used worldwide, and presume a large company network, namely a broadcast multi-access network with 400 OSPF routers.

OSPF works with 2 kinds of router, namely, the Designated Router (DR) and its neighboring routers (neighbors) on broadcast multi-access networks. An adjacency should be formed with the DR and its neighbor. The DR also has a list of all other routers attached to the network. In this case, when the DR has ceased the routing operation, neighbors attempt to cast hello packets

© Springer-Verlag Berlin Heidelberg 2014
M.S. Obaidat and J. Filipe (Eds.): ICETE 2012, CCIS 455, pp. 21–35, 2014.
DOI: 10.1007/978-3-662-44791-8_2

to the DR. If the DR does not respond to 4 hello packets from a neighbor, a neighbor detects DR failure and all neighbors start to elect new DR among their own neighbors. The hello packet interval is 10 sec (*Hello Interval*, default value), hence it takes 40 sec (*Router Dead Interval*) for neighbors to detect the DR failure. After the DR failure, it takes more than 40 sec to reroute all paths by original OSPF. General speaking, this time length of communication failure is very long for many applications on networks. Thus, when the DR has ceased the routing operation on OSPF networks by the network failure, it takes long time to recover the network operation.

There is a simple method to reduce *Router Dead Interval*. We can set the value of the hello packet interval under 10 sec on an OSPF router. However, paper [3] reports that any *Hello Interval* value less than 10 sec leads to unacceptable number of false alarms, meaning neighbors mistakenly DR failure due to the successive discards of hello packets.

There are another methods to detect OSPF failures. When the links fail, OSPF multicasts LSA (Link State Advertisement) packets. The Paper [4] proposed a method of OSPF failure identification based on LSA flooding analysis taking these aspects into account. However, if the OSPF on a router ceases the operation or the Layer-2 (L2) link fails (in this case, network topology contains L2-network), the other OSPF routers cannot detect this failure and send LSA packets. Thus, this proposed method cannot detect OSPF failure in these cases by monitoring LSA packets and avoid *Router Dead Interval*.

To avoid this *Router Dead Interval*, we propose an enhanced OSPF with a new DR failure detection mechanism added without the hello packet. Our method uses user IP packets to detect the DR failure and monitors user IP packets from the DR. When the DR has ceased the operation, it no longer sends user IP packets. Our method can detect DR failure faster than the original OSPF by monitoring the behavior of those IP packets.

This paper is organized as follows. In Sect. 2, we first indicate our objective for original OSPF. In Sect. 3, we describe the mechanism of original OSPF and its *Router Dead interval* problem and show our proposed method to solve this problem. In Sect. 4, we show the behavior examples of our proposed method for several network facility failures. In Sect. 5, we evaluate path reroute processing time of our proposed method and original OSPF in typical network model. Finally, in Sect. 6, the effect of our proposal method is summarized and future works mentioned.

2   OSPF Behavior for the DR Failure

OSPF can adapt to many network configurations, peer-to-peer networks, point-to-multipoint networks, broadcast multi-access networks and so on. We focus on the broadcast multi-access network, because it is a major network configuration of company private networks. OSPF works with 2 kinds of OSPF router, DR and neighbors on broadcast multi-access networks. The router will attempt to form adjacencies with some of its newly acquired neighbors. Link-state databases are synchronized between pairs of adjacent routers. On broadcast multi-access networks, the DR determines which routers should become adjacent. Adjacencies control the distribution of routing information. Routing updates are only sent and received on adjacencies, hence the DR plays an important role in OSPF networks.

If the DR has ceased routing operation due to failure, neighbors cannot detect this failure immediately and cannot receive new link-state information from the DR. Under these circumstances, the OSPF cannot reroute paths to avoid failing routers or links until the successful detection of DR failure. Neighbors send hello packets to the DR to confirm such failure. *Hello interval* is 10 sec as the default value on an OSPF router. If the DR does not respond to 4 hello packets from a neighbor, the neighbor detects DR failure, meaning it takes 40 sec is required for neighbors to detect DR failure. This time interval is called the *Router Dead Interval*.

Of course, the *Hello Interval* is one of the OSPF parameters and there is a simple way for *Hello Interval* to be set to under 10 sec to reduce *Router Dead Interval*. However, this is not feasible for commercial ISPs. This method was analyzed by paper [3] by measuring ISPs topologies and it was reported that any *Hello Interval* value under 10 sec led to an unacceptable number of false alarms. Thus, we think that the *Hello Interval* should remain 10 sec and need to adapt a different method.

There is also a backup DR in the general OSPF network. When the DR has ceased operation, the backup DR becomes the DR and a new backup DR is elected among other neighbors. In this paper, we assume that a DR and a backup DR have ceased the operation due to simultaneous multiple failure.

3 Enhancement OSPF for the Router Dead Interval

3.1 Outline for Enhancement OSPF

Our objective is to avoid using the hello packet to realize the faster path reroute mechanism. To achieve this objective, we enhance the DR failure detection mechanism part of OSPF.

We have 2 simple key ideas as follows for this enhancement

1. When a link or router fails, the flow of IP packets stops or changes immediately.
2. An IP packet which traverses the DR has a hello function.

For key idea 1, if the DR fails, a neighbor does not receive IP packets from the DR. Also, in the case of Fig. 1, if the DR or an L2-link fails, a neighbor does not receive IP packets. In other words, a neighbor can detect DR failure by monitoring IP packets from the DR.

For key idea 2, we can substitute a user IP packet for a hello packet to detect DR failure, because we can use an IP header option within the private network and the IP is at the same layer as the OSPF.

We show the outline of the new DR failure detection mechanism based on the ideas.

Case 1 : OSPF failure on the DR

Case 2 : L2 link failure and OSPF failure on the DR

Fig. 1. Typical OSPF network failures.

1. The user IP packet which traverses the DR is marked on an option of the IP header.
2. The neighbor monitors the marked IP packets.
3. If the receiving rate of user IP packets on the DR is less than the threshold value (R_{DR}), the DR sends a marked dummy IP packet to its neighbor.
4. If the local time exceeds the threshold value (R_i) on an neighbor i, this neighbor casts missing message packets to all neighbors.
5. If another neighbor j receives a missing message packet, it monitors the arrival interval time of marked IP packets. If the marked IP packet interval time is under the threshold value (R_j), this neighbor sends an alive message packet.
6. If the neighbor i does not receives an alive message packet, this neighbor detects the DR failure. A new DR is elected among all neighbors and reconstructs the new routing table.

Here, we presume the DR writes 1 as a mark in an option of the IP packet header, which is sent from the DR to a neighbor. When a neighbor receives a marked IP packet, it writes 0 as an unmark in an option and sends the user IP packet.

Next, we define the threshold value R. To calculate R, we borrow the idea of the TCP timeout mechanism [5].

TCP monitors all RTT (Round Trip Time) of TCP packets at the TCP interfaces and calculates the average RTT and its deviation. The time out value is the average RTT + 2×deviation [6]. (In 1990, the paper [7] revised this equation, average RTT + 4×deviation. We select the former equation for the performance of our method.) TCP decides on the packet loss event based on this time out value and retransmits the packet.

Our proposed method decides the DR failure event by comparing the threshold value R with the arrival interval time of the marked IP packets. R is calculated by the following equation

$$Err = M - A$$
$$A \rightarrow A + gErr$$
$$D \rightarrow D + h(|Err| - D)$$
$$R = A + 2D$$

Neighbor side   DR side

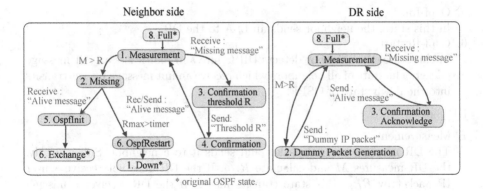

Fig. 2. Proposed state transition diagram.

where M is the arrival interval time of the marked IP packet (measurement value), A is the average of M, g is the coefficient $1/8$, Err is the difference M and A, h is the coefficient $1/4$, D is the mean deviation. The value of coefficients is equal to one of the original TCP timeout mechanism.

3.2 Our Proposal Algorithm

We describe our proposed new DR failure detection mechanism. We show the state transitions diagram of DR and its neighbor in Fig. 2.

Neighbor Side

1. Measurement
   The neighbor monitors the marked IP packets and calculates M and R. If the local time exceeds R, this state transits into state 2. If M is less than R, there is no transition of state. If a missing message packet is received, this state transits into state 3.
2. Missing
   The neighbor multicasts a missing message packet to all OSPF routers. It corrects the R_i of other neighbors i and calculates the maximum value R_{max} among R_i If an alive message packet is received by R_{max}, the neighbor knows that the DR is alive and there is path failure on an adjacency path. This state transits into state 5 to reconstruct adjacency with the DR. If an alive message packet is not received by R_{max}, the neighbor detects DR failure and this state transits into state 6.
3. Confirm R
   The neighbor i having received the missing message packet confirms R_i and sends it to the sender of the missing message packet, whereupon this state transits into state 4.
4. Confirmation
   If a marked IP packet is received by R_i, an alive message packet is multicast. Also, if an alive message packet is received from the other neighbor, this state transits into state 1.

5. Ospf-Init

In this state, the neighbor sends an LSA to the DR.

6. Ospf-Restart

In this state, the neighbor detects DR failure and multicasts an init message packet. The state of all neighbors which receive an init message packet transits into the down state of OSPF.

DR Side

1. Measurement

The DR marks a user IP packet and sends it to a neighbor. Subsequently, the DR measures M and calculate R_{DR}. If the DR does not receive a user IP packet by R_{DR}, this state transits into 2. If the DR receives a missing message packet, this state transits into 3.

2. Dummy Packet Generation

The DR generates a dummy marked IP packet and sends it to a neighbor.

3. Confirmation Acknowledgement

The DR multicasts alive message packets and this state transits into state 1.

3.3   Path Reroute Processing Time

In this section, we mention the path reroute processing flow of our proposed method for various network facility failure. Various network facilities and OSPF network configuration patterns exist. We assume a DR, neighbor, L2 switch and link to comprise the main network facilities for simplicity and show the path reroute processing flow of our proposed method for failure of those facilities in Fig. 3.

The *Path reconstruction* process is the original OSPF process, SPF calculation, SPF Delay and LSA processing and so on, but this process is used by our proposed method. The *DR election* includes hello processing.

The Fig. 3 shows that there are 3 cases of processing flow, namely, (1) *Path reconstruction*, (2) *Path reconstruction + DR failure detection* and (3) *Path reconstruction + DR failure detection + DR election*. But there are only 2 processing time cases (2) and (3) for the failure of those facilities to evaluate our proposed method. We will evaluate the case (2) in Sect. 5.2 and the case (3) in Sect. 5.1.

4   Examples of Enhancement of OSPF Behavior

In this section, we show some examples of working mechanisms of our proposed method in the event of failure of various network facilities.

4.1   Example 1: The DR Failure

We assume that the DR is connected to a neighbor, whereupon the DR has ceased operation due to OSPF function failure but not link failure. For the original OSPF, *Router Dead Interval* occurs in this case. We explain our method with Fig. 4 in this case.

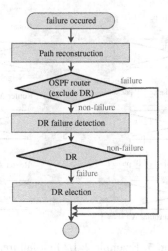

Fig. 3. Processing flow for network facilities failure.

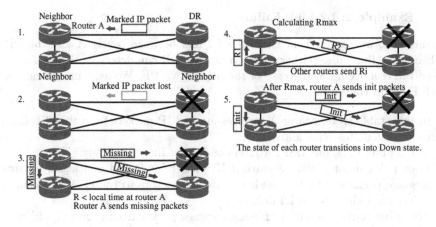

Fig. 4. Example 1: the DR failure.

1. In a stable state, router A receives marked IP packets from the DR. Each router calculates R_{DR} and R.
2. The OSPF function on the DR stops due to failure, but the link state is ready.
3. Router A cannot receive a marked IP packet by R and multicasts missing message packets.
4. The other routers multicast their R. Router A calculates R_{max}.
5. The other routers cannot receive a marked IP packet from the DR by R and does not send an alive message packet. Router A cannot receive an alive message packet by R_{max} and multicast init message packets. Subsequently, the state of all routers transits into the down state of OSPF.

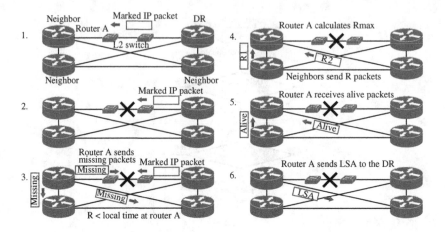

Fig. 5. Example 2: L2 link failure.

4.2   Example 2: L2 Link Failure

In this case, we assume that there is a L2 link between router A and the DR.
When an L2 link fails, neither router A nor the DR can detect it. Hence, *Router
Dead Interval* occurs in the case of the original OSPF. We explain our method
with Fig. 5 in this case.

1. In this stable state, router A receives marked IP packets from the DR. Each
   router calculates R_{DR} and R.
2. The L2 link fails, but OSPF routers and other links are ready.
3. Router A cannot receive a marked IP packet by R and multicasts missing
   message packets. The DR sends marked IP packets to router A and cannot
   detect the failure on an L2 link.
4. The other routers receive a missing message packet from router A and multicast R.
5. The other routers receive marked IP packets from the DR and multicast alive
   message packets.
6. Router A receives an alive message packets and sends LSA to the DR.

4.3   Example 3: Few User IP Packets

In this example, there is no network failure. However, few user IP packets traverse
the DR. The detection time of our proposed method depends on the average
packet arrival interval time. If the amount of user IP packets declines further,
the packet arrival interval time increases to an ever greater extent, and hence the
detection time of our proposed method follows suit. We confirm the mechanism
of our proposal in this situation with Fig. 6.

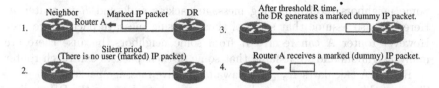

Fig. 6. Example 3: few user IP packets.

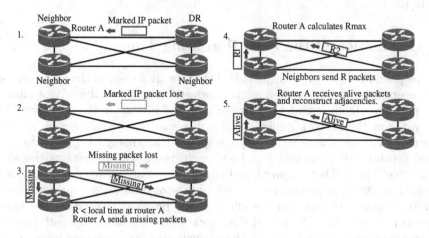

Fig. 7. Example 4: message packets lost.

1. In this stable state, router A receives marked IP packets from the DR. Each router calculates R_{DR} and R.
2. The user applications temporarily stop communications.
3. When the DR does not receive a user IP packet by R, it generates a marked dummy IP packet and sends it to the router A.
4. Router A receives a marked dummy IP packet and can confirm that the DR is alive.

4.4 Example 4: Loss of Message Packets

In this example, we assume that some of the marked IP packets, missing message packets and alive message packets are lost. We confirm the mechanism of our proposal in this situation with Fig. 7.

1. In a stable state, router A receives marked IP packets from the DR. Each router calculates R_{DR} and R.
2. Marked IP packets are lost due to some failures.
3. Router A cannot receive a marked IP packet by R and multicasts missing message packets. However, we assume that certain missing message packets are lost due to some failures.

4. Some neighbors receive missing message packets and send R to router A. Here, we also assume that some of those missing message packets are lost. However router A can receive R from some neighbors, because there are many neighbors and we assume that some of their packets can reach router A. Router A calculates R_{max} and awaits an alive message packet.
5. Some neighbors can multicast alive message packets, because the DR is alive, some of which can be received by router A Subsequently, router A sends LSA to the DR.

5 Evaluation of the Path Rerouting Time

In the previous Sect. 3.3, we explained that there are 2 cases of the path reroute processing time of our proposed method for network facility failure. We evaluate the path reroute processing time for our proposed method in those 2 cases.

We show the network configuration in Fig. 8 as the typical network model. There are 2 types of network, a backbone network and many local networks. All local networks are connected to a backbone network. OSPF manages the network *area*. The backbone is *area* 0 and local networks are *area* i ($i = 1, 2, \ldots, N$) on typical OSFP networks. But we set only *area* 0 on all networks for simplicity. Because we focus on the effect of our proposal method on the path reroute processing time. If the OSPF networks have many *areas*, the path reroute processing time needs to include path information propagation time from a area to the other area.

We assume that each local and backbone network has a DR, a backup DR and 18 OSPF neighbor routers. In this network configuration, we evaluate the processing time for path rerouting from router A to router B. We assume that backup DR and DR fail at the same time in this evaluation.

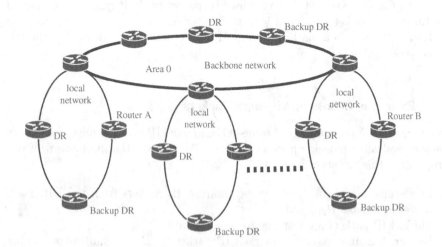

Fig. 8. Evaluation network model.

Table 1. Various delays affecting the operation of OSPF protocol [3,8].

Name	Processing time and description
Hello interval	The time delay between successive Hello packets. Usually 10 sec
Router dead interval	The time delay since the last Hello before a neighbor is declared to be down. Usually 4 times the *Hello Interval*.
SPF delay	The delay between the shortest path calculation and the first topology change that triggered the calculation. Used to avoid frequent shortest path calculations. Usually 5 sec
SPF calculation delay	$0.00000247 \times x^2 + 0.000978$ sec (Cisco 3600 series)
Route install delay	The delay between shortest path calculation and update of forwarding table. Observed to be 0.2 sec
LSA processing delay	<0.001 sec
Hello processing delay	<0.001 sec[a]

[a] In [8], CISCO Systems, Inc. showed the OSPF processing log with time stamp. The time resolution of this log is 0.001 sec. and we can see that hello processing delay is less than 0.001 sec. Thus, we set that hello processing delay is less than 0.001 sec)

Next, we set the evaluation parameters. The paper [3] lists different standards and vendor introduced delays that affect the OSPF operation in networks of popular commercial routers. We show those delays which are used in our evaluation in Table 1.

Also, the DR failure detection time of our proposal methods depends on the arrival interval time of user IP packets. In this evaluation, we set the following constant arrival interval time of user IP packets on each link for simplicity.

- Arrival interval: 1, 0.5, 0.1 sec

5.1 Case 1: DR Failure

Initially, we evaluate the path reroute processing time for both our proposed method and the original OSPF in the case of DR failure on the backbone network as a typical case.

In the case of the original OSPF, new DR and backup DR are elected among neighbors after *Router Dead Interval*, whereupon OSPF routers reconstruct the path table.

In the case of our proposed method, new DR and backup DR are elected without *Router Dead Interval* by a new failure detection mechanism using marked IP packets.

We sum up the overall processing delay time of the path rerouting according to the original OSPF algorithm and our proposed method. The Fig. 9 shows the path reroute processing time for the original OSPF and proposed method. When the number of OSPF routers increases, so does the SPF calculation delay.

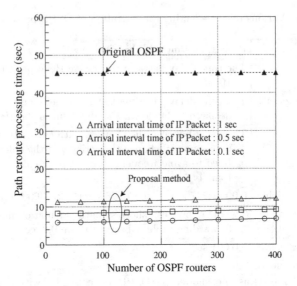

Fig. 9. Path reroute processing time for case 1.

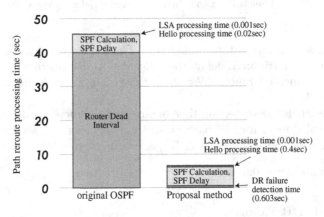

Fig. 10. The details of path reroute processing time for case 1. (Number of OSPF routers is 400).

However, this increase is minor in terms of total processing delay. The Fig. 10 shows the details of processing time in the case of 400 routers. The major contribution to path reroute processing time is SPF delay and *Router Dead Interval*. Thus, we can say that our proposed method reduces this processing time very effectively, because it avoids *Router Dead Interval*.

Also, if the arrival interval time of the marked IP packets exceeds 0.1 sec, our proposed method can send dummy marked IP packets every 0.1 sec In this case, the bandwidth consumed is 5.12 kbps (The size of a dummy packet is 64 bytes). This bandwidth consumption can be considered negligible.

5.2   Case 2: Marked Packet Loss

In this case, we assume that certain marked IP packets, missing message packets and alive message packets are lost in the network. This case is similar to example 4 in Sect. 4.4.

Both the DR and backup DR are operating normally. However, the original OSPF and proposed method determine that the DR and backup DR have stopped the OSPF operation, because hello packets and marked IP packets are lost.

In the case of the original OSPF, both the DR and backup DR are elected among OSPF routers after *Router Dead Interval* and the path table is reconstructed.

In the case of the proposed method, some neighbors cannot detect either the DR or backup DR. However, there are many OSPF routers (neighbors) and all routers monitoring the marked IP packets. We cannot assume that all marked IP packets are lost. Thus, neighbors can receive some marked IP packets and multicast alive message packets. Also, we assume that some alive message packets can reach neighbors, if some alive message packets are lost. Neighbors which receive alive message packets send the LSA packets to the DR and reconstruct the routing table. In the case of the proposed method, the DR election process is omitted, because the neighbor can confirm that the DR is alive.

The Fig. 11 shows the results of the path reroute processing time for the original OSPF and proposed method in this case and Fig. 12 shows the detail of results. We confirm that our proposed method can reduce the path reroute processing time, because it avoids *Router Dead Interval*.

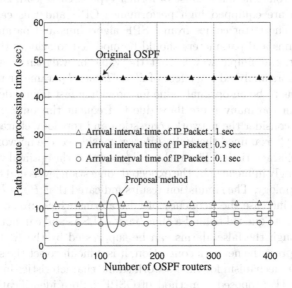

Fig. 11. Path reroute processing time for case 2.

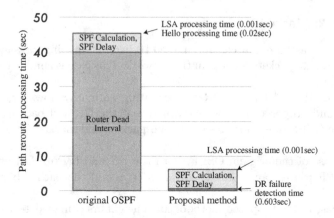

Fig. 12. The details of path reroute processing time for case 2. (Number of OSPF routers is 400).

6   Related Work

There have been several approches and proposals for the network failure detection method on OSPF networks. OSPF has the complex processing algorithms and many factors of processing delay to recover the link failure. There are mainly 2 kinds of delay type. One is compute part, such as generation of routing and forwarding tables, processing hello packets or link state packets (LSP) and so on. The other is wait or time out part, such as SPF hold delay, *Router Dead Interval* and so on. The main cause of former type is CPU load. But the newest OSPF routers are equipped high performance CPU and this case should be neglected [3]. The latter comes from OSPF algorithms and parameters. Thus, OSPF algorithms and parameters should be modified to achieve the fast failure recovery. First, the simple way is that the value of wait timer is reduced. In paper [9], authors analyzed the effect of *Hello Interval* parameter reduction and reported 275 ms to be an optimal value for providing fast failure detection while not resulting in too many route flaps due to frequent timeouts. However, this paper did not consider the network congestion and topology characteristics.

The paper [3] examined the *Hello Interval* considered the network congestion and topology characteristics. The authors claimed that the optimal value for *Hello Interval* is strongly influenced by the expected congestion levels and the number of links in the topology. The simulation results indicated that *Hello Interval* under 10 sec leads to increase the frequency of false alarms which are generated if the *Hello* message gets queued behind a huge burst of LSAs and can not be processed in time. Although the false alarms can be suppressed by the RED mechanism which can suppress the network congestion, it is difficult to set the suitable parameters of RED mechanism for the network traffic characteristics in general.

The Paper [4] proposed a method of OSPF failure identification based on LSA flooding analysis taking these aspects into account. This approach works suitable on OSPF networks. Also, the paper [10] proposed the failure insensitive routing (FIR). This proposal method is proactive routing approach and computes interface - specific forwarding and backwarding tables for link failures. When this method detects link failures, it can avoid link failures and reroute effectively. However, if the OSPF on a router ceases the operation or the L2 link failures (in this case, network topology contains L2-network), these proposed method cannot detect those failures and avoid *Router Dead Interval*.

7   Conclusions

We proposed a fast DR failure detection mechanism for OSPF to reroute paths when the DR has ceased operation. The original OSPF uses hello packets to detect DR failure, but it takes *Router Dead Interval*. Our new DR failure detection mechanism substitutes user IP packets for the hello packets to avoid *Router Dead Interval*.

Our proposed method involves the 2 processing procedures for network facility failures. We evaluated it in each case on the typical OSPF network models and results showed that our proposed method can reduce the path reroute processing time, due to avoiding *Router Dead Interval*. Our proposed method is very effective in rerouting paths when the DR and backup DR fails.

In this paper, we showed the results by the calculating the sum of processing the time according to the original algorithms and the proposed method. We will install our proposed method on a test OSPF router and evaluate the performance in the event of network failure.

References

1. Moy, J.T.: RFC 2328: OSPF version 2 (1998)
2. Moy, J.T.: OSPF: Anatomy of an Internet Routing Protocol. Addison-Wesley Professional, Reading (1998)
3. Goyal, M.: Achieving faster failure detection in ospf networks. In: Proceedings of the International Conference on Communications (ICC), pp. 296–300
4. Yuichiro, H., Tomohiko, O., Shigehiro, A., Hasegawa, T.: OSPF failure identification based on lsa flooding analysis. In: 10th IFIP/IEEE International Symposium on Integrated Network Management (IM), pp. 717–720 (2007)
5. Stevens, W.R.: TCP/IP Illustrated. Protocols, vol. 1. Addison Wesley Longman, Reading (1994)
6. Jacobson, V.: Congestion avoidance and control. ACM Comput. Commun. Rev. 18(4), 314–329 (1988)
7. Jacobson, V.: Berkeley tcp evolution from 4.3-tahoe to 4.3-reno. In: Proceedings of the Eighteenth Internet Engineering Task Force, p. 365 (1990)
8. CISCO Systems: Troubleshooting the routing protocols: Rst-3901. In Cisco Networkers (2007)
9. Basu, A., Riecke, J.: Stability issues in ospf routing. In: Proceedings of the 2001 Conference on Applications, Technologies, Architectures, and Protocols for Computer Communications, SIGCOMM '01, pp. 225–236. ACM, New York (2001)
10. Nelakuditi, S., Lee, S., Yu, Y., Zhang, Z.-L., Chuah, C.-N., Member, S.: Fast local rerouting for handling transient link failures. IEEE/ACM Trans. Networking 15, 359–372 (2007)

Intelligent Monitoring System for Bird Behavior Study

D.F. Larios[1(✉)], C. Rodríguez[2], J. Barbancho[1], M. Baena[3],
F. Simón[1], J. Marín[2], C. León[1], and J. Bustamante[2]

[1] Departamento de Tecnología Electrónica,
Universidad de Sevilla, Seville, Spain
{dlarios,jbarbancho,cleon}@us.es
[2] Department of Wetland Ecology,
Doñana Biological Station (EDB-CSIC), Seville, Spain
horus@csic.ebd.es
[3] ICTS, Singular Scientific and Technological Infrastructure,
Doñana Biological Station, Seville, Spain

Abstract. Until now, the best way to obtain relevant information about the behaviour of animals is capturing them. However, the procedure to capture individuals cause them stress and introduces an effect on the measurement that can affect the behaviour of the animals. To solve this problems this paper describes a novel intelligent motoring system for birds breeding in nest boxes. This system is based in a network of smart-nest boxes that allows access to the acquired data all over the world through internet. A prototype of the proposed system has been implemented for the evaluation of a lesser kestrel breeding colony in Southern Spain. This prototype has offered in a short time more valuable information that several years of manual captures. This prototype has demonstrated that the proposed system allows short and log time animal behaviour evaluation without interferences or causing stress.

Keywords: Neuronal network · Computational intelligence · Data fusion · Environmental monitoring · Sensor networks

1 Introduction

For zoologists, one of the most important periods for a bird is the breeding period, being this period one of the most frequently studied. Mate acquisition, nest defence, mate feeding, incubation, and chick rearing (including provisioning flights) are studied in the surroundings of the nest. Many of these aspects help us understand key topics in ecology, such as what factors influencing lifetime reproductive success (LRS: [17]), the parent-offspring conflict [21, 23], or evolutive stable strategies (ESS: [16]) regarding sex roles in reproduction [15].

Classic monitoring methods that require the capturing of individuals or close-up observations limit the amount and quality of data that can be obtained. Therefore, in this paper a remote monitoring system based on smart nest-boxes is proposed. These smart nest-boxes allow acquiring high amount of data without stressing the animals, gathering long-term and highly reliable information on the species.

© Springer-Verlag Berlin Heidelberg 2014
M.S. Obaidat and J. Filipe (Eds.): ICETE 2012, CCIS 455, pp. 36–51, 2014.
DOI: 10.1007/978-3-662-44791-8_3

The proposed system, called HORUS, permits gathering basic information on the identity of individuals, studying its behaviour and the temporal changes in individual body mass. All this information can be made accessible through the internet to scientist all over the world.

Some of the information recorded by the system can be used to study, without in terference, the behaviour of species during the breeding period. One of the most important biometric parameters in birds is body mass. It allows us to measure the impact of parental care on breeding individuals. Manually, it is impossible to develop a continuous monitoring of this parameter. Capturing causes too much stress on the individual in its most sensitive period. Another important parameter is the measurement of the amount of food brought to the nest by individuals to feed their offspring.

The proposed system allows us to perform a continuous monitoring of the reproduction without stressing the individuals, e.g. obtaining reliable body mass measurements every time a bird enters or leaves the nest. The main problem obtaining the measurements is the movement of the animal, which produces unstable values. These values have been calibrated using a neuronal network processing, obtaining high accurate measurements.

The rest of the paper is organized as follows: Sect. 2 focuses on the lesser kestrel behaviour study, especially comparing a traditional approach versus automated data reading. Section 3 briefly describes the HORUS system infrastructure. A detailed description of the information treatment developed in this project can be found in Sect. 4. The results obtained with our system are shown in Sect. 5. Finally, Sect. 6 sum-up conclusions and provides remarks.

2   Lesser Kestrel Breeding Behavior Study

The lesser kestrel (Falco naumanni) is a small (body mass around 150 g) migratory falcon inhabiting open landscapes [6]. It is a colonial species that breeds in old buildings, such as churches or castles within urban areas in Western Europe. The species experienced a marked decline in its Western Palearctic breeding range in the middle of the 20th century [1, 6]. Considered previously one of the most abundant raptors in Europe [2] the lesser kestrel became extinct in several countries (e.g. Austria, Hungary, Poland) and practically disappeared in others (e.g. France, Portugal, Bulgaria).

Mediterranean Spain constitutes its stronghold in the Western Palearctic [1]. However, the Spanish population also suffered a precipitous decline, as it dropped from an estimated 20,000–50,000 pairs in the 1970s [9] to 4,000–5,000 breeding pairs in 1988 [10]. This decline has been attributed to the reduction in both the extent and quality of foraging habitats [18]. The species is also sensitive to climate warming [20]. So it makes for a good model species to study the impact of global change on an endangered species.

2.1 Traditional Monitoring

The *"Estación Biológica de Doñana"* (EDB-CSIC) has been monitoring lesser kestrel colonies since 1988. It has been recording colony occupancy and breeding success in terms of number of fledglings and proportion of successful nests. Regarding individual monitoring, birds have been marked with metal and PVC rings with a unique alpha-numeric code that allows identifying individuals by using telescopes. Biometric mea-sures were taken sporadically for all marked individuals when captured. Due to ethical reasons, however, the number of captures in the nest is limited (the capture alters breeding behaviour and may jeopardize the survival of the offspring) and the majority of resightings were made with telescopes. This causes high differences in the frequency of recaptures among individuals mainly due to differences in detectability. In a classic data base monitoring, 2,135 birds figured as recaptured (including resightings with telescope). On average they were captured 3 times on the same breeding season (range: 1–70). In approximately 45 % of cases, body mass was measured and maximum number of measurements per bird and year was 4.

Because of that, the pattern of body mass variation of breeding adults from arrival to the colony in mid-February to the end of the nestling period in mid-July is not well known. The proposed remote monitoring system aims to bridge the above detailed logistic and ethic gaps, thus allowing us to get enough information to document both patterns.

2.2 Automated Data Reading

Habitat monitoring has evolved greatly evolution due to the boom of sensor networks technology.

Several consequences have been caused due to the increase of sensors: Firstly the quality of information grows in time and on the spatial domain; secondly the possibility of transmitting the measured data through the network increases the need of having high bandwidth communications; and thirdly, it to the reduction of the cost of the data storage makes possible to save huge amounts of data.

All these consequences imply some negative effects: an increase of data traffic and increase of power consumption.

Some authors have taken these effects into account [4, 22] and have expressed the need to employ processing techniques in order to reduce these handicaps.

There are different approaches to habitat monitoring. Some of them use wireless sensor network technology in order to acquire and process the physical information [3, 8, 11, 24]. Others focus on the needed middleware that allows access to the physical information [7, 12].

In our approach, both aspects are considered.

3 Horus Infraestructure

The proposed infrastructure is a distributed system as Fig. 1 depicts. This figure shows the most important devices of the proposed architecture.

These devices will now bebriefly described.

3.1 Network Infrastructure

The HORUS infrastructure is made up of different subsystems interconnected through a low data rate communication network.

This network has been designed considering the following restrictions:

- The devices that provided information to the network are deployed in a spread way without any previous planning.
- The data rate associated with the data sources is low (< 250 kbps)
- The system could be easily scalable.

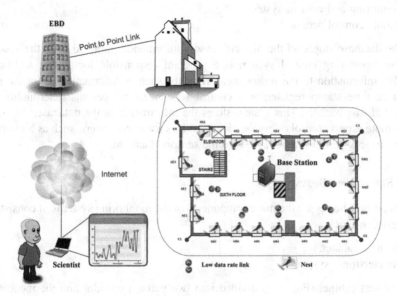

Fig. 1. HORUS network scheme.

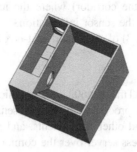

Fig. 2. Nest cabinet.

The network used in HORUS can be accessible through different physical media (wireless or wired based).

Robustness of the network is very important, for the proposed application: during the breeding period, it is not possible to realize maintenance tasks, because it can disturb and stress the colony. All detected failures would be repaired in winter, after the birds have left the colony.

3.2   Base Station

The process server is a system that offers the following services:

- Database server.
- Monitoring and control system.
- Remote control access.

The database stores all the historic sensors information gathered from the system.

The monitoring control system is a program responsible for adding additional valuable information to the sensor measurements, such as information about the nest sender, a time stamp register or a control sequence, that permits determining the number of loss packets. This system stores the information in the database.

Remote access control offers the cloud services for remote users, such as biologists. These services permit remote access to the sensors database.

3.3   Smart Nest-Boxes

The smart nest-boxes are the main components of the monitoring systems. It consists of the next two blocks:

- The nest cabinet.
- The electronic system

The nest cabinet (Fig. 2) is divided into two parts: a corridor and the incubation chamber. This nest cabinet has a smart design to ensure that the birds pass the corridor each time they enter or leave the nest. The advantage of this is to allow the distribution the sensors in a small area (the corridor) where the animal is forced to pass and, therefore, it ensures obtaining the sensor information.

The electronic system (Fig. 3) of each smart nest-box is accomplished with the next subsystems:

Microcontroller Board

This board is based on the ATmega2560, an economic, low power and robust microcontroller. It controls and processes the nest's sensor information. This board communicates with sensors and other components, and processes the collected information that is sent to the process server over the communication interface.

The program implemented in the microcontroller performs the following tasks:

- Communicates with the process server over a communication interface, and synchronize clock time with this.
- Checks infra-red barriers. Each nest-box has two infra-red barriers at both extremes of the corridor. The sequence in which they are activated indicates whether birds enter or leave the nest-box.

- Checks if the RFID reader has read a code from ringed kestrels.
- Obtains the body mass measurement from a digital balance.
- Reads the temperature and humidity of the nest.
- Controls the RFID reader to identify individuals.

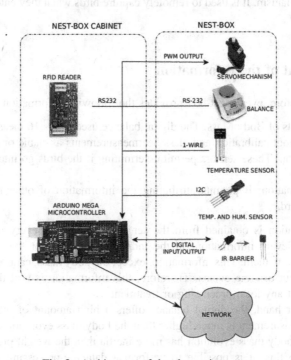

Fig. 3. Architecture of the electronic system.

Sensors Board

A sensor board adapts the logic levels from the nest sensors to the microcontroller board's requirements.

All the nest's sensors are spread onto the corridor of the nest. Positions of sensors are designed to ensure that every time the birds pass the corridor the system registers at least one record per sensor.

The deployed sensors are:

- A Digital Balance. It allows a maximum weight of 600 g and an accuracy of 0.01 g, offering 16 measures per second. It permits getting an estimate of the body mass of the individuals in movement. Although the pan is round, it has been modified to be rectangular in order to fit the shape of the corridor.
- An integrated temperature sensor located in the window. It is calibrated to operate in environmental temperature range. It is used to measure the nest temperature.
- An integrated Humidity Sensor. It is used to measure the nest humidity.
- Two infra-red barriers, used to trace the direction of birds' movements.

- A RFID reader. It communicates via RS-232C and offers a reading on the unique ID of a tagged bird, when it is passing through the nest entrance. This system has mechanisms to avoid collisions, permitting operation even when there are several birds around the entrance.
- A Servomechanism. It is used to remotely capture birds when they enter in the nest-box.

4   Treatment of the Information

As described before, every nest-box provides the following information:

- Measurements of Body Mass: The digital balance used offers 16 measurements per seconds without calibration and classifies measurements as stable or unstable.
- IR Information: These sensors permit determining if the birds go into or go out of the nest.
- RFID Information: It permits attributing the information of other sensors to an individual bird.

All this information is obtained from the sensors deployed in every nest-box. The sensors offer relevant information on the individual breeding at the colony to the biologists that study them. This information, except the body mass, cannot be added, as they inform about discrete events. Therefore, this information is sent directly to the database without any local processing or treatment.

On the other hand, the digital balance offers a high amount of information. Its frequency of measurement is much higher than the body mass evolution of the animal. i.e., the animal body mass evolution has more inertia than the weight provided by the balance. Due to this, it is possible to perform a data pre-processing about weight information, reducing with that the amount of information send to the central processing.

4.1   Weight Pre-processing

The algorithm described in this paper, is focused on locally pre-processing the weight information, to reduce the amount of unnecessary information and increase its accuracy. It is designed to be executed in each nest-box, in the microcontroller board. It has been designed to fulfil the next goals:

- To reduce the amount of useless information in the database using local pre-processing.
- To increase the accuracy of the measurements, calibrating the results obtained.
- To increase accuracy of the communication network, reducing the amount of packet loss, the delays and the collisions.
- To increase the amount of useful information in the database, estimating a body mass from each pattern with non-stable measurements.
- To permit its execution on devices with low resources.

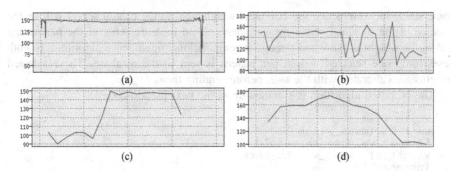

Fig. 4. Different weight pattern Y-axis, weight in grams. X-axis, samples.

To increase the accuracy a tare calibration is necessary. The balance used offers measurements without a tare calibration. This calibration would be obtained consulting the body mass measured by the balance, when there is no animal on the pan i.e., when the measured weight is below a certain threshold. This threshold can be obtained as a function of the body mass of the animals to monitor. In our deployment for the Lesser Kestrel (with a body mass range of 100–190 g) a threshold of 100 g of has been used.

In the real deployment we have proven that the tare does not change significantly during a year. Therefore, measuring the tare only once per day offers enough accuracy for the proposed system.

On the other hand, as described before, the balance offers 16 weight measurements tagging them every second by itself as stable (i.e., measurements that remain a same value during a long period of time) or unstable. But birds usually do not pass over the balance slow enough to obtain stable measurements. This causes the database to have a high amount of the information as unstable measures. In the real prototype only about 15.25 % of the measured patterns had a stable measurement, considering a pattern as the collection of measurements obtained from the time the bird gets on the balance (i.e., when the balance acquires a weight over the threshold) until the animal gets out of balance (i.e., when the balance acquires during 5 s weights below the threshold). Figure 4 shows different examples of weight patterns obtained in the real deployment with these conditions.

This figure shows different real weight patterns obtained from the same animal in different days. Only pattern (a) has some stable measurement. These stable measurements have been compared with measurements of the animal done manually capturing the bird. The stable tare measurements are correct, but not frequent enough to obtain a long term sequence of body mass temporal change of the birds at the colony.

To solve this, a computational intelligence algorithm to estimate the body mass of animals from the patterns with non-stable weights has been developed, increasing the amount of useful information. This neuronal network algorithm is described below.

Initially, the system has been designed to store, in the central server, all weight measurements of the pattern acquired by the balance, stable or unstable, but it causes high bandwidth consumption in the communications interface.

To reduce the amount of useless information, the proposed algorithm only sends one estimated weight to the database for each measured patterns. If the pattern has some stable measurements, the estimated weight sent to the central server will be the average of the obtained stable measurements. If no measurements of the pattern are stable, the weight is estimated through a computational intelligence algorithm. In both cases, only one selected weight per pattern is sent to the database. These selected weights are calibrated with the tare, before sending them.

The proposed algorithm is summed-up in the next pseudo-code:

```
while 1:
wait new(meas_weight);
if meas_weight>=threshold
weight[i]:=meas_weight-tare;
increase I;
if stable(meas_weight)==1
stable :=1;
end if
else
if i!=0
if stable==1
est_weight:=average(
stable_weight);
stable:=0;
else
est_weight:=model(weigth);
end if
send_server(est_weight);
i:=0;
else
new_tare:=meas_weight;
tare:=Iter_RMS(prev_tares,
new_tare);
end if
end if
end while
```

Applying Machine Learning for Weight Recognition

For this application, an algorithm has been evaluated. Initially, an algorithm without machine learning based on the differences between consecutives measurements has been considered. This algorithm considers a weight stable if there are more than a certain number of measurements of the same weight. This is similar to the internal algorithm of the balance for tagging measurements as stable or unstable, but it is less restrictive: the balance requires a high number of measurements with the same value to consider a measurement stable. It permits the retrieval of some weights from the unstable patterns, but it fails with complex patterns. Our proposal of using computational intelligence (machine learning) increases the percentage of success.

Machine learning is widely used in pattern recognition, but its use in animal monitoring is less widespread. Other supervised learning techniques apart of the neuronal network have been considered. Non supervised techniques, such as Self-Organized maps (SOM, [14]) or Support Vector Machine (SVM, [5]) were discarded, because we have some stable measurements that permit performing training.

One example of the considered supervised machine learning techniques is the use of Artificial Neuro-Fuzzy Inference Systems (ANFIS; [13]). ANFIS has many applications in the evaluation of complex systems, but it requires a previous knowledge of the system to design the rules and the initial system. This system was discarded; due to the complex forms of the patterns that do not easily permit acquire this initial system.

Expert systems or case based experts system were not considered, due to the amount of previous information gathered from the smart nest-box was not sufficient for these kinds of systems.

For these reasons, a neuronal network model was finally chosen. The variables used as inputs of the model are as follows:

- Max_1: The most repeated weight in a pattern (the largest if multiple).
- N_1: Number of repetitions of the previous variable in a pattern.
- Max_2: The second most repeated weight in a pattern (the largest if multiple).
- N_2: Number of repetitions, in a pattern, of the previous variable.
- Max_C1: The most consecutively repeated weight in a pattern.
- NC_1: Number of repetitions of the previous variable in a pattern,
- Max_C2: The second most repeated weight, consecutively, in a pattern.
- NC_2: Number of repetitions, in a pattern, of the previous variable.
- N_EL: Total number of weight measures in a pattern.

In order to obtain these parameters, a pattern with at least 5 weight measurements is needed. As an value output, the neuronal network model offers a value, called "Output weight". This output reflects the estimated weight of the neuron model and it is the information sent through the network to the server database.

The steps execution of this neuronal network model is summed-up in the next pseudo-code, where the neuronal network is the execution of a three layer network.

Neuronal network needs a set of parameters for its training. These sets have been obtained for each pattern with stable measures, by executing the following steps:

1. A variable name "Target weight" was defined for every pattern. This variable stores the average value of all stable weights. This is the target result of the training of the neuronal network.
2. For every pattern, a new pattern has been created, eliminating all stable measurements.
3. The inputs have been obtained from this new pattern without stable values.
4. The input values for each pattern were stored, together with their respective Target weight into a table, named "Training information"

With these tables two sets of information were obtained, one for training and the other for evaluating the accuracy of the system. In total, the training information table has 1163 sets of values. 50 % of these values (randomly selected) were used for training, and the other 50% were used for validation.

5 Simulation, Tests and Results

The results obtained with this system can be classified in two types: analysis of the network performance and weight estimation accuracy obtained with the real deployment.

This section summarizes these two types of results.

Table 1. Analysis of the database.

Caption	Value
Measurement weight	2583565
Number of pattern	51517
Patterns with stable weights	7856
Average pattern time	23,18 s
Days of test	399 days

5.1   Network Performance

During the first year of the deployment (2010), the prototype was sending information from all sensors, even the 16 records per second of the balance, to the database of the central server. The main characteristic of the gathered information in the database is summarized in Table 1.

After a year of deployment, the analysis of data allowed us to detect some network conflicts. For example, if different nest-boxes are acquiring weights from individuals at the same time, they are competing for control of the bus, causing data collisions and delays in transmitting information. The proposed system allows avoiding these conflicts, using the proposed data fusion.

In this section we are going to quantify the advantage of data fusion against the classical centralized systems. Due to that, in this kind of applications it is important to reduce the use of bandwidth as much as possible.

The analysis of database information has been summed-up in the Table 1. It shows that only a 15.25 % of the acquired patterns have any stable measurement.

Knowing that the balance offers 16 Samples Per Second (SPS), the average payload of the application layer per pattern of the system without data fusion can be obtained with the Eq. 1.

$$N_{T,raw} = 16_{sps} \cdot P_T \cdot N_{Bytes} \cdot N_{msg} \qquad (1)$$

Where $N_{T,raw}$ is the number of bytes to send per day at application layer; P_T is the length of the pattern in seconds; N_{Bytes} is the number of bytes to send. 16 bytes in this case and N_{msg} is the number of messages per day.

On the other hand, with the proposed algorithm, only one message per pattern is sent. In this case, the payload per pattern can be obtained according to Eq. 2.

$$N_{T,raw} = N_{Bytes} \cdot N_{msg} \qquad (2)$$

This shows that the amount of information sent to the database varies in function of the number of patterns and the length (in time) of the pattern. Figure 5 depicts these results.

Concluding, the local processing permits one to drastically reduce the used throughput of the network, especially in days with a high number of patterns.

This data fusion and aggregation scheme is especially important for its use in low bandwidth systems, due to it permitting one to save energy. With the proposed system, only one message per pattern is sent, instead of 16 measurements per second during the capture of the pattern. These results are summed-up in Table 2. They consider the average pattern length of 23.18 s, i.e. the average time while the bird is on the balance.

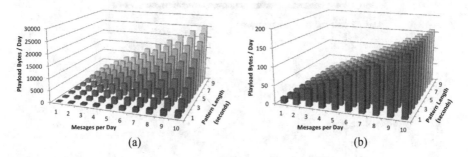

(a)   (b)

Fig. 5. Bytes per day send, at application layer, to the central server. (a) Without data fusion. (b) With data fusion.

With these conditions and with the CC2420 radio transceiver, widely used in wireless sensor network, permit saving 99.76 % of the energy used in data transmissions, considering a power consumption of 38 mW in transmission mode [19].

Using all weight patterns obtained in the year 2010, the proposed body mas s estimation algorithm permits the retrieval of around 56.21 % of the patterns without stable measurements.

This is a good result that permits us to obtain an average of 4 body mass estimations per day and nest, which is 4 times higher than using only patterns with stable measurements. It permits to have a continuous tracing of body mass in individuals.

As a conclusion, the local processing permits us to drastically reduce the used throughput of the network, especially in the days with a high number of patterns.

5.2   Body Mass Estimation Accuracy

Based on the training and verification set described in Sect. 4.1, some analysis has been done to the proposed algorithm for body mass estimation.

With the evaluation set, the system offers an accuracy of 98.7 %, i.e., an error in the order of 2 g, which is quite small considering the typical body mass of these animals (150 g).

This accuracy permits analysis of a long series for the evaluation of temporal changes in body mass, and sometimes to determine the body mass of prey, when birds bring medium-sized animals to the nest to feed the nestlings.

Table 2. Cost per message with CC2420 Radio transceiver.

Caption	Energy (J)
Without data fusion	255.3
With data fusion	0.608

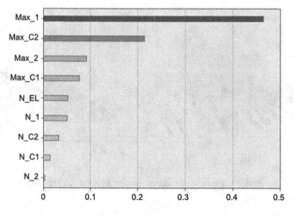

Fig. 6. Neural network model: importance of the variables in the calculation of the estimated weights.

From the training procedure, an analysis of the importance of the input parameters in relationship with the target body mass can be obtained. Figure 6 shows these results. This analysis concludes that the selected parameters are valid to effectively estimate the body mass of animals.

5.3   Real Deployment

A prototype, for a real validation of the proposed system, has been deployed in the grain elevator of "La Palma del Condado (Huelva Province, SW Spain". At this site, researchers of the Estación Biológica de Doñana have been studying the lesser kestrel colony since 1994. At this colony, kestrels nested on the windowsills of the grain elevator that are sheltered and sufficiently enclosed to make a suitable nesting site.

For the prototype installation we select the windows on the 6th floor of the building where smart nest-boxes were installed, and readily accepted, by kestrels during preliminary checking (3 and 4 nest-boxes during 2008 and 2009, respectively) and also when the definitive prototype installation was made in 2010.

Nest-boxes are placed in all the windows along the sixth floor. They are named "6XY", where X refers to the cardinal point and Y is an ordinal number. Each box has two separate entrances and two incubation chambers (I. left and D: right) in a symmetrical distribution. Entrances are placed at the extremes of the box to avoid potential aggressions between neighbours, thus maximizing the number of potential breeding pairs. Nonetheless, the right part has not been opened yet.

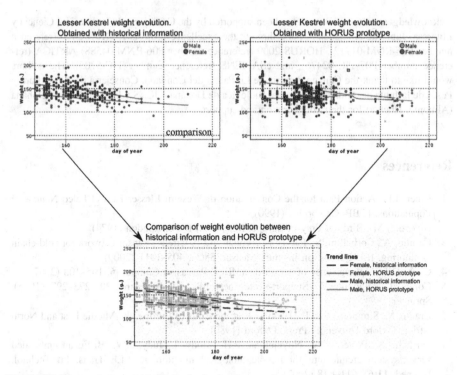

Fig. 7. Weight evolution obtained on the basis of manual measurements along several years of monitoring. Each point represents a single measurement of an individual.

Until now, the proposed system has offered the following qualitative conclusions:

- 18 of the 20 installed nests-boxes were used by breeding kestrels. This leads to the conclusion that the proposed system effectively allows one to gather a high amount of information about the behaviour of breeding individuals without stressing them. If the nest and its sensors were hostile, it would not have been chosen by lesser kestrels breeding pairs.
- The lesser kestrel mainly feeds on insects, but sometimes can catch slightly bigger prey, such as small rodents, birds or lizards (with around a dozen of grams). The proposed system would permit an analysis of the frequency of big prey captures.

As said before, the proposed system allows obtain in a short period of time similar data than the obtained by recapturing the individuals during a lot of time. Figure 7 depicts a comparison of the body weight evolution, using both the proposed system and historical data from manual captures. Historical data took 24 years (1988–2012 breeding periods) for the acquisition of data with sporadic captures of different individuals. Different years of manual captures are overlaid. As it can be seen, the results obtained from the historical data are similar to the obtained with the proposed prototype. The HORUS prototype offers in a year similar data to that obtained in 24 years of manual captures.

Acknowledgements. This work has been supported by the Consejería de Innovación, Ciencia y Empresa, Junta de Andalucía, Spain, through the excellence projects HORUS 2006 (reference number P06-RNM-01712), HORUS 2009 (reference number P06-RNM-04588) ARTICA (reference number P07-TIC-02476), and eSAPIENS (reference number TIC-5705). The authors would like to thank the Cámara Agraria de La Palma del Condado, Consejería de Agricultura y Pesca de la Junta de Andalucía, Reserva Biológica de Doñana – ICTS y Espacio Natural Doñana (Almonte, Huelva) for their collaboration and support.

References

1. Biber, J.P.: Action Plan for the Conservation of Western Llesser Kestrel Falco Naumanni Populations. ICBP, Cambridge (1990)
2. Bijleveld, M.: Birds of Prey in Europe. Macmillan Press, London (1974)
3. Carullo, A., Corbellini, S., Parvis, M., Vallan, A.: A wireless sensor network for cold-chain monitoring. IEEE Trans. on Instrum. Measur. **58**(5), 405–1411 (2009)
4. Cook, D.J.: Making sense of sensor data. IEEE Pervasive Comput. **6**, 105–108 (2007)
5. Cortes, C., Vapnik, V.: Support-vector networks. Mach. Learn. **20**, 273–297 (1995). Springer
6. Cramp, S., Simmons, K.E.L.: Handbook of the Birds of Europe, the Middle East and North Africa. Oxford University Press, Oxford (1980)
7. Farshchi, S., Pesterev, A., Nuyujukian, P.H., Mody, I., Judy, J.W.: Bi-Fi: an embedded sensor/system architecture for remote biological monitoring. IEEE Trans. Inf Technol. Biomed. **11**(6), 611–618 (2007)
8. Garcia-Sanchez, A.-J., Garcia-Sanchez, F., Losilla, F., Kulakowski, P., Garcia-Haro, J., Rodríguez, A., López-Bao, J.-V., Palomares, F.: Wireless sensor network deployment for monitoring wildlife passages. Sensors **10**, 7236–7262 (2010)
9. Garzón, J.: Birds of prey in Spain. The present situation. World Conference on Birds of Prey. Report of Proceedings, International Council for Bird Preservation, Cambridge, UK, pp. 159–170 (1977)
10. González, J.L., Merino, M.: El cernícalo primilla (Falco naumanni) en la Península Ibérica. Situación, Problemática Y Aspectos Biológicos. ICONA, Madrid (1990)
11. Handcock, R.N., Swain, D.L., Bishop-Hurley, G.J., Patison, K.P., Wark, T., Valencia, P., Corke, P., O'Neill, C.J.: Monitoring animal behaviour and environmental interactions using wireless sensor networks, gps collars and satellite remote sensing. Sensors **9**, 3586–3603 (2009)
12. Hwang, J., Shin, C., Yoe, H.: Study on an agricultural environment monitoring server system using wireless sensor networks. Sensors **10**, 11189–11211 (2010)
13. Jang, R.J.-S.: ANFIS: adaptive-network-based fuzzy inference system. IEEE Trans. Syst. Man Cybern. **23**, 665–685 (1993)
14. Kohonen, T.: The Self-organizing map. Proc. IEEE **78**(9), 1464–1480 (1990)
15. Kokko, H., Wong, B.B.M.: What determines sex roles in mate searching? Evolution **61**, 1162–1175 (2007)
16. Maynard Smith, J., Price, G.R.: The logic of animal conflict. Nature **246**, 15–18 (1973)
17. Newton, I.: Lifetime Reproduction in Birds. Academic Press, London (1992)
18. Peet, N.B., Gallo-Orsi, U.: Action plan for the Lesser Kestrel Falco naumanni. Council of Europe and BirdLife International, Cambridge, U.K. (2000)

19. Polastre, J., Szewczyk, R., Culler, D.: Telos: enabling ultra-low power wireless research. In: 4th International Symposium on Information Processing in Sensor Networks (IPSN), Los Angeles, CA, pp. 364–369, April 2005
20. Rodríguez, C., Bustamante, J.: The effect of weather on Lesser Kestrel breeding success: can climate change explain historical population declines? J. Anim. Ecol. **72**, 793–810 (2003)
21. Schlomer, G.L., Ellis, B.J., Garber, J.: Mother-child conflict and sibling relatedness: a test of hypotheses from parent-offspring conflict theory. J. Res. Adolesc. **20**, 287–306 (2010)
22. Sridhar, P.: Hierarchical Aggregation and Intelligent Monitoring and control in fault-tolerant wireless sensor networks. University of New Mexico (2007)
23. Trivers, R.L.: Parent-offspring conflict. Am. Zool. **14**, 249–264 (1974)
24. Valente, J., Sanz, D., Barrientos, A., Cerro, J., Ribeiro, A., Rossi, C.: An air-ground wireless sensor network for crop monitoring. Sensors **11**, 6088–6108 (2011)

e-Business

Three Dimensional Components
of e-Business Sustainability

Mohammed Naim A. Dewan[✉], Md. Maruf Hossan Chowdhury,
and Mohammed A. Quaddus

Curtin Graduate School of Business, Curtin University, Perth, WA, Australia
{mohammed.dewan,md.chowdhury}@postgrad.curtin.edu.au,
mohammed.quaddus@gsb.edu.curtin.edu.au

Abstract. e-Business modelling is a prevalent term now days as it converts technology into economic value. The sustainability of the business is another global contemporary issue. Although e-business modelling and sustainability are the two major global trends now but still there is no common understanding about the elements that need to be used for a sustainable e-business model. Surprisingly, none of the e-business modelling approaches even consider sustainability as a major element. In this paper, therefore, after extensive literature review on e-business modelling and sustainability of the business we carefully identify and determine the required elements for a sustainable e-business model. The elements are three dimensional and selected from customer value area, business value area, and process value area so that the modelling elements safeguard the interests of all stakeholders (customer, business, society, and environment) while maintaining the sustainability.

Keywords: e-Business · Sustainability · Business model · Blended value

1   Introduction

The term e-business modelling is widespread but it is considered that only some views of e-business have been investigated. Now days, to be competitive it has become very important that all businesses carefully validate their business objectives, requirements, and strategies through a careful process of formal business modelling with the current global e-business and e-commerce initiatives. But a very few business models talks about the sustainability of the businesses. Although sustainability issues are considered in some modelling approaches, they are mainly in strategic level and not in operational level. To develop a better understanding about sustainable business and to enhance the confidence in the feasibility of these ideas such a modelling framework needs to be developed that can be easily implemented by the stakeholders successfully and that will truly contribute to the innovative e-business modelling ideas. For the long run sustainability business modelling approaches only with strategic directions are not sufficient, instead, a complete sustainable e-business model with operational directions is essential.

Blended value or shared value is introduced by the scholars lately. According to the literature [20] blended value is the integration of economic value, social value, and environmental value. Blended value which is also referred as "shared value can be

© Springer-Verlag Berlin Heidelberg 2014
M.S. Obaidat and J. Filipe (Eds.): ICETE 2012, CCIS 455, pp. 55–71, 2014.
DOI: 10.1007/978-3-662-44791-8_4

defined as policies and operating practices that enhance the competitiveness of a company while simultaneously advancing the economic and social conditions in the communities in which it operates" [43]. But these blended value definitions in the literature do not directly include the business value or the process value. Business value is vital in the sense that it safeguards the interest of the organisation and helps to keep in track for achieving goals. Similarly, process value is another vital element as it supports to produce both customer value and business value. Therefore, we define blended value as the integration of economic value, social value, and environmental value for both customer and business. It is different from CSR (Corporate Social Responsibility) value in the sense that CSR value is separate from profit maximization and agenda is determined by external reporting, whereas blended value is integral to profit maximization and agenda is company specific and internally generated. In such a theoretical lacuna regarding blended value and e-business modelling the aim of this paper is to identify the required elements necessary to develop a sustainable e-business model that will encapsulate economic, environmental and social aspects in the strategic and operational settings of organisations. We termed them as 'blended value elements'. We, in this paper: (i) explore and determine the important elements in developing e-business model; and (ii) investigate how the sustainability dimensions can be integrated with the value dimensions in developing sustainable e-business model. The following section of the article covers extensive literature review on business modelling, e-business modelling and sustainability of the business. Section 3 explicate the importance of the three dimensional elements in e-business modelling. The identification of three dimensional elements and their comprehensive explanation is covered in Sect. 4. Section 5 is consists of discussion on findings and further research direction; and finally, Sect. 6 concludes the article.

2 Literature Review

2.1 Business Modelling

The modelling approaches by [40] and [6] are very similar, who view a business model as a model that "describes the logic of a 'business system' for creating value that lies behind the actual processes". Reference [52] provide a typology of business models that they call b-webs. In the methodology proposed by Afuah and Tucci [1], one can find a list of business model components. Osterwalder and Pigneur [37] conceive the business model as the description of the value a company offers to one or several segments of customers and the architecture of the firm and its network of partners. There are some more researchers who have worked on business modelling. Among them the research works of Zott et al., [58], Hawkins [26], Stabell and Fjeldstad [49], Linder and Cantrell [32], Applegate [5], Hamel [24], Papakiriakopoulos et al. [38] are worth mentioning.

What is found from the literature is that there are number of terms used in business modelling. Business model has been referred to as a statement [82], a description [5, 55], a representation [75, 80], an architecture [16, 53], a conceptual tool or model [76, 77, 83], a structural template [61], a method [1], a framework [60], a pattern [64], and as a set [79] found by Zott et al. [59]. There are even different aspects that are used by the scholars for business modelling, such as, product/revenue aspects, business actor/network aspects, and marketing specific aspects, etc. Although a number of researchers tried to include value aspect in their modelling but none of them precisely point out the contents of the value that will be able to make a business sustainable.

2.2   e-Business Modelling

It has been found by a study of Zott et al., [59] that in a total of 49 conceptual studies in which the business model is clearly defined, almost one fourth of the studies are related to e-business. That means, the majority of research into business models in the information systems field has been concerned with e-business and e-commerce; and there have been some attempts to develop convenient classification schemas [3]. Table 1 shows the elements that are used for business and e-business modelling by different researchers. For example, definitions, components, and classifications into e-business models have been suggested [1, 4]. Timmers [53] was the first who defined e-business model in terms of the elements and their interrelationships. Applegate [5] introduces the following six e-business models: focused distributors, portals, producers, infrastructure distributors, infrastructure portals, and infrastructure producers. Weill and Vitale [55], suggest a subdivision into so called atomic e-business models, which are analyzed according to a number of basic components. Rappa [44] provides taxonomy of e-business models based on the value offerings and mode of generating revenues. Dubosson-Torbay et al. [16] identify the following principal dimensions for classifying business models: user's role, interaction pattern, nature of the offering, pricing system, level of customization, and economic control.

2.3   e-Business and Sustainability

A sustainable business maintains a balance among economic development, environmental stewardship, and social equity [47]. In other words, sustainable business means a business with dynamic balance among three mutually inter dependent elements: (i) protection of ecosystems and natural resources; (ii) economic efficiency; and (iii) consideration of social wellbeing such as jobs, housing, education, medical care and cultural opportunities [8]. It has been evident that there is a positive correlation between environmental and social sustainability and economic return [11]. Even though many scholars enlightened their study on sustainability incorporating economic, social, and environmental perspective but still "most companies remain stuck in social responsibility mind-set in which societal issues are at the periphery, not the core. The solution lies in the principle of shared (blended) value, which involves creating economic value in a way that also creates value for society by addressing its needs and challenges" [43]. Moreover, most of the scholars provide with hypothetical ideas for maintaining sustainability. A comprehensive business model for sustainability with operational directions is still not present.

e-Business is the point where economic value creation and information technology/ ICT come together [2]. ICT can have both positive and negative impact on the society and the environment. But ccorporations have the knowledge, resources, and power to

Table 1. Business modelling elements (adapted from [3]).

Authors	Element indicators
Timmers [53, p. 4]	Architecture, Value proposition, Business actors and roles, Revenue sources
Venkatraman & Henderson [84, pp. 33–34]	Architecture, Organisation strategy, Customers, Asset configuration, Knowledge leverage
Linder & Cantrell [73, pp. 1–2]	Business logic, Value capture, Revenue sources
Gordijn et al. [67, p. 41]	Value proposition/exchange, Stakeholder network
Petrovic et al. [40, p. 2]	Business logic, Value proposition, Intermediate theoretical layer
Amit&Zott [61, p. 4]	Value proposition, Structure, Governance
Torbay et al. [16, p. 3]	Value proposition, Architecture, Network of partners, Relationship capital
Stahler [81, p. 6]	Abstract, Simplification of current and future business reality
Chesbrough & Rosenbloom [66, p. 532]	Coherent framework, Mediating construct, Technology, Economic Value
Magretta [74, p. 4]	Value proposition, Customers, Revenue sources
Bouwman [63, p. 3]	Roles and relationships: company, customer, partners, Value proposition
Hedman & Kalling [69, pp. 49, 52–53]	Key business components, Resources, Customers, Value proposition, Network, Architecture, Structure, Dynamic
Campanovo & Pigneur [65, p. 4]	Conceptual, Intermediate theoretical layer
Leem et al. [72, p. 78]	Strategy, Revenue, Alliances
Shafer et al. [80, p. 202]	Business logic, Strategy, Value proposition, Value network
Osterwalder et al. [77, pp. 17–18]	Conceptual tool, Business logic, Value proposition, Customer segments, Architecture, Network of partners, Revenue
Haaker et al. [68, p. 646]	Blueprint, Network of firms, Customers, Value proposition
Andersson et al. [62, pp. 1–2]	Business actors and relations, Value exchange
Kallio et al. [71, pp. 282–283]	Value proposition: information/goods/services, Industry participants: customers/partners/competitors/government
Rajala & Westerlund [78, p. 118]	Value proposition, Set of actors, Revenue
Janssen et al. [70, p. 204]	Business logic, Value proposition, Customers; Current or future business
Rappa [44]	Revenue sources, Position in the value chain

bring about enormous positive changes in the earth's ecosystems [46]. In consistent with the definition of environmental sustainability of IT [17], sustainability of e-business can be defined as the activities within the e-business domain to minimize the negative impacts and maximize the positive impacts on the society and the environment through the design, production, application, operation, and disposal of information technology and information technology-enabled products and services throughout their life cycle.

3 Why Three Dimensional Elements in Sustainable e-Business Modelling?

In the past, businesses limited their view of business profitability as they were only aware of economic gain and were focused on sound financial systems to maintain that gain. Similarly, businesses were only concerned about economic value even when delivering value to the customers. Then slowly the trend for socially conscious businesses started and now a day to compete in the market businesses need to deliver not only the economic value but the blended value. Customers now want to know what total value they are receiving from the businesses. Therefore, to deliver a total or complete value to the customers businesses need to include economic, social, and environmental value in their value propositions.

As there are multiple stakeholders involved in e-business modelling this research approach sincerely considered the stakeholder theory while identifying the elements of sustainable e-business modelling. Stakeholder theory holds the idea that businesses shall take decision considering the interest and impact of all stakeholders. If a balance cannot be ensured among the stakeholders, organisational sustainability will be questioned [23]. A sustainable organisation try to maximize economic, social, and environmental performance for a sustainable and value based stakeholder relation [39]. To provide adequate value to stakeholders and to manage relation with them organisations need to develop specific processes at different levels of organization [23]. Such type of process development shall be based on considering the economic, social, and environmental interests of the stakeholders. Hence, it can be summed up that stakeholder theory indicates the development of a business model that recognizes the value requirements of multiple stakeholders to sustain the business.

Now if we look at the previous research in this area what we see is that most of the business models research in information systems field has been concerned with e-business and e-commerce [3]. A number of ideas exist about e-business models of which most of them provide only conceptual overview and concentrate only on economic aspects of the business. None of them exclusively considers the sustainability aspects. Similarly, there is a growing number of literature available about the sustainability of businesses (i.e. [8, 21, 50, 51], etc.) which do not focus on e-business. But the intersection of these two global trends, e-business and sustainability, need to be addressed. Although recently a very few researchers talks about green IT/ICT concept (i.e. [17, 18, 22, 27, 29, 34], etc.) but none of them clearly explains how that concept will fit in an e-business model to make it sustainable and at the same time, to protect the interests of the customers.

It is said that all firms, whether non-profit or for-profit, create blended value—the only issue up for debate is the degree to which they maximize the component elements of value [19]. According to the literature, the sustainable value must include values from three areas: (a) Economic value, (b) Social value, and (c) Environmental value.

Importantly, businesses must also realize that to be competitive in the market this value needs to be measured from three dimensions:

Dimension 1: What Value is demanded by the Customers?
This means, the requirements that need to be fulfilled to minimize gap of what value the customers are receiving and what value they are expecting. Businesses need to see whether the customers are receiving the total value that they are expecting, or not. If not, the businesses must identify all the existing discrepancies and try to fulfil those discrepancy requirements to deliver the total value to the customers effectively.

Dimension 2: What Value is required by the Businesses based on their Strategy to reach their Goals?
Traditionally, customer requirements were the only concern for the businesses to compete successfully in the market and still now there is no doubt about the importance of customer requirements in business. But now only fulfilment of customer requirements does not guarantee the long term competency and profitability for the businesses. To compete successfully every business must have their own clear goal defined in their strategy that they want to achieve in time. This dimension includes with all the business requirements necessary to reach the organisation goals.

Dimension 3: What Value is required by the Businesses to have efficient Value processes?
Just producing and delivering the value is not enough to be competitive now a day. Rather, value need to be produced effectively by the businesses to compete and to ensure profitability for the long run. To produce value effectively, efficient process is a must. All the inefficiencies of the value processes must be identified and corrected to produce the value effectively. The requirements that are necessary to make all the processes of a business to be efficient are included in this dimension of measurement.

4   The Three Dimensional Elements

Now, based on the discussion in Sect. 3 if the sustainable value is measured from the above three dimensions value requirements of a business can be categorised into 9 (nine) groups as follows:

(a) Customer Value Requirements (CVR): VOC based
  1. Economic requirements (EcVR1)
  2. Social requirements (SoVR1)
  3. Environmental requirements (EnVR1)
(b) Business Value Requirements (BVR): Strategy based
  4. Economic requirements (EcVR2)
  5. Social requirements (SoVR2)
  6. Environmental requirements (EnVR2)
(c) Process Value Requirements (PVR): Process based
  7. Economic requirements (EcVR3)
  8. Social requirements (SoVR3)
  9. Environmental requirements (EnVR3)

4.1   Dimension 1: Customer Value Requirements for Sustainability (CVR)

Generally, customer requirements indicate voices of the customers (VOCs). Since rich literature is available about VOCs, we are not explaining it further. In a number of research approaches VOCs are translated as customer requirements through evaluation and validation [12, 13, 25, 30, 54]. But we, more specifically, by customer requirements, mean the total value (economic, social, and environmental) that is demanded by the customer. This requirement can be any or any combination of the economic, social and environmental value.

Customers can be of different types, such as, internal customers (shareholders, managers, employees), intermediate customers (wholesale people), ultimate customers (recipient of service, purchasers, institutional purchasers), etc. 12. When identifying customer requirements, every organisation should ask itself few general questions [33]:

– Which customer will help them the most in achieving their business goals?
– Are all customer equally important to them, or some are more valuable to them than others?

Usually, there are too many customer requirements to be manageable and that is why of classification of customer requirements is beneficial [25] and necessary to limit the budget of investments. According to our approach, customer requirements can be of 3 (three) types:

4.1.1   Economic Value Requirements for 'Customer Requirements' (Ecvr1)

Economic value of a product or service has number of different definition and explanation in the past literature. Therefore, we are not going to define it further; rather we focus on economic value requirements for customer requirements. In our approach, this customer requirement means any of the customer's value requirements which is somehow economically related directly or indirectly to the product or service that is to be delivered to the customer. These economic requirements are not the factors from business's point of view which are mentioned by Porter in his classical work on Competitive Strategy (1980) and Competitive Advantage (1985), instead these economic requirements are the demands from the customer's point of view. In other words, these requirements mean all types of economic benefits that the customers are looking for. For example, price of the product or service is directly related to the product or service economically. Even quality, after-sales-service, availability or ease of access, delivery, etc. also appear under this category.

Generally, economic value requirements are considered as the top prior requirement from the customers' point of view within all of the value requirements except some product and services whose value dimensions are different. From the previous research it has been found that majority of the customers look for economic value requirements of the product or service before any other requirements. For example, [45] and [9] identified customers that equate value with price. Zeithaml [57] identified from a study that customer's equated value of the product or service with low price. According to Porter [43], value for the customer is defined as benefits relative to costs. In another study by Hoffman [28] reveals the salience of price in the value equations of customers.

Zeithaml [57] also found that number of customers consider value as price first and quality second.

4.1.2   Social Value Requirements for 'Customer Requirements' (Sovr1)

Social value requirement for the customer means any value for the customer's society. Almost all of the products or services produce some sort of value impact to the society. It will be very difficult to identify many products or services which do not have any social value impact, direct or indirect. Also, there will be very few business activities which are totally detached from producing some kind of social value. If it is true that most of the businesses produce some kind of social value, positive or negative, then the social value requirements also must be encountered at the core of the business model. Today's customers are interested to see the contribution or impact of the product or service or operations of the business organisations to the society they are living. These social value requirements are not the social responsibilities that the business organi-sations are thinking to perform; rather these are the requirements that the customers are demanding or expecting from the products or services or from the supplier of the products or services when they consume that product or service (Fig. 1).

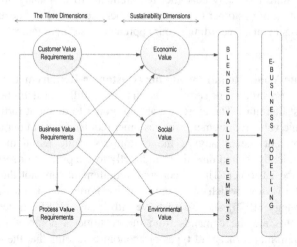

Fig. 1. Proposed elements of e-business modelling.

Social value requirements can be of different dimensions. Such as, it can be directly related to the product or service of the business, such as, knowledge of the customers' society, customers' safety of the product, customers' health (fresh food, harmful packaging or ingredients in the food, life-saving medicines), etc.; or it can be indirectly related to the business, such as, generating local employment, supporting education, health and welfare, loans and assistance to the charities, etc. Social value requirements may also include employment policies of the organisation that ensure diversity, including gender, race and religion, proper work environment for all the staff that meets social necessities, encouraging or allowing organisation's staff to get involved in fundraising and volunteer activities for the disadvantaged within the society, offering business education, community training programs, etc. Porter [43] identifies three ways to create economic value for the customer by creating social value- by re-conceiving products and markets, by re-defining productivity in the value chain, and by building supportive industry clusters at the company's locations.

4.1.3 Environmental Value Requirements for 'Customer Requirements' (EnVR1)

Customers, suppliers, and public are increasingly demanding that businesses minimize any negative impact of their products and operations on the natural environment [31]. Customers now a day do not just look at the economic value of the product or service, they also want to know whether that product or service or the supplier of that product or service cause any impact on the environment. Because they believe 'business have major role to play in helping and enhancing the environment' and thus, every business should develop sound environmental management policies for processes and products [14]. It is also believed now by the customers that there are number of ways how businesses can reduce the impact on the environment, for example, sourcing responsibly, such as, using recycled materials and sustainable timber, creating an efficient and fuel-efficient distribution network, creating recyclable products, minimising packaging, working with suppliers and distributors who take steps to minimise their environmental impact, buying locally to save fuel costs, etc. As a whole, the customers want the businesses to act more responsibly by performing an important and positive role in the society through creating additional environmental value for the future generations.

Bovea and Vidal [10] suggest how more value can be added to the product for the customer by integrating environmental impact, costs and customer evaluation during the product design process. Munoz and Sheng [35] present a model which they believe can serve as a framework for decision-making in environmentally conscious manufacturing.

4.2 Dimension 2: Business Value Requirements for Sustainability (BVR)

It is proven that better quality of the products or services lead to the fulfilment of customer requirements or higher customer satisfaction. But only fulfilment of customer requirements does not guarantee the future profitability of the businesses as the market changes. Therefore, businesses need to think in advance about how to sustain the profitability in the long run. Strategic managers will be mainly responsible to identify the business requirements by evaluating the current situations and the future directions of the businesses. Managers must clearly define their goals and targets when identifying these requirements. The businesses must consider its future strategy and all the cost drivers relative to its operations when selecting these business requirements. For example, there can be a number of different business goals that businesses may aim to achieve in the long run based on their current circumstances. But whatever the goals are, to achieve them there are always relative business requirements that need to be fulfilled. Porter [41, 42] provides with a list of common cost drivers which may guide all the businesses during the business requirements selection to achieve their goals. Business requirements can be of different types depending on what type of business that is. All business requirements can be classified into 3 (three) groups:

4.2.1   Economic Value Requirements for 'Business Requirements' (EcVR2)

Economic value requirements for business requirements are those requirements which add some economic value to the business directly or indirectly if they are fulfilled. These economic value requirements are very similar to the requirements explained in the section EcVR1 except that those economic requirements are demanded by the customers and these economic requirements (EcVR2) are identified by the businesses to be fulfilled to achieve the planned future goals. For example, reducing the cost of production, increase of sales and/or profit, getting cheaper raw materials, minimizing packaging and delivery cost, replacing the employees with more efficient machinery, reducing costs by implementing more efficient supply chain management systems, saving of time and energy, etc. add some sort of economic value to the businesses. Generally, the ultimate goal of adding some economic value to business is to pass the savings to the customers in the competitive market and maximise profit.

4.2.2   Social Value Requirements for 'Business Requirements' (SoVR2)

These social value requirements are to add some value to the society from business's point of view if they are fulfilled. Types of social values are discussed in the section SoVR1. These value requirements (SoVR2) reflect what social value the business is planning and willing to deliver to the customers' society in time regardless of the customers' demand. For building societal value, Nelson [36] proposes an approach based on three elements: (i) efficient and ethical pursuit of core business activities, such as, creating local jobs, paying taxes and royalties, implementing social human resource policies, etc. (ii) social investment and philanthropy, such as, offering training program to the community, running employee volunteering schemes, business education projects, sponsoring community development trusts, civic improvement, etc. and (iii) contribution to the public policy debate, such as, supporting progress for good governance including anti-corruption initiatives and human rights standards, contribution to the social policies including education, training, local economic development, employment management, etc. Adding social value by the businesses can be a part of different types of business goals depending on the business natures. Part of the goals can be simply for the wellbeing of the society, or can be for the competition in the market. For instance, Lever Bros Ltd. uses few principles to focus on social value, such as, emphasising on employees' personal development, training, health, and safety; improving well-being of the society at large; using world class expertise base human safety to ensure consumer safety; improving living conditions of its employees, etc. [56]. Through participation in community-based programs such as sponsorships, donations, and employee volunteer programs, global firm Fortis commit to work to fight illness and disease, promote education, aid and protect children, and prevent homelessness and hunger [48] to add social value.

4.2.3   Environmental Value Requirements for 'Business Requirements' (EnVR2)

To be competitive in the market businesses need to act environmental friendly now a day. According to Denton [15], adding environmental value can be a competitive advantage for the businesses since businesses can differentiate themselves by creating products or processes that offer environmental benefits. As mentioned in the section

EnVR1 above, there are number of ways how businesses can minimise the impact on the environment. By implementing environmental friendly operations businesses may achieve cost reductions, too. For example, minimum use of environmentally-toxic chemicals, reduced contaminations, recycling of materials, improved waste management and reuse or recycling of waste, using fuel efficient machineries, minimize packaging, using recycled water, etc. reduce the impact on the environment and at same time they may reduce the costs of the businesses. One of the principles of Lever Bros Ltd. is to take great care to minimize the environmental impact of all their operations-from raw material procurement, product design, manufacture and distribution- to use and disposal [56]. In the section EnVR1, we discussed environmental value requirements that are demanded by the customers but these environmental value requirements are identified by the businesses for their different business goals that they aim to achieve in time.

4.3   Dimension 3: Process Value Requirements for Sustainability (PVR)

Process value requirements are the requirements that need to be fulfilled to have an efficient value creating process within the existing business processes. Even though customer satisfaction can be obtained effectively and efficiently for some time by fulfilling various customer requirements, an organisation still cannot ensure future profitability if it lacks value creating capability [54]. Process value requirements are identified from the gap between what is being achieved and what need to be achieved from the existing value processes. These requirements are not demanded or identified by the customers rather they are identified by the business itself by looking at what amount of value it is currently producing and what amount of value it is supposed to produce to safeguard the interest of customer value and business value. For example, inaccurate or slow manufacturing of a product or service by employee or machinery, untimed delivery, inefficient processes caused by lack of training, social misconducts, unproductive waste management, unplanned pollution (air, water, sound) management, etc. and any other inaccuracies within the existing processes which can be corrected without or with very low efforts and/or investments are identified as value requirements. Common steps for optimizing business processes which are analysing, designing, implementing and evaluating can be followed to have an efficient value creating system within the organisation. The 'Process value requirements' can be any of the following 3 (three) types:

4.3.1   Economic Value Requirements for 'Process Requirements' (EcVR3)

Economic value requirements for value requirements are mainly related to the cost savings within the existing business processes which can be later transferred to the customers. Again, this additional value (cost savings) is not demanded by the customers, instead the managers identify those value creating inefficiencies within the existing processes and try to correct them which result in some sort of economic benefits for the organisations. Then those economic benefits can be passed to the customers as economic value by the organisations. For example, employing skilled workers, keeping up with the up-to-date technologies, providing adequate amount of training, using efficient energies, improved supply chain management systems, etc. can increase the efficiency of the value processes that can certainly add some economic value to the organisation that can be transferred to the customers, if required.

4.3.2   Social Value Requirements for 'Process Requirements' (SoVR3)

Recent expectation from each society is that every business should act honestly and ethically. Value for the society can be of different types: basic value, ethical value, voluntary value, etc. To identify the social value requirements for value requirements managers look at the whole value process of the organisation and see whether there is any scope to add some value to the society they are operating within the existing value process systems. Sometimes the businesses even do not hesitate to spend some extra (investment) or to give some extra effort if there are chances to add some social value. In the sections SoVR1 and SoVR2, we have already explained about what the social value is and their examples. SoVR3 is different from SoVR1 and SoVR2 in the sense that SoVR1 requirements are demanded by the customers, SoVR2 requirements are identified by the managers that they are planning to deliver to the customers in the future, and SoVR3 requirements are identified by the managers but they are identified within the current value process system so that they can be fulfilled and delivered immediately. For instance, educating disadvantaged children, organising skills training for unemployed people, employing disabled people, establishing schools and colleges, sponsoring social events, organising social gathering, organising awareness programs etc. can add value to the society and most of these requirements can be easily fulfilled by the businesses without or with a little investments or efforts.

4.3.3   Environmental Value Requirements for 'Process Requirements' (EnVR3)

These value requirements need to be fulfilled to minimize the impact of current value processes on the environment. To fulfil these requirements, the businesses try to find and implement all the necessary steps within the existing processes that will stop or reduce the chances of effecting the environment, thus, adding some value to the environment. Similar to SoVR3, these requirements are also identified within the current value process system by the managers so that they can be fulfilled and can start adding more value immediately. EnVR1 requirements are demanded by the customers but EnVR3 and EnVR2 are identified by the businesses themselves to increase the value by increasing the efficiencies in the business processes now and in the future respectively. For example, leakage of water/oil/heat, incompetent waste management, inefficient disposal and recycling of materials, unplanned pollution (air, water, sound) management, uncontrolled ecosystem stress, heating and lighting inefficiency, etc. will result in incompetency in the value processes for the businesses. Thus, by fulfilling these requirements businesses may get rid of these inefficiencies and add value to the value creation processes.

5   Discussion and Further Research

It has been found from the above discussion that focusing only on the customers' demand is not enough to be competitive regardless of whether the demand is economic, social, or environmental. As mentioned above, customer satisfaction can be obtained effectively and efficiently for some time by fulfilling various customer requirements but still an organisation cannot ensure future profitability if it lacks value creating capability. Moreover, only fulfilment of customer requirements does not guarantee the future profitability of the businesses as the market changes. To be competitive and to maintain the sustainability an e-business must consider values (economic, social, and environmental) from all three dimensions: customer value requirements, business value requirements, and process value requirements. It is also found that each of the blended value elements (customer value, business value, and process value) need to be related to all of the sustainability elements (economic, social, and environmental). What is also realised that within the blended value elements the customer value and the business value are partially dependant on process value as the process value supports the customer value and the business value.

Based on the three dimensional elements of e-business model our further research will be directed at the development of an e-business model based on blended value which will be sustainable and simultaneously will safeguard the interests of all the stakeholders. Therefore, the main objectives of the further research in this area can be defined as follows:

- To investigate how the concept of blended value dimensions can be used in developing an e-business model.
- To investigate how these three dimensional elements can be used to determine the optimal/appropriate design requirements in developing an e-business model.
- To develop a 'value-sustainability' framework for modelling e-business in conjunction with 'blended value' and 'sustainability' concepts.

6 Conclusions

There can be found a number of ideas and proposals about business modelling and e-business modelling in the literature and few of them used 'value' as the main element of their modelling. But in their approaches 'value' is measured mainly from the customer's point of view and not from the business point of view or the process point of view. Which means 'business value' and 'process value' is fully ignored in the previous approaches. Recently some scholars are talking about 'sustainable value', 'shared value, or 'blended value'; even them did not consider 'business value' or 'process value'. Moreover, none of them clearly explicated the value elements that will protect the interests of the customer and the business. In this paper, we have shown the important elements that should be used for a sustainable e-business model after extensive literature review. From the literature we have explored and determined that the three dimensional elements should be used in developing sustainable e-business model. We have also shown why these three dimensional elements should be used for sustainable e-business modelling. Furthermore, we have investigated and shown how the sustainability dimensions can be integrated with the value dimensions in developing sustainable e-business model.

References

1. Afua, A., Tucci, C. (eds.): Internet Business Models and Strategies. Mcgraw-Hill, New York (2001)
2. Akkermans, H.: Intelligent e-business: from technology to value. IEEE Intell. Syst. **16**, 8–10 (2001)
3. Al-Debei, M.M., Avison, D.: Developing a unified framework of the business model concept. Eur. J. Inf. Syst. **19**, 359–376 (2010)
4. Alt, R., Zimmerman, H.: Introduction to special section - business models. Electron. Mark. **11**, 3–9 (2001)
5. Applegate, L.M.: Emerging e-Business Models: Lessons Learned From The Field. Harvard Business Review (2001)
6. Auer, C., Follack, M.: Using action research for gaining competitive advantage out of the internet's impact on existing business models. In: Proceedings of the 15th Bled Electronic Commerce Conference - Ereality: Constructing the Economy, 17–19 June (2002)
7. Bled, Slovenia. Bled, Slovenia (2002)
8. Bell, S., Morse, S.: Sustainability Indicators: Measuring The Immeasurable. Earthscan Publications, London (2009)
9. Bishop, W.R.: Competitive intelligence. Progressive Groc. **63**, 19–20 (1984)
10. Bovea, M.D., Vidal, R.: Increasing product value by integrating environmental impact, costs and customer valuation. Resour. Conserv. Recycl. **41**, 133–145 (2004)
11. Carter, C.R., Rogers, D.S.: A framework of sustainable supply chain management: moving toward new theory. Int. J. Phys. Distrib. Logist. Manag. **38**, 360–387 (2008)
12. Chan, L.-K., Wu, M.-L.: A systematic approach to quality function deployment with a full illustrative example. Omega: Int. J. Manag. Sci. **33**, 119–139 (2005)
13. Chien, T.-K., Su, C.-T.: Using the QFD concept to resolve customer satisfaction strategy decisions. Int. J. Qual. Reliab. Manag. **20**, 345–359 (2003)
14. Demirdogen, R.E.: The role, responsibility and impact of business in eco-efficient technologies and bio-trade. In: International Conference on Environment: Survival and Sustainability Nicosia-Northern Cyprus, Nicosia-Northern Cyprus, 19–24 February 2007
15. Denton, D.K.: Enviro-Management: How Smart Companies Turn Environmental Costs Into Profits. Prentice Hall, New Jersey (1994)
16. Dubosson-Torbay, M., Osterwalder, A., Pigneur, Y.: Ebusiness model design, classification and measurements. Thunderbird Int. Bus. Review **44**, 5–23 (2001)
17. Elliot, S.: Transdisciplinary perspectives on environmental sustainability: a resource base and framework for it-enabled business transformation. Mis. Q. **35**, 197–236 (2011)
18. Elliot, S., Binney, D.: Environmentally sustainable ICT: developing corporate capabilities and an industry-relevant is research agenda. In: Pacific Asia Conference on Information Systems. Suzhou, China (2008)
19. Emerson, J.: The blended value proposition: integrating social and financial results. Calif. Manag. Rev. **45**, 35 (2003)
20. Emerson, J. (ed.): Moving ahead together: implications of a blended value framework for the future of social entrepreneurship. Oxford University Press, Oxford (2006)
21. Epstein, M.J., Wisner, P.S.: Using a balanced scorecard to implement sustainability. Environ. Qual. Manage. **11**, 1–10 (2001)
22. Erek, K.: From green it to sustainable information systems management: managing and measuring sustainability in it organisations. In: European, Mediterranean & Middle Eastern Conference on Information Systems. Athens, Greece (2011)
23. Freeman, R.E.: Strategic Management: A Stakeholder Approach. Pitman, Boston (1984)

24. Hamel, G.: Leading The Revolution. Harvard Business School Press, Boston (2000)
25. Han, S.B., Chen, S.K., Ebrahimpour, M., Sodhi, M.S.: A conceptual QFD planning model. Int. J. Qual. Reliab. Manag. **18**, 796 (2001)
26. Hawkins, R.: The business model as a research problem in electric commerce. Spru - Science and Technology Policy Research (2001)
27. Hilty, L.M., Hercheui, M.D.: ICT and sustainable development. In: Berleur, J., Hercheui, M. D., Hilty, L.M. (eds.) HCC9 2010. IFIP AICT, vol. 328, pp. 227–235. Springer, Heidelberg (2010)
28. Hoffman, G.D.: Our Competitor Is Our Environment. Progressive Grocer – Value. Executive Report, pp. 28–30 (1984)
29. Houghton, J.W.: ICT and the environment in developing countries: A review of opportunities and developments. In: Berleur, J., Hercheui, M.D., Hilty, L.M. (eds.) HCC9 2010. IFIP AICT, vol. 328, pp. 236–247. Springer, Heidelberg (2010)
30. Hwarng, H.B., Teo, C.: Translating customers' voices into operations requirements-A QFD application in higher education. Int. J. Qual. Reliab. Manag. **18**, 195–225 (2001)
31. Klassen, R.D., Whybark, D.C.: The impact of environmental technologies on manufacturing performance. Acad. Manag. J. **42**, 599–615 (1999)
32. Linder, J.C., Cantrell, S.: Changing business models: surveying the landscape (2001)
33. Mazur, G.: Voice of the customer (Define): QFD to define value. In: Proceedings of the 57th American Quality Congress. Kansas City (2003)
34. Melville, N.P.: Information systems innovation for environmental sustainability. Mis. Q. **34**, 1–21 (2010)
35. Munoz, A.A., Sheng, P.: An analytical approach for determining the environmental impact of machining processes. J. Mater. Process. Technol. **53**, 736–758 (1995)
36. Nelson, J.: Leadership companies in the 21st century: creating shareholder value and societal value. Vis. Ethical Bus. **1**, 21–26 (1998)
37. Osterwalder, A., Pigneur, Y.: An e-business model ontology for modeling e-business. In: The Proceedings of the 15th Bled Electronic Commerce Conference, Slovenia, 17–19 June 2002
38. Papakiriakopoulos, D., Poulymenakou, A., Doukidis, G.: Building e-business models: an analytical framework and development guidelines. In: The Proceedings of 14th Bled Electronic Commerce Conference, Bled, Slovenia, 25–26 June 2001 (2001)
39. Perrini, F., Tencati, A.: Sustainability and stakeholder management: the need for new corporate performance evaluation and reporting systems. Bus. Strat. Environ. **15**, 296–308 (2006)
40. Petrovic, O., Kittl, C., Teksten, R.D.: Developing business models for ebusiness. In: Proceedings of the International Conference on Electronic Commerce, Vienna, Austria (2001)
41. Porter, M.E.: Competitive Strategy: Techniques For Analysing Industries And Competitors. The Free Press, New York (1980)
42. Porter, M.E.: Competitive Advantage: Creating and Sustaining Superior Performance. Free Press, New York (1985)
43. Porter, M.E.: The big idea: creating shared value. Harv. Bus. Rev. **89**, 62–77 (2011)
44. Rappa, M.: Managing the digital enterprise - business models on the web. http://digitalenterprise.org/models/models.html (2008). Accessed 4 April 2011
45. Schechter, L.: A normative conception of value. Progressive Grocer, Executive Report, pp. 12–14 (1984)
46. Shrivastava, P.: The role of corporations in achieving ecological sustainability. Acad. Manag. Rev. **20**, 936–960 (1995)

47. Sikdar, S.K.: Sustainable development and sustainability metrics. AIChE J. **49**, 1928–1932 (2003)
48. Snider, J., Hill, R.P., Martin, D.: Corporate social responsibility in the 21st century: a view from the world's most successful firms. J. Bus. Ethics **48**, 175–187 (2003)
49. Stabell, C.B., Fjeldstad, O.D.: Configuring value for competitive advantage: on chains, shops, and networks. Strateg. Manag. J. **19**, 413–437 (1998)
50. Stead, J.G., Stead, E.: Eco-enterprise strategy: standing for sustainability. J. Bus. Ethics **24**, 313–329 (2000)
51. Tanzil, D., Beloff, B.R.: Assessing impacts: overview on sustainability indicators and metrics. Environ. Qual. Manag. **15**, 41–56 (2006)
52. Tapscott, D., Lowy, A., Ticoll, D.: Digital capital: harnessing the power of business webs. Thunderbird Int. Bus. Rev. **44**, 5–23 (2000)
53. Timmers, P.: Business models for electronic markets. Electron. Mark. **8**, 3–8 (1998)
54. Wang, H.-F., Hong, W.-K.: An integrated service strategy by QFD approach: a case of a telecom company in Taiwan. Int. J. Manag. Decis. Making **8**, 251–267 (2007)
55. Weill, P., Vitale, M.: What it infrastructure capabilities are needed to implement e-business models? MIS Q. **1**, 17–34 (2002)
56. Zairi, M., Peters, J.: The impact of social responsibility on business performance. Manag. Audit. J. **17**, 174–178 (2002)
57. Zeithaml, V.A.: Consumer perceptions of price, quality, and value: a means-end model and synthesis of evidence. J. Mark. **52**, 2–22 (1988)
58. Zott, C., Amit, R., Massa, L.: The Business Model: Theoretical Roots, Recent Developments, and Future Research. Iese Business School, University Of Navarra, Pamplona (2010)
59. Zott, C., Amit, R., Massa, L.: The business model: recent developments and future research. J. Manag. **37**, 1019–1042 (2011)
60. Afuah, A.: Business Models: A Strategic Management Approach. Irwin/McGraw-Hill, New York (2004)
61. Amit, R., Zott, C.: Value creation in e-business. Strateg. Manag. J. **22**, 493–520 (2001)
62. Andersson, B., Bergholtz, M., Edirisuriya, A., Ilayperuma, I., Johannesson, P., Gre´Goire, B., Schmitt, M., Dubois, E., Abels, S., Hahn, A., Gordijn, J., Weigand, H., Wangler, B.: Towards a reference ontology for business models. In: Proceedings of the 25th International Conference on Conceptual Modeling (ER2006), 6–9 November, Tucson, AZ, USA, pp. 1–16 (2006)
63. Bouwman, H.: The sense and nonsense of business models. In: International Workshop on Business Models, HEC Lausanne 6 p. cat. O, Projectcode: ICT (2002)
64. Brousseau, E., Penard, T.: The economics of digital business models: a framework for analyzing the economics of platforms. Rev. Netw. Econ. **6**(2), 81–110 (2006)
65. Campanovo, G., Pigneur, Y.: Business model analysis applied to mobile business. In: Proceedings of the 5th International Conference on Enterprise Information Systems, 23–26 April, pp. 1–10. Angers (2003)
66. Chesbrough, H.W., Rosenbloom, R.S.: The role of the business model in capturing value from innovation: evidence from xerox corporation's technology spin-off companies. Ind. Corp. Change **11**(3), 529–555 (2002)
67. Gordijn, J., Akkermans, H., van Vliet, H.: Business Modelling Is Not Process Modelling. In: Mayr, H.C., Liddle, S.W., Thalheim, B. (eds.) ER Workshops 2000. LNCS, vol. 1921, pp. 40–51. Springer, Heidelberg (2000)
68. Haaker, T., Faber, E., Bouwman, H.: Balancing customer and network value in business models for mobile services. Int. J. Mobile Commun. **4**(6), 645–661 (2006)

69. Hedman, J., Kalling, T.: The business model concept: theoretical underpinnings and empirical illustrations. Eur. J. Inf. Syst. **12**(1), 49–59 (2003)

70. Janssen, M., Kuk, G., Wagenaar, R.W.: A survey of web-based business models for e-government in the Netherlands. Government Inf. Q. **25**(2), 202–220 (2008)

71. Kallio, J., Tinnila, M., Tseng, A.: An international comparison of operator-driven business models. Bus. Process Manag. J. **12**(3), 281–298 (2006)

72. Leem, C.S., Suh, H.S., Kim, D.S.: A classification of mobile business models and its applications. Ind. Manag. Data Syst. **104**(1), 78–87 (2004)

73. Linder, J., Cantrell, S.: Changing business models: surveying the landscape. In: Working paper, Accenture Institute for Strategic Change (2001)

74. Magretta, J.: Why business models matter. Harvard Bus. Rev. **80**(5), 86–92 (2002)

75. Morris, M., Schindehutte, M., Allen, J.: The entrepreneur's business model: toward a unified perspective. J. Bus. Res. **58**, 726–735 (2005)

76. Osterwalder, A.: The business model ontology—A proposition in a design science approach. University of Lausanne, Switzerland (2004)

77. Osterwalder, A., Pigneur, Y.: Clarifying business models: Origins, present, and future of the concept. Commun. Assoc. Inf. Syst. **16**(1), 1–25 (2005)

78. Rajala, R., Westerlund, M.: Business models – a new perspective on firms' assets and capabilities: observations from the Finnish software industry. Int. J. Entrepreneurship Innov. **8**(2), 115–126 (2007)

79. Seelos, C., Mair, J.: Profitable business models and market creation in the context of deep poverty: a strategic view. Acad. Manag. Perspect. **21**, 49–63 (2007)

80. Shafer, S.M., Smith, H.J., Linder, J.: The power of business models. Bus. Horiz. **48**, 199–207 (2005)

81. Stahler, P.: Business models as a unit of analysis for strategizing. In: Proceedings of 1st International Workshop on Business Models Lausanne, Switzerland. [WWW document] (2002). http://www.business-model-innovation.com/english/definitions.html

82. Stewart, D.W., Zhao, Q.: Internet marketing, business models and public policy. J. Pub. Policy Market. **19**, 287–296 (2000)

83. Teece, D.J.: Business models, business strategy and innovation. Long Range Plan. **43**, 172–194 (2010)

84. Venkatraman, M., Henderson, J.C.: Real strategies for virtual organizing. Sloan Manag. Rev. **40**(1), 33–48 (1998)

Consumer Online Search Behavior: A Cross-Industry Analysis Based on User-Level Data

Florian Nottorf[(✉)], Andreas Mastel, and Burkhardt Funk

Leuphana Universität Lüneburg, Scharnhorststr. 1, 21335 Lüneburg, Germany
{nottorf,mastel,funk}@uni.leuphana.de
http://www.leuphana.de

Abstract. Understanding consumer online search behavior is crucial to optimize companies' paid search advertising campaigns. Standard measures such as the click-through rate do not account for this search behavior over time, which may favor a certain group of search type and, therefore, may mislead managers in allocating their financial spending efficiently. We analyzed a large query log for the occurrence of user-specific interaction patterns within and across three different industries and were able to show that consumers' online search behavior is indeed a multi-stage process that heavily depends on industry-specific characteristics. For example, whereas a product search within the clothing industry typically begins with general keywords ("sneakers") and that search process becomes narrowed as it proceeds by including more specific, e.g. brand-related ("sneakers adidas"), keywords, this behavior is a relatively rare event in other industries (e.g., the healthcare industry). Our method to analyze consumer search processes helps companies to identify the role of specific activities within a respective industry and to allocate their financial spending in paid search advertising accordingly.

Keywords: Online search · Online advertising · Consumer behavior · Query log

1 Introduction

Selling advertising linked to user-generated queries, the so-called paid search advertising has become a critical component of companies marketing campaigns [1]. Although more than half of all search processes by individual users consist only of one query [2], consumers that have a transactional intention often do not reach their goals by conducting only a single search [3]. An aspect also confirmed by [4,5]. They demonstrate the so-called "spillover effect" from generic to brand-related searches for multiple companies and its industry-specific dependencies: the generic search (e.g., "hotel") and the corresponding advertisements by the company in question significantly contributed to the fact that users later turned to brand-related searches for this company (e.g. "hotel hilton"). Their works

© Springer-Verlag Berlin Heidelberg 2014
M.S. Obaidat and J. Filipe (Eds.): ICETE 2012, CCIS 455, pp. 72–87, 2014.
DOI: 10.1007/978-3-662-44791-8_5

clarify how traditional metrics in online advertising such as the click-through rate are alone no adequate tools to control for paid search advertising campaigns: they only take into account the users' search activities singularly and do not consider any interactions between them.

Our analysis is based on a complete query log published by AOL in 2006 [6] and explains users' search activities in more behavioral detail. Unlike [4,5], who mainly used keyword-level data aggregated on a daily basis of a paid search advertising campaign of a single company for each industry, we analyze users' individual queries within and across entire industries in order to determine whether the resulting user journey shows behavior indicating spillover effects. As evidence of such a spillover we regard a user journey that, for example, started with a generic and was followed by a brand-related search. We investigated and confirmed the spillover effect and its occurrence in users' online search behavior for several industries and, by doing so, highlighted the role of generic activities as gatekeepers for companies' online advertising. To the best of our knowledge, our work is the first to analyze a complete query log for the occurrence of the spillover effect and thus makes a contribution to research on consumer online search behavior. In addition, an improved understanding of the role of generic activities and of how consumers actually search for products and brands to satisfy their needs will help advertisers to allocate their budget on online advertising more efficiently.

The paper is structured as follows: first, we will review existing work on consumer online search behavior in general as well as in the specific context of paid search advertising. In the next chapters we will describe our method of analyzing spillover effects in query logs and introduce our dataset together with the filtering procedures applied. Next, we focus on the results of spillover effects across several industries. The last sections contain a discussion of our findings and will close this paper by mentioning the limitations of our study and by giving suggestions for further investigations.

2   Related Work

The detailed records of users' Internet activities opened up the possibility of analyzing a variety of topics, such as consumers' online search behavior (see, for example, [7] for a review and discussion of strengths and limitations of clickstream data for marketing research). General research classifies consumers' online searches into navigational, transactional, and informational purposes [8,9]. According to [10], searches heavily depend on the individual purchase intent such as involvement: while directed-buying sessions present very narrowly aimed shopping behavior, consumers with low purchase intention exhibit much broader search patterns for unspecific products. Reference [11] confirm that the depth of consumer search is generally low and shows no increase with a consumer's growing experience. This aspect is confirmed by analyses showing that the click-through rate on a search engine's (sponsored) link decreases with its position [12–15]. Despite the amount of literature focusing on users' search behavior no work has yet considered possible differences of this behavior across industries - an aspect considered and analyzed in more detail in the present paper.

The empirical analysis of sponsored search has only recently begun to become the focus of the scientific community. Reference [14] examine the general impact of paid search advertising on measures such as the relationship between the type and length of keywords and different variables on consumers' click and conversion behavior. Although the authors uncover important differences in the click and purchasing intensity regarding a specific group of keywords, they miss to account for users' interactions between them. Reference [16] build an integrated model of customer lifetime, transaction rate, and gross margin accounting for spillovers from sponsored search on customer acquisition and behavior in offline channels. Their results indicate that customers who were originally acquired through paid search advertising on Google have a significant higher lifetime value (about 20 %) than customers acquired from other channels. In a recent study, [15] criticize the common assumption that users respond homogeneously to keywords. The authors formulate a consumer-level approach to especially evaluate textual properties of paid search ads on consumers' responses and account in this way for heterogeneity. Besides several findings referring to the consumer-integrated focus, the authors confirm that keyword-specific factors, like the distinction between broad and narrow purposes, are important when linking searches to a click-through rate (see also [14]). This stream of research typically uses aggregated-level data. Although the majority of papers discussed above claim a more behavioral focus on how users respond and act in the context of search engines, they only scratch the surface of an analysis of consumers' actual online search behavior (see [17] for discussion of aggregation bias in sponsored search data).

This paper is most closely related to [4,5], who are able to demonstrate the spillover effect from generic to brand-related searches for companies of multiple industries. The generic search (e.g., "hotel") and the corresponding ads of the advertising company significantly contribute to the fact that users later turn to brand-related searches for this company (e.g. "hotel hilton"). We will explore the differences between the research methods of [4] as well as [5] and our approach in the following chapter more closely.

3   Data and Methodology

Our analysis is based on a log published by AOL which consists of over 35 million queries from about 650,000 users over a three month period (March to May) [6].[1] Although this dataset dates back to 2006, it is still an unique and comprehensive query log containing extraordinary information about users' search and click behavior, which may be found in todays search engines like Google or Bing.[2]

---

[1] Since the users who represent the queries are mostly located in the United States of America, our work is mainly based on the US region.

[2] We would like to thank an anonymous reviewer for pointing out this more clearly.

In terms of analyzing user journeys for specific behavioral aspects, such as the spillover effect from generic to brand-related searches, we, first, needed to define industries and, second, companies within these. It was only then that we were able to categorize user queries into generic and brand-related types of searches respectively and to make a definite statement about both the existence and the extent of industry-specific interaction effects between generic and brand-related search activities.

We will explain this process in more detail in the following chapters. Please find all additional data and information such as the list of selected companies, keywords, or our final filtered query log on the author's website[3].

3.1   The Initial Query Log

The log includes 36,389,567 records structured in five columns (see Table 1 for a short excerpt of the data):

- *AnonID*: A unique identification number of an anonymized user.
- *Query*: The user's query.
- *QueryTime*: The point of time at which the query was submitted for search.
- *ItemRank*: In case a user clicked on one of the result pages, the "ItemRank" shows the site's position in the result pages. If no page was selected, this field remained empty.
- *ClickURL*: Shows the URL of the clicked result [6].

We focused on three industries: the *hotel and hospitality industry* to make our findings comparable with those of [4]; the *clothing industry* as a representative of nondurable goods with the influence of brand strength being assumed to be strong; and the *healthcare industry* as a representative of the insurance sector. We further restricted our analysis to the top ten companies in 2006, their ranking being based on revenue and brand strength within a certain industry [18]. We did so on the assumption that these companies represented the major number of possible brand-related search activities within a specific industry. The consequences of this approach will be discussed later, for example of the fact that

Table 1. Extract from the AOL dataset.

AnonID	Query	QueryTime	ItemRank	ClickURL
1927	does bcbs cover ci	03.05.2006 00:24		
1927	does bcbs fl cover ci	03.05.2006 00:25		
7117	www.anthem.com	09.05.2006 09:33	3	www.maine.nea.org
7117	www.anthem.com	09.05.2006 09:33	4	hr.nd.edu
7117	www.anthem.com	10.04.2006 06:57	1	www.myuhc.com

---

[3] http://www.nottorf.org

we did not consider the total number of brand-related or generic search activities recorded in the query log.

On the basis of the industries selected and each of the ten companies we filtered out generic and brand-related queries from the initial query log.

3.2 The Filtering Process for Queries

For each of the ten companies within each industry we defined **brand-related keywords** to analyze a specific query for their occurrence and, as the case may be, marked the query as a branded search. Because of the fact that many of the selected companies have subsidiaries, we had to define a set of keywords that were related to the parent-company.[4] We organized the brand names and keywords in hierarchical order as shown in Fig. 1. Based on this structure we applied tools (e.g. the online toolset given by Google AdWords) to identify keywords that are often searched for in the context of the brand names mentioned.

We started with the company names (e.g. "Nike Inc."), which were placed in the root section of this structure. Next to it we put brand and product names which we derived from the company's information itself (e.g. "NIKEDiD" or "Air Jordan") and from the help of the keyword tools mentioned above. On the basis of these subcategories was defined the final set of keywords (e.g. "nikeid", "nikid", or "jordans") for our analysis (see the right column of Fig. 1). In this section were also taken into account variant names and typing errors. However, we defined 120 brand-related keywords for the healthcare, 228 for the hotel, and 720 for the clothing industry.

Defining the set of **generic keywords** required us to limit which queries could directly be related to the mentioned industries. Therefore, we may have had to consider those queries that had no direct relationship to a specific industry and its companies or products, but still were able to generate clicks on links to these companies. For example, the analysis of the hotel industry raised the question whether the search for a country or a flight could have already be

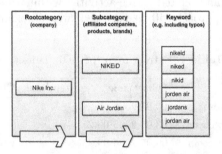

Fig. 1. Structure of the filtering process of brand-related keywords.

---

[4] The Harrah's Entertainment Inc., for example, had about 21 hotels and hotel chains in 2006.

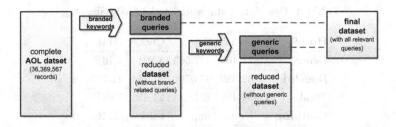

Fig. 2. Schematic illustration of the filtering procedure for a given industry.

seen as a generic query or not. It is possible that a selection of a final dataset that is too comprehensive may also cover users who do not have the intention to purchase something at all. This is a problem every paid search advertising campaign has to face to some extent, since advertisers want to become displayed and ranked when a possible consumer searches for products or services that the respective company offers. The consequences of a potentially incorrect or incomplete selection will be discussed later.

We proceeded from the advertiser's point of view and defined generic keywords that reflected the intention to gather information about the product or to purchase it. Hence, we restricted our set of generic keywords to directly product-related terms, their synonyms and variations. To achieve this, we also made use of the keyword tools referred to above but mostly we derived the keywords manually by gathering general information from the companies' websites. Thus, we defined 196 generic keywords for the healthcare (e.g. "health care", "dental insurance", "medicare"), 335 for the hotel (e.g. "hotel", "motel", "suites"), and 197 for the clothing industry (e.g. "shoes", "shorts", "underwear").

On the basis of our brand-related and generic keywords we **filtered and categorized** the query log records (see Fig. 2). First, all log records whose "Query"-columns contained brand-related keywords were moved into an industry-specific table and were marked as brand-related queries. This ensured that a record with both brand-related and generic keywords appearing in the same query was not duplicated. The second step was to filter the reduced dataset (without brand-related queries) on the basis of generic keywords, which were moved to the three industry-specific tables with only generic queries. Ideally, the remaining dataset should no longer have contained any relevant queries. It is important to mention that our procedure also filtered out log records that were not related to the industries selected. This was due to the fact that some queries occur also within an irrelevant context. We handled this problem by manually scanning the filtered data and by deleting records giving information about an irrelevant context (e.g. queries in a pornographic context).

The records not only contain information about a user's query itself but also the URL of a **clicked result**. We distinguished between URLs on pages that were related to the ten companies defined above and between URLs that were not, such as websites of retailers (e.g. "www.ebay.com" or "www.amazon.com"). Thus, we were able to separate relevant clicks (from the perspective of the

Table 2. Descriptive statistics on the final dataset.

Hotel	Users	Imp.	Clicks	CTR
Generic	71,405	327,563	3,801	1.16 %
Branded	32,039	97,070	21,154	21.79 %
Total	84,408	424,633	24,955	5.88 %
Clothing	Users	Imp.	Clicks	CTR
Generic	51,105	293,645	350	0.12 %
Branded	14,225	46,586	5,695	12.22 %
Total	58,166	340,231	6,045	1.78 %
Healthcare	Users	Imp.	Clicks	CTR
Generic	10,876	33,115	719	2.17 %
Branded	9,304	20,516	7,896	38.49 %
Total	18,255	53,631	8,615	16.01 %

ten companies) from irrelevant ones and were in a position to make more precise statements about the effects of generic and/or brand-related searches. To determine those (relevant) clicks we analyzed the information contained in the "ClickURL"-column of our final dataset and manually checked whether the clicked pages were related to the companies examined. Following this procedure, we identified 244 websites for the clothing, 298 for the healthcare, and 838 for the hotel industry.

The total number of unique users, of impressions, and of (relevant) clicks in our final dataset for each industry following our filtering procedure are shown in Table 2. The resulting **descriptive statistics** confirm strong differences in efficiency between generic and brand-related keywords. Although we filtered out far more generic than brand-related queries from the initial query log, the number of clicks in response to branded searches was much higher. This fact results in quite different CTRs as already shown by e.g. [4,14,19,20]. Companies focusing only on these statistics might conclude that the concentration on brand-related keywords and the neglect of generic terms would increase profitability since the metrics for keywords containing brand-specific information seem to be more effective than for those keywords describing generic purposes. The major problem of these types of keyword-based analyses is, however, that they only link users' actions to a specific keyword one at a time and do not consider any interactions between several searches and clicks. We, on the other hand, aimed at a processual analysis of the data and considered the development of users' search activities over time.

3.3 Indicating Spillover Behavior in Query Logs

The development of the search process from generic to brand-related searches may be attributed to the fact that individual brands gain the users' attention during the search process. We defined two levels of the spillover effect in user journeys:

Spillover Behavior Level 1. A user journey shows a generic-to-branded spillover effect, when a user first searches for generic and next, at any further time, for brand-related terms.

Spillover Behavior Level 2. A user journey shows a generic-to-branded spillover effect, when a user first searches for a generic term and her last search that leads to a (relevant) click is a brand-related one.

For each of the two definitions we assigned all considered user journeys to the four fields in a 2×2 matrix (generic→branded, generic→generic, branded→branded, branded→generic). For the level 2 spillover effect we obviously had less user journeys than for level 1, since we required those users to had at least one (relevant) click in their journeys.

Our analysis is different from the one of [4] as we utilize user-level instead of keyword-level data. Rutz and Bucklin use the daily number of generic searches and clicks as independent variables modeling a latent construct of awareness which in turn affects the number of brand-related searches. In addition, they use data from a paid search advertising campaign of one company – thus having a clear boundary of the study.

The fact that we built our analysis on a complete query log further enabled us to consider user-specific behavior within a whole industry instead of analyzing keyword-level data aggregated on a daily basis for just one company. We captured all search activities for three different industries and determined the number of users who searched for either generic or brand-related terms only, alternatively, performed spillovers from generic to brand-related searches and vice versa. In addition, we were able to establish the point of time when a user performed an action and analyzed the exact time span in which possible spillover effects might occur.

4 Results

4.1 Spillover Results

The results of the spillover analysis for each industry following the **level 1 spillover definition** are shown in Table 3. It shows the proportion of all unique users in relation to each group of user journeys, resulting in a 2×2 matrix for each industry.

The results indicate that the interaction effects between generic and brand-related searches differ across industries. Take, for instance, the healthcare industry. Here, 41.1 % of all users conducted only brand-related and 48.3 % only generic searches. Note that these homogeneous groups also contain user journeys with only a single search. The remaining 10.6 % of all users who switched either from generic to branded or from branded to generic searches during their

Table 3. Proportions of first search activities within user journeys per industry (Spillover Behavior Level 1).

Hotel	to generic		to branded	
from branded	8.6 %	(7,258)	20.8 %	(17,523)
from generic	56.7 %	(47,849)	13.9 %	(11,778)
Clothing	to generic		to branded	
from branded	4.7 %	(2,720)	15.0 %	(8,784)
from generic	72.6 %	(42,218)	7.7 %	(4,444)
Healthcare	to generic		to branded	
from branded	4.9 %	(897)	41.1 %	(7,509)
from generic	48.3 %	(8,821)	5.7 %	(1,028)

Note: Both the percentage and the total number (in brackets) of all unique users within one of the journey-groups are represented for each industry.

user journeys divide nearly equally into the two hybrid groups. There is no clear sign of users' favoring one specific interaction direction within the healthcare industry.

The results for the clothing industry, on the other hand, indicate at least a small spillover behavior from generic to brand-related search activities. We found a large number of users searching only for generic terms (72.6 %) while a much smaller group searched only for brand-related ones (15.0 %). Although there were no more than 12.4 % of users in total conducting hybrid searches, there were 3.0 % more user journeys starting with a generic search that was followed by a brand-related one (7.7 %) than in the opposite group (4.7 %). Users looking for articles in the clothing industry, such as shirts, shoes, or underwear, seemed to switch more likely their type of search from generic to brand-related terms than from brand-related to generic ones.

An obvious sign of spillover behavior was shown by the results for the hotel industry. Here, nearly 14 % of all users switched to brand-related searches after they initially searched for generic terms. Although the opposite group, starting with branded and switching to generic terms, was also relatively large (8.6 %), it significantly differed from the actual spillover group. This can be seen as evidence for the fact that users' search behavior within the hotel industry initially started with broad and general search terms (e.g. "hotel", "bed and breakfast", "suite") which became more (brand-)specific as the search proceeded (e.g. "harrah", "sheraton", "hyatt").

Table 4 shows the results for the **level 2 spillover effect**. The focus in this spillover definition on users' clicks on (relevant) links led to a shift in favor of brand-related keywords. This is not surprising since the brand-related queries received far more clicks compared to generic ones (see Table 2). But, similar to the differentiation into an exploratory and a goal-directed searching mode (e.g. [10, 21]), this alternative spillover analysis has the ability to differentiate between

Table 4. Percentages of first search activity and last search activity before a click within user journeys per industry (Spillover Behavior Level 2).

Hotel	to generic		to branded	
from branded	2.7 %	(338)	50.9 %	(6,428)
from generic	12.7 %	(1,602)	33.7 %	(4,206)
Clothing	to generic		to branded	
from branded	0.9 %	(36)	63.9 %	(2,532)
from generic	6.2 %	(244)	29.0 %	(1,150)
Healthcare	to generic		to branded	
from branded	1.0 %	(58)	80.0 %	(4,206)
from generic	9.0 %	(471)	10.0 %	(523)

Note: Both the percentages and the total number (in brackets) of all unique users within one of the journey-groups are represented for each industry.

users intending to purchase something (which results in a click) and users behaving in a less goal-directed manner (resulting in no click on a company's website). We acknowledge that there might be a purchase intention even if a user did not click on a link to a company's website (e.g., that a user clicks on a third party's link, such as Amazon or Ebay).

This analysis shows very strong evidence for spillover behavior. See, for example, the results for the hotel industry. Here, 33.7 % of all users that clicked on a company's link started their user journeys with a generic search and switched to a brand-related one. This means that more than one third of these users first looked for generic terms before they specified their searches using brand-related keywords and finally clicked and ended their search-to-click-processes. The magnitude of the effect for the hotel industry becomes even more pronounced, since the reverse-spillover effect (users that first searched for brand-related keywords before they conducted a generic search and clicked on a company's link) was the smallest of all four groups by far.

Similar findings to the hotel industry can be found for the clothing sector. Here, about 29 % of all users that clicked on a company's link looked for brand-related terms after they conducted generic searches. The reverse-spillover is insignificantly small, since less than 1 % of the users first searched for brand-related and afterwards for generic terms before they clicked.

Focusing on the healthcare industry, the findings of the level 1 spillover analysis can be partly confirmed. Again, a large number of users seemed to search only for brand-related or generic terms before clicking on a respective link. Nearly 90 % of all users who clicked on a company's link did not switch their type of search, that is they searched only for either brand-related or generic terms. This fact had an immediate influence on the strength of the spillover effect from generic to brand-related search: only a relatively small number of users' (nearly 10 %) first searched for generic terms and next conducted a brand-related one before they clicked on a corresponding link.

We are not able to fully explain this relatively small number of interactions between generic and branded terms, especially when compared to our findings for the hotel and clothing industry. Still, there are some differences in the data of the three industries (see Table 2) that may at least give a clue to this relative lack of interactions. For example, the total number of impressions within the healthcare industry is considerably smaller than in the two others. In particular, there are about ten times fewer generic impressions. Also, the CTR of the brand-related keywords is by far the highest. This can already be seen as an indicator for a relatively small interaction-rate between generic and brand-related searches, since these two metrics indicate that searches of a single type alone seem to be able to lead to a possible solution for the user.

4.2   Time Differences Between Actions

Table 5 shows the time spans and the quantiles for each industry within which the generic-to-branded spillover effects occurred. "Level 1" denotes the time differences of spillover behavior from (first) generic to (first) brand-related searches (see the above definition of "Spillover Behavior Level 1"). The time that elapsed between the users' first generic search and last brand-related one that resulted in a click on a company's link is denoted by "Level 2" ("Spillover Behavior Level 2").

Let us first focus on the hotel industry. The results of the analysis of the time differences for the first spillover definition suggest that 25 % of all users switched from generic to brand-related searches within only 2.4 hours. These users changed their search behavior very quickly when compared with the average time span of about 9 days (8.95) in which the generic-to-branded spillover

Table 5. Time spans for each industry in which the Spillovers occurred.

| Industries | Quantiles of time difference in days | | | | |
	10 %	25 %	50 %	75 %	90 %
Hotel					
Level 1	0.01	0.10	8.95	30.13	55.47
Level 2	0.03	4.85	22.87	51.17	70.15
Clothing					
Level 1	0.01	1.73	14.91	37.54	59.07
Level 2	0.04	6.86	23.12	47.86	66.70
Healthcare					
Level 1	0.00	0.02	4.95	22.01	49.91
Level 2	0.01	0.72	12.07	37.26	60.90

Note: "Level 1" denotes the time differences in "Spillover Behavior Level 1". "Level 2" denotes the time differences in "Spillover Behavior Level 2" accordingly.

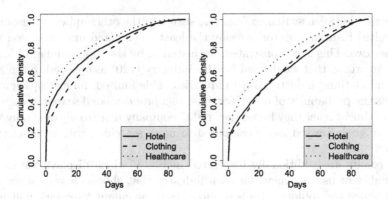

Fig. 3. Time Spans within which "Spillover Behavior Level 1" (Left) and "Spillover Behavior Level 2" (Right) Occurred.

occurred. As expected, the "Level 2"-results indicate a longer time difference since we focused on users' last brand-related search that led to a click on a company's link. Overall, our findings are consistent with the results of [4] who find that the search process for lodging seems to be short and to occur mainly in between a couple of days to two weeks. We confirm an even shorter time difference on the basis of our results since we found many users who switched their type of search in between only a few hours and up to one day. That rest of the users spread their search process over the further investigation period, see Fig. 3, seems likely to be a coincidence.

The results for the clothing industry show some deviations from those for the hotel industry. Although we expected a search process for garments to change in a shorter period of time from generic to brand-related terms, as it does in searches for the right hotel, this was not borne out by the findings for this industry. Indeed, the mean time span of the spillover behavior was about 2 to 3 weeks. This can be explained by the possibility of users being confronted with far more possibilities of choice compared to the hotel industry since competition in the clothing industry is not restricted to a certain location. In other words, a user searching for a hotel in a specific location (e.g. "hotel barcelona") might not have as many choice alternatives when searching for an appropriate room as a user looking for a specific garment (e.g. "hoodie jacket"). This circumstance could reduce the time users needed to spend on finding the right hotel. Another explanation of the relatively long time differences compared to the hotel industry is that searching for the garments might not be that selectively intensive and target-oriented as looking for the right hotel.

In the healthcare industry, the time spans in which the spillover occurred were the shortest by far. Focusing on the "Level 1"-results, 25 % of all users whose journey showed spillover behavior switched the type of search within half an hour (0.02). The results of "Level 2" confirm this short interaction period since more than one out of four of all spillovers did not take more than one day even though considering the clicks. Following our previous chain of reasoning, this short period between switching from one search to the other appears reasonable: the (health) insurance sector is easily the least fragmented in comparison with the other two. This is demonstrated, for instance, by the total number of brand-related keywords that we defined for this industry (120) as opposed to the hotel (190) and clothing industry (720) industries. This limited number of keywords increases the probability of users switching to a brand-related search in a shorter period of time. Either they found the "right" company more easily or simply were in a more goal-directed mode compared to users searching within the clothing industry.

All results are additionally illustrated in Fig. 3, which displays the respective number of user journeys for each industry that showed a very short time span in which the spillover effects occurred (see the cumulative density at point "0 Days"). Further, it can be seen that each time span slowly approximates the total investigation period of 90 days. The analysis of the time difference provides evidence for both a substantial percentage of users that switched from generic to brand-related searches in a very short period of time (less than one day or several hours) and the average percentage of users that changed their type of search over several days or weeks.

5   Discussion

Our results emphasize the role of generic search activity in the users' search and decision process since it is crucially important for companies and individual brands to gain the users' attention during the search process and thus probably to be considered a potential solution.

By investigating online search behavior we were able to show that traditional research vindicates and can be applied in the online setting. Following this literature, consumers' decision processes can be divided into at least two stages: the first is a set of products or brands a consumer is aware of at any given point of time. This is referred to as the "awareness set". In the second, the so-called "evoked set", a consumer is likely to reduce his or her set of products that the final decision is based upon [22]. Therefore, the chance of a brand being considered for purchase does not exist if that brand is not part of a consumer's awareness set [23]. When a consumer does not know which brand may satisfy his or her initial need (e.g., has no distinctive evoked or awareness set), a search-process will more likely begin with general searches and show a narrowing by becoming (brand-)specific as it proceeds. We can confirm this assumption within the setting of online search, since it is indeed crucial for companies to gain the users' attention during the early stage of their search and decision processes.

With respect to understanding users' search behavior in general and with respect to paid search advertising in specific, we agree with the work of [4], since we found the generic search activities of primary importance for the users' search and decision process: although generic searches receive far less clicks as brand-related ones, they are indeed indispensable in managing online advertising campaigns. Since there are also strong differences in the extent of the spillover effects (e.g. hotel vs. healthcare industry), it is recommended for each company to identify the degree of this interaction effect between generic and brand-related activities and adjust their spending accordingly.

The differences of the extent of the spillover behavior across industries might not only result from different market and competition set-ups, but might also be due to different factors influencing users' search behavior, such as involvement.

Searching for the right hotel room or for the best health insurance may be more functionally driven than choosing the right sneakers or underwear. A further differentiation into users with a goal-directed searching mode and those with a low purchase intention may reveal some more insights into the extent of the spillover effect. We focused on that circumstance by considering clicks on companies' websites (definition Spillover Behavior Level 2) and have found a much stronger spillover behavior in the first group compared to users that search only. Further research should investigate this differentiation in more detail.

The opportunity of investigating users' search behavior upon a very large query log suffers from a variety of drawbacks. Turning to our filtering and categorization procedures, there may be several sources that could skew our findings. Although we have been very detailed on the keyword-creation-process, we still might not have captured all of the generic and brand-related search activities. For instance, we may have defined too few brand-related keywords, which would result in too few brand-related queries being filtered out of the initial query log. If, on the other hand, we had filtered out more brand-related queries, this would have, under constant conditions and chargeable to the generic homogeneous group, increased both the hybrid and the homogeneous ("from branded - to branded") search groups proportionally. We also could have picked out more (unknown) companies instead of focusing on the top ten for each industry. Unknown brands might not receive as many homogeneous searches as the top ten industries. Additionally, users would be more likely to become aware of these unknown brands through generic searches, which probably would have increased the spillover effect from generic to branded searches. Restricting our study to the top companies therefore can be seen as resulting in conservative figures since it more likely leads to an underestimation than an overestimation of the spillover effect.

6 Conclusions

To better understand consumer online search behavior we analyzed the query log published by AOL in 2006 [6] for the occurrence of the spillover effect first described by [4,5]. Our results confirm the occurrence of spillover effects in online search behavior, but also show that these effects differ between industries.

Starting from the initial AOL query log we (1) filtered out every brand-related log record that could refer to one of the selected companies or their products, and (2) filtered out log records of the remaining queries that contained generic terms for a specific industry. Within our analysis we found more user journeys starting with generic and switching to brand-related searches than the other way round. Among the three industries selected, the effect is most noticeable in the hotel, closely followed by the clothing industry. The weakest degree of a spillover was detected in the healthcare industry.

We could prove the key role of generic activities and the early anchoring of companies and brands within user journeys. Both our understanding of users' search activity as a process and our findings of the spillover effect within user journeys allowed us to transfer the theoretical concepts of the evoked and (un-)awareness set of [22,23] to the user's search and decision process in the context of search engines: the development of the search process from generic to brand-related searches may at least partially be attributed to the fact that individual brands gain the users' attention during the search process, who thus "become aware" of these companies or brands. The focus on generic activities becomes indispensable since they seem to play the role of gatekeeper for companies in online advertising.

This paper has several limitations. Although we have been very detailed on the data filtering process there might be effects that blurred our results, since the manually selected and revisited generic keywords for each industry as well as the brand-related ones for each company might not capture all users and his or her search intentions. Another limitation is the missing information on conversions which would have enabled us to formulate a more specific occurrence of the spillover effect. Our approach, therefore, neglects the fact that one user might have made several purchases during the investigation period within one industry. An alternate dataset might overcome these limitations in a further investigation.

Although we analyzed several industries in this paper, we neither considered possible interactions between them nor between companies within these (e.g. spillovers from company A to company B). Since, for example, [19] found that there are cross-category purchases within one company for several keywords in sponsored search, a complete query log to some extent contains information for such a further analysis. Our work can be seen as a first step in directing attention more to the behavioral aspects of users' online search activities.

References

1. Ghose, A., Yang, S.: Comparing performance metrics in organic search with sponsored search advertising. In: Proceedings of the 2nd International Workshop on Data Mining and Audience Intelligence for Advertising, ADKDD '08, pp. 18–26. ACM, New York (2008)
2. Jansen, B.J., Mullen, T.: Sponsored search: an overview of the concept, history, and technology. Int. J. Electron. Bus. **6**, 114–131 (2008)
3. Search Engine Watch: Delving deep inside the searcher's mind (2006). http://searchenginewatch.com/3406911
4. Rutz, O.J., Bucklin, R.E.: From generic to branded: a model of spillover in paid search advertising. J. Mark. Res. **48**, 87–102 (2011)
5. Nottorf, F., Funk, B.: A cross-industry analysis of the spillover effect in paid search advertising. Electron. Mark. **23**, 205–216 (2013)

6. Pass, G., Chowdhury, A., Torgeson, C.: A picture of search. In: Proceedings of the 1st International Conference on Scalable Information Systems, InfoScale '06. ACM, New York (2006)
7. Bucklin, R.E., Sismeiro, C.: Click here for internet insight: advances in clickstream data analysis in marketing. J. Interact. Mark. **23**, 35–48 (2009)
8. Broder, A.: A taxonomy of web search. SIGIR Forum **36**, 3–10 (2002)
9. Jansen, B.J., Spink, A.: The effect on click-through of combining sponsored and non-sponsored search engine results in a single listing. In: Proceedings of 2007 Workshop on Sponsored Search Auctions, Banff, AB, Canada (2007)
10. Moe, W.W.: Buying, searching, or browsing: differentiating between online shoppers using in-store navigational clickstream. J. Consum. Psychol. **13**, 29–39 (2003)
11. Johnson, E.J., Moe, W.W., Fader, P.S., Bellman, S., Lohse, G.L.: On the depth and dynamics of online search behavior. Manag. Sci. **50**, 299–308 (2004)
12. Agarwal, A., Hosanagar, K., Smith, M.D.: Location, location, location: an analysis of profitability of position in online advertising markets. J. Mark. Res. **48**, 1057–1073 (2011)
13. Animesh, A., Viswanathan, S., Agarwal, R.: Competing "creatively" in sponsored search markets: the effect of rank, differentiation strategy, and competition on performance. Inf. Syst. Res. **22**, 153–169 (2011)
14. Ghose, A., Yang, S.: An empirical analysis of search engine advertising: sponsored search in electronic markets. Manag. Sci. **55**, 1605–1622 (2009)
15. Rutz, O.J., Trusov, M., Bucklin, R.E.: Modeling indirect effects of paid search advertising: which keywords lead to more future visits? Mark. Sci. **30**, 646–665 (2011)
16. Chan, T.Y., Xie, Y., Wu, C.: Measuring the lifetime value of customers acquired from google search advertising. Mark. Sci. **30**, 837–850 (2011)
17. Abhishek, V., Hosanagar, K., Fader, P.S.: On aggregation bias in sponsored search data: existence and implications. In: Proceedings of the 13th ACM Conference on Electronic Commerce (2011)
18. Interbrand & Business Week: Interbrand's best global brands 2006 (2006)
19. Ghose, A., Yang, S.: Modeling cross-category purchases in sponsored search advertising (2010)
20. Yang, S., Ghose, A.: Analyzing the relationship between organic and sponsored search advertising: positive, negative, or zero interdependence? Mark. Sci. **29**, 602–623 (2010)
21. Janiszewski, C.: The influence of display characteristics on visual exploratory search behavior. J. Consum. Res. **25**, 290–301 (1998)
22. Howard, J.A., Sheth, J.N.: A theory of buyer behavior. Rivista internazionale di scienze economiche e commerciali **15**, 589–618 (1968)
23. Narayana, C.L., Markin, R.J.: Consumer behavior and product performance: an alternative conceptualization. J. Mark. **39**, 1–6 (1975)

eGovernment Interventions: The Multiple Projects Evaluation Problem

Fabrizio d'Amore and Luigi Laura[✉]

Department of Computer, Control, and Management Engineering,
Sapienza University of Rome, Via Ariosto 25, 00185 Rome, Italy
{damore,laura}@dis.uniroma1.it

Abstract. Consider the scenario where an organ of a public administration, which we refer as the *decision-maker*, is requested to plan one or
more interventions in some framework related to the Information Society or the eGovernment set of actions. The above scenario has been
addressed in a recent work [1], where the authors propose a methodology to support the decision-maker in orienting, planning, and evaluating
multiple (partially overlapping) interventions. Furthermore, the problem
has been formally modeled, and it has been proved that it belongs to the
NP-complete class.

In this paper we study the above problem, i.e., the Multiple Projects
Evaluation, focusing on its approximability. In particular, we show that
the problem admits a $O(1 - \frac{1}{e})-$approximation algorithm.

Keywords: eGovernment · Interventions planning

1   Introduction

We consider the scenario, from [1], aimed at planning and/or designing *interventions*, namely the definition of thematic areas, categories of users and beneficiaries, geographic locations and specific goals constituting a framework in which
a *decision-maker* wants to fund new projects, during the process of setting up
an explicit call. The decision-maker is typically a specific organ of the (central
or local) public administration.

Such decision-maker, in charge of assigning a give amount of money, has to
select the type of intervention by mean of an articulated and complex decision
process, which includes kind of users to benefit, type of services and level of
their interactivity, state/level of existing and expected services, geographical
and socio-economical context, etc. It is clear that such a decision process cannot
be fully automated, but it can get benefits from the definition of guidelines and
from the availability of supporting tools that make faster the so called "what-if"
analysis.

Although the interventions we consider pertain the eGovernment, the Information Society and the ICT areas, the results we present may apply to several
other areas.

© Springer-Verlag Berlin Heidelberg 2014
M.S. Obaidat and J. Filipe (Eds.): ICETE 2012, CCIS 455, pp. 88–100, 2014.
DOI: 10.1007/978-3-662-44791-8_6

Table 1. Summary of the notation used in this paper.

Notation	Meaning
B	Available budget for all the interventions
q	Number of interventions
B_i	Budget for intervention i
p_i	Number of projects to be funded in the intervention i
$B_{i,j}$	Funding for project j of intervention i
r_i	$B_{i,1}/B_{i,p_i}$ ratio between min and max funding in intervention i
R	B_1/B_q ratio between the budgets of the interventions with min and max budget

In [1], the above problem has been formally modeled and the authors showed that the corresponding optimization problem, i.e. the Multiple Projects Evaluation problem, belongs to the NPO complexity class.[1]

In this paper we present an approximation algorithms, based on a reduction to the Budgeted Maximum Coverage Problem, that has been studied by Khuller, Moss, and Naor in [8].

This paper is organized as follows: the necessary background is provided in the following sections, where we address, respectively, the formal definition of interventions and budget (Sect. 2), the impact analysis (Sect. 3), and the scoring function (Sect. 4). Then, in Sect. 5, we present the main result of the paper: an approximation algorithms, based on a reduction to the Budgeted Maximum Coverage Problem [8]. We address some conclusive remarks in Sect. 6.

2 Interventions and Budget

In this section we briefly present an overview, from [1], of formal definitions of interventions and budget, that will be the basis of the analysis described in the rest of the paper. A summary of the notation used in this paper is shown in Table 1.

An intervention can be characterized by: the available budget, to be granted to co-funded projects; constraints on the employment of the budget, deriving from laws and rules; types of objectives of fundable projects; category of beneficiaries and their socio-economical/territorial positions; type and impact of the expected results.

The available budget is often an amount not subjected to decision. This happens when an external organization (e.g., the European Committee) makes available to the decision-maker an amount for co-funding projects satisfying some specific requirements. The budget defines natural constraints on the amounts to be assigned to the projects[2] and so it allows to approximately dimension the interventions.

---

[1] Interested readers may find detailed discussions in the classical reference books on computational complexity [10], NP-Completess [7], and approximation algorithms [2].

[2] In the case of co-funding, the amount assigned to each project is at least the 30–35 % of the budget of the whole project and therefore it determines its size.

If resources are fairly distributes, it is easy to estimate the number of projects to be funded, by defining the ratio between maximum and minimum funding. Denoting the available budget by B, the number of projects to be funded by p, the fund to be assigned to the i-th project by B_i and the ratio between the minimum and the maximum funding by

$$r = \frac{\min_i\{B_i\}}{\max_i\{B_i\}}$$

being $0 < r \leq 1$, it is possible to exploit mathematical interpolation to dimension the amounts of the fundings. In the case of linear interpolation we have

$$B = \sum_{i=1}^{p} B_i = \frac{(\max_i\{B_i\} + \min_i\{B_i\})p}{2}$$

from which we get

$$\max_i\{B_i\} = \frac{2B}{p(1+r)}$$

If we re-number the projects accordingly to increasing fundings we get

$$B_j = B_1 + \frac{B_p - B_1}{p-1}(j-1)$$

for $j = 1, 2, \ldots, p$, with

$$B_1 = \frac{2rB}{p(1+r)}$$

Even if we have obtained these amounts by means of a simple and arbitrary linear interpolation, they are suitable to be the starting scheme of the decision-maker. Subsequent refinements will not cause, most likely, substantial changes of the amounts.

In some cases, the decision-maker can program interventions by means of more than one call. Our approach still allows to determine the (base) amounts to be assigned to the projects. We introduce in a more compact form the used notation, assuming without loss of generality that both interventions and projects are numbered by increasing fundings. The linear interpolation immediately gives

$$B_{i,p_i} = \frac{2B_i}{p_i(1+r_i)}$$

Such formula requires to know B_i, which can be determined by an analogous procedure.

$$B_q = \frac{2B}{q(1+R)}, \quad B_1 = \frac{2RB}{q(1+R)}$$

The searched value is

$$B_i = B_1 + \frac{B_q - B_1}{q-1}(i-1)$$

The decision-maker can therefore fix a few important parameters, such as B, q, R and the r_i's, and use them to compute the p_i's and $B_{i,j}$'s. The whole process could require some iterations, but allows to quickly estimate the rough value of a few important quantities. This can be efficiently done exploiting a simple spreadsheet.

We conclude remarking the importance of recognizing the relationships existing among different interventions. In practice, if each intervention was independently planned, there would be no difference between to plan q interventions and to plan q times an intervention. What will make the quantum leap is identifying the dependencies existing among different types of interventions, setting up a hierarchical system that will allow to start well-coordinated and highly correlated tasks, according to a bottom-up approach aiming at privileging the construction of basic common infrastructures.

3   Impact Analysis

In this section we recall, from [1], the methodology for carrying out the analysis of the impact of a planned intervention. It is based on the concept of *indicator*. Indicators have been introduced in statistics and are currently used in a variety of areas, among which the management control [11]; here we use indicators for carrying out the analysis of the impact of interventions. An indicator is a mathematical function defined over a finite or infinite domain commonly defined as $D = D_1 \times D_2 \times \cdots \times D_n$, where each D_i is a finite set of numbers (real, integer or natural) and $n \in \mathbb{N}$ describes the quantity of homogeneous data which we want to get concise information from. In the management control, statistical indicators are used to get concise information about some specific aspect of reality; depending on the type of analysis we are carrying on — pre-analysis, post-analysis, feasibility analysis, benchmarking etc. — many different categories of indicators can be used. In the recent literature there are several proposals providing sets of indicators, organized by category, level of aggregation, homogeneity, correlation etc. (see, e.g., [5,6,9,12]).

From what we discussed before, it is clear that the Indicators Set (IS) plays a critical role in the whole process of planning, designing, and evaluating interventions; the following points are therefore crucial:

1. The definition of a *correct* and *complete* Indicators Set able to model the scenario.
2. The indicators in the IS must be easily *measured* and constantly *monitored* before, during, and after the intervention. Information sources must be reliable for the whole duration of the process.
3. In order to improve the reliability, the IS should be chosen to be partially redundant, i.e. there should be some correlation between different indicators and, if possible, information sources should be chosen to obtain independently values of correlated indicators.

With distinct information sources providing the values of the indicators, it is possible on one side to have a precise picture of the real evolution of the intervention/project, on the other a variation in the correlation between related indicators might point out some errors in the measure or in the update of an indicator and, in the long run, can help in the assessment of the information sources themselves.

Given an indicators set $I = \{i_1, i_2, \ldots, i_n\}$, we define an *aggregation* (of the indicators) $A = \{A_1, A_2, \ldots, A_k\}$, where $A_i \subseteq I$ for any i and $A_i \cap A_j = \emptyset$ for $i \neq j$; in other words, an aggregation is a partition of I, conceptually based on a high level of homogeneity. From the decision-maker point of view, both indicators and aggregations belong to conceptual categories whose level is not sufficiently high. The decision-maker prefers to reason about concrete objectives, directly related to benefits for citizens, enterprises, concerns, public administration etc. When defining a main topic for an intervention (e.g., the area of ICT) it is easy to define a set of (concrete) possibly interesting objectives $O = \{o_1, o_2, \ldots, o_m\}$. Once O has been defined, we expect it very slowly changes as time passes, so that we can assume without loss of generality O is fixed. For each item $o_i \in O$ it is possible to identify its correlations to some indicators in I or, more simply, to elements in A.

In this way, when interested in an objective o_i, the decision-maker can be easily informed about the involved indicators, related to o_i. It will be sufficient to make explicit all the correlations and store them into some suitable supporting system. Notice that we can consistently extend our assumption of static sets, what leads us to static correlations. Identifying elements of sets and their correlations can be done once; later, only limited maintenance will be required.

The decision-maker is also interested in contextualizing information (according territory, socio-economics, politics etc.). We assume for simplicity one semantic coordinate of contextualization. Hence, we introduce a set of contexts $R = \{r_1, r_2, \ldots, r_\ell\}$ (e.g., the main politic units, or regions, of a given country). It is possible to introduce more sets of contexts, all of them to be considered as orthogonal. On the base of the context analysis, and of laws and rules, high priority objectives can defined, immediately identifying the involved indicators.

In order to describe all this knowledge we exploit the mathematical concept of *graph*; for basic definitions on graphs (simple graph, tree, forest, walk etc.) see for instance [4]. In particular we are interested in the notion of *multipartite graph*, defined as a simple graph $G = (V, E)$ where

- V is partitioned into k subsets $V_i \subseteq V$, with $\bigcup_i V_i = V$ and $V_i \cap V_j = \emptyset$ for $i \neq j$;
- there is no edge $\{u, v\}$ if u and v belong to the same subset of vertices.

In this case the graph is said to be k-parted.

We can use a 4-parted graph to represent sets I, A, O and R, and to model the correlations existing among their elements. We define a 4-parted graph whose set of vertices is defined as $I \cup A \cup O \cup R$ and it is partitioned into I, A, O and R, and whose edges are of three types:

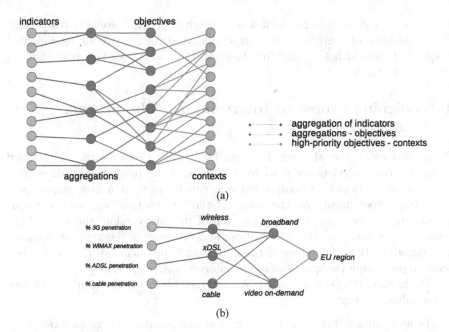

Fig. 1. (a) A possible 4-parted graph, showing sets O, I, A and R. (b) Example of tree of monotonous walks.

- Edges incident to vertices of A and I. They model the structure of the aggregation of indicators.
- Edges incident to vertices of O and R. They model the correlations between contexts and high-priority objectives.
- Edges incident to vertices of A and O. They model the correlations between high-priority objectives and aggregations of indicators.

An example is given in Fig. 1(a). Given such a graph, by selecting any vertex all related information can be automatically selected: it suffices to find the appropriate set of walks.

Given a multipartire graph, we define a *monotonous walk* as a walk having exactly one vertex in every subsets of vertices. In the 4-parted graph each monotonous walk is constituted by an indicator, an aggregation of indicators, a context and an objective. When the decision-maker selects objective o_i, the set of all monotonous walks containing o_i is immediately identified. It is easy to see that such a set of walks define a tree, which we call "tree of monotonous walks rooted at o_i." An example is shown in Fig. 1(b).

Our approach allows to capture the correlations among the important concepts. Notice that the model could be strengthened by quantifying the correlations, so introducing a measure that can depend not only on the two related concepts, but also on additional information (contextualization, other strongly related indicators etc.). A hypergraph [3], that generalizes the concept of graph, seems to be a candidate for such a quantitative model, however most of natural problems on hypergraphs are intractable. A simpler way is to use weighted graphs, by introducing a weighting function associating positive real numbers (weights) to edges.

4   Assigning Scores to Interventions: The Scoring Function

Before discussing the Multiple Projects Evaluation Problem, that is detailed in the following section, we need to briefly recall the properties of its scoring function; in particular, a Scoring System, can be seen, at a first glance, as a block box whose input are: the target of the intervention (e.g. school, public administration, concern etc.), the location of the intervention, the state of the indicators *pre* and *post* the intervention, and the state of the average (national or international) of the values of the indicators. The output of the system is a score, representing the goodness of the intervention/project.

The input of the Scoring System, as described above, can be formally detailed in the following way:

- The intervention target $t \in T = \{$ set of all the possible intervention targets $\}$.
- The Indicator Domain $D = D_1 \times D_2 \times \cdots \times D_n$, where each D_j is a subset of $\mathbb{R}$, the set of real numbers. Without loss of generality we can normalize all the domains to the interval $[0,1] \subset \mathbb{R}$.
- The state *pre* intervention is a vector $i_A = (i_1, i_2, \ldots i_n)$, where $i_1 \in D_1$, $i_2 \in D_2$, $\ldots, i_n \in D_n$.
- The state *post* intervention is a vector $i_P = (i_1, i_2, \ldots i_n)$, where $i_1 \in D_1$, $i_2 \in D_2$, $\ldots, i_n \in D_n$.
- The (national or international) average is a vector $i_M = (i_1, i_2, \ldots i_n)$, where $i_1 \in D_1$, $i_2 \in D_2$, $\ldots, i_n \in D_n$.
- The locality of the intervention is completely described by the vector i_A (state of the indicators before the intervention).

The output of the System is a score that, without loss of generality, we can assume between 0 and 1; therefore a Scoring System can be seen as a function $f : T \times [0,1]^3 \rightarrow [0,1]$. Some natural requirements for a scoring system are:

- If $i_P = i_A$, then $f(t, i_A, i_P, i_M) = 0$ (zero score): if a project does not improve any of the indicators then its score is 0.
- If $i_P = (1, 1 \ldots, 1)$, then $f(t, I_A, i_P, i_M) = 1$ (maximum score): if an intervention/project raises all the indicator the maximum then its score is maximum.
- Given two projects $P1$ and $P2$, with $i_{P1} = (i_1, i_2, \ldots i_j + \Delta i_j \ldots i_n)$ and $i_{P2} = (i_1, i_2, \ldots i_j \ldots i_n)$, then $f(t, i_A, i_{P1}, i_M) \geq f(t, i_A, i_{P2}, i_M)$ (non decreasing property): if two different projects bring all the indicators to the same values, except one, the project better performing on that indicator should score better (or equal[3]).

---

[3] The score can be equal when, given a set of weights representing the relative importance of the indicators, the corresponding weight is 0.

4.1   The Scoring Function

In this section we recall, from [1], the scoring system that satisfies the requirements described previously. The intervention target is modeled as a vector of n weights $t = (w_1, w_2, \ldots, w_n)$, where $w_j \in [0,1]$ for $j = 1, 2, \ldots, n$. Here n is the number of indicators and each weight w_j represents the relative importance of the indicator for the given target. The vector of weights can be derived from the tree of monotonous walks previously introduced, by identifying the objective (element of set O) which the target is aiming at. In the case of more than objectives, the associated forest of monotonous walks will be considered.

That being stated, the scoring system can be represented by the following function:

$$f(t, i_A, i_P, i_M) = \frac{t \cdot (i_P - i_A)}{t \cdot (\overline{1}_n - i_A)} \tag{1}$$

where we have denoted by $\overline{1}_n$ the vector whose n components are all equal to 1, by "$\cdot$" the vector product and by "$-$" the vector difference. We recall that, given two vectors $v = (v_1, v_2, \ldots, v_n)$ e $w = (w_1, w_2, \ldots, w_n)$ it holds that

$$v \cdot w = v_1 \cdot w_1 + v_2 \cdot w_2 + \cdots + v_n \cdot w_n$$

and

$$v - w = (v_1 - w_1, v_2 - w_2, \ldots, v_n - w_n)$$

We prove now that this function satisfies all the requirements:

- If $i_P = i_A$, then $f(t, i_A, i_P, i_M) = 0$ (zero score):

$$f(t, i_A, i_P, i_M) = \frac{t \cdot (i_A - i_A)}{t \cdot (\overline{1}_n - i_A)} = \frac{t \cdot \overline{0}_n}{t \cdot (\overline{1}_n - i_A)} = 0$$

where we have denoted by $\overline{0}_n$ the vector whose n components are all equal to 0.
- If $i_P = (1, 1 \ldots, 1)$, then $f(t, I_A, i_P, i_M) = 1$ (maximum score):

$$f(t, i_A, i_P, i_M) = \frac{t \cdot (\overline{1}_n - i_A)}{t \cdot (\overline{1}_n - i_A)} = 1$$

- Given two projects $P1$ and $P2$, with $i_{P1} = (i_1, i_2, \ldots i_j + \Delta i_j \ldots i_n)$ and $i_{P2} = (i_1, i_2, \ldots i_j \ldots i_n)$, then $f(t, i_A, i_{P1}, i_M) \geq f(t, i_A, i_{P2}, i_M)$ (non decreasing property):

$$f(t, i_A, i_{P1}, i_M) - f(t, i_A, i_{P2}, i_M) =$$

$$= \frac{t \cdot (i_{P1} - i_A)}{t \cdot (\overline{1}_n - i_A)} - \frac{t \cdot (i_{P2} - i_A)}{t \cdot (\overline{1}_n - i_A)} =$$

$$= \frac{t \cdot (i_{P1} - i_A) - t \cdot (i_{P2} - i_A)}{t \cdot (\overline{1}_n - i_A)} =$$

$$= \frac{t \cdot (i_{P1} - i_A - i_{P2} + i_A)}{t \cdot (\bar{1}_n - i_A)} = \frac{t \cdot (i_{P1} - i_{P2})}{t \cdot (\bar{1}_n - i_A)} =$$

$$= \frac{t \cdot ((i_1, i_2, \ldots, i_j + \Delta i_j, \ldots, i_n) - (i_1, i_2, \ldots, i_j, \ldots, i_n))}{t \cdot (\bar{1}_n - i_A)} =$$

$$= \frac{t \cdot (0, 0, \ldots, \Delta i_j, \ldots, 0)}{t \cdot (\bar{1}_n - i_A)} \geq 0$$

We notice that this function does not keep into account the national (or international) average of the indicators; the above definitions can be easily adapted to include it.

5   The Multiple Projects Evaluation Problem

In this section we detail the approximation algorithm for the Multiple Projects Evaluation Problem, that is formally defined as follows (see [1] for more details).

MULTIPLE PROJECTS EVALUATION (MPE)
Given in input:

- an initial scenario S, represented by the values of a set of indicators $I = (i_1, i_2, \ldots i_n)$;
- a set of projects $P = (p_1, p_2, \ldots p_m)$, each associated with a cost $(c_1, c_2, \ldots c_m)$ and a post intervention vector $(v_1, v_2, \ldots v_m)$; with $I(p_j)$ we denote the (estimated) values of the indicators after the completion of project p_j; if $R \subseteq P$ with $I(R)$ we denote the (estimated) values of the indicators after the completion of all the projects in R.
- a scoring function $f : I \to \mathbb{R}$;
- a real number b, representing the available budget;

we look for a projects subset $P' \subseteq P$, whose overall cost is less than or equal to the budget, to maximize the scoring function; more formally we look for a subset P' such that:

- $\sum_{j:p_j \in P'} c_j \leq b$ (budget constraint)
- $\forall P'' \subseteq P, P'' \neq P', \sum_{j:p_j \in P''} c_j \leq b, \ f(P') \geq f(P'')$ (optimality constraint)

Before discussing the approximation algorithm let us recall, from [1], an example. It is important to mention that, when planning multiple projects, the value of the indicators after the projects must be carefully analysed. Let us provide an example: assume that, in a given area, the broadband penetration is 30 %; we have two distinct projects, using distinct technologies, that have been estimated to raise that value by, respectively, 35 % and 45 %. It is clear that, when estimating the overall improvement of both projects, we cannot simply add the values, since this would lead to an unfeasible value of 110 %; neither we can estimate it to 100 %, because it is reasonable that there should be some overlapping in the population reached by both projects, and therefore the real value might be something slightly bigger than 75 %.

Therefore it is important to analyze the effect of the multiple projects together, rather than simply summing up all the (estimated) effects. We now provide an example of a somewhat of a paradoxical effect: given a ranking of projects, it might happen that, when we want to fund some of them, the best outcome is when we choose the worst (in the ranking) projects.

Let us assume that we have 4 projects and 3 indicators; for the sake of simplicity we assume that (i) all the weights in the target vector are equal to 1 ($t = (1, 1, 1)$), (ii) the initial value of all the indicators is equal to 0 ($i_A = (0, 0, 0)$), (iii) the cost of each project is unitary, and (iv) our budget is 2, i.e. we can choose at most two projects amongst them. The post intervention vectors for the projects are as follows:

- $i_{P1} = (1.0, 0.0, 0.0)$
- $i_{P2} = (0.9, 0.0, 0.0)$
- $i_{P3} = (0.5, 0.3, 0.0)$
- $i_{P4} = (0.5, 0.0, 0.2)$

It is easy to see that, if we compute the scoring function as defined in Sect. 4, the outcome is

$$f(t, i_A, i_{P1}) > f(t, i_A, i_{P2}) > f(t, i_A, i_{P3}) > f(t, i_A, i_{P4})$$

Since there is budget for two projects, it would seem natural to fund $P1$ e $P2$; but let us now consider the post intervention vectors for all the possible pairs:

- $i_{(P1+P2)} = (1.0, 0.0, 0.0)$
- $i_{(P1+P3)} = (1.0, 0.3, 0.0)$
- $i_{(P1+P4)} = (1.0, 0.0, 0.2)$
- $i_{(P2+P3)} = (1.0, 0.3, 0.0)$
- $i_{(P2+P4)} = (1.0, 0.0, 0.2)$
- $i_{(P3+P4)} = (1.0, 0.3, 0.2)$

It is clear that, if we have to choose only two projects, the best outcome is when we fund $P3$ and $P4$, that, considered alone are worst than $P1$ and $P2$, but together are better.

Can we design efficient algorithms able to solve this problem? Unfortunately, the problem belongs to the NPO complexity class, as stated in the following theorem:

Theorem 1. *[1] The optimization problem MPE, as defined above, belongs to the NPO complexity class.*

We derive an approximation algorithm for the MPE problem using a reduction to the following problem, i.e., the Budgeted Maximum Coverage Problem, that has been studied by Khuller, Moss, and Naor in [8].

BUDGETED MAXIMUM COVERAGE (BMC):
INSTANCE: A collection of sets $S = \{S_1, \ldots, S_m\}$, with associated costs $\{c_1, \ldots, c_m\}$, is defined over a domain of elements $X = \{X_1, \ldots, X_n\}$ with associated weights $\{w_1, \ldots, w_n\}$.
QUESTION: Find a subset $S' \subseteq S$, such that the total cost of the elements in S' does not exceed a given budget L, and the total weights of elements of X covered by the elements of S' is maximized.

It is easy to verify that is possible to reduce the MPE problem into the BMC problem in the following way; the key idea is, for each indicator, to split the contribution into distinct *pieces* that can be covered by the projects. Informally:

- Each project P_i becomes a set; in particular, it becomes the set of all the improvements in the indicators.
- The cost of project P_i becomes the cost of the corresponding set S_i.
- For each indicator, the contribution of each problem is split into a (bounded) number of distinct elements. The weight of each element corresponds to the *marginal* increment of the scoring function.

Let us clarify with an example. Let us refer to the previously mentioned MPE instance, where we have 4 projects, 3 indicators, budget $b = 2$, unitary cost for all the projects and the initial value of all the indicators is equal to 0 ($i_A = (0, 0, 0)$); the post intervention vectors for the projects are as follows:

- $i_{P1} = (1.0, 0.0, 0.0)$
- $i_{P2} = (0.9, 0.0, 0.0)$
- $i_{P3} = (0.5, 0.3, 0.0)$
- $i_{P4} = (0.5, 0.0, 0.2)$

We turn this MPE instance into the following BMC instance: each project become a set, and the cost is unitary for each set. Now, the delicate part, is to split the contribution of each indicator. We recall that the post intervention vectors for all the possible pairs are:

- $i_{(P1+P2)} = (1.0, 0.0, 0.0)$
- $i_{(P1+P3)} = (1.0, 0.3, 0.0)$
- $i_{(P1+P4)} = (1.0, 0.0, 0.2)$
- $i_{(P2+P3)} = (1.0, 0.3, 0.0)$
- $i_{(P2+P4)} = (1.0, 0.0, 0.2)$
- $i_{(P3+P4)} = (1.0, 0.3, 0.2)$

We can assume that the first indicator has three distinct parts, valued respectively 0.5, 0.4 and 0.1. For example, we can assume that the P_1 achieves all the three parts, P_2 achieves the first and the second part, P_3 achieves only the first one, whilst P_4 achieves the second and the third one. To each of this parts we associate an element of X, and therefore we have $\{X_1, X_2, X_3\}$ that are the elements derived from the first indicator. The second and third indicators, as we can see, are simpler, i.e. there is no need to split them, and therefore we add one element for the second indicator (X_4) and one element for the third indicator (X_5). In summary, these are the four sets:

- $S_1 = \{X_1, X_2, X_3\}$ (P_1 achieves all the three parts of the first indicator);
- $S_2 = \{X_1, X_2\}$ (P_2 achieves the first and the second part of the first indicator);
- $S_1 = \{X_1, X_4\}$ (P_3 achieves only the first part of the first indicator, and the unique part of the second indicator);
- $S_1 = \{X_2, X_3, X_5\}$ (P_4 achieves the second and the third part of the first indicator, and the unique part of the third indicator).

As we defined, the weight of each element of X corresponds to the marginal increment of the scoring function due to that element. It is easy to see that, therefore, that the weights of the five elements are $\{\frac{0.5}{3}, \frac{0.4}{3}, \frac{0.1}{3}, \frac{0.3}{3}, \frac{0.2}{3}\}$.

Now, we can state the following theorem.

Theorem 2. *The optimization problem MPE admits an $O(1-\frac{1}{e})$-approximation algorithm.*

Proof. The statement derives immediately from the reduction above and the $O(1-\frac{1}{e})$-approximation algorithm for the BMC problem [8].

Note that the $O(1-\frac{1}{e})$-approximation algorithm for the BMC problem, that achieves a $\frac{1}{2} \cdot (1 - \frac{1}{e})$ factor of approximation, is a greedy algorithm that can be directly turned into the following simple algorithm for the MPE problem: at each step we select the project that maximizes the ratio between the marginal increment to the scoring function and the cost of the project. If there is budget for including this project in the solution, we do so; otherwise we drop it and examine the next project.

If we apply the above greedy algorithm to the MPE example instance, it is easy to see that the first problem to be selected is P_1, and after it the project that maximizes the marginal value of the scoring function is P_3. Therefore, this greedy solution $Sol^G = \{P_1, P_3\}$ achieves an overall value of $\frac{1.3}{3}$, whilst the optimum solution $Sol^* = \{P_3, P_4\}$ achieves $\frac{1.5}{3}$. It holds that

$$Sol^G > \frac{1}{2} \cdot (1 - \frac{1}{e}) \cdot S^*$$

6   Conclusions

We addressed the scenario from [1], where an organ of a public administration, i.e. the *decision-maker*, is requested to plan one or more interventions in some framework related to the Information Society or the eGovernment set of actions.

In particular, we study the Multiple Projects Evaluation problem, focusing on its approximability. We show that the problem admits a $(1 - \frac{1}{e})$–approximation algorithm.

It remains open the question of whether this approximation is the best possible.

References

1. d'Amore, F., Laura, L., Luciani, L., Pagliarini, F.: Planning, designing and evaluating multiple eGovernment interventions. In: Proceedings of the International Conference on e-Business (DCNET/ICE-B/OPTICS), pp. 85–92 (2012)
2. Ausiello, G., Protasi, M., Marchetti-Spaccamela, A., Gambosi, G., Crescenzi, P., Kann, V.: Complexity and Approximation: Combinatorial Optimization Problems and Their Approximability Properties. Springer-Verlag New York Inc., Secaucus (1999)
3. Berge, C.: Graphes et Hypergraphes. Dunod, Paris (1970)
4. Diestel, R.: Graph Theory. Graduate Texts in Mathematics. Springer, Heidelberg (2006)
5. eGEP. eGovernment Unit - DG Information Society and Media - European Commission. eGovernment Economics Projects - Measurements Framework. Final Deliverable, http://rso.it/eGEP
6. European Commission. Key ICT indicators for the Member States, Norway and Iceland. i2010 Annual Information Society Report 2007, vol. 3 (2007)
7. Garey, M.R., Johnson, D.S.: Computers and Intractability: A Guide to the Theory of NP-Completeness. W. H. Freeman and Company, New York (1979)
8. Khuller, S., Moss, A., Naor, J.: The budgeted maximum coverage problem. Inf. Process. Lett. **70**(1), 39–45 (1999)
9. Ojo, A.K., Janowski, T., Estevez, E.: Determining progress towards e-government: What are the core indicators? In Proceedings of the 5th European Conference on e-Government, pp. 312–322. ACL, Reading (2005)
10. Papadimitriou, C.M.: Computational Complexity. Addison-Wesley, Reading (1994)
11. Smith, C.: Economic indicators. In: Wankel, C. (ed.) Encyclopedia of Business in Today's World. SAGE Publications Inc., California (2009)
12. Understand. Understand (European regions UNDER way towards STANDard indicators for benchmarking information society). Methodological Handbook (2006), http://www.understand-eu.net/

Strategizing and Revenue Creation in Dynamic Paradigms: A Model to Support Revenue Analysis for Mobile Incumbent Telcos

Antonio Ghezzi[1], Angela Malanchini[1], Raffaello Balocco[1],
Marcelo Cortimiglia[2(✉)], and Alejandro G. Frank[2]

[1] Department of Management, Industrial Engineering Department,
Politecnico Di Milano, Via Lambruschini 4B, 20156 Milan, Italy
{antoniol.ghezzi, angela.malanchini,
raffaello.balocco}@polimi.it
[2] Department of Industrial Engineering,
Federal University of Rio Grande Do Sul, Porto Alegre, Brazil
{cortimiglia, frank}@producao.ufrgs.br

Abstract. The growth of the Mobile telecommunications business in Italy has largely offset the decrease in revenues coming from fixed telephony. More specifically, we are witnessing a significant growth in data services, mainly driven by connectivity. The competitive landscape is also evolving, thanks to the growing convergence between the markets of Telecommunications, Media and Consumer Electronics. In consideration of the above scenario, this study aims to develop a strategic model in to analyze revenue streams generated by Telcos in the Italian Mobile services segment. This model describes the variation of the main factors influencing income and creates three possible future scenarios (optimistic, pessimistic and expected), affecting these variables in the next 5 years. The goal of the model is to support Telco executives in the identification of any critical areas that may create large gaps in revenue in the coming years and in the formulation of the right strategies.

Keywords: Strategy · Business model · Revenue model · Revenue analysis mobile telecommunications · Dynamic paradigms · Forecasting

1 Introduction

In recent years, the growth of the Mobile telecommunications business in Italy has largely offset the decrease in revenues coming from fixed telephony.

In the last two years there was a weight increase of expenditure on telecommunications (services and terminals) in the basket of consumer prices, equal to 2.65 % in 2011, due mainly to the broadband incidence [2]. Within this market, the distribution of smartphones allowing access to services so far typical of fixed location use, is one of the factors which contribute to explain the aforementioned increase.

However, today the Mobile market is increasingly saturated and mature in its traditional voice and messaging components [11, 13]. The market is characterized by strong competitive pressure at both retail and wholesale level, which leads to traditional services

© Springer-Verlag Berlin Heidelberg 2014
M.S. Obaidat and J. Filipe (Eds.): ICETE 2012, CCIS 455, pp. 101–115, 2014.
DOI: 10.1007/978-3-662-44791-8_7

losses [10, 20]. For this reason, Telcos started to develop innovative applications and services in order to balance the effects of competition. In this market Telco have yet to understand which strategy they should adopt [7, 8, 15].

For Operators there are growth prospects on the connectivity side, thanks to both smartphone and Internet Key-based browsing, and Value Added Services (VAS) area as Mobile Content, Mobile Advertising and Mobile Payment.

The competitive landscape of Mobile telecommunications is also evolving, thanks as well to the growing convergence between the markets of Telecommunications, Media and Consumer Electronics – a phenomenon giving rise to a "cross" competition that opened up competition to converging markets and their Operators, creating growth opportunities for Mobile Operators and, at the same time, competitive threats [Ghezzi…][Peppard, Rylander]. Another important element is the presence of so-called Over The Top (e.g. Google) characterized by their ability to compete in multiple markets across the board and global levels.

For the Media Company, the scenario is dominated by vertically integrated players, but with a growing importance of Web and Mobile as a complementary distribution platform - hence the importance of a direct relationship with Telcos.

In Consumer Electronics market, smartphone operating systems with a high quality and effectiveness and application store manned by the device manufacturer, create a new ecosystem in which the role of Telcos is marginal.

The Over The Top, finally, are the most significant threat for Telcos, due to the ability of diversification, the ability to rapidly scale model of disruptive advertising based and intensive use of customer knowledge.

In consideration of the aforementioned scenario, this work aims to:

- identify main factors that enable new Mobile paradigms and summarize the main differences as compared to the past, to quantify Mobile Internet and Application store Italian markets and to analyze current trends and future scenarios;
- conduct an empirical analysis based on studies of Italian companies selected from among main actors in the Mobile sector: Mobile Operators, Media Companies and Device Manufacturers;
- Develop a strategic model in order to analyze revenue streams generated by Telcos in the Italian Mobile services segment. This model describes the variation of the main factors influencing income and creates three possible future scenarios (optimistic, pessimistic and expected), affecting these variables in the next 5 years. The goal of the model is to provide support to Telco executives in the identification of any critical areas that may create large gaps in revenue in the coming years and in the formulation of the right strategies.

2 Literature Review

The first part of the presented research aims to frame the Mobile telecommunications market and the new paradigms of Mobile Internet and Application stores in the reference literature, enshrining the actors, the main strategies and current trends.

First, the Telecommunications Industry was analyzed through the secondary sources analysis - such as reports (e.g. [1, 2, 14]) and academic studies (e.g. [6, 8, 9, 15–18, 20–22, 24, 25]). Different phenomena characterizing the market will be illustrated. In particular, we will provide a framework and a quantification of the Mobile industry in Italy and on the international level, identifying the main trends.

Main issues coming out from the analysis are:

- International scenario:
  - continuous and progressive decline in fixed line segment;
  - slowdown in the Mobile segment;
  - increasing demand on data segment, used by both fixed and Mobile line.

- National scenario:
  - contraction of the final overall total expenditure of households and firms;
  - drop in investments in Mobile network infrastructure and a modest growth for the fixed network;
  - increased pressure from the competition, with a decrease in the concentration of the telecommunications markets;
  - progressive entry into the Mobile market to new entrants (such as Mobile Virtual Network Operators - MVNO), including some already active in the fixed telephony (BT Italy, Fastweb, Tiscali, etc.);
  - gradual reduction of prices charged by companies to end users;
  - decline of traditional services for the fixed network and growing diffusion of broadband services, but less intense than in other European countries;
  - diffusion of broadband applications in the Mobile network as a strategic factor, both - the growth of the sector for the development of other markets linked to the chain of information and audio and video content.

The market is also characterized by trends that are widely changing its strategic structure.

- One of the most important trends of the moment is the merger and acquisition process, that in the last year has mainly involved the Mobile phone industry and broadband services provision.
- Another trend is telecommunications operators orientation towards solutions that enable efficiency gains and operating costs reductions. This happens especially in the Mobile industry, where operators are increasingly concentrated in services, while resort to technical solutions for infrastructure sharing (so-called network sharing) and / or 'external subcontracting network operations (cd network outsourcing).
- The evolution of the market - more and more oriented towards the use of data and Internet services - as well as influence the development of next-generation fixed networks, in the same way also influence the choices of actors in the markets for Mobile communications. Characteristic in this sector is the rapid expansion of Mobile broadband.
- In recent years, wireless has become increasingly pervasive, as well as voice service for data service. The indoor environment has also assumed great importance for

network operators, because it is home to a large portion of Mobile traffic. The combination of these two factors, combined with the benefit that you are approaching the transmitting antenna to the terminal in terms of improvement of the radio channel and, therefore, the actual performance that the customer can experience, they tend to think of Mobile network deployments future according to a paradigm that shifts from macro-cell current in cells gradually smaller as micro, pico and femto.

- Up to now, the paradigm of Mobile portal has always been considered a successful model by the Operators in order to reach their customer base efficiently and effectively and in order to maximize revenues from the sale of services and content. By offering online portals, Telcos aimed at making their offer exclusive and at the same time, they made sure to keep third parties (MCSP in the first place) far from the customer base. This strategy is currently no longer profitable, even with offers from Mobile Content Provider through Application site and store. Hence the gradual "transformation" from the online portal to off portal paradigm occurred, where the Telco delegated the processes of overseeing and monitoring the services available to third party service providers.

- The Mobile Payment can be defined as a new challenge for the Telcos [12]: it is a phenomenon that is widely available and constitutes for the telecom industry in the Mobile industry a new source of revenues and a new option that can push subscribers to intensify further the use of cell phones and this trend provides, in fact, the possibility of diversifying the business, in a context in which the high Mobile penetration and increasing end-user familiarity with the instrument is in favor of Mobile operators, the profitability of this business, however, are much smaller than those of traditional services.

- Finally, the increasing spread of Mobile Virtual Network Operators (MVNOs) amplifies the degree of competition in the market. They are created to provide different offer models: traders who are turning to certain foreign communities (market "ethnic" supermarket chains operators that combine Mobile telephony services with special offers and promotions within their chain, offering Mobile operators that integrate the financial services as their core competence, and finally, integration of services of telecommunication companies are already present in the fixed network).

A second phase of the study is focused on secondary sources analysis - such as reports, press releases, reviews, etc. - and some academic paper analysis aimed to investigate on Internet and Mobile applications market development and to identify development opportunities about various Mobile market players. These new paradigms are changing Mobile telecommunications industry and supply chain relationships with Media Companies and Device Manufacturers.

The objective of this phase is to show how the Mobile Internet market has triggered a virtuous cycle driven by several factors: introduction by all operators of attractive flat rate offer, significant investments in communication with Telco asset; agreements between Mobile Operators and major web portals (Social Networks, in particular), increasing smartphones diffusion with good navigation skills. These factors push a growing number of users to Mobile Internet, leading an increasing number of Content

Provider (Web Companies, Media Companies, etc.) to develop a range of content optimized for Mobile use.

Regarding Mobile Internet and Mobile Content market, these Mobile market segments follow two opposing dynamics: Mobile Internet has seen a growth in recent years; Mobile Content has recorded a negative trend, a part Games and Media components.

A study on new Mobile Internet and Application store paradigm is accompanied by the analysis of these "enablers" [4]:

- Smartphones diffusion with good navigation skills (OS, browser, etc.).
- Flat offer penetration;
- Available bandwidth increase;
- Application store model introduction;
- Browser importance to enhance Mobile Surfer experience;
- Mobile sites and applications offer explosion;
- Communication pushed by involved players.

New Mobile Internet and Application stores dynamic paradigms are changing relationship between Telco and Content Providers and, generally, among all other players in the process.

- On one hand we proceed to a "healthy" relationship-enabled dispenser, characterized by distinct and well defined roles: Telco, the type rating, and Content providers to content providers.
- On the other, their paths are separating because, at this time, Telco are aiming primarily to increase their revenues from Mobile Internet and Content Providers are trying to understand ways to generate revenues from interesting content premium sales on Mobile site and Application store and from Mobile Advertising. In this scenario, the situation is as follows:

  - While revenues from Mobile Internet, today, are in absolute value substantial (equivalent to nearly 400 million € in 2011) and growing, Content Providers revenues derived from new paradigms are still very low (equal to a few tens of million €, including applications sales and advertising on Mobile sites and applications);
  - An interesting virtuous circle is still in place: the more you spread the Mobile Internet, the more chance there is for Content Providers to generate revenue by selling premium content and advertising (both with Mobile sites and Mobile applications).

- As well as Telco and Content Providers, a key role is played by two other types of players: Mobile handsets manufacturers and operating systems manufacturers and technology platforms providers.

Sector applications and sector Operating Systems is expected to grow, with strong opportunities for all players in the sector. In this market that are going to be major events:

- iPhone launch, which gave rise to new Mobile Internet and Application store paradigms;
- Android Operating System introduction that marks "bully" entrance by Google in Mobile world;
- New players offer entry or expansion into Pc world (Acer, HP with Palm purchase, etc.).

These changes are creating many problems to traditional player, because they not only must invest heavily to guard Operating System and application interface (from browsing capabilities), but they must also understand what role playing in the new world of Application store, knowing that App Store success will not be easily imitated: this boom, in fact, is not based so much on technological innovation introduced, but on innovation business made possible by complex and unique Apple ecosystem.

The third phase of the study required a review of strategic research streams, to understand strategic changes that Mobile telecommunications field is experiencing.

More specifically, topics identified describe current situation and possible future strategies developments adopted by Mobile operators; they also describe how they relate to other players, in particular with Media Company and Device Manufacturer.

The discussed themes in this chapter are the following:

- *Business Model and Strategy;*
- *Co-opetition;*
- *Value Network Analysis;*
- *Open Innovation.*

This academic literature analysis stage, as mentioned, aims to understand, through assessing a number of strategic models: (i) how Telcos' strategic paradigms and positioning will change; (ii) how Telcos can leverage their assets in coming years; (iii) how the identified endogenous and exogenous variables affect Telco revenues tree representation; (iv) how the dynamic paradigm can affect the activity of Scenario Planning in the industry.

This choice is dictated by the fact that the strategic model proposed is to identify, for each income item, three scenarios types (optimistic, expected, pessimistic) that Telcos could face a 4–5 years horizon depending evolution of endogenous and exogenous variables.

3 Research Methodology

After literature analysis, an empirical analysis has been conducted to understand the approach, strategies, positioning and trends of Italian companies: 4 Mobile Network Operators, 7 Media Company and 2 Mobile Device Manufacturer.

The analysis was based on case studies [3, 5, 26], carried out through interviews with Mobile strategies Heads in the case of Mobile media companies and handset manufacturers and the VAS areas director with respect to Telcos.

The questions asked to respondents were based on corporate strategy framework in Mobile market and, in particular, towards an understanding of the following units of analysis (Tables 1, 2 and 3).

Table 1. Scheme of analysis for interviews on Mobile Telcos.

General business profile Business Model and Strategy	• Core competences and business diversification • Organizational Structure • Full year results • Portal evolution strategies • New strategies born with Application store paradigm • Mobile Internet strategy • Content Provider relationship • Traditional services (egSms premium) • Evoluzionedelle flat offers evolution flat about Mobile navigation • Strategies in face of Authority regulations

Table 2. Scheme of analysis for interviews on Media Companies.

General Business profile
 	
Business model for digital strategies
 	
Business model for Mobile services
 	
Investment and future development plans
	• Core competences and business diversification
	• Organizational Structure and Human Resources
	• Relevant geographic markets
	• Mobile Offer features
	• Customers and suppliers role in the supply chain
	• Revenues and business model
	• Mobile Market Mission
	• Mobile Content offer features:
	  o Platforms (Sms, Mms, Download, Applications, Video)
	  o Mobile Contents development
	• Mobile Internet offer features:
	  o Content Management Systems
	  o on portal/off portal offer
	• Offer innovation level
	• Customers and suppliers role in the supply chain
	• Revenues and Mobile business model
	• Mobile human resources
	• Long term strategy
	• Choosing whether to invest on Applications or on Mobile Site
	• Supply chain relationship
	• View on future devices (boom tablet, etc.)

Table 3. Scheme of analysis for interviews on Device Manufacturers.

General Business Profile	• Core competences and business diversification • Investment in innovation
Business Model and Strategy	• New strategies born with Application store paradigm • Store services offer • Revenue mode Application store offer • Store payment mode • Sales terminals sales strategies

The companies and the case studies are:

- Mobile Operators: Vodafone, Tim, Wind, H3G;
- Media Company: RCS Media Group, Il Sole24ORE, Gruppo Editoriale L'Espresso, Editoriale Domus, SKY Italia, RAI, Seat Pagine Gialle;
- Device Manufacturer: Nokia, Research In Motion – BlackBerry.

To complete the empirical analysis, in addition to case studies, a census of the Mobile Internet tariffs offered by Mobile operators was conducted. This will provide a range of quantitative data on supply trying to understand the dynamics that govern over it. The census was based on secondary sources, in order to gather information which allowed to do an Operators tariffs benchmarking.

Empirical analysis objectives are:

- Getting the information to read critically, in strategic terms, the Mobile operators approach and orientation for Mobile Internet "new" market, the traditional market for Mobile content and Application store innovative paradigm, in particular addressing the attention to supply chain relationships with Media Companies and Device Manufacturers;
- Understanding how media companies are facing new Mobile paradigms, analyzing their role within the sector (with particular reference to the relationship with Telco) and developing business models;
- Assessing the role that Device Manufacturers play in this market as enablers of technology to deliver increasingly rich user experiences for end users;

Analyzing current services offer on the operators portal and to measure the growth of the role of third parties in the provision of Mobile services.

4   The Revenue Analysis Strategic Model

Ultimate objective of the present study is the strategic model development in order to determine Mobile Telcos revenue tree representation, identifying for each income item the driving factors - external and internal - trying also to trace three possible scenarios for future evolution. With scenarios analysis, critical revenues areas that require, a coherent strategy declination in the coming years were identified. Also, the revenue model stands as a core parameter of Mobile firm's business model [7, 19, 23].

The strategic model was constructed following the steps outlined below, in sequence:

1. For each revenue function area (voice, messaging, connectivity, VAS), function that describes revenues has been identified.
2. For each variable within each function identified in point 1, the main factors that influence trend in coming years has been highlighted.
3. For all the major key factors (e.g., VoIP, Mobile Number Portability, proliferation of offers "bundled" service penetration of Mobile Internet users, etc.), were followed the steps listed below:

   (a) three possible scenarios identification (optimistic, pessimistic and expected) over the next 5 years;
   (b) impact of three possible scenarios calculation on variable that is affected by this specific factor (calculated for variables in a quantitative way).

4. For each variable, delta between optimistic scenario value at 2015 and pessimistic scenario value at 2015 was calculated. Later the delta value impact about variable is considered, and thus impact on total functions revenues.

The "revenue tree" on which we base the model construction is shown below (Fig. 1).

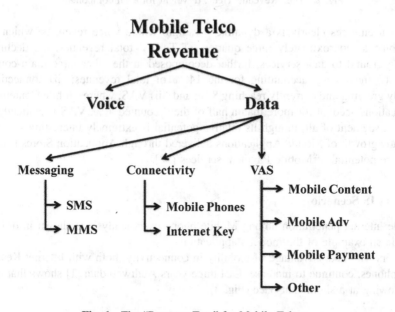

Fig. 1. The "Revenue Tree" for Mobile Telcos.

The empirical analysis carried out on Telcos balance sheets and financial reports, coupled with the data gathered during the direct interviews with the informants, allowed to calculate the relative weight α of each component of Telco's revenues (Fig. 2).

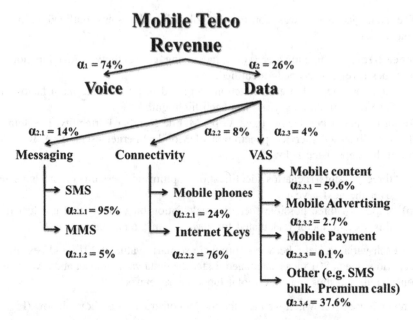

Fig. 2. The "Revenue Tree": α weight for each component.

What emerges clearly is a dynamic paradigm where voice revenues, which still contribute to approximately three quarters of Telcos' total revenues, are declining, leaving ground to data services, further decomposed in the other three main components: (i) messaging, accounting for the 14 % of total revenues; (ii) connectivity, quickly growing and currently reaching 8 %; and (iii) VAS, where Mobile Content and Applications account for more than a half of the accounted 4 %. VAS is evidently the smallest segment of all, though its relative potential is extremely interesting – see the dramatic growth of Mobile Applications delivered through Application Stores [4], and the huge potential of Mobile Payment services [12].

4.1 As IS Scenario

Mobile Internet penetration among Mobile phone users analysis is shown in order to provide an example of the model's application.

Users who take advantage of mobility in connectivity, both with Internet Key and smartphones, continue to increase. Last three years Audiweb data [1] shows that users are growing at a significant pace (Fig. 3).

4.2 Future Scenarios Description

- Optimistic Scenario:
  - Users who currently use services from a Mobile phone connectivity are the "pioneers", and then the real service "boom" is yet to come;

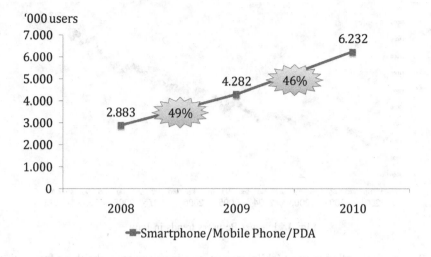

Fig. 3. Mobile Internet users trend in Italy.

– In short term users number connecting to Internet with Mobile phones is growing exponentially.

• Expected Scenario:

 – The connectivity service is already in a full development stage, and growth in the coming years will be straight and it will reach saturation in ten years;
 – In short term users number connecting to Internet with Mobile phones will grow at the same current rate of progress.

• Pessimistic Scenario:

 – The connectivity service will not develop as the current trend leads one to believe, but it arrive early to an asymptote, leading to a relatively low penetration of the number of Mobile phone users;
 – In short term users number connecting to Internet with Mobile phones will grow at progressively lower rates.

To construct the curve trend penetration of smartphone users was estimated. Then connectivity penetration was estimated during 10 years:

• Optimistic scenario – 70 % Mobile phone users;
• Expected scenario – 50 % users;
• Pessimistic scenario – 35 % Mobile phone users (current smartphone penetration).

Subsequently for each cases regression curve was applied:

• For all scenarios an exponential curve similar to Internet with Pc users trend were applied (Fig. 4).

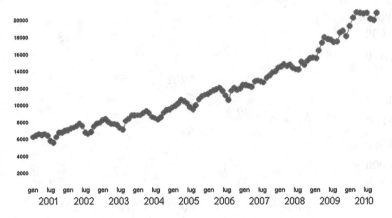

Fig. 4. Internet Pc users trends in Italy.

Such curve applied to the Mobile ecosystem allows to obtain the three forecasting scenarios presented in Fig. 5.

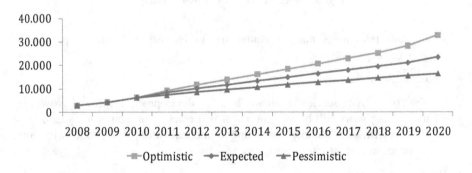

Fig. 5. Mobile Internet penetration scenarios predicted.

4.3   Impact Analysis of the Scenarios

A revenue delta calculation was hence based on scenarios analysis on current connectivity revenues (Table 4).

Table 4. Connectivity deltas.

Variable	Delta	Delta rate on 2010 users	Revenue delta	Delta rate on current connectivity revenues
Mobile Internet service penetration on Mobile phone users	6.600 users	105,9 %	582,5 million €	148,6 %

5 Conclusions

The study allows to shed light the definition and proposition of a comprehensive set of strategic ideas set that Mobile Telcos could pursue in order to increase their earnings, based on the evidences collected through the empirical research and the Revenue tree.

- **Voice and Messaging Segments.** Not so many actions are available to raise revenues, since these segments are increasingly saturated and mature. However, to contain the negative trend Telos can abandon the "price war" and continue studying flat fares that do not incorporate the two traditional services (Voice and Sms) as they are adversely affected by traditional "package volume" (increased volume, lower revenue per unit).

- **Connectivity Segment.** Despite low revenues, volume generated with this service (8 %) show that Operators have the largest growth prospects as the market is changing. Telcos should focus their strategies on Internet service differentiation (for both phone and Internet Key) by means of:

  - offering lower consumption prices than current consumption prices in order to capture users lion's share who consider essential only a few weeks access;
  - introducing flat packages for access to specific services, as not all clients use all services available online (e.g. e-mail, Social Networks, News).
  - keeping flat package offers on market.

These strategic offers are essential also for high congestion that is affecting more and more Mobile networks [8]. In this way, bandwidth "waste" from useless services that generate high traffic is limited.

There are also two other directions that are strategic for Telcos:

  - create cooperation agreements with the Mobile industry players (Media and Device Manufacturer Company);
  - invest heavily in next generation networks in order to increase connectivity service use.

- **VAS Segment.** Compared to the excellent results achieved in recent years and since a few years, the traditional Mobile Content are experiencing downward trend, Telcos must try to restore lifecycle to this market with following strategies:

  - focusing on services that are growing, like sweepstakes and voting services via Sms, to increase revenue from premium Sms and try to encourage the industry players to innovate in this direction;
  - trying to turn on the Mobile portal strategies so that, on one hand, to avoid the risk of generating losses resulting from that area, and the other hand to understand what could be the role of Telco in determining access to Mobile Internet;
  - despite being a very profitable channel, Telcos should not divest Wap Billing on Mobile Site off portal service because it is expected that content providers will more and more take the road of offering pay content on Mobile Site;

- focusing on Billing to other stores service because it offers excellent growth prospects, thanks to the possibility of entering into agreements directly with Content Providers;
- it is difficult, despite significant Italian Telco market shares, to consider Billing on Telcos store a winning strategy (e.g. Vodafone 360).
- with regards to Mobile Advertising, with the gradual portals disposal and Sms database saturation, there are no strategies to generate sufficient revenues in short term that could justify any investment to be made in that market so that it expands;
- regarding Mobile Payment, Telco revenues from this service are practically zero; as this service is widespread among foreign Telcos, Italian operators should pursue the same path in order to enable payment systems via remote payment through phone bills; all Telco are under study for this new segment revenues.

Finally, Operators should strive to increase the number of customer owning a SIM (Single Identity Module) card on subscription over customers owning a prepaid SSIM card, as the small average credit for SIM cards affects the ability to purchase premium content, severely limiting VAS segment's growth.

The strategies and choices for Telcos put forward in this study only aim at enhancing incumbents' revenue generation ability, while they do not take into full consideration the costs structure (CAPEX and OPEX) related to their implementation. Future developments of this work could consider these outflows' impact, reassessing and prioritizing these strategies in terms of investment requirements.

References

1. Audiweb: AW trends. Online diffusion in Italy. Research report (2010)
2. Assinform: Assinform report on informatics, telecommunications and multimedia content. Research report (2012)
3. Bonoma, T.V.: Case research in marketing: opportunities, problems, and a process. J. Mark. Res. **22**, 199–208 (1985)
4. Cortimiglia, M., Ghezzi, A., Renga, F.: Mobile applications and their delivery platforms. IT Prof. **13**(5), 51–56 (2011)
5. Eisenhardt, K.M., Graebner, M.E.: Theory building from cases: opportunities and challenges. Acad. Manag. J. **50**(1), 25–32 (2007)
6. Fjeldstad, Ø.D., Becerra, M., Narayanan, S.: Strategic action in network industries: an empirical analysis of the European mobile phone industry. Scand. J. Manag. **20**, 173–196 (2004)
7. Ghezzi, A.: Revisiting business strategy under discontinuity. Manag. Decis. **51**(7), 1326–1358 (2013)
8. Ghezzi, A., Georgadis, M., Reichl, P., Di-Cairano, G.C., Mangiaracina, R., Le-Sauze, N.: Generating innovative business models for the future internet. Info **15**(4), 43–68 (2013)
9. Dell'Era, C., Frattini, F., Ghezzi, A.: The role of the adoption network in the early market survival of innovations: the Italian mobile VAS industry. Eur. J. Innov. Manag. **13**(1), 118–140 (2013)
10. Ghezzi, A.: Emerging business models and strategies for mobile platforms providers: a reference framework. Info **14**(5), 36–56 (2012)

11. Ghezzi, A., Cortimiglia, M., Balocco, R.: Mobile content & service delivery platforms: a technology classification model. Info **14**(2), 72–88 (2012)
12. Ghezzi, A., Renga, F., Balocco, R., Pescetto, P.: Mobile payment applications: offer state of the art in the Italian market. Info **12**(5), 3–22 (2010)
13. Ghezzi, A.: emerging business models and strategies for mobile middleware technology providers. In: Proceedings of the 17th European Conference on Information Systems (ECIS '09), Verona, Italy (2009)
14. IDC: Worldwide quarterly mobile phone tracker. Research report (2010)
15. Kuo, Y., Yu, C.: 3G Telecommunication operators' challenges and roles: a perspective of Mobile commerce value chain. Technovation **26**, 1347–1356 (2006)
16. Li, F., Whalley, J.: Deconstruction of the telecommunications industry: from value chain to value network. Telecommun. Policy **26**, 451–472 (2002)
17. Normann, R., Ramirez, R.: Designing Interactive Strategy: From the Value Chain to the Value Constellation. Wiley, Chichester (1994)
18. Olla, P., Patel, N.V.: A value chain model for mobile data service providers. Telecommun. Policy **26**, 551–571 (2002)
19. Osterwalder, A.: The business model ontology. A proposition in a design science approach. Ph.D. thesis, Ecole des Hautes Etudes Commerciales de l'Université de Lausanne (2004)
20. Peppard, J., Rylander, A.: From value chain to value network: an insight for mobile operators. Eur. Manag. J. **24**(2), 128–141 (2006)
21. Sabat, H.K.: The evolving Mobile wireless value chain and market structure. Telecommun. Policy **26**, 505–535 (2002)
22. Seaberg, J.G., Hawn, J., Dincerler, G.E., Eugster, C.C., Rao, N.: Attackers versus incumbents: the battle for value in an IP-networked world. McKinsey Q. **4**, 138–153 (1997)
23. Teece, D.J.: Business models, business strategy and innovation. Long Range Plan. **43**(2–3), 172–194 (2010)
24. Weill, P., Vitale, M.: Place to Space: Migrating to E-Business Models. Harvard Business School Press, Boston (2001)
25. Wirtz, B.W.: Reconfiguration of value chains in converging media and communications markets. Long Range Plan. **34**, 489–506 (2001)
26. Yin, R.: Case Study Research: Design and Methods. Sage Publishing, Thousand Oaks (2003)

Optical Communication Systems

Iteratively Detected and SVD-assisted MIMO Multimode Transmission Schemes

Sebastian Aust[(⊠)], Andreas Ahrens, and Steffen Lochmann

Department of Electrical Engineering and Computer Science,
Communications Signal Processing Group, Hochschule Wismar,
University of Technology, Business and Design,
Philipp-Müller-Straße 14, 23966 Wismar, Germany
aust.seba@googlemail.com,
{andreas.ahrens,steffen.lochmann}@hs-wismar.de
http://www.hs-wismar.de

Abstract. In the recent past the concept of MIMO (multiple input multiple output) transmission over multimode fibers has attracted increasing interest in the optical fiber transmission community, targeting at increased fiber throughput or improved bit-error rate performance. In this contribution a coherent (2×2) MIMO (multiple input multiple output) transmission with iterative detection over a measured multimode fiber channel at 1325 nm as well as at 1570 nm operating wavelength is studied under the constraint of a given fixed data throughput and integrity. For the channel measurements a fibre length of 1,4 km were chosen. Extrinsic information transfer (EXIT) charts are used for analyzing and optimizing the convergence behaviour of the iterative demapping and decoding. Our results show that in order to achieve the best bit-error rate, not necessarily all MIMO layers have to be activated.

Keywords: Multiple-Input Multiple-Output (MIMO) system · Singular-Value Decomposition (SVD) · Bit allocation · Optical fibre transmission · Multimode Fiber (MMF) · Bit-Interleaved Coded Modulation (BICM)

1 Introduction

Wireless communication is nowadays one of the areas attracting a lot of research activity due to the strongly increasing demand in high-data rate transmission systems. The use of multiple antennas at both the transmitter and receiver side has stimulated one of the most important technical breakthroughs in recent communications allowing increasing the throughput and dropping the bit-error rate. The concept of MIMO transmission has been investigated since decades now for both, twisted-pair copper cable transmission – suffering from crosstalk between neighbouring wire pairs – [4,21], as well as for multi-antenna radio systems – where signal interference occurs on the radio interface [11,20].

© Springer-Verlag Berlin Heidelberg 2014
M.S. Obaidat and J. Filipe (Eds.): ICETE 2012, CCIS 455, pp. 119–134, 2014.
DOI: 10.1007/978-3-662-44791-8_8

In the recent past the concept of MIMO (multiple input multiple output) transmission over multimode fibers has attracted increasing interest in the optical fiber transmission community, e.g. [7,8,19], targeting at increased fiber throughput or improved bit-error rate performance.

A MIMO approach where modal dispersion is exploited, rather than avoided, is a promising solution. Note that for a long time the multipath nature of wireless channels was viewed as a limiting factor to be avoided. In recent years it has been realized that the multipath nature of a channel can actually enhance throughput and improve the quality of the data transmission (i.e. minimize the bit-error rate) if it is properly exploited [2].

Bit-interleaved coded modulation (BICM) was designed for bandwidth efficient transmission over fading channels [9,10]. Wireless MIMO-BICM transmission schemes for both non-frequency and frequency selective MIMO channels have attracted a lot of attention and reached a state of maturity [1,14]. By contrast, MIMO-aided optical systems require substantial further research [13,15,18]. That is why in addition to bit loading algorithms in this contribution the benefits of channel coding are also investigated. The proposed iterative decoder structures employ symbol-by-symbol soft-output decoding based on the Bahl-Cocke-Jelinek-Raviv (BCJR) algorithm and are analyzed under the constraint of a fixed data throughput [6].

However, their parameters have to be carefully optimized. The well-known water-filling technique is virtually synonymous with adaptive modulation and it is used for maximizing the overall data rate. However, delay-critical applications, such as voice or video transmission schemes, may require a certain fixed data rate. For these fixed-rate applications it is desirable to design algorithms, which minimize the bit-error rate at a given fixed data rate.

Against this background, the novel contribution of this paper is that we jointly optimize the number of activated MIMO layers and the number of bits per symbol combined with powerful error correcting codes under the constraint of a given fixed data throughput and integrity. The performance improvements are exemplarily studied by computer simulations at a measured 1,4 km multimode MIMO fiber channel at 1325 nm and at 1570 nm operating wavelength.

Since the "design-space" is large, a two-stage optimization technique is considered. Firstly, the uncoded MIMO scheme is analyzed, investigating the allocation of both the number of bits per modulated symbol and the number of activated MIMO layers at a fixed data rate. Secondly, the optimized uncoded system is extended by incorporating bit-interleaved coded modulation using iterative detection (BICM-ID), whereby both the uncoded as well as the coded systems are required to support the same user data rate within the same bandwidth.

The remaining part of this contribution is organized as follows: Sect. 2 introduces our system model, while the proposed uncoded solutions are discussed in Sect. 3. In Sect. 4 the channel encoded MIMO system is introduced. The associated performance results are presented and interpreted in Sect. 5. Finally, Sect. 6 provides our concluding remarks.

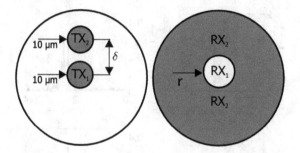

Fig. 1. Forming the optical MIMO channel (left: light launch positions at the transmitter side with a given eccentricity δ, right: spatial configuration at the receiver side as a function of the mask diameter r).

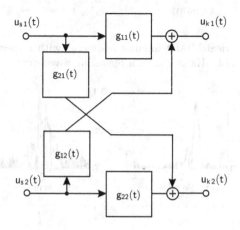

Fig. 2. Electrical (2×2) MIMO system model.

2   Channel Measurements and MIMO System Model

Forming the MIMO (multiple input multiple output) system, the corresponding optical transmitter as well as receiver side configuration is depicted in Fig. 1. At the receiver side different spatial filters have been produced by depositing a metal layer at fiber end-faces and subsequent ion milling [16]. Details on the transmission model, which has been determined by channel measurements, are given in [16].

2.1   MIMO Channel Measurements

For the investigated optical MIMO channel an eccentricity δ of $10\,\mu$m and a mask diameter r of $15\,\mu$m were chosen (Fig. 1). The arising electrical (2×2) MIMO channel is highlighted in Fig. 2.

The obtained MIMO channel impulse responses at 1325 nm and 1570 nm operating wavelength are depicted in Figs. 3 and 4, respectively and show the

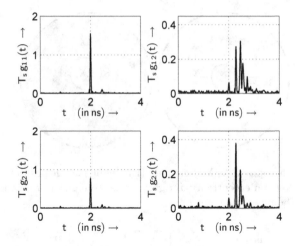

Fig. 3. Measured electrical MIMO impulse responses with respect to the pulse frequency $f_T = 1/T_s = 5,12$ GHz at 1325 nm operating wavelength.

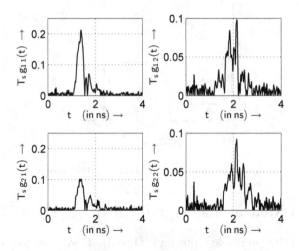

Fig. 4. Measured electrical MIMO impulse responses with respect to the pulse frequency $f_T = 1/T_s = 5,12$ GHz at 1570 nm operating wavelength.

expected dependency from the operating wavelength. The measured MIMO channel impulse responses at 1325 nm operating wavelength are highlighted in Fig. 3 and illustrate the activation of different mode groups according to the transmitter side light launch conditions (Fig. 1). The individual mode groups are clearly separated since almost no chromatic dispersion is imminent at the wavelength of 1325 nm. At a higher operating wavelength, i.e. 1570 nm, the separation of the different mode groups disappears based on the additional effect of the chromatic dispersion (Fig. 4).

2.2   MIMO Channel Parameters

In MMF two different sources of dispersion take place, i.e. modal and chromatic dispersion. The modal dispersion can be approximated by a weighted Dirac delta impulse response

$$g_{\mathrm{m}}^{(\nu\,\mu)}(t) = \sum_{\kappa=0}^{N-1} g_{\mathrm{m}\,\kappa}^{(\nu\,\mu)}\,\delta(t - \tau_0 - \tau_\kappa) \ . \tag{1}$$

Therein, N is the number of propagating modes (i.e. mode groups), $g_{\mathrm{m}\,\kappa}^{(\nu\,\mu)}$ describes the attenuation of the κth propagation mode (i.e. mode group) between the μth input and the νth output, τ_κ is the differential modal delay with respect to the overall baseline delay of τ_0. In the presence of modal coupling, the attenuation factor $g_{\mathrm{m}\,\kappa}^{(\nu\,\mu)}$ would become time-varying. Taking the different SISO (single input single output) channels into consideration, the value $g_{\mathrm{m}\,\kappa}^{(\nu\,\mu)}$ expresses the different contributions of the individual mode groups to the SISO channels within the MIMO system. Since almost no chromatic dispersion is imminent at the wavelength of 1325 nm, the individual mode groups are clearly separated as highlighted in Fig. 3.

As a result of the modal dispersion at the receiver side, a single transmitted pulse may spread into a number of adjacent symbol periods, depending on the data rate, distance traveled, and fiber properties [19]. Practically, the weighted Dirac delta pulses can be approximated by Gaussian pulses. Figure 5 shows the obtained impulse responses by using Matlabs® curve fitting tool.

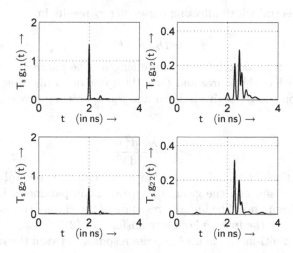

Fig. 5. Approximated electrical MIMO impulse responses with respect to the pulse frequency $f_{\mathrm{T}} = 1/T_{\mathrm{s}} = 5, 12$ GHz at 1325 nm operating wavelength by using Matlabs® curve fitting tool.

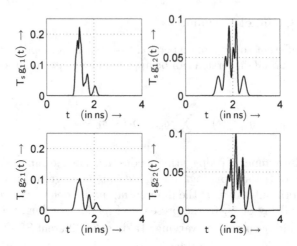

Fig. 6. Approximated electrical MIMO impulse responses with respect to the pulse frequency $f_T = 1/T_s = 5,12$ GHz at 1570 nm operating wavelength by using Matlabs® curve fitting tool.

Another limit for MMF is given by the chromatic dispersion, based on the frequency-dependence of the phase velocity of a wave. The transfer function of the chromatic dispersion is given by

$$G_c(f) = e^{(\pi f \tau_c)^2} . \tag{2}$$

Therein, the spectral width affecting parameter τ_c results in

$$\tau_c = D_c \cdot \delta_\lambda \cdot \ell , \tag{3}$$

with the parameter ℓ describing the fibre length. The parameter δ_λ represents the spectral width of the source and D_c is the group delay dispersion parameter, which depend on the refractive index n and the operating wavelength λ, and is described as

$$D_c = -\frac{\lambda}{c} \cdot \frac{d^2 n}{d\lambda^2} . \tag{4}$$

In this work a fibre length of $\ell = 1,4$ km is chosen. The spectral width of the source is $\delta_\lambda = 11$ nm and the group delay dispersion parameter is assumed to be $D_c = 18$ ps/(nm·km). The impulse response of the chromatic dispersion $g_c(t)$ can be obtained by the inverse Fourier transform of (2).

Finally, the multi-mode channel impulse response between the μth input and the νth output can be obtained as

$$g_{\nu \mu}(t) = g_m^{(\nu \mu)}(t) * g_c(t) . \tag{5}$$

Figure 6 shows the obtained SISO impulse responses with modal and chromatic dispersion within the MIMO system by using Matlabs® curve fitting tool.

2.3   MIMO System Model

Figure 7 illustrates the MIMO related single input single output (SISO) channels. Rectangular pulses are used for transmit and receive filtering. The baseband finite-length impulse response of the MIMO channel between the μth input and the νth output is given by

$$h_{\nu\,\mu}(t) = g_{\rm s}(t) * g_{\nu\,\mu}(t) * g_{\rm ef}(t) \; . \tag{6}$$

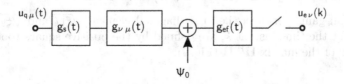

Fig. 7. Mathematical representation of the MIMO related single input single output (SISO) channels.

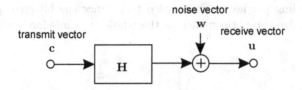

Fig. 8. Transmission system model.

The impulse responses of the transmit and receive filtering are described by $g_{\rm s}(t)$ and $g_{\rm ef}(t)$.

The block diagram of the transmission model is shown in Fig. 8: Coherent transmission and detection is assumed together with the modulation format QAM (quadrature amplitude modulation) per MIMO transmission mode. The block-oriented system for frequency selective channels is modelled by:

$$\mathbf{u} = \mathbf{H} \cdot \mathbf{c} + \mathbf{w} \; . \tag{7}$$

In (7), the transmitted signal vector $\mathbf{c}$ is mapped by the channel matrix $\mathbf{H}$ onto the received vector $\mathbf{u}$. Finally, the vector of the additive, white Gaussian noise (AWGN) is defined by $\mathbf{w}$ [16,17]. Details on the transmission model are given in [16].

In MIMO communication, singular-value decomposition (SVD) has been established as an efficient concept to compensate the interferences between the different data streams transmitted over a dispersive channel: SVD is able to transfer the whole system into independent, non-interfering layers exhibiting unequal gains per layer as highlighted in Fig. 9.

The singular-value decomposition (SVD) [12] of the system matrix $\mathbf{H}$ results in: $\mathbf{H} = \mathbf{S} \cdot \mathbf{V} \cdot \mathbf{D}^{\mathrm{H}}$, where $\mathbf{S}$ and $\mathbf{D}^{\mathrm{H}}$ are unitary matrices and $\mathbf{V}$ is a real-valued diagonal matrix of the positive square roots of the eigenvalues of the matrix $\mathbf{H}^{\mathrm{H}} \mathbf{H}$ sorted in descending order[1].

The MIMO data vector $\mathbf{c}$ is now multiplied by the matrix $\mathbf{D}$ before transmission. In turn, the receiver multiplies the received vector $\mathbf{u}$ by the matrix $\mathbf{S}^{\mathrm{H}}$. In doing so, neither the transmit power budget nor the noise power characteristic is changed. The overall transmission relationship is defined as

$$\mathbf{y} = \mathbf{S}^{\mathrm{H}} \left(\mathbf{H} \cdot \mathbf{D} \cdot \mathbf{c} + \mathbf{w} \right) = \mathbf{V} \cdot \mathbf{c} + \tilde{\mathbf{w}} \ . \tag{8}$$

The unequal gains per layer, i.e., the diagonal element $\sqrt{\xi_{1k}}$ and $\sqrt{\xi_{2k}}$ of the matrix $\mathbf{V}$ at the time instant k, are defined by the positive square roots of the eigenvalues of the matrix $\mathbf{H}^{\mathrm{H}} \mathbf{H}$ (Fig. 9).

3   Optimization Approach

By taking the different layer-specific weighting, introduced by the positive square roots of the eigenvalues of the matrix $\mathbf{H}^{\mathrm{H}} \mathbf{H}$, into account (Fig. 9), bit- and power loading per layer can be used to balance the bit-error probabilities and thus optimize the performance of the whole transmission system. Given a

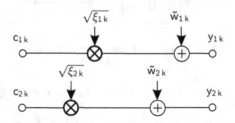

Fig. 9. SVD-based layer-specific transmission model.

Table 1. Parameters for bitloading: Investigated QAM transmission modes for fixed transmission bit rate.

Throughput	Layer 1	Layer 2
4 bit/s/Hz	16	0
4 bit/s/Hz	4	4
2 bit/s/Hz	4	0
2 bit/s/Hz	2	2

---

[1] The transpose and conjugate transpose (Hermitian) of $\mathbf{D}$ are denoted by $\mathbf{D}^{\mathrm{T}}$ and $\mathbf{D}^{\mathrm{H}}$, respectively.

fixed transmission bit rate, the optimization target is a minimum BER: Therefore the bit loading to the different transmission modes is optimized according to the options shown in Table 1.

4   Channel-encoded MIMO System

BICM is constituted by the concatenation of an encoder, an interleaver and a mapper, which is extended here to a BICM-MIMO scheme, where different signal constellations are mapped appropriately to different layers.

The channel-encoded transmitter structure is depicted in Fig. 10. The encoder employs a half-rate non-systematic, non-recursive convolutional (NSNRC) code using the generator polynomials $(7, 5)$ in octal notation. The uncoded information is organized in blocks of N_i bits, consisting of at least 3000 bits, depending on the specific QAM constellation used. Each data block $\mathbf{i}$ is encoded and results in the block $\mathbf{b}$ consisting of $N_b = 2\, N_i + 4$ encoded bits, including 2 termination bits. The encoded bits are interleaved using a random interleaver and stored in the vector $\tilde{\mathbf{b}}$. The encoded and interleaved bits are then mapped to the MIMO layers. The task of the multiplexer and buffer block of Fig. 10 is to divide the vector of encoded and interleaved information bits, i.e. $\tilde{\mathbf{b}}$, into subvectors according to the chosen transmission mode (Table 1). The individual binary data vectors are then mapped to the QAM symbols $c_{1\,k}$ and $c_{2\,k}$ according to the specific mapper used (Figs. 9 and 10).

The iterative demodulator structure is shown in Fig. 11 [5].

When using the iteration index ν, the first iteration of $\nu = 1$ commences with the soft-demapper delivering the N_b log-likelihood ratios (LLRs) $L_2^{(\nu=1)}(\tilde{\mathbf{b}})$ of the encoded and interleaved information bits, whose de-interleaved version $L_{a,1}^{(\nu=1)}(\mathbf{b})$ represents the input of the convolutional decoder as depicted in Fig. 11 [6,14]. This channel decoder provides the estimates $L_1^{(\nu=1)}(\mathbf{i})$ of the original uncoded information bits as well as the LLRs of the N_b NSNRC-encoded bits in the form of

$$L_1^{(\nu=1)}(\mathbf{b}) = L_{a,1}^{(\nu=1)}(\mathbf{b}) + L_{e,1}^{(\nu=1)}(\mathbf{b}) \ . \tag{9}$$

As seen in Fig. 11 and (9), the LLRs of the NSNRC-encoded bits consist of the receiver's input signal itself plus the extrinsic information $L_{e,1}^{(\nu=1)}(\mathbf{b})$, which is generated by subtracting $L_{a,1}^{(\nu=1)}(\mathbf{b})$ from $L_1^{(\nu=1)}(\mathbf{b})$. The appropriately ordered, i.e. interleaved extrinsic LLRs are fed back as *a priori* information $L_{a,2}^{(\nu=2)}(\tilde{\mathbf{b}})$ to the soft demapper of Fig. 11 for the second iteration.

Following the detailed structure of the soft-demapper in Fig. 12, the N_b LLRs $L_2^{(\nu)}(\tilde{\mathbf{b}})$ are composed of sub-blocks $(L_2^{(\nu)}(\tilde{\mathbf{b}}_1), L_2^{(\nu)}(\tilde{\mathbf{b}}_2))$. Each vector $L_2^{(\nu)}(\tilde{\mathbf{b}}_\ell)$ (with $\ell = 1, 2$) is generated by the soft demapper from the MIMO channels' output $y_{\ell,k}$ and the *a priori* information $L_{a,2}^{(\nu)}(\tilde{\mathbf{b}}_\ell)$ (with $\ell = 1, 2$) provided by the channel decoder. After the first iteration, this *a priori* information emerges from the N_b LLRs $L_{a,2}^{(\nu)}(\tilde{\mathbf{b}})$.

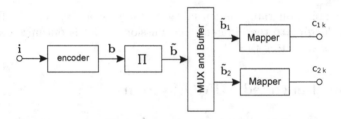

Fig. 10. The channel-encoded MIMO transmitter structure.

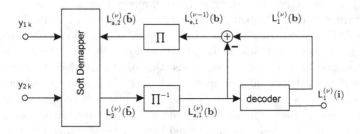

Fig. 11. Iterative demodulator structure.

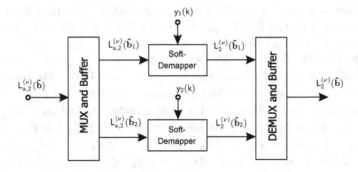

Fig. 12. Detailed soft demapper demodulator structure.

5   Results

The numerical analysis targets at BER results. For this purpose it is assumed, that each optical input within the multimode fiber is fed by a system with identical mean properties with respect to transmit filter and pulse frequency $f_{\mathrm{T}} = 1/T_{\mathrm{s}}$. For numerical assessment within this paper, the pulse frequency is chosen to be $f_{\mathrm{T}} = 5{,}12$ GHz, the average transmit power is supposed to be $P_{\mathrm{s}} = 1\,\mathrm{V}^2$ – this equals 1 W at a linear and constant resistance of $1\,\Omega$ – and as an external disturbance a white Gaussian noise with power spectral density N_0 is assumed [16]. In order to transmit at a fixed data rate while maintaining the best possible integrity, i.e., bit-error rate, an appropriate number of MIMO layers has to be used, which depends on the specific transmission mode, as detailed in Table 1.

5.1   Uncoded MIMO System

The optimization results, obtained by computer simulation at an overall data rate of 20,48 Gbps, are shown in Fig. 13 for different operating wavelength: The BER becomes minimal in case of an optimized bit loading (Fig. 13) with highest bit loading in the layer with largest singular values. The optimized MIMO transmission exhibits an improvement with respect to SISO transmission, but a non-optimized MIMO transmission leads to a significant degradation of the system performance. Furthermore, the simulation results show that in order to minimize the overall BER at a fixed data rate, not necessarily all MIMO layer should be activated. Instead, only the strongest MIMO layers should be used with appropriate modulation levels in the considered example.

Furthermore, as obtained by the channel measurements (Figs. 3 and 4), at a higher operating wavelength, i.e. 1570 nm, the separation of the different mode groups disappears based on the effect of the chromatic dispersion. Since the chromatic dispersion affects all mode groups almost equally, MIMO isn't able to generate an additional diversity gain (in comparison to wireless channels, where delay-spread isn't any longer a limiting parameter [2,3]). The advantage of a higher signal-to-noise-ratio due to lower attenuation in the third optical window is diminished by the chromatic dispersion. Therefore, the obtained bit-error rate results are higher at 1570 nm compared to 1325 nm. However, dispersion compensation schemes are well established in optical communications and they are not considered as a practical limitation.

However, uncoded systems have reached a state of maturity. By contrast coded MIMO configurations require substantial further research.

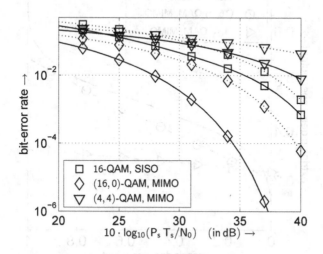

Fig. 13. BER performance at 1570 nm operating wavelength (dotted line) and at 1325 nm operating wavelength (solid line) when using the transmission modes introduced in Table 1 and transmitting 4 bit/s/Hz over frequency selective optical MIMO channels.

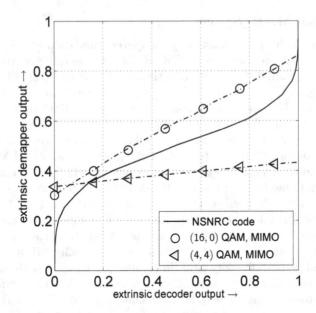

Fig. 14. EXIT chart for an effective user-data throughput of 2 bit/s/Hz and the different QAM constellations at $10\log_{10}(P_s\,T_s/N_0) = 18$ dB (1325 nm operating wavelength and anti-Gray mapping on all activated MIMO layers).

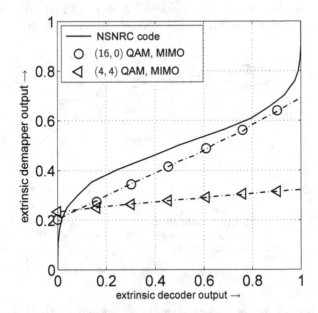

Fig. 15. EXIT chart for an effective user-data throughput of 2 bit/s/Hz and the different QAM constellations at $10\log_{10}(P_s\,T_s/N_0) = 18$ dB (1570 nm operating wavelength and anti-Gray mapping on all activated MIMO layers).

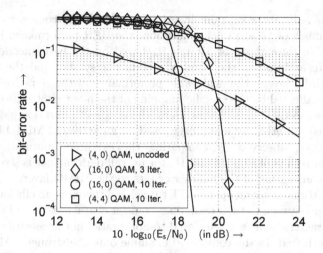

Fig. 16. BERs assuming anti-Gray mapping scheme on the activated MIMO layers for an effective user-data throughput of 2 bit/s/Hz (1325 nm operating wavelength).

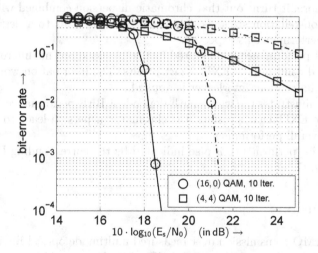

Fig. 17. BER comparison at 1325 nm operating wavelength (solid line) and at 1570 nm operating wavelength (dotted line) assuming anti-Gray mapping scheme on the activated MIMO layers for an effective user-data throughput of 2 bit/s/Hz.

5.2   Channel encoded MIMO System

The joint optimization of the number of activated MIMO layers as well as the number of bits per symbol was found to be effective at high SNRs. However, iterative receivers are able to work in a much lower SNR region. Therefore it would be interesting to see how the design criteria change when coding is added to the transmission system.

Using the half-rate, constraint-length $K_{cl} = 3$ NSNRC code with the generator polynomials of $(7,5)$ in octal notation, the BER performance is analyzed for an effective throughput of 2 bit/s/Hz based on the best uncoded schemes of Table 1. In addition to the number of bits per symbol and the number of activated MIMO layers, the achievable performance of the iterative decoder is substantially affected by the specific mapping of the bits to both the QAM symbols as well as to the MIMO layers. Here, the maximum iteration gain can only be guaranteed, if anti-Gray mapping is used on all activated MIMO layers [10].

Furthermore, observed by comparing the extrinsic information transfer (EXIT) chart results of Figs. 14 and 15, the overall performance is strongly influenced by the allocation of the number of bits to the MIMO layers.

In order to guarantee an open EXIT tunnel and therefore an efficient information exchange between the soft demapper transfer characteristic and the decoder transfer characteristic at a given signal-to-noise ratio, not necessarily all MIMO should be activated. In the considered example only the strongest MIMO layer should be used with appropriate modulation level. Activating all MIMO layers the information exchange between the soft demapper and the decoder stops relatively early, resulting in a reduced BER performance.

Furthermore, it turns out that chromatic dispersion combined with the specific QAM constellation sizes, as detailed in Table 1, leads to a degradation of the overall performance as expected.

The BER performance is presented in Fig. 16 based on the different schemes of Table 1 and confirms the EXIT chart results. The information word length is 3000 bits and a random interleaver is applied.

Figure 17 illustrates the wavelength-dependent BER performance. As already stated by the EXIT charts results, the chromatic dispersion leads to a degradation of the overall performance.

The inferior performance is also indicated by the corresponding BER curves shown in Fig. 17.

6   Conclusions

Coherent MIMO transmission over measured multimode optical fibers has been investigated targeting at minimized BER while keeping the transmission bitrate constant. The results show that MIMO transmission based on SVD is a promising approach, in particular when the bit loading is optimized. In that case significant BER improvements can be achieved compared to a conventional SISO system. The proposed MIMO-BICM scheme includes an adaptation of the transmit parameters. EXIT charts are used for analysing and optimizing the convergence behaviour of iterative demapping and decoding. Here, the choice of the number of bits per symbol and the number of MIMO layers combined with powerful error correcting codes substantially affects the performance of a MIMO system, suggesting that not all MIMO layers have to be activated in order to achieve the best BERs.

References

1. Ahrens, A., Benavente-Peces, C.: Modulation-mode and power assignment for broadband MIMO-BICM Schemes. In: Proceedings of the IEEE 20th Personal, Indoor and Mobile Radio Communications Symposium (PIMRC), Tokyo, Japan (2009a)

2. Ahrens, A., Benavente-Peces, C.: Modulation-mode and power assignment in broadband MIMO systems. Facta Univ. (Series Electronics and Energetics) **22**(3), 313–327 (2009b)

3. Ahrens, A., Benavente-Peces, C.: Modulation-mode assignment in iteratively detected and SVD-assisted broadband MIMO schemes. In: Obaidat, M.S., Filipe, J. (eds.) ICETE 2009. CCIS, vol. 130, pp. 307–319. Springer, Heidelberg (2011)

4. Ahrens, A., Lange, C.: Exploitation of far-end crosstalk in MIMO-OFDM twisted pair transmission systems. In: IASTED International Conference on Wireless Networks and Emerging Technologies (WNET), Banff, Alberta, Canada (2006)

5. Ahrens, A., Ng, S.X., Kühn, V., Hanzo, L.: Modulation-mode assignment for SVD-aided and BICM-assisted spatial division multiplexing. Phys. Commun. (PHYCOM) **1**(1), 60–66 (2008)

6. Bahl, L.R., Cocke, J., Jelinek, F., Raviv, J.: Optimal decoding of linear codes for minimizing symbol error rate. IEEE Trans. Inf. Theory **20**(3), 284–287 (1974)

7. Bülow, H., Al-Hashimi, H., Schmauss, B.: Stable coherent MIMO Transport over few mode fiber enabled by an adiabatic mode splitter. In: European Conference and Exhibition on Optical Communication (ECOC), Torino, Italy. page. P4.04 (2010)

8. Bülow, H., Al-Hashimi, H., Schmauss, B.: Coherent multimode-fiber MIMO transmission with spatial constellation modulation. In: European Conference and Exhibition on Optical Communication (ECOC), Geneva, Switzerland (2011)

9. Caire, G., Taricco, G., Biglieri, E.: Bit-interleaved coded modulation. IEEE Trans. Inf. Theory **44**(3), 927–946 (1998)

10. Chindapol, A., Ritcey, J.A.: Design, analysis, and performance evaluation for BICM-ID with square QAM constellations in Rayleigh fading channels. IEEE J. Sel. Areas Commun. **19**(5), 944–957 (2001)

11. Foschini, G.J.: Layered space-time architecture for wireless communication in a fading environment when using multiple antennas. Bell Labs Tech. J. **1**(2), 41–59 (1996)

12. Haykin, S.S.: Adaptive Filter Theory. Prentice Hall, New Jersey (2002)

13. Hsu, R.C.J., Tarighat, A., Shah, A., Sayed, A.H., Jalali, B.: Capacity enhancement in coherent optical MIMO (COMIMO) multimode fiber links. IEEE Commun. Lett. **10**(3), 195–197 (2006)

14. Kühn, V.: Wireless Communications over MIMO Channels - Applications to CDMA and Multiple Antenna Systems. Wiley, Chichester (2006)

15. Lenz, D., Rankov, B., Erni, D., Bächtold, W., Wittneben, A.: MIMO channel for modal multiplexing in highly overmoded optical waveguides. In: International Zurich Seminar on Communications (IZS), Zurich, Switzerland (2004)

16. Pankow, J., Aust, S., Lochmann, S., Ahrens, A.: Modulation-mode assignment in SVD-assisted optical MIMO multimode fiber links. In: 15th International Conference on Optical Network Design and Modeling (ONDM), Bologna, Italy (2011)

17. Raleigh, G.G., Cioffi, J.M.: Spatio-temporal coding for wireless communication. IEEE Trans. Commun. **46**(3), 357–366 (1998)

18. Shah, A., Hsu, R.C.J., Tarighat, A., Sayed, A.H., Jalali, B.: Coherent Optical MIMO (COMIMO). J. Lightwave Tech. **23**(8), 2410–2419 (2005)
19. Singer, A.C., Shanbhag, N.R., Bae, H.-M.: Electronic dispersion compensation - an overwiew of optical communications systems. IEEE Signal Process. Mag. **25**(6), 110–130 (2008)
20. Telatar, E.: Capacity of multi-antenna Gaussian channels. Eur. Trans. Telecommun. **10**(6), 585–595 (1999)
21. van Etten, W.: An optimum linear receiver for multiple channel digital transmission systems. IEEE Trans. Commun. **23**(8), 828–834 (1975)

Security and Cryptography

Use of SIMD Features to Speed up Eta Pairing

Anup Kumar Bhattacharya[1]([✉]), Sabyasachi Karati[1], Abhijit Das[1],
Dipanwita Roychowdhury[1], Bhargav Bellur[2], and Aravind Iyer[2]

[1] Department of Computer Science and Engineering,
Indian Institute of Technology Kharagpur, Kharagpur, India
{anup,skarati,abhij,drc}@cse.iitkgp.ernet.in
[2] General Motors Technical Centre India, India Science Lab, Bangalore, India
bhargav_bellur@yahoo.com, aravind.iyer@gm.com

Abstract. Eta pairing over supersingular elliptic curves is widely used
in designing many cryptographic protocols. Because of efficiency considerations, curves over finite fields of small characteristics are preferred. In
this paper, we report several of our implementations of eta pairing
over finite fields of characteristics two and three. We exploit SIMD
features available in Intel processors to speed up eta-pairing computations. We study two ways of vectorizing the computations: horizontal
(intra-pairing) and vertical (inter-pairing). We report our experimental
results using SSE2 and AVX2 features supported by the Haswell microar-
chitecture. Our implementations use two popular curves. Recently proposed discrete-logarithm algorithms make these curves less secure than
previously thought. We discuss the implications of these developments
in the context of our implementations.

Keywords: Supersingular elliptic curves · Eta pairing · Software
implementation · SIMD · SSE intrinsics · AVX intrinsics

1 Introduction

Pairing over algebraic curves are extensively used [11,12,23] in designing cryptographic protocols. There are two advantages of using pairing in these protocols.
Some new functions are realized using pairing [11,23]. Many other protocols [12]
achieve small signature sizes at the same security level.

Miller's algorithm [31] is an efficient way to compute pairing. Tate and Weil
are two main variants of pairing functions on elliptic curves, with Tate pairing computation being significantly faster than Weil pairing for small fields. In
the last few years, many variants of Tate pairing [8,20,28] are proposed to reduce
the computation complexity of Tate pairing substantially. Eta pairing [8] is one
such variant defined for supersingular curves. Some pairing-friendly families [15]
of curves are defined over prime fields and over fields of characteristics two and
three. Vercauteren [38] proposes the concept of optimal pairing which gives lower
bounds on the number of Miller iterations required to compute pairing.

© Springer-Verlag Berlin Heidelberg 2014
M.S. Obaidat and J. Filipe (Eds.): ICETE 2012, CCIS 455, pp. 137–154, 2014.
DOI: 10.1007/978-3-662-44791-8_9

There have been many attempts to compute pairing faster. Barreto et al. [9] propose many simplifications of Tate-pairing algorithms. Final exponentiation is one such time-consuming step in pairing computation. Scott et al. [35] propose elegant methods to reduce the complexity of final exponentiation. Ahmadi et al. [3] and Granger et al. [18] describe efficient implementations of arithmetic in fields of characteristic three for faster pairing computation. Multi-core implementations of Tate pairing are reported in [5,10]. Beuchat et al. [10] provide an estimate on the optimal number of cores needed to compute pairing in a multi-core environment. GPU-based implementations of eta pairing are reported in [13,25].

Many low-end processors are released with SIMD facilities which provide the scope of parallelization in resource-constrained applications. SIMD-based implementations of pairing are reported in [5,10,19]. All these data-parallel implementations vectorize individual pairing computations, and vary in their approaches to exploit different SIMD intrinsics in order to speed up the underlying field arithmetic. This technique is known as horizontal vectorization.

The other SIMD-based vectorization technique, vertical vectorization, has also been used for efficient implementation purposes. Montgomery [32] applies vertical vectorization to Elliptic Curve Method to factor integers. For RSA implementations using SSE2 intrinsics, Page and Smart [33] use two SIMD-based techniques called inter-operation and intra-operation parallelisms. Grabher et al. [17] propose digit slicing to reduce carry-handling overhead in the implementation of ate pairing over Barreto-Naerhig curves defined over prime fields. Implementation results with both inter-pairing and intra-pairing parallelism techniques are provided and a number of implementation strategies are discussed.

Intuitively, so long as different instances of some computation follow fairly the same sequence of basic CPU operations, parallelizing multiple instances (vertical vectorization) would be more effective than parallelizing each such instance individually (horizontal vectorization). Computation of eta pairing on curves over fields of small characteristics appears to be an good setting for vertical vectorization. This is particularly relevant because all the parties in a standard elliptic-curve-based protocol typically use the same curve and the same base point (unlike in RSA where different entities use different public moduli).

Each of the two vectorization models (horizontal and vertical) has its private domains of applicability. Even in the case of pairing computation, vertical vectorization does not outperform horizontal vectorization in every step. For example, comb-based multiplication [29] of field elements is expected to be more efficient under vertical vectorization than under horizontal vectorization. On the contrary, modular reduction using polynomial division seems to favor horizontal vectorization more than vertical vectorization, since the number of steps in the division loop and also the shift amounts depend heavily on the operands. This problem can be bypassed by using defining polynomials with a small number of non-zero coefficients (like trinomials or pentanomials). However, computing inverse by the extended polynomial gcd algorithm cannot be similarly tackled. Moreover, vertical vectorization is prone to encounter more cache misses compared to horizontal vectorization and even to non-SIMD implementation. The effects of cache misses are rather pronounced for algorithms based upon lookup tables (like comb methods).

Despite all these potential challenges, vertical vectorization may be helpful in certain cryptographic operations. Our experimentation with SSE2 and AVX2 intrinsics reveals that this is the case for eta pairing on supersingular curves over fields of characteristics two and three. More precisely, horizontal vectorization leads to speedup of up to 30 % over non-SIMD implementation. Vertical vectorization, on the other hand, yields speedup in the range 25–55 %. In short, the validation of the effectiveness of vertical vectorization in pairing computations is the main technical contribution of this paper.

We take two popular supersingular elliptic curves defined over the fields $\mathbb{F}_{2^{1223}}$ and $\mathbb{F}_{3^{509}}$. At the time we started this work, eta pairing over these curves were believed to offer 128-bit security. Recently proposed finite-field discrete-logarithm algorithms [6,24] indicate that their security guarantees are much less. For example, Adj et al. [2] estimate that the curve over $\mathbb{F}_{3^{509}}$ offers slightly more than 80-bit security. As a result, we have to use curves over much larger fields in order to restore the security level to 128 bits. In another paper, Adj et al. [1] demonstrate that a curve defined over $\mathbb{F}_{2^{3041}}$ provides 129-bit security. All our SIMD-based techniques can be ported *mutatis mutandis* to curves defined over fields larger than what we study in this paper. However, larger fields imply slower implementations of eta pairing, and that in turn highlights the necessity of achieving better speedup figures. We expect that our SIMD-based implementations of eta pairing appropriately address this necessity.

The rest of the paper is organized as follows. Section 2 reviews the notion of pairing, and lists the algorithms used to implement field and curve arithmetic. Section 3 describes horizontal and vertical vectorization models. We intuitively explain which of the basic operations are likely to benefit more from vertical vectorization than from horizontal vectorization. We give special attention to field multiplication. Our experimental results are tabulated in Sect. 4. We conclude the paper in Sect. 5 after highlighting some potential areas of future research.

2 Background on Eta Pairing

In this section, we briefly describe standard algorithms that we have used for implementing arithmetic in extension fields of characteristics two and three. We subsequently state Miller's algorithm for the computation of eta pairing on supersingular curves over these fields.

2.1 Eta Pairing in a Field of Characteristic Two

We implemented eta pairing over the supersingular elliptic curve $y^2 + y = x^3 + x$ defined over the binary field $\mathbb{F}_{2^{1223}}$ represented as an extension of $\mathbb{F}_2$ by the irreducible polynomial $x^{1223} + x^{255} + 1$. An element of $\mathbb{F}_{2^{1223}}$ is packed into an array of 64-bit words. The basic operations on such elements are done as follows.

- Addition: We perform word-level XOR to add multiple coefficients together.
- Multiplication: Computing products $c = ab$ in the field is costly, but needed most often in Miller's algorithm. Comb-based multiplication [29] with four-bit windows is used in our implementations.
- Inverse: We use the extended Euclidean gcd algorithm for polynomials to compute the inverse of an element in the binary field.
- Square: We use a precomputed table of square values for all possible 8-bit inputs.
- Square Root: The input element is written as $a(x^2) + xb(x^2)$. Its square root is computed as $a(x) + x^{1/2}b(x)$, where $x^{1/2} = x^{612} + x^{128}$.
- Reduction: Since the irreducible polynomial defining $\mathbb{F}_{2^{1223}}$ has only a few non-zero coefficients, we use a fast reduction algorithm (as in [34]) for computing remainders modulo this polynomial.

The embedding degree for the supersingular curve stated above is four. So we need to work in the field $\mathbb{F}_{(2^{1223})^4}$. This field is represented as a tower of two quadratic extensions over $\mathbb{F}_{2^{1223}}$. The basis for this extension is given by $(1, u, v, uv)$, where $g(u) = u^2 + u + 1$ is the irreducible polynomial for the first extension, and $h(v) = v^2 + v + u$ defines the second extension. The distortion map is given by $\psi(x, y) = (x + u^2, y + xu + v)$.

Addition in $\mathbb{F}_{(2^{1223})^4}$ uses the standard word-wise XOR operation on elements of $\mathbb{F}_{2^{1223}}$. Multiplication in $\mathbb{F}_{(2^{1223})^4}$ can be computed by six multiplications in the field $\mathbb{F}_{2^{1223}}$ [19].

Algorithm 1 describes the computation of eta pairing η_T. This is an implementation [19] of Miller's algorithm for the supersingular curve $E_2 : y^2 + y = x^3 + x$ under the above representation of $\mathbb{F}_{2^{1223}}$ and $\mathbb{F}_{(2^{1223})^4}$. Here, the point $P \in E_2(\mathbb{F}_{2^{1223}})$ on the curve has prime order r. Q too is a point with both coordinates from $\mathbb{F}_{2^{1223}}$. The distortion map is applied to Q. Algorithm 1 does not explicitly show this map. The output of the algorithm is an element of μ_r, the order-r subgroup of $\mathbb{F}^*_{(2^{1223})^4}$.

Algorithm 1. Eta Pairing Algorithm for a Field of Characteristic Two.

Input: $P = (x_1, y_1), Q = (x_2, y_2) \in E(\mathbb{F}_{2^{1223}})[r]$
Output: $\eta_T(P, Q) \in \mu_r$

$T \leftarrow x_1 + 1$
$f \leftarrow T \cdot (x_1 + x_2 + 1) + y_1 + y_2 + (T + x_2)u + v$

for $i = 1$ **to** 612 **do**
   $T \leftarrow x_1$
   $x_1 \leftarrow \sqrt{x_1}, y_1 \leftarrow \sqrt{y_1}$
   $g \leftarrow T \cdot (x_1 + x_2) + y_1 + y_2 + x_1 + 1 + (T + x_2)u + v$
   $f \leftarrow f \cdot g$
   $x_2 \leftarrow x_2^2, y_2 \leftarrow y_2^2$
end for

return $f^{(q^2 - 1)(q - \sqrt{2q} + 1)}$, where $q = 2^{1223}$.

The complexity of Algorithm 1 is dominated by the 612 iterations (called Miller iterations), and exponentiation to the power $(q^2 - 1)(q - \sqrt{2q} + 1)$ (referred to as the final exponentiation). In each Miller iteration, two square roots, two squares, and seven multiplications are performed in the field $\mathbb{F}_{2^{1223}}$. In the entire Miller loop, 1224 square roots and 1224 squares are computed, and the number of multiplications is 4284. Evidently, the computation of the large number of multiplications occupies the major portion of the total computation time. Each multiplication of $\mathbb{F}_{(2^{1223})^4}$ (computation of $f \cdot g$) is carried out by six multiplications in $\mathbb{F}_{2^{1223}}$. In these six multiplications, three variables appear as one of the two operands. Therefore only three precomputations (instead of six) are sufficient for performing all these six multiplications by the Lopez-Dahab method. For characteristic-three fields, such a trick is proposed in [37]. Using Frobenius endomorphism [19,35], the final exponentiation is computed, so this operation takes only a small fraction of the total computation time.

2.2 Eta Pairing in a Field of Characteristic Three

The irreducible polynomial $x^{509} - x^{318} - x^{192} + x^{127} + 1$ defines the extension field $\mathbb{F}_{3^{509}}$. The curve $y^2 = x^3 - x + 1$ defined over this field is used. Each element of the extension field is represented using two bit vectors [36]. The basic operations on these elements are implemented as follows.

- Addition and subtraction: We use the formulas given in [26].
- Multiplication: Comb-based multiplication [3] with two-bit windows is used in our implementations.
- Inverse: We use the extended Euclidean gcd algorithm for polynomials to compute the inverse of an element in the field.
- Cube: We use a precomputed table of cube values for all possible 8-bit inputs.
- Cube Root: The input element is first written as $a(x^3) + xb(x^3) + x^2c(x^3)$. Its cube root is computed as $a(x) + x^{1/3}b(x) + x^{2/3}c(x)$, where $x^{1/3} = x^{467} + x^{361} - x^{276} + x^{255} + x^{170} + x^{85}$, and $x^{2/3} = -x^{234} + x^{128} - x^{43}$ [3,7]. We have not used the cube-root-friendly representation of $\mathbb{F}_{3^{509}}$ prescribed in [4].
- Reduction: We use a fast reduction algorithm [34] for computing remainders modulo the irreducible polynomial.

The embedding degree in this case is six, so we need to work in the field $\mathbb{F}_{(3^{509})^6}$. A tower of extensions over $\mathbb{F}_{3^{509}}$ is again used to represent $\mathbb{F}_{(3^{509})^6}$. The first extension is cubic, and is defined by the irreducible polynomial $u^3 - u - 1$. The second extension is quadratic, and is defined by $v^2 + 1$. The basis of $\mathbb{F}_{(3^{509})^6}$ over $\mathbb{F}_{3^{509}}$ is therefore $(1, u, u^2, v, uv, u^2v)$. The distortion map in this case is $\psi(x, y) = (u - x, yv)$.

For multiplying two elements of $\mathbb{F}_{(3^{509})^6}$, we have used 18 multiplications in $\mathbb{F}_{3^{509}}$ [27]. The method reported in [16], which uses only 15 such multiplications, is not implemented.

Algorithm 2 describes the computation of eta pairing [10] in the case of characteristic three. P and Q are points with both coordinates from $\mathbb{F}_{3^{509}}$.

The distortion map is applied to Q. Algorithm 2 does not show this map explicitly. The order of P is a prime r, and μ_r is the order-r subgroup of $\mathbb{F}^*_{(3^{509})^6}$.

The first **for** loop of Algorithm 2 is a precomputation loop. The second **for** loop implements the Miller iterations. The final exponentiation in the last line uses Frobenius endomorphism [19,35]. The most time-consuming operations involved in Algorithm 2 are 508 cubes, 508 cube roots and 3556 multiplications in the field $\mathbb{F}_{3^{509}}$ (given that one multiplication of $\mathbb{F}_{(3^{509})^6}$ is implemented by 18 multiplications in $\mathbb{F}_{3^{509}}$). The final exponentiation again does not incur a major computation overhead in Algorithm 2.

Algorithm 2. Eta Pairing Algorithm for a Field of Characteristic Three.

Input: $P = (x_P, y_P), Q = (x_Q, y_Q) \in E(\mathbb{F}_{3^{509}})[r]$
Output: $\eta_T(P, Q) \in \mu_r$

$x_P \leftarrow \sqrt[3]{x_P} + 1$
$y_P \leftarrow -\sqrt[3]{y_P}$
$t \leftarrow x_P + x_Q$
$R \leftarrow -(y_P t - y_Q v - y_P u)(-t^2 + y_P y_Q v - tu - u^2)$
$X_P[0] \leftarrow x_P, Y_P[0] \leftarrow y_P$
$X_Q[0] \leftarrow x_Q, Y_Q[0] \leftarrow y_Q$

for $i = 1$ **to** 254 **do**
  $X_P[i] \leftarrow \sqrt[3]{X_P[i-1]}$
  $X_Q[i] \leftarrow X_Q^3[i-1]$
  $Y_P[i] \leftarrow \sqrt[3]{Y_P[i-1]}$
  $Y_Q[i] \leftarrow Y_Q^3[i-1]$
end for

for $i = 1$ **to** 127 **do**
  $t \leftarrow X_P[2i-1] + X_Q[2i-1]$
  $w \leftarrow Y_P[2i-1]Y_Q[2i-1]$
  $t' \leftarrow X_P[2i] + X_Q[2i]$
  $w' \leftarrow Y_P[2i]Y_Q[2i]$
  $S \leftarrow (-t^2 + wv - tu - u^2)(-t'^2 + w'v - t'u - u^2)$
  $R \leftarrow R \cdot S$
end for

return $f^{(q^3-1)(q+1)(q+\sqrt{3q}+1)}$, where $q = 3^{509}$.

---

3 Horizontal and Vertical Vectorization

Many modern CPUs, even in desktop machines, support a set of data-parallel instructions operating on SIMD registers. For example, Intel has been releasing SIMD-enabled CPUs since 1999 [21,30]. As of now, most vendors provide support for 128-bit SIMD registers and parallel operations on 8-, 16-, 32- and 64-bit data. Recently, CPUs with 256-bit SIMD registers are also available. We work with

Intel's SSE2 (128-bit) and AVX2 (256-bit) registers. Since we use 64-bit words for packing of data, using these SIMD intrinsics can lead to speedup of nearly two or four. In practice, we expect less speedup for various reasons. First, all steps in a computation do not possess inherent data parallelism. Second, the input and output values are usually available in chunks of machine words which are 32 or 64 bits in size. Before the use of an SIMD instruction, one needs to pack data stored in normal registers or memory locations to SIMD registers. Likewise, after using an SIMD instruction, one needs to unpack the content of an SIMD register back to normal registers or memory locations. Frequent conversion of data between scalar and vector forms may be costly. Finally, if the algorithm is memory-intensive, SIMD features do not help much.

We use SIMD-based vectorization techniques for the computation of eta pairing. These vectorization techniques provide speedup by reducing the overheads due to packing and unpacking. We study two common SIMD-based vectorization techniques called horizontal and vertical vectorization. Though vertical vectorization is capable of reducing data-conversion overheads substantially, it encounters an increased memory overhead in terms of cache misses. Experimental results of eta pairing computation over fields of characteristics two and three validate the claim that vertical vectorization achieves better performance gains compared to horizontal vectorization.

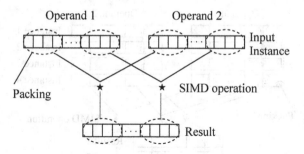

Fig. 1. Horizontal vectorization.

3.1   Horizontal Vectorization

Figure 1 explains the working of horizontal vectorization using AVX2 (256-bit) registers. One single operation ⋆ between two multi-word operands is to be performed. Four 64-bit machine words of individual operands are first packed into SIMD registers, and one SIMD instruction for ⋆ is used to compute the output in a single SIMD register. The result stored in the output SIMD registers can further be used in remaining computations.

As an example, consider operands a and b each stored in an array of twenty 64-bit words. Suppose that we need to compute the bit-wise XOR of a and b, and store the result in c. A usual 64-bit implementation calls for twenty invocations of the CPU instruction for XOR. AVX2-based XOR handles 256 bits of the operands in one CPU instruction, and finishes after only five invocations of this instruction. The output array c of SIMD registers is available in the packed format required in future data-parallel operations in which c is an input.

There are, however, situations where horizontal vectorization requires unpacking of data after a CPU instruction. Consider the unary left-shift operation on an array a of twenty 64-bit words. Let us index the words of a as $a_1, a_2, \ldots, a_{20}$. The words $a_{4i-3}, a_{4i-2}, a_{4i-1}, a_{4i}$ are packed into an SIMD register R_i. Currently, SIMD intrinsics do not provide facilities for shifting R_i as a 256-bit value by any amount (except in multiples of eight). What we instead obtain in the output SIMD register is a 256-bit value in which all the 64-bit components are individually left-shifted. The void created in the shifted version of a_{4i-k} needs to be filled by the most significant bits of the pre-shift value of a_{4i-k+1}. More frustratingly, the void created in a_{4i} by the shift needs to be filled by the most significant bits of the pre-shift value of a_{4i+1} which is a 64-bit member of a separate SIMD register R_{i+1}. The other 64-bit members in R_{i+1} must not interfere with the shifted value of R_i. Masking out these members from R_{i+1} eats up a clock cycle. To sum up, horizontal vectorization may result in frequent scalar-to-vector and vector-to-scalar conversions, and suffer from packing and unpacking overheads.

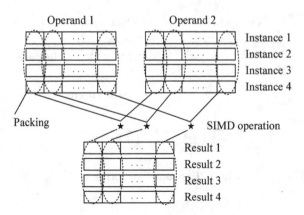

Fig. 2. Vertical vectorization.

3.2   Vertical Vectorization

Vertical vectorization using AVX2 (256-bit) registers and 64-bit words works as shown in Fig. 2. Four instances of the same operation are carried out on two different sets of data. Data of matching operands from the four instances are packed into SIMD registers, and the same sequence of operations is performed on these registers using SIMD intrinsics. Each one-fourth of an SIMD register pertains to one of the instances. After an SIMD instruction, each one-fourth of the output SIMD register contains the result for one of the four instances. Thus, data from four separate instances are maintained in 64-bit formats in these SIMD registers throughout a sequence of operations. When the sequence is completed, data from the final output SIMD registers are unpacked into the respective 64-bit storage outputs for the four instances.

The advantage of this vectorization technique is that it adapts naturally to any situation where two identical sequences of operations are performed on four separate sets of data. The algorithm does not need to possess inherent data parallelism. However, the sequence of operations must be identical (or nearly identical) on four different sets of data. Finally, a computation using vertical vectorization does not require data conversion after every SIMD operation in the CPU, that is, potentially excessive packing and unpacking overheads associated with horizontal vectorization are significantly eliminated.

Let us now explain how vertical vectorization gets rid of the unpacking requirement after a left-shift operation. Suppose that four operands a, b, c, d need to be left-shifted individually by the *same* number of bits. The i-th words a_i, b_i, c_i, d_i are packed in an SIMD register R_i. First, a suitably right-shifted version of R_{i+1} is stored in another SIMD register S_{i+1}. After that, R_i is left-shifted by a single SIMD instruction causing all of a_i, b_i, c_i, d_i to be left-shifted individually. This shifted SIMD register is then XOR-ed with the SIMD register S_{i+1}. The individual 64-bit words $a_{i+1}, b_{i+1}, c_{i+1}, d_{i+1}$ are not needed in the unpacked form.

3.3   Vectorization of Eta Pairing

Eta pairing on supersingular curves defined over fields of characteristics two and three can be computed using bit-wise operations only (that is, no arithmetic operations are needed). More precisely, only the XOR, OR, AND, and the left- and right-shift operations on 64-bit words are required. As explained earlier, both horizontal and vertical vectorizations behave gracefully for the XOR, OR and AND operations. On the contrary, shift operations are efficient with vertical vectorization only. Therefore the presence and importance of shift operations largely determine the relative performance of the two vectorization methods. We now study each individual field operation (in $\mathbb{F}_{2^{1223}}$ or $\mathbb{F}_{3^{509}}$) in this respect.

- Addition/Subtraction: Only XOR, OR and AND operations are needed to carry out addition and subtraction of two elements in both types of fields. So both the vectorization models are suitable for these operations.
- Multiplication (without reduction): We use comb-based multiplication algorithms in which both left- and right-shift operations play a crucial role. Consequently, multiplication should be faster for vertical vectorization than horizontal vectorization.
- Square/Cube (without reduction): Since we have used precomputations in eight-bit chunks, byte-level shifts suffice, that is, both models of vectorization are efficient for these operations.

- Modular reduction: Reduction using the chosen irreducible polynomials call for bit-level shift operations, so vertical vectorization is favored.
- Square-root/Cube-root with modular reduction: Extraction of the polynomials a, b (and c for characteristic three), and multiplication by $x^{1/2}$ (or $x^{1/3}$ and $x^{2/3}$) involve several shift operations. So vertical vectorization seems to be the better choice.
- Inverse: The extended Euclidean algorithm is problematic for both horizontal and vertical vectorization models. On the one hand, bit-level shifts impair the performance of horizontal vectorization. On the other hand, the sequence for a gcd calculation depends heavily on the operands, rendering vertical vectorization infeasible to implement. We therefore use only non-SIMD implementations for the inverse operation.

Multiplication (with modular reduction) happens to be the most frequent operation in Algorithms 1 and 2. Vertical vectorization is therefore expected to outperform horizontal vectorization for these algorithms. We present our horizontal and vertical multiplication algorithms as Algorithms 3 and 4. These pertain to the curve over $\mathbb{F}_{2^{1223}}$. Multiplication in $\mathbb{F}_{3^{509}}$ can be similarly handled.

Algorithms 3 and 4 implement comb-based multiplication [29] with four-bit windows. We take 64-bit words and 256-bit SIMD registers (AVX2). We pack four words in an SIMD register. In the algorithms, word variables are denoted by lower-case letters, and SIMD registers by upper-case letters. We use the subscripts 64 and 256 to differentiate between word-level and SIMD-level operations. For example, $a[i][j] \ll_{64} 41$ indicates 41-bit left-shift of the word $a[i][j]$. Likewise, $T_1 \oplus_{256} T_2$ stands for an AVX2 XOR operation. Switching between word-based and SIMD representations is denoted by pack and unpack. Comb-based multiplication has three stages: precomputation, intermediate product computation, and reduction. The reduction stage is shown separately as Algorithm 5.

An element of $\mathbb{F}_{2^{1223}}$ is stored in twenty 64-bit words. The inputs of horizontal vectorization are two arrays A, B of five 256-bit values. The intermediate product is output as an array c of forty 64-bit words (actually, 39 words suffice). Precomputations are done on the second input B. A 16×20 table t is prepared in this stage. During intermediate product computation, we use 256-bit XOR, but both the operands of this operation are packed and the result is unpacked, inside the loop. Finally, the shift-intensive reduction of c (see Algorithm 5) would proceed at the 64-bit word level. As a consequence, horizontal vectorization is expected to show poor performance.

In vertical vectorization, four pairs of inputs are packed in two arrays, each consisting of 20 SIMD registers. The intermediate products are output as an array of 40 SIMD registers. Since four pairing computations now proceed in parallel, the precomputed table t is now a 64×20 array of 64-bit words. During intermediate product computation, entries from t are packed in an SIMD register P and XOR-ed with an appropriate register in the output array C. This entry in C does not need to be packed inside the loop. Likewise, after the XOR operation, there is no need to unpack the entry in C inside the loop. We can pass the packed intermediate product C straightaway to the reduction function which can now

---

Algorithm 3. Horizontal Vectorization of Multiplication in $\mathbb{F}_{2^{1223}}$.

Input: $A[0, \ldots, 4], B[0, \ldots, 4]$.
Output: $c[0, \ldots, 39]$.

Initialize all the words of c to 0, $U \leftarrow \text{pack}(0xF, 0xF, 0xF, 0xF)$, and $v[0] \leftarrow 0$.
for $i = 0$ **to** 4 /* Precomputation loop */ **do**
$\quad j \leftarrow i \ll_{64} 2, \ k \leftarrow j + 1, \ T \leftarrow B[i], \ u \leftarrow \text{unpack}(T)$.
$\quad v[1] \leftarrow u[1] \gg_{64} 61, v[2] \leftarrow u[2] \gg_{64} 61, v[3] \leftarrow u[3] \gg_{64} 61$.
$\quad V \leftarrow \text{pack}(v[0,1,2,3]), \ t[0][j, j+1, j+2, j+3] \leftarrow (0,0,0,0)$
$\quad T_1 \leftarrow T, \ t[1][j, j+1, j+2, j+3] \leftarrow \text{unpack}(T_1)$.
$\quad T_2 \leftarrow (T \ll_{256} 1) \oplus_{256} (V \gg_{256} 2), \ t[2][j, j+1, j+2, j+3] \leftarrow \text{unpack}(T_2)$.
$\quad T_3 \leftarrow T \oplus_{256} T_2, \ t[3][j, j+1, j+2, j+3] \leftarrow \text{unpack}(T_3)$.
$\quad T_5 \leftarrow (T \ll_{256} 2) \oplus_{256} (V \gg_{256} 1)$.
$\quad$ **for** $k = 1$ **to** 3 **do**
$\quad\quad$ **if** $(k = 1)$ **then** $T_4 \leftarrow T_5$,
$\quad\quad$ **else if** $(k = 2)$ **then** $T_4 \leftarrow (T \ll_{256} 3) \oplus_{256} V$, **else** $T_4 \leftarrow T_4 \oplus_{256} T_5$.
$\quad\quad t[4k][j, j+1, j+2, j+3] \leftarrow \text{unpack}(T_4)$.
$\quad\quad t[4k+1][j, j+1, j+2, j+3] \leftarrow \text{unpack}(T_4 \oplus_{256} T_1)$.
$\quad\quad t[4k+2][j, j+1, j+2, j+3] \leftarrow \text{unpack}(T_4 \oplus_{256} T_2)$.
$\quad\quad t[4k+3][j, j+1, j+2, j+3] \leftarrow \text{unpack}(T_4 \oplus_{256} T_3)$.
$\quad$ **end for**
$\quad v[0] \leftarrow t[0][0] \gg_{64} 61$.
end for
$j \leftarrow 15$.
while $(j \geq 0)$ /* Intermediate product computation loop */ **do**
$\quad l \leftarrow j \ll_{64} 2$.
$\quad$ **for** $i = 0$ **to** 4 **do**
$\quad\quad T \leftarrow (A[i] \gg_{256} l) \text{ AND}_{256} U$.
$\quad\quad$ **for** $k = 0, 4, 8, 12, 16$ **do**
$\quad\quad\quad T_1 \leftarrow \text{pack}(c[4i+k, 4i+k+1, 4i+k+2, 4i+k+3])$.
$\quad\quad\quad T_2 \leftarrow \text{pack}(t[u[0]][k], t[u[0]][k+1], t[u[0]][k+2], t[u[0]][k+3])$.
$\quad\quad\quad T_3 \leftarrow T_1 \oplus_{256} T_2$.
$\quad\quad\quad c[4i+k, 4i+k+1, 4i+k+2, 4i+k+3]) \leftarrow \text{unpack}(T_3)$.
$\quad\quad$ **end for**
$\quad\quad$ **for** $l = 1$ **to** 3 **do**
$\quad\quad\quad$ **for** $k = 0$ **to** 19 **do**
$\quad\quad\quad\quad c[4i+k+l] \leftarrow c[4i+k+l] \oplus_{64} t[u[l]][k]$.
$\quad\quad\quad$ **end for**
$\quad\quad$ **end for**
$\quad$ **end for**
$\quad$ **if** $(j = 0)$ **then** break.
$\quad v_1 \leftarrow 0$.
$\quad$ **for** $i = 0$ **to** 39 **do**
$\quad\quad t_1 \leftarrow c[i], \ v_0 \leftarrow t_1 \gg_{64} 60, \ c[i] \leftarrow (t_1 \ll_{64} 4) \oplus_{64} v_1, \ v_1 \leftarrow v_0$.
$\quad$ **end for**
$\quad j \leftarrow j - 1$.
end while

Algorithm 4. Vertical Vectorization of Multiplication in $\mathbb{F}_{2^{1223}}$.

Input: $A[0, \ldots, 19], B[0, \ldots, 19]$
Output: $C[0, \ldots, 39]$

$L_1 \leftarrow \text{pack}(0x1, 0x1, 0x1, 0x1), \; L_2 \leftarrow \text{pack}(0x3, 0x3, 0x3, 0x3),$
$L_3 \leftarrow \text{pack}(0x7, 0x7, 0x7, 0x7). \; V_0 \leftarrow \text{pack}(0, 0, 0, 0).$
$T_{63} \leftarrow \text{pack}(0xF^{15}E, 0xF^{15}E, 0xF^{15}E, 0xF^{15}E),$
$T_{62} \leftarrow \text{pack}(0xF^{15}C, 0xF^{15}C, 0xF^{15}C, 0xF^{15}C),$
$T_{61} \leftarrow \text{pack}(0xF^{15}8, 0xF^{15}8, 0xF^{15}8, 0xF^{15}8).$
for $i = 0$ **to** 19 /* Precomputation loop */ **do**
    $T_1 \leftarrow ((V_0 \gg_{256} 2) \; \text{AND}_{256} \; L_1) \; \text{OR}_{256} \; ((B[i] \ll_{256} 1) \; \text{AND}_{256} \; T_{63}),$
    $T_2 \leftarrow ((V_0 \gg_{256} 1) \; \text{AND}_{256} \; L_2) \; \text{OR}_{256} \; ((B[i] \ll_{256} 2) \; \text{AND}_{256} \; T_{62}),$
    $T_3 \leftarrow (V_0) \; \text{OR}_{256} \; ((B[i] \ll_{256} 3) \; \text{AND}_{256} \; T_{61}).$
    $S_1 \leftarrow B[i] \oplus_{256} T_1, \; S_2 \leftarrow T_2 \oplus_{256} T_3.$
    $t_0[0, 1, 2, 3] \leftarrow \text{unpack}(B[i]), \; t_1[0, 1, 2, 3] \leftarrow \text{unpack}(T_1),$
    $t_2[0, 1, 2, 3] \leftarrow \text{unpack}(T_2), \; t_3[0, 1, 2, 3] \leftarrow \text{unpack}(T_3).$
    $s_1[0, 1, 2, 3] \leftarrow \text{unpack}(S_1), \; s_2[0, 1, 2, 3] \leftarrow \text{unpack}(S_2).$
    for $j = 0$ **to** 3 **do**
        $t[16j][i] \leftarrow 0, \; t[16j + 1][i] \leftarrow t_0[j], \; t[16j + 2][i] \leftarrow t_1[j], \; t[16j + 3][i] \leftarrow s_1[j],$
        $t[16j + 4][i] \leftarrow t_2[j], \; t[16j + 5][i] \leftarrow t_2[j] \oplus_{64} t_0[j], \; t[16j + 6][i] \leftarrow t_2[j] \oplus_{64} t_1[j],$
        $t[16j + 7][i] \leftarrow t_2[j] \oplus_{64} s_1[j], \; t[16j + 8][i] \leftarrow t_3[j], \; t[16j + 9][i] \leftarrow t_3[j] \oplus_{64} t_0[j],$
        $t[16j + 10][i] \leftarrow t_3[j] \oplus_{64} t_1[j], \; t[16j + 11][i] \leftarrow t_3[j] \oplus_{64} s_1[j],$
        $t[16j + 12][i] \leftarrow s_2[j], \; t[16j + 13][i] \leftarrow s_2[j] \oplus_{64} t_0[j],$
        $t[16j + 14][i] \leftarrow s_2[j] \oplus_{64} t_1[j], \; t[16j + 15][i] \leftarrow s_2[j] \oplus_{64} s_1[j].$
    end for
end for
Initialize C to zero, $U \leftarrow \text{pack}(0xF, 0xF, 0xF, 0xF)$, and $j \leftarrow 15$.
while $(j \geq 0)$ /* Intermediate product computation loop */ **do**
    $l \leftarrow j \ll_{64} 2$
    for $i = 0$ **to** 19 **do**
        $U \leftarrow (A[i] \gg_{256} l) \; \text{AND}_{256} \; U, \; (u_1, u_2, u_3, u_4) \leftarrow \text{unpack}(U), \; ival \leftarrow i, \; k \leftarrow 0.$
        while $k < 20$ **do**
            $P \leftarrow \text{pack}(t[u_4][k], t[u_3][k], t[u_2][k], t[u_1][k]),$
            $C[ival] \leftarrow C[ival] \oplus_{256} P.$
            $P \leftarrow \text{pack}(t[u_4][k + 1], t[u_3][k + 1], t[u_2][k + 1], t[u_1][k + 1]),$
            $C[ival + 1] \leftarrow C[ival + 1] \oplus_{256} P.$
            $P \leftarrow \text{pack}(t[u_4][k + 2], t[u_3][k + 2], t[u_2][k + 2], t[u_1][k + 2]),$
            $C[ival + 2] \leftarrow C[ival + 2] \oplus_{256} P.$
            $P \leftarrow \text{pack}(t[u_4][k + 3], t[u_3][k + 3], t[u_2][k + 3], t[u_1][k + 3]),$
            $C[ival + 3] \leftarrow C[ival + 3] \oplus_{256} P.$
            $k \leftarrow k + 4, \; ival \leftarrow ival + 4.$
        end while
    end for
    if $(j = 0)$ break.
    Initialize V_0 to zero.
    for $i = 0$ **to** 39 **do**
        $V_1 \leftarrow C[i] \gg_{256} 60, \; C[i] \leftarrow V_0 \oplus_{256} (C[i] \ll_{256} 4), \; V_0 \leftarrow V_1.$
    end for
    $j \leftarrow j - 1.$
end while

Algorithm 5. Reduction of the Intermediate Product.

Input: The intermediate product $\gamma[0 \ldots 38]$
Output: The reduced product stored in $\gamma[0 \ldots 19]$

for $i = 38$ **down to** 20 **do**
   $\alpha \leftarrow \gamma[i]$, $\gamma[i-20] \leftarrow \gamma[i-20] \oplus (\alpha \ll 57)$, $\gamma[i-19] \leftarrow \gamma[i-19] \oplus (\alpha \gg 7)$,
   $\gamma[i-16] \leftarrow \gamma[i-16] \oplus (\alpha \ll 56)$, $\gamma[i-15] \leftarrow \gamma[i-15] \oplus (\alpha \gg 8)$.
end for
$\alpha \leftarrow \gamma[19] \gg 7$, $\gamma[0] \leftarrow \gamma[0] \oplus \alpha$, $\gamma[3] \leftarrow \gamma[3] \oplus (\alpha \ll 63)$,
$\gamma[4] \leftarrow \gamma[4] \oplus (\alpha \gg 1)$, $\gamma[19] \leftarrow \gamma[19]$ AND δ.

operate on SIMD registers. This is how vertical vectorization shows the promise of improved performance. It would be nice if we could additionally avoid the packing of entries of t in P. But since the indices in t of the words to be packed depend very much on the four inputs in A, this overhead seems unavoidable.

Algorithm 5 shows the reduction of the intermediate product for both models of vectorization. In horizontal vectorization, γ is the array c of 64-bit words, α a 64-bit variable, $\delta = 0x7F$, and all operations are on 64-bit words. In vertical vectorization, γ is the array C of 256-bit SIMD registers, α a 256-bit variable, $\delta = \text{pack}(0x7F, 0x7F, 0x7F, 0x7F)$, and all operations are on SIMD registers.

4   Experimental Results

We have carried out our experiments on an Intel Corei7-4770S platform (CPU clock 3.10 GHz) running the 64-bit Ubuntu operating system version 13.10. The programs are compiled by version 4.8.1 of the gcc compiler with the -O3 optimization flag. In some of our experiments, the widely available SSE2 (Streaming SIMD Extension) intrinsics are used [21,30]. SSE2 uses 128-bit SIMD registers, so we can pack two 64-bit words in a single SIMD register. The Sandy Bridge architecture released by Intel in 2011 introduces 256-bit SIMD registers AVX (Advanced Vector Extension). AVX supports 256-bit floating-point vector operations only. The Haswell architecture released in 2013 introduces another extension AVX2 which supports 256-bit integer vector operations. Our machine supports all these SIMD features. In addition to SSE2, we have also worked with AVX2 intrinsics [21]. With AVX2, we can pack four 64-bit words in a register and hope to exploit data parallelism more than what can be achieved with SSE2.

The timing results are reported in clock cycles. For non-SIMD and horizontal-SIMD implementations, the timings correspond to the execution of one field operation or one eta-pairing computation. For the vertical-SIMD implementation, two (for SSE2) or four (for AVX2) operations are performed in parallel. The times obtained by our implementation are divided by two or four in the tables below in order to indicate the average time per operation. This is done to make the results directly comparable with the results from the non-SIMD and horizontal-SIMD implementations. We use gprof and valgrind to profile our program. Special cares are adopted to minimize cache misses [14].

Tables 1 and 2 summarize the average computation times of basic field operations in $\mathbb{F}_{2^{1223}}$ and $\mathbb{F}_{3^{509}}$. For the addition and multiplication operations, SIMD-based implementations usually perform better than the non-SIMD implementation. For the square, square-root, cube and cube-root operations, the performance of the horizontal implementation is often poorer than that of the non-SIMD implementation, whereas the performance of the vertical implementation is noticeably better than that of the non-SIMD implementation. The experimental results tally with our theoretical observations discussed in Sect. 3.3. That is, field operations involving bit-level shifts significantly benefit from the vertical model of vectorization. In particular, with SSE2, the time of each multiplication operation can be reduced by up to 25 % using horizontal vectorization. For vertical vectorization, this reduction is in the range 25–50 %. AVX2 can produce an additional speedup of 30–50 % over SSE2.

In Table 3, we mention the average times for computing one eta pairing for non-SIMD, horizontal-SIMD and vertical-SIMD implementations. The speedup figures tabulated are with respect to the non-SIMD implementation. Vertical vectorization is seen to significantly outperform both non-SIMD and horizontal-SIMD implementations. Once again, we obtain noticeably higher benefits if we use AVX2 in place of SSE2.

In Tables 1, 2 and 3, we also mention other reported implementation results on finite-field arithmetic and eta-pairing computation. Hankerson et al. [19] use only SIMD features, and our implementations are already faster than their implementations in both characteristics two and three. Our implementations are, however, slower than the implementations reported in the other two papers [5, 10]. In fact, these two papers employ other parallelization techniques (multi-threading in multi-core machines). SIMD-based parallelization is not incompatible with multi-core implementations. Indeed, these two parallelization techniques can go hand in hand, that is, SIMD techniques may provide additional speedup in the computation of every individual core. The scope of our work is to compare the performances of horizontal and vertical vectorization techniques in the context

Table 1. Timing for field operations in $\mathbb{F}_{2^{1223}}$ (clock cycles).

Mode	Addition	Multiplication*	Square*	Square root*
Non-SIMD	52.5	10546.2	279.7	2806.9
SSE2 (H)	27.2	11780.3	415.0	2565.1
SSE2 (V)	27.5	8192.6	285.5	1663.7
AVX2 (H)	10.3	5525.1	276.9	3140.5
AVX2 (V)	6.6	5478.9	244.4	853.7
Hankerson et al. [19]		8200	600	500
Beuchat et al. [10]		5438.4	480	748.8
Aranha et al. [5]		4030	160	166

*Including modular reduction

Table 2. Timing for field operations in $\mathbb{F}_{3^{509}}$ (clock cycles).

Mode	Addition	Multiplication*	Cube*	Cube root*
Non-SIMD	132.3	14928.4	773.9	4311.9
SSE2 (H)	64.1	11025.2	835.4	5710.6
SSE2 (V)	54.4	6494.6	442.8	1953.3
Hankerson et al. [19]		7700	900	1200
Beuchat et al. [10]		4128	900	974.4

*Including modular reduction

Table 3. Times for computing one eta pairing (in millions of clock cycles).

Implementation	Characteristic	Time	Speedup
Non-SIMD	2	40.6	
	3	53.7	
SSE2 (H)	2	41.5	−2.2 %
	3	37.7	29.8 %
SSE2 (V)	2	29.5	27.3 %
	3	24.9	53.6 %
AVX2 (H)	2	29.1	28.3 %
AVX2 (V)	2	27.2	33.0 %
Hankerson et al. [19]	2	39	
	3	33	
Beuchat et al. [10]	2	26.86	
	3	22.01	
Aranha et al. [5]	2	18.76	

of eta pairing over finite fields of small characteristics. To this end, our experimental results, although slower than the best reported implementations, appear to have served our objectives.

5 Conclusions

In this paper, we establish the superiority of the vertical model of SIMD vectorization over the horizontal model for eta-pairing computations over finite fields of small characteristics. Some possible extensions of our work are stated now.

- We have studied vectorization for bit-wise operations only. It is unclear how the two models compare when arithmetic operations are involved. Eta pairing on elliptic curves defined over prime fields heavily use multiple-precision integer arithmetic. These form a class of curves still immune to the recent attacks [1,2,6,24]. Other types of pairing and other cryptographic primitives also require integer arithmetic. Managing carries and borrows during addition and subtraction stands in the way of effective vectorization. Multiplication poses a more potent threat to data-parallelism ideas.

- Porting our implementations to curves over larger fields of small characteristics (in order to achieve 128-bit security) is important.
- In near future, Intel is going to release the Broadwell architecture which is promised to feature 512-bit SIMD registers (AVX-512) [22]. These registers should produce some additional speedup in eta-paring computations.
- It needs experimentation to understand the extent to which multi-threaded implementations of [5,10] additionally benefit from the application of SIMD-based vectorization techniques.

References

1. Adj, G., Menezes, A., Oliveira, T., Rodríguez-Henríquez, F.: Weakness of $\mathbb{F}_{3^{6\cdot1429}}$ and $\mathbb{F}_{2^{4\cdot3041}}$ for discrete logarithm cryptography. In: IACR Eprint Archive (2013). http://eprint.iacr.org/2013/737
2. Adj, G., Menezes, A., Oliveira, T., Rodríguez-Henríquez, F.: Weakness of $\mathbb{F}_{3^{6\cdot509}}$ for discrete logarithm cryptography. In: IACR Eprint Archive (2013). http://eprint.iacr.org/2013/446
3. Ahmadi, O., Hankerson, D., Menezes, A.: Software implementation of arithmetic in $\mathbb{F}_{3^m}$. In: Carlet, C., Sunar, B. (eds.) WAIFI 2007. LNCS, vol. 4547, pp. 85–102. Springer, Heidelberg (2007)
4. Ahmadi, O., Rodriguez-Henriquez, F.: Low complexity cubing and cube root computation over $\mathbb{F}_{3^m}$ in polynomial basis. IEEE Trans. Comput. **59**, 1297–1308 (2010)
5. Aranha, D.F., López, J., Hankerson, D.: High-speed parallel software implementation of the η_T pairing. In: Pieprzyk, J. (ed.) CT-RSA 2010. LNCS, vol. 5985, pp. 89–105. Springer, Heidelberg (2010)
6. Barbulescu, R., Gaudry, P., Joux, A., Thomé, E.: A quasi-polynomial algorithm for discrete logarithm in finite fields of small characteristic. In: IACR Eprint Archive (2013). http://eprint.iacr.org/2013/400
7. Barreto, P.S.L.M.: A note on efficient computation of cube roots in characteristic 3. In: IACR Eprint Archive (2004). http://eprint.iacr.org/2004/305
8. Barreto, P.S.L.M., Galbraith, S.D., OÉigeartaigh, C., Scott, M.: Efficient pairing computation on supersingular Abelian varieties. Des. Codes Crypt. **42**(3), 239–271 (2007)
9. Barreto, P.S.L.M., Kim, H.Y., Lynn, B., Scott, M.: Efficient algorithms for pairing-based cryptosystems. In: Yung, M. (ed.) CRYPTO 2002. LNCS, vol. 2442, pp. 354–368. Springer, Heidelberg (2002)
10. Beuchat, J.-L., López-Trejo, E., Martínez-Ramos, L., Mitsunari, S., Rodríguez-Henríquez, F.: Multi-core implementation of the tate pairing over supersingular elliptic curves. In: Garay, J.A., Miyaji, A., Otsuka, A. (eds.) CANS 2009. LNCS, vol. 5888, pp. 413–432. Springer, Heidelberg (2009)
11. Boneh, D., Franklin, M.: Identity-based encryption from the Weil pairing. In: Kilian, J. (ed.) CRYPTO 2001. LNCS, vol. 2139, pp. 213–229. Springer, Heidelberg (2001)
12. Boneh, D., Lynn, B., Shacham, H.: Short signatures from the Weil pairing. J. Cryptology **17**, 297–319 (2004)

13. Bose, U., Bhattacharya, A.K., Das, A.: GPU-based implementation of 128-bit secure eta pairing over a binary field. In: Youssef, A., Nitaj, A., Hassanien, A.E. (eds.) AFRICACRYPT 2013. LNCS, vol. 7918, pp. 26–42. Springer, Heidelberg (2013)

14. Drepper, U.: What every programmer should know about memory (2007). http://lwn.net/Articles/250967/

15. Freeman, D., Scott, M., Teske, E.: A taxonomy of pairing-friendly elliptic curves. J. Cryptology **23**, 224–280 (2010)

16. Gorla, E., Puttmann, C., Shokrollahi, J.: Explicit formulas for efficient multiplication in $\mathbb{F}_{3^{6m}}$. In: Adams, C., Miri, A., Wiener, M. (eds.) SAC 2007. LNCS, vol. 4876, pp. 173–183. Springer, Heidelberg (2007)

17. Grabher, P., Großschädl, J., Page, D.: On software parallel implementation of cryptographic pairings. In: Avanzi, R.M., Keliher, L., Sica, F. (eds.) SAC 2008. LNCS, vol. 5381, pp. 35–50. Springer, Heidelberg (2009)

18. Granger, R., Page, D., Stam, M.: Hardware and software normal basis arithmetic for pairing-based cryptography in characteristic three. IEEE Trans. Comput. **54**(7), 852–860 (2005)

19. Hankerson, D., Menezes, A., Scott, M.: Software Implementation of Pairings. Identity Based Cryptography, pp. 188–206. IOS Press, Amsterdam (2008)

20. Hess, F., Smart, N.P., Vercauteren, F.: The eta pairing revisited. IEEE Trans. Inf. Theor. **52**(10), 4595–4602 (2006)

21. Intel: Intel® C++ compiler XE 13.1 user and reference guide: compiler reference: intrinsics (2013). http://software.intel.com/sites/products/documentation/doclib/iss/2013/compiler/cpp-lin/GUID-712779D8-D085-4464-9662-B630681F16 F1.htm

22. Intel: Intel Instruction Set Architecture Extensions (2014). http://software.intel.com/en-us/intel-isa-extensions

23. Joux, A.: A one round protocol for tripartite Diffie-Hellman. J. Cryptology **17**, 263–276 (2004)

24. Joux, A.: Faster index calculus for the medium prime case application to 1175-bit and 1425-bit finite fields. In: Johansson, T., Nguyen, P.Q. (eds.) EUROCRYPT 2013. LNCS, vol. 7881, pp. 177–193. Springer, Heidelberg (2013)

25. Katoh, Y., Huang, Y. J., Cheng, C. M., Takagi, T.: Efficient implementation of the η_T pairing on GPU. In: IACR Eprint Archive (2011). http://eprint.iacr.org/2011/540

26. Kawahara, Y., Aoki, K., Takagi, T.: Faster implementation of η_T pairing over GF(3^m) using minimum number of logical instructions for GF(3)-addition. In: Galbraith, S.D., Paterson, K.G. (eds.) Pairing 2008. LNCS, vol. 5209, pp. 282–296. Springer, Heidelberg (2008)

27. Kerins, T., Marnane, W.P., Popovici, E.M., Barreto, P.S.L.M.: Efficient hardware for the tate pairing calculation in characteristic three. In: Rao, J.R., Sunar, B. (eds.) CHES 2005. LNCS, vol. 3659, pp. 412–426. Springer, Heidelberg (2005)

28. Lee, E., Lee, H.S., Park, C.M.: Efficient and generalized pairing computation on Abelian varieties. IEEE Trans. Inf. Theor. **55**, 1793–1803 (2009)

29. López, J., Dahab, R.: High-speed software multiplication in F2m. In: Roy, B., Okamoto, E. (eds.) INDOCRYPT 2000. LNCS, vol. 1977, pp. 203–212. Springer, Heidelberg (2000)

30. Microsoft: MMX, SSE, and SSE2 Intrinsics (2010). http://msdn.microsoft.com/en-us/library/y0dh78ez(v=vs.90).aspx

31. Miller, V.: The Weil pairing and its efficient calculation. J. Cryptology **17**, 235–261 (2004)

32. Montgomery, P.L.: Vectorization of the elliptic curve method. ACM (1991)
33. Page, D., Smart, N.P.: Parallel cryptographic arithmetic using a redundant Montgomery representation. IEEE Trans. Comput. **53**, 1474–1482 (2004)
34. Scott, M.: Optimal irreducible polynomials for $GF(2^m)$ arithmetic. In: IACR Eprint Archive (2007). http://eprint.iacr.org/2007/192
35. Scott, M., Benger, N., Charlemagne, M., Dominguez Perez, L.J., Kachisa, E.J.: On the final exponentiation for calculating pairings on ordinary elliptic curves. In: Shacham, H., Waters, B. (eds.) Pairing 2009. LNCS, vol. 5671, pp. 78–88. Springer, Heidelberg (2009)
36. Smart, N.P., Harrison, K., Page, D.: Software implementation of finite fields of characteristic three. LMS J. Comput. Math. **5**, 181–193 (2002)
37. Takahashi, G., Hoshino, F., Kobayashi, T.: Efficient $GF(3^m)$ multiplication algorithm for η_T pairing. In: IACR Eprint Archive (2007). http://eprint.iacr.org/2007/463
38. Vercauteren, F.: Optimal pairings. IEEE Trans. Inf. Theor. **56**, 455–461 (2010)

Redactable Signature Schemes for Trees with Signer-Controlled Non-Leaf-Redactions

Hermann de Meer[1,3], Henrich C. Pöhls[2,3](✉), Joachim Posegga[2,3], and Kai Samelin[3]

[1] Chair of Computer Networks and Communications,
University of Passau, Passau, Germany
[2] Chair of IT-Security, University of Passau, Passau, Germany
[3] Institute of IT-Security and Security Law (ISL),
University of Passau, Passau, Germany
demeer@fim.uni-passau.de, {hp,jp,ks}@sec.uni-passau.de

Abstract. Redactable signature schemes (RSS) permit to remove parts from signed documents, while the signature remains valid. Some RSSs for trees allow to redact non-leaves. Then, new edges have to be added to the tree to preserve it's structure. This alters the position of the nodes' children and may alter the semantic meaning encoded into the tree's structure. We propose an extended security model, where the signer explicitly controls among which nodes new edges can be added. We present a provably secure construction based on accumulators with the enhanced notions of indistinguishability and strong one-wayness.

Keywords: Redactable signatures · Malleable signatures · Trees

1 Introduction

Trees are commonly used to structure data. XML is one of today's most prominent examples. To protect these documents against unauthorized modifications, digital signatures are used. They protect two important properties: integrity of the data itself and also the data's origin. In certain scenarios it is desirable to *remove* parts of a signed document without invalidating the protecting signature. However, classical signatures prevent any alteration of data.

The straight-forward solution to this problem is to request a new signature with the parts in question removed. This round-trip allows to satisfy the above

This is an extended and heavily revised version of [1]

The research leading to these results has received support from the European Union's Seventh Framework Programme (FP7/2007–2013) under grant agreement n° 609094. Was supported by "Regionale Wettbewerbsfähigkeit und Beschäftigung", Bayern, 2007–2013 (EFRE) as part of the SECBIT project (http://www.secbit.de) and the European Community's Seventh Framework Programme through the EINS Network of Excellence under grant agreement n° 288021, while at the University of Passau.

© Springer-Verlag Berlin Heidelberg 2014
M.S. Obaidat and J. Filipe (Eds.): ICETE 2012, CCIS 455, pp. 155–171, 2014.
DOI: 10.1007/978-3-662-44791-8_10

requirements. However, what happens if the original signer is not reachable, or communication is too costly? The "digital document sanitization problem" [2] therefore asks for two additional requirements: (1) the original signer must not be involved for derivation of signatures, and (2) the removed parts must remain private. This is also useful in cases where the signer must not know which parts of a signed document are passed to other parties. Redactable signature schemes (RSS) address the above constellation. As standard signatures schemes, they prohibit *unauthorized* changes: only removal is allowed. This possibility comes in handy in many scenarios, e.g., privacy-preserving handling of medical records becomes simpler [3–6]. There are many more applications given in the literature. References [7–9] provide additional scenarios.

State of the Art and Related Work. The concept of RSSs has been introduced in [10,11]. Both describe a signature scheme that allows removing parts from signed data without invalidating the signature. Reference [10] termed this functionality "redactable signatures". Constructions emerged in the following years calling this same functionality differently, e.g., in the following work it is termed close to or as "sanitizing" [2,12–15]. For example, *Izu* et al. call this functionality "sanitized signatures" [12,13]. We follow the terminology from [10], describing the functionality as "redactable signatures" [10]. Hence, this paper disagrees with the classification from [13], which states that [11] are "sanitized signatures". This is especially important for a clear separation from the concept of "sanitizable signature schemes" [16–21], coined by *Ateniese* et al. [16]. They are, however, to some extend, related. In sanitizable signatures, elements are not redacted, but (admissible) ones can be altered to arbitrary strings. To do so, sanitizers require to know a secret. Even though the primitives seem to be very related, the aims and security models substantially differ on a detailed level [22,23].

Following the first ideas, RSSs have been proposed to work for lists [24,25], and have extended to trees [3,26] and graphs [3]. *Brzuska* et al. derived a set of desired properties for redactable tree-structured documents including a formal model for security notions [26]. Following their definitions, most of the schemes proposed are not secure, e.g., the work done in [2,3,6,10,11,27]. In particular, a third party can see that something has been redacted, which impacts on the intention of an RSS. However, their model is limited to leaf-redaction only.

Recently, schemes with *context-hiding*, a very strong privacy notion, and variations thereof, e.g., [28–30] appeared. In those schemes, a derived signature does not leak whether it corresponds to an already existing signature in a statistical sense. Most recent advances generalize similar ideas, e.g., [28–33].

Flexibility of Non-Leaf Redactions. Consider the tree depicted in Fig. 1, ignoring the numbers in brackets for now. To remove the leaf n_4, the node n_4 itself and the edge $e_{3,4}$ is removed. By consecutive removal of leaves, complete sub-trees can be redacted [26]. However, schemes only allowing redaction of leaves fail to redact the data stored in, e.g., n_3 only. The wanted tree is depicted

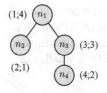

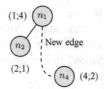

Fig. 1. Original tree with traversal numbers.

Fig. 2. Transitive closure of the child-of relation.

Fig. 3. After removal of n_3; with orig. traversal numbers.

Fig. 4. Added explicitly authorized potential edge.

in Fig. 3: to connect n_4 to the remaining tree, the third party requires to add a *new* edge $e_{1,4}$, which was not present before. However, $e_{1,4}$ is in the *transitive closure* of the original tree, as shown in Fig. 2. The scheme introduced in [3] allows redaction of non-leaves, stating that this flexibility is useful in many scenarios. One may think of redacting hierarchies. We model non-leaf redaction as a two step process: first, all children of the to-be-redacted node are re-located to its parent. The to-be-redacted node is now a leaf and can be redacted as such. Allowing non-leaf removal has its merits, but generally allowing this behavior can lead to a reduced structural integrity protection, as we describe next.

Structural Integrity Protection. Let us consider a chart encoding employees' names as nodes and their position within the companies hierarchy is encoded in the trees structure. Hence, protecting structural integrity is equal to protecting the correctness of the employees' hierarchical positions. If one only signs the ancestor relationship of the nodes, all edges that are part of the transitive closure are part of the signature. This is depicted in Fig. 2. This allows a third party to add edges to the tree. This possibility was named "Level Promotion" in [25]. In our prior example, this translates easily: an employee can be "promoted". This may not *always* be wanted (Fig 4).

The scheme introduced in [3] behaves like this: it builds upon the idea that having all pre- and post-order traversal numbers of the nodes in a tree, one can uniquely reconstruct it. To make their scheme hiding occurred redactions, the traversal numbers are randomized in an order-preserving manner, which does not have an impact on the reconstruction algorithm, as the relation between nodes does not change. For our discussion, this step can be left out.[1] Assume we redact n_3, as depicted in Fig. 3: the traversal-numbers are still in the correct relation. Hence, the edge $e_{1,4}$, which has not explicitly been present before, passes verification. One might argue that nesting of elements must adhere to a specific codified structure, i.e., XML-Schema. Henceforth, possibilities like level-promotions are detected by any XML-Schema validation. However, elements may contain itself, like hierarchically structured employees or treatments composed of

---

[1] Indeed, the randomization step does not hide anything [26,34].

treatments. Hence, redaction of non-leaves is not acceptable in the generic case and may lead to several new attack vectors, similar to the ones of XPath [35]. We conclude that the signer must *explicitly* sign only the authorized transitive edges, if the aforementioned behavior is not wanted, or use an RSS which only permits leaf-redactions.

Our Contribution. We present a security model where the signer has the flexibility to allow redaction of any node. Our model allows level promotions due to re-locations of specified sub-trees, which resembles the *implicit* possibility of previous schemes. The signer is *explicitly* prohibiting the redaction of nodes individually, as the signer must explicitly sign an edge for re-locations. Re-locations of sub-trees can be used to emulate non-leaf redactions, but allow even more flexibility: we can relocate sub-trees without redactions. We also allow that a sanitizer can prohibit such re-locations by redacting the authorized potential edge.

While [34] either allows or disallows non-leaf redactions completely, this work allows the signer to decide which non-leaves can be redacted: the signer defines to which "upper-level node" the "dangling" sub-tree's root can be connected to.

We derive a provably secure construction, based on cryptographic accumulators [36,37], in combination with *Merkle*'s Hash-Tree-Technique. Thus, our construction requires only standard cryptographic primitives. However, we need to strengthen existing definitions of accumulators. In particular, we introduce the notions of indistinguishability and strong one-wayness of accumulators.

In our construction, the signer controls the protection of the order of siblings. Hence, our scheme is capable of signing both ordered and unordered trees. Finally, we present some new attacks on existing schemes.

2   Preliminaries and Security Model

Nodes are addressed as n_i. The root is denoted as n_1. With c_i, we refer to all the content of node n_i, which is additional information that might be associated with a node, i.e., data, element name and so forth. We use the work done in [26] as our starting point. Their model only allows removing *a single leaf* at a time and does not support non-leaf redactions.

Flexible RSS. An RSS consists of four efficient (PPT) algorithms: $\mathcal{RSS} :=$ (KeyGen, Sign, Verify, Modify). All algorithms output $\perp$ in case of an error. Also, they take an implicit security parameter λ (in unary).

KeyGen. The algorithm KeyGen outputs the key pair of the signer, i.e., $(\mathsf{pk}, \mathsf{sk}) \leftarrow$ KeyGen(1^λ), λ being the security parameter.

Sign. On input of sk, T, and ADM, Sign outputs a signature σ. ADM controls what changes by Modify are admissible. In detail, ADM is the set containing all signed edges, including the ones where a sub-tree can be re-located to. In particular, $(n_i, n_j) \in$ ADM, if the edge (n_i, n_j) must verify. These edges cannot be derived from T alone. Let $(T, \sigma, \text{ADM}) \leftarrow$ Sign($\mathsf{sk}, T, \text{ADM}$).

Verify. On input of pk, the tree T and a signature σ, Verify outputs a bit $d \in \{0,1\}$, indicating the validity of σ, w.r.t. pk and T: $d \leftarrow$ Verify(pk, T, σ). Note, ADM is not required.

Modify. The algorithm Modify takes pk, the tree T, a signature σ and ADM, and an instruction MOD. MOD contains the actual change to be made: redact a sub-tree, relocate a sub-tree, or prohibit relocating a sub-tree. On modification, ADM is adjusted. If a node n_i is redacted, the edge to its father needs to be removed. Moreover, if there exists a sub-tree which can be re-located under the redacted node, the corresponding edges need to be removed from ADM as well. The alteration of ADM is crucial to maintain privacy and transparency. Hence, we have: $(T', \sigma', \text{ADM}') \leftarrow$ Modify(pk, T, σ, ADM, MOD).

We require the usual correctness requirements to hold [26]. A word of clarification: we assume that ADM is always correctly derivable from σ. However, we always explicitly denote ADM to increase readability of our security definitions.

The Extended Security Model. We build around the framework given in [26], extending it to cater for the flexibility of non-leaf redactions and re-locations.

Unforgeability. No one should be able to compute a valid signature on a tree T^* verifying for pk outside span$_\vdash(T, \sigma, \text{ADM})$, without access to the corresponding secret key sk. Here, span$_\vdash(T_i, \sigma_i, \text{ADM}_i)$ expresses the set of trees derivable by use of Modify on T_i, σ_i and ADM$_i$. This is analogous to the standard unforgeability requirement for signature schemes [38]. A scheme RSS is unforgeable, if for any PPT adversary $\mathcal{A}$, the probability that the game depicted in Fig. 5 returns 1, is negligible.

Privacy. No one should be able to gain any knowledge about parts redacted. This is similar to the standard indistinguishability notation for encryption schemes [39]. An RSS is private, if for any PPT adversary $\mathcal{A}$, the probability that the game shown in Fig. 6 returns 1, is negligibly close to $\frac{1}{2}$. In a nutshell, privacy says that everything which has been redacted remains hidden. However, if in real documents redactions are obvious, e.g., due to missing structure, one may trivially be able to decide that not the complete tree was given to the verifier. However, this cannot be avoided: our definitions assume that no other sources of knowledge apart from (several) σ_i', T_i' and ADM$_i'$ are available to the attacker.

Experiment Unforgeability$_{\mathcal{A}}^{\text{RSS}}(\lambda)$

    (pk, sk) $\leftarrow$ KeyGen(1^λ)

    $(T^*, \sigma^*) \leftarrow \mathcal{A}^{\text{Sign}(\text{sk}, \cdot, \cdot)}(\text{pk})$

        let $i = 1, 2, \ldots, q$ index the queries/answers to/from Sign

    return 1, if

        Verify(pk, T^*, σ^*) = 1 and

        for all $1 \le i \le q$, $T^* \notin$ span$_\vdash(T_i, \sigma_i, \text{ADM}_i)$

Fig. 5. Unforgeability.

Experiment $\text{Privacy}_{\mathcal{A}}^{\text{RSS}}(\lambda)$

    $(\text{pk}, \text{sk}) \leftarrow \text{KeyGen}(1^{\lambda})$

    $b \xleftarrow{\$} \{0, 1\}$

    $d \leftarrow \mathcal{A}^{\text{Sign}(\text{sk},\cdot,\cdot),\text{LoRModify}(\cdot,\cdot,\cdot,\cdot,\cdot,\cdot,\text{sk},b)}(\text{pk})$

    where oracle $\text{LoRModify}(T_{j,0}, \text{ADM}_{j,0}, \text{MOD}_{j,0}, T_{j,1}, \text{ADM}_{j,1}, \text{MOD}_{j,1}, \text{sk}, b)$

        if $\text{MOD}_{j,0}(T_{j,0}) \neq \text{MOD}_{j,1}(T_{j,1})$ return $\perp$

        $(T_{j,0}, \sigma_0, \text{ADM}_{j,0}) \leftarrow \text{Sign}(\text{sk}, T_{j,0}, \text{ADM}_{j,0})$

        $(T_{j,1}, \sigma_1, \text{ADM}_{j,1}) \leftarrow \text{Sign}(\text{sk}, T_{j,1}, \text{ADM}_{j,1})$

        $(T'_{j,0}, \sigma'_0, \text{ADM}'_{j,0}) \leftarrow \text{Modify}(\text{pk}, T_{j,0}, \sigma_0, \text{ADM}_{j,0}, \text{MOD}_{j,0})$

        $(T'_{j,1}, \sigma'_1, \text{ADM}'_{j,1}) \leftarrow \text{Modify}(\text{pk}, T_{j,1}, \sigma_1, \text{ADM}_{j,1}, \text{MOD}_{j,1})$

        if $\text{ADM}'_{j,0} \neq \text{ADM}'_{j,1}$, abort returning $\perp$

        return $(T'_{j,b}, \sigma'_b, \text{ADM}'_{j,b})$

    return 1, if $b = d$

Fig. 6. Privacy.

Experiment $\text{Transparency}_{\mathcal{A}}^{\text{RSS}}(\lambda)$

    $(\text{pk}, \text{sk}) \leftarrow \text{KeyGen}(1^{\lambda})$

    $b \xleftarrow{\$} \{0, 1\}$

    $d \leftarrow \mathcal{A}^{\text{Sign}(\text{sk},\cdot,\cdot),\text{ModifyOrSign}(\cdot,\cdot,\cdot,\text{sk},b)}(\text{pk})$

    where oracle $\text{ModifyOrSign}(T, \text{ADM}, \text{MOD}, \text{sk}, b)$

        if $\text{MOD} \notin \text{ADM}$, return $\perp$

        $(T, \sigma, \text{ADM}) \leftarrow \text{Sign}(\text{sk}, T, \text{ADM})$

        $(T', \sigma', \text{ADM}') \leftarrow \text{Modify}(\text{pk}, T, \sigma, \text{ADM}, \text{MOD})$

        if $b = 1$:

            $(T', \sigma', \text{ADM}') \leftarrow \text{Sign}(\text{sk}, T', \text{ADM}')$

        return $(T', \sigma', \text{ADM}')$

    return 1, if $b = d$

Fig. 7. Transparency.

Transparency. A party who receives a signed tree T should not be able to tell whether it received a freshly signed tree (case $b = 1$ in Fig. 7) or a tree derived by Modify [26]. We say that an RSS is transparent, if for any PPT adversary $\mathcal{A}$, the probability that the game shown in Fig. 7 returns 1, is negligibly close to $\frac{1}{2}$.

Relations. The implications and separations between the security properties given in [26] do not change — the proofs are very similar and therefore omitted in this work. In particular, transparency implies privacy, while transparency and unforgeability are independent.

Cryptographic Accumulators. For our construction, we deploy accumulators. They have been introduced in [37]. The basic idea is to hash a set S into a short value a, normally referred to as the accumulator. For each element $y_i \in S$ a short witness w_i is generated, which allows to verify that y_i has actually been accumulated into a. We only need the basic operations of an accumulator, e.g., neither trapdoor-freeness [40,41] nor dynamic updates [42], or revocation techniques [43] are required. A basic accumulator consists of four efficient algorithms, i.e., $\mathcal{AH} := \{\mathsf{KeyGen}, \mathsf{Hash}, \mathsf{Proof}, \mathsf{Check}\}$:

KeyGen. Outputs the public key pk on input of a security parameter λ:
   $\mathsf{pk} \leftarrow \mathsf{KeyGen}(1^\lambda)$

Hash. Outputs the accumulator a, and an auxiliary value aux, given a set $\mathcal{S}$, and pk:
   $(a, \mathsf{aux}) \leftarrow \mathsf{Hash}(\mathsf{pk}, \mathcal{S})$

Proof. On input of an auxiliary value aux, the accumulator a, a set $\mathcal{S}$, and an element $y \in \mathcal{S}$, Proof outputs a witness w, if y was actually accumulated:
   $w \leftarrow \mathsf{Proof}(\mathsf{pk}, \mathsf{aux}, a, y, \mathcal{S})$

Check. Outputs a bit $d \in \{0, 1\}$, indicating if a given value y was accumulated into the accumulator a with respect to pk and a witness w:
   $d \leftarrow \mathsf{Check}(\mathsf{pk}, y, w, a)$

All correctness properties must hold [36]. Next, we define the required security properties of accumulators.

Strong One-Wayness of Accumulators. It must be hard to find an element not accumulated, even if the adversary can chose the set to be accumulated. The needed property is strong one-wayness of the accumulator [36]. We say that an accumulator is strongly one-way, if the probability that the game depicted in Fig. 8 returns 1, is negligibly close to 0. Note, in comparison to [36,44], we consider probabilistic accumulation and allow to query adaptively.

Indistinguishability of Accumulators. We require that an adversary cannot decide how many additional members have been digested. We say that an accumulator is indistinguishable, if the probability that the game depicted in Fig. 9 returns 1, is negligibly close to $\frac{1}{2}$. Here, the adversary can choose three sets, and has to decide, which sets have been accumulated (either the first and the second, or the first and the third). Note, only the witnesses for the first set are returned. An accumulator not fulfilling these requirements has been proposed by *Nyberg* in [44]; the underlying *Bloom*-Filter can be attacked by probabilistic methods and therefore leaks the amount of members [45]. This is not acceptable for our construction, as it impacts on privacy. A concrete instantiation of such an accumulator achieving our requirements is the probabilistic version of [36]. In a

---

Experiment $\mathsf{Strong-One-Wayness}_{\mathcal{A}}^{\mathcal{AH}}(\lambda)$
   $\mathsf{pk} \leftarrow \mathsf{KeyGen}(1^\lambda)$
   $(a^*, y^*, p^*) \leftarrow \mathcal{A}^{\mathsf{Hash}(\mathsf{pk}, \cdot)}(1^\lambda, \mathsf{pk})$
      where oracle **Hash** for input $\mathcal{S}_i$:
         $(a_i, \mathsf{aux}_i) \leftarrow \mathsf{Hash}(\mathsf{pk}, \mathcal{S}_i)$
         return $(a_i, \{(y_j, p_j) \mid y_j \in \mathcal{S}_i, p_j \leftarrow \mathsf{Proof}(\mathsf{pk}, \mathsf{aux}_i, a_i, y_j, \mathcal{S}_i)\})$
   look for k s.t. $a_k = a^*$. If such k does not exist, return 0.
   return 1, if $\mathsf{Check}(1^\lambda, \mathsf{pk}, y^*, p^*, a^*)$ and $y^* \notin \mathcal{S}_k$

Fig. 8. Accumulator strong one-wayness.

Experiment Indistinguishability$_{\mathcal{A}}^{\mathcal{AH}}(\lambda)$

$\quad$ pk $\leftarrow$ KeyGen(1^λ)

$\quad$ $b \overset{\$}{\leftarrow} \{0, 1\}$

$\quad$ $d \leftarrow \mathcal{A}^{\mathsf{LoRHash}(\cdot,\cdot,\cdot,b,\mathrm{pk})}(1^\lambda, \mathrm{pk})$

$\qquad$ where oracle LoRHash for input $\mathcal{S}, \mathcal{R}_0, \mathcal{R}_1$:

$\qquad\quad$ $(a, \mathsf{aux}) \leftarrow \mathsf{Hash}(\mathrm{pk}, \mathcal{S} \cup \mathcal{R}_b)$

$\qquad\quad$ return $(a, \{(y_i, p_i) \mid y_i \in \mathcal{S}, p_i \leftarrow \mathsf{Proof}(\mathrm{pk}, y_i, \mathsf{aux})\})$

$\quad$ return 1, if $d = b$

Fig. 9. Accumulator privacy.

nutshell, instead of fixing the base for the RSA-function, it is drawn at random. A more detailed discussion is given in [45]. We do note that our definition of indistinguishability already assumes a probabilistic hash algorithm; [45] also accounts for deterministic ones. Additional information about accumulators can be found in [36, 37, 42].

3   A New Flexible RSS

Our construction makes use of *Merkle*-Hash-Trees. The *Merkle*-Hash $\mathcal{MH}$ of a node x is calculated as: $\mathcal{MH}(x) = \mathcal{H}(\mathcal{H}(c_x)||\mathcal{MH}(x_1)|| \ldots ||\mathcal{MH}(x_n))$, where $\mathcal{H}$ is a collision-resistant hash-function, c_x the content of the node x, x_i a child of x, n the number of children of the node x, while $||$ denotes a uniquely reversible concatenation of strings. $\mathcal{MH}(n_1)$'s output depends on all nodes' content and on the *right order* of the siblings. Hence, signing $\mathcal{MH}(n_1)$ protects the integrity of the nodes in an ordered tree and the tree's structural integrity. Obviously, this technique does not allow to hash unordered trees: an altered order most likely causes a different digest value.

Hash-Trees and Privacy. Removing sub-trees requires to give a hash of the removed node to the verifier, in order to calculate the same $\mathcal{MH}(n_1)$. This directly impacts on privacy and transparency, because the hash depends on removed information that shall remain private. One example for an RSS which suffers from this problem is given in [46]. It can be attacked in the following way: the attacker asks its left-or-right oracle to sign a root with one child only, but without redacting anything. The other input is a tree with the root and two children, while the *left* child is to redacted. This results in the same tree: the root with one child. However, in the case the first input is used, their "fake-digest" is the right node, while in the other case the fake-digest is the left node. This can clearly be distinguished and privacy is broken.

A more detailed analysis of the *Merkle*-Hash-Tree is given in [3], which also gives an introduction on the possible attacks on non-private schemes. To overcome the limitation of *Merkle*-Hash-Trees, we use accumulators instead of standard collision-resistant hash-functions. We do note that the idea to use accumulators has already been proposed in [3]. However, they state that accumulators are not able to achieve the desired functionality. We show that they are sufficient by giving a concrete construction. Note, compared to the old version of this paper [1], we do not permit a redaction of the root, as this may lead to problematic behavior as well [34]. Moreover, this small constraint reduces the number of signatures to be generated to only one.

Construction. We allow explicit re-location of sub-trees. If a non-leaf is subject to redaction, all sub-trees of the node need to be re-located. If this is possible and what their new ancestor will be must be under the sole control of the signer. We limit re-locations directing towards the root to avoid forming loops, which was possible in the original publication [1]. We now sketch our solution, and give the concrete algorithms afterward. Our re-location definition does not require to delete the ancestor node. This behavior of re-locating only is discussed later on.

Sketch. In our solution, the signer replicates all re-locatable nodes and the underlying sub-trees to all locations where a sanitizer is allowed to relocate the sub-tree to. The replicas of the nodes are implicitly used to produce the re-locatable edges. Each additional edge is contained in ADM. To prohibit simple copy attacks, i.e., leaving a re-located sub-tree in two locations, each node n_i gets an associated unique nonce r_i. The whole tree gets signed using a *Merkle*-Hash-Tree, but using an accumulator instead of a standard hash. To redact parts, the sanitizer removes the nodes in question, and no longer provides the corresponding witnesses. As accumulators work on sets, it does not matter in what order the members are checked. However, if ordered trees are present, the ordering between siblings has to be explicitly signed. To do so, we sign the "left-of" relation, as already used and proposed in [24–26]. Note, this implies a quadratic complexity in the number n of siblings, i.e., $\frac{n(n-1)}{2}$. To relocate a sub-tree, one only applies the necessary changes to T, without any further changes. However, a sanitizer can prohibit consecutive re-locations by altering ADM. This control is similar to consecutive sanitization control [2]. Verification is straight forward: for each node x inside the tree check, if x's content, x's children and x's order to other siblings is contained in x's *Merkle*-Hash. This is done recursively. Further, all node's nonces must be unique for this tree. Finally, the root's signature is checked.

The Algorithmic Description. $\Pi := (\mathsf{KeyGen}, \mathsf{Sign}, \mathsf{Verify})$ denotes a standard unforgeable signature scheme [38]. Note, to shorten the *algorithmic* description, we abuse notation and define that Hash directly works on a set and returns all witness/element pairs (w_i, y_i). We denote the accumulation as $(a, \mathcal{W} = \{(w_i, y_i)\}) \leftarrow \mathcal{AH}(\mathsf{pk}, \{y_1, \ldots, y_n\})$. In the following algorithms we use //*comment* to indicate comments (Fig. 10).

KeyGen(λ):
    $\mathsf{pk}_{\mathcal{AH}} \leftarrow \mathcal{AH}.\mathsf{KeyGen}(1^\lambda)$
    $(\mathsf{pk}_S, \mathsf{sk}_S) \leftarrow \Pi.\mathsf{KeyGen}(1^\lambda)$
    return $((\mathsf{pk}_S, \mathsf{pk}_{\mathcal{AH}}), \mathsf{sk}_S)$

Expand(T, ADM):
    For all edges $e_i \in \mathsf{ADM} \setminus T$ (must be done *bottom-up*)

Replicate the sub-tree underneath the node addressed by e_i
to the designated position. //*Note: this is recursive!*
Return this expanded tree

Sign(sk, T, ADM):
  // *We implicitly assume a parameter $s \in \{\text{ordered}, \text{unordered}\}$,*
  // *denoting if the order must be protected*
  For each node $n_i \in T$:
    $r_i \overset{\$}{\leftarrow} \{0,1\}^\lambda$
  Append r_i to each node $n_i \in T$
  Expand tree: $\Omega \leftarrow$ Expand(T, ADM) //*Note: r_i is copied as well*
  Do the next step with the expended tree Ω:
    If $s =$ unordered: //$\mathcal{MH}(\cdot)$ *denotes the digest calculated by* $\mathcal{AH}$
      $(d_1, \{(y_k, w_k)\}) \leftarrow \mathcal{AH}(\text{pk}, \{c_1 \| r_1, \mathcal{MH}(x_1), \dots, \mathcal{MH}(x_n)\})$
    Else ($s =$ ordered): //*ordered tree*
      $(d_1, \{(y_k, w_k)\}) \leftarrow \mathcal{AH}(\text{pk}, \{c_1 \| r_1, \mathcal{MH}(x_1), \dots, \mathcal{MH}(x_n), \Xi_x\})$,
      where $\Xi_x = \{r_i \| r_j \mid 0 < i < j \leq n\}$
  Sign the root-hash: $\sigma_s \leftarrow \Pi.\text{Sign}(\text{sk}_S, d_1 \| s)$
  $\mathcal{W} = \{(y_k, w_k)\}$ denotes the set of **all** witness/element pairs returned
  return $\sigma = (\sigma_s, \mathcal{W}, \text{ADM})$

Modify(pk, T, σ, ADM, MOD):
  use Verify to verify the tree T
  Expanded tree $\Omega \leftarrow$ Expand(T, ADM)
  Case 1: MOD instruction to redact sub-tree T_s (only via leaf-redaction):
    //*1. remove all $n_l \in T_s$ (incl. replicas) from Ω:*
    Set $\Omega' \leftarrow \Omega \setminus n_l$
    //*2. remove all $n_l \in T_s$ from T:*
    Set $T' \leftarrow T \setminus T_s$
    Create ADM' by removing all ingoing edges all nodes in T_s from ADM
    return $\sigma' = (T', \sigma_s, \mathcal{W} \setminus \{(y_k, w_k) \mid y_k \in \Omega'\}, \text{ADM}')$
  Case 2: MOD instruction to re-locate T_s:
    Set $T' \leftarrow \text{MOD}(T)$
    return σ
  Case 3: MOD instruction to remove re-location edges e:
    Set ADM' $\leftarrow$ ADM $\setminus e$
    //*Note: This expansion is done with the modified ADM'.*
    Let $\Omega' \leftarrow$ Expand(T, ADM')
    return $\sigma' = (T, \sigma_s, \mathcal{W} \cap \{(y_k, w_k) \mid y_k \in \Omega'\}, \text{ADM}')$

Verify(pk, T, σ):
  Check if each $r_i \in T$ is unique.
  Check σ using $\Pi.$Verify
  Let the value protected by σ_s be $d_1' = d_1 \| s$
  For each node $x \in T$:

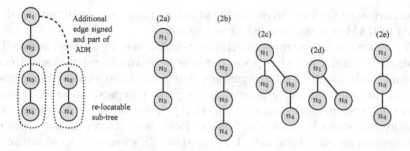

Fig. 10. Left: expanded tree with duplicates, (2a–e) Examples of valid trees after redactions or re-locations.

For all children x_i of x do:
  //*Note: checks if children are signed*
  Let $d \leftarrow$ Check(pk, d_i, w_i, d_x) //d_x denotes the node's digest
  If $d = 0$, return 0
  If $s =$ ordered:
    //*Is every "left-of"-relation signed?*
    //*Note: only linearly many checks*
    For all $0 < i < n$:
      $d \leftarrow$ Check(pk, $r_i\|r_{i+1}, w_{x,x+1}, d_x$)
      If $d = 0$, return 0
return 1

Arguably, allowing re-location without redaction may also be too much freedom. However, it allows the signer to allow a flattening of hierarchies, i.e., to remove the hierarchical ordering of treatments in a patient's record. We want to stress that copying complete sub-trees may lead to an exponential blow-up in the number of nodes to the signed. This happens, in particular, if re-locations are nested. However, if only used sparely, our construction remains useable, as a performance analysis shows next.

Performance. We have implemented our scheme to demonstrate its usability using the old algorithm given in [1], i.e., where every accumulator is signed, not only the root. As the accumulator, we chose the original construction [37] in its randomized form. Tests were performed on a *Lenovo Thinkpad T61* with an *Intel* T8300 Dual Core @2.40 GHz and 4 GiB of RAM. The OS was *Ubuntu* Version 10.04 LTS (64 Bit) with Java-Framework 1.6.0_26-b03 (OpenJDK). We took the median of 10 runs: we only want to demonstrate that our construction is practical as a proof-of-concept. We measured trees with unordered siblings and one with ordered siblings. Trees were randomly generated in an iterative fashion. Re-locations were not considered: only leaf-removal has been implemented. Time for generation of keys for the hash is included. We excluded the time for creating the required signature key pair. However, both becomes negligible in terms of the performance for large trees. On digest calculation, we store all intermediate results in RAM to avoid any disk access impact.

As shown, our construction runtime remains within useable limits. The advanced features come at a price; our scheme is considerably slower than a standard hash like SHA-512. Signatures are more often verified than generated, so the overhead for verification has a greater impact. All other provable secure and transparent schemes, i.e., [24, 26], have the same complexity and therefore just differ by a constant factor. References [24, 26] do not provide a performance analysis on real data. Compared to [34], where a performance analysis of a prototype is provided, this construction offers equal speed or is faster (Table 1).

Table 1. Median runtime in ms.

Nodes	Generation of σ			Verification of σ		
	10	100	1,000	10	100	1,000
Ordered	276	6,715	57,691	26	251	2,572
Unordered	103	599	5,527	21	188	1,820
SHA-512	4	13	40	4	13	40

Security of the Construction. Our scheme is unforgeable, private and transparent. Assuming $\mathcal{AH}$ is strongly one-way, and the signature scheme Π is UNF-CMA, our scheme is unforgeable, while the indistinguishability of $\mathcal{AH}$ implies privacy and transparency. The formal proofs are relegated to Appendix 4.

4   Conclusions

We have shown that redacting arbitrary nodes of a tree can lead to severe problems. Our security model captures that the signer has to explicitly mark redactable nodes. We derived a new construction based on accumulators. Our construction can handle ordered and unordered trees. We have implemented our scheme, and as our performance measurements show, it is reasonably fast. It remains unclear how we can make RSSs accountable [47, 48], and if more efficient schemes exist.

Appendix

Security Proofs of the Construction

We now show that our construction fulfills the given definitions. Namely, these are unforgeability, privacy, and transparency. We prove each property on its own.

Our Scheme is Unforgeable. If $\mathcal{AH}$ is strongly one-way, while the signature scheme Π is unforgeable, our scheme is unforgeable.

Proof. Let $\mathcal{A}$ be an algorithm winning the unforgeability game. We can then use $\mathcal{A}$ in an algorithm $\mathcal{B}$ to either to forge the underlying signature scheme Π or to break the strong one-wayness of $\mathcal{AH}$. Given the game in Fig. 5 we can derive that a forgery must fall in at least one of the two following cases, for at least one node d in the tree:

- Type 1 Forgery: The value d protected by σ_s has never been signed by the signing oracle.
- Type 2 Forgery: The value d protected by σ_s has been signed, but $T^* \notin \operatorname{span}_\vdash(T, \sigma, \mathsf{ADM})$ for any tree T signed by the signing oracle.

Type 1 Forgery. In the first case, we can use the forgery generated by $\mathcal{A}$ to create $\mathcal{B}$ which forges a signature. We construct $\mathcal{B}$ using $\mathcal{A}$ as follows:

1. $\mathcal{B}$ generates the key pair of $\mathcal{AH}$, i.e., $\mathsf{pk} \leftarrow \mathsf{KeyGen}(1^\lambda)$. It passes pk to $\mathcal{A}$. This is also true for pk_S of the signature scheme to forge.
2. All queries to the signing oracle from $\mathcal{A}$ are genuinely answered with one exception: instead of signing digests itself, $\mathcal{B}$ asks it own signing oracle to generate the signature. Afterward, $\mathcal{B}$ returns the signature generated to $\mathcal{A}$.
3. Eventually, $\mathcal{A}$ outputs a pair (T^*, σ^*). $\mathcal{B}$ looks for the message/signature pair (m^*, σ_s^*) inside the transcript not queried to its own signing oracle, i.e., the accumulator value with the signature σ_s^* of the root of (T^*, σ^*). Hence, there exists a value not signed by $\mathcal{B}$'s signing oracle. This pair is then returned as $\mathcal{B}$'s own forgery attempt.

As every tree/signature pair was accepted as valid, but not signed by the signing oracle, $\mathcal{B}$ breaks the unforgeability of the signature algorithm. Here, we have a tight reduction for the first case.

Type 2 Forgery. In the case of a type 2 forgery, we can use $\mathcal{A}$ to construct $\mathcal{B}$, which breaks the strong one-wayness of the underlying accumulator. We construct $\mathcal{B}$ using $\mathcal{A}$ as follows:

1. $\mathcal{B}$ generates a key pair of a signature scheme Π.
2. It receives pk of $\mathcal{AH}$. Both public keys are forwarded to $\mathcal{A}$.
3. For every request to the signing oracle, $\mathcal{B}$ uses its hashing oracle to generate the witnesses and the accumulators. All other steps are genuinely performed. The signature is returned to $\mathcal{A}$.
4. Eventually, $\mathcal{A}$ outputs (T^*, σ^*). Given the transcript of the simulation, $\mathcal{A}$ searches for a pair (w^*, y^*) matching an accumulator a, while y^* has not been queried to hashing oracle under a. Note, the root accumulator has been returned: otherwise, we have a type 1 forgery. $\mathcal{B}$ outputs (a, w^*, y^*).

As every new element accepted as being part of the accumulator, while not been hashed by the hashing oracle, breaks the strong one-wayness of the accumulator, we have a tight reduction again.

Our Scheme is Private. If $\mathcal{AH}$ is indistinguishable our scheme is private. Note: the random numbers do not leak any information, as they are distributed uniformly and are not ordered. Hence, we do not need to take them into account.

Proof. Let $\mathcal{A}$ be an algorithm winning the privacy game. We can then use $\mathcal{A}$ in an algorithm $\mathcal{B}$ to break the indistinguishability of the accumulator $\mathcal{AH}$. We construct $\mathcal{B}$ using $\mathcal{A}$ as follows:

1. $\mathcal{B}$ generates a key pair of a signature scheme Π.
2. It receives pk of $\mathcal{AH}$. Both public keys are forwarded to $\mathcal{A}$.
3. For every request to the signing oracle, $\mathcal{B}$ produces the expanded trees given ADM. Then, it uses its hashing-oracle to generate the accumulators, and then proceeds honestly as the original algorithm would do. Finally, it returns the generated signature σ to $\mathcal{A}$.
4. For queries to the Left-or-Right oracle, $\mathcal{B}$ extracts the common elements to be accumulated for both trees — this set is denoted $\mathcal{S}$. Note, $\mathcal{S}$ may be empty. The additional elements for the first hash are denoted $\mathcal{R}_0$, and $\mathcal{R}_1$ for the second one. $\mathcal{B}$ now queries its own Left-or-Right oracle with $(\mathcal{S}, \mathcal{R}_0, \mathcal{R}_1)$ for each hash. The result is used as the accumulator and the witnesses required: $\mathcal{B}$ genuinely performs the rest of the signing algorithm and hands over the result to $\mathcal{A}$.
5. Eventually, $\mathcal{A}$ outputs its own guess d.
6. $\mathcal{B}$ outputs d as its own guess.

As we only pass queries, $\mathcal{B}$ succeeds, whenever $\mathcal{A}$ succeeds.

Our Construction is Transparent. We already know that our scheme is private. As neither the underlying signature, nor the witness' values, nor the accumulator itself change during a redaction, no building block leaks additional information. Transparency follows.

References

1. Pöhls, H.C., Samelin, K., de Meer, H., Posegga, J.: Flexible redactable signature schemes for trees - extended security model and construction. In: SECRYPT, pp. 113–125 (2012)
2. Miyazaki, K., et al.: Digitally signed document sanitizing scheme with disclosure condition control. IEICE Trans. **88–A**, 239–246 (2005)
3. Kundu, A., Bertino, E.: Privacy-preserving authentication of trees and graphs. Int. J. Inf. Sec. **12**, 467–494 (2013)
4. Pöhls, H.C., Samelin, K., Posegga, J.: Sanitizable signatures in XML signature — performance, mixing properties, and revisiting the property of transparency. In: Lopez, J., Tsudik, G. (eds.) ACNS 2011. LNCS, vol. 6715, pp. 166–182. Springer, Heidelberg (2011)
5. Slamanig, D., Rass, S.: Generalizations and extensions of redactable signatures with applications to electronic healthcare. In: De Decker, B., Schaumüller-Bichl, I. (eds.) CMS 2010. LNCS, vol. 6109, pp. 201–213. Springer, Heidelberg (2010)
6. Wu, Z.Y., Hsueh, C.W., Tsai, C.Y., Lai, F., Lee, H.C., Chung, Y.: Redactable Signatures for Signed CDA Documents. J. Med. Syst. **36**(3), 1795–1808 (2012)
7. Becker, A., Jensen, M.: Secure combination of xml signature application with message aggregation in multicast settings. In: ICWS, pp. 531–538 (2013)

8. Hanser, C., Slamanig, D.: Blank digital signatures. In: AsiaCCS, pp. 95–106. ACM (2013)
9. Rass, S., Slamanig, D.: Cryptography for Security and Privacy in Cloud Computing. Artech House, Boston (2013)
10. Johnson, R., Molnar, D., Song, D., Wagner, D.: Homomorphic signature schemes. In: Preneel, B. (ed.) CT-RSA 2002. LNCS, vol. 2271, pp. 244–262. Springer, Heidelberg (2002)
11. Steinfeld, R., Bull, L., Zheng, Y.: Content extraction signatures. In: Kim, K. (ed.) ICISC 2001. LNCS, vol. 2288, pp. 285–304. Springer, Heidelberg (2002)
12. Izu, T., Kanaya, N., Takenaka, M., Yoshioka, T.: PIATS: a partially sanitizable signature scheme. In: Qing, S., Mao, W., López, J., Wang, G. (eds.) ICICS 2005. LNCS, vol. 3783, pp. 72–83. Springer, Heidelberg (2005)
13. Izu, T., Takenaka, M., Yajima, J., Yoshioka, T.: Integrity assurance for real-time video recording. In: 2012 Sixth International Conference on Innovative Mobile and Internet Services in Ubiquitous Computing (IMIS), pp. 651–655. IEEE (2012)
14. Miyazaki, K., Hanaoka, G.: Invisibly sanitizable digital signature scheme. IEICE Trans. Fundam. Electron. Commun. Comput. Sci. 91, 392–402 (2008)
15. Miyazaki, K., Hanaoka, G., Imai, H.: Digitally signed document sanitizing scheme based on bilinear maps. In: ASIACCS, pp. 343–354. ACM (2006)
16. Ateniese, G., Chou, D.H., de Medeiros, B., Tsudik, G.: Sanitizable signatures. In: di Vimercati, S.C., Syverson, P.F., Gollmann, D. (eds.) ESORICS 2005. LNCS, vol. 3679, pp. 159–177. Springer, Heidelberg (2005)
17. Brzuska, C., Fischlin, M., Freudenreich, T., Lehmann, A., Page, M., Schelbert, J., Schröder, D., Volk, F.: Security of sanitizable signatures revisited. In: Jarecki, S., Tsudik, G. (eds.) PKC 2009. LNCS, vol. 5443, pp. 317–336. Springer, Heidelberg (2009)
18. Brzuska, C., Fischlin, M., Lehmann, A., Schröder, D.: Sanitizable signatures: How to partially delegate control for authenticated data. In: Proceedings of BIOSIG. LNI, vol. 155, pp. 117–128. GI (2009)
19. Brzuska, C., Fischlin, M., Lehmann, A., Schröder, D.: Unlinkability of sanitizable signatures. In: Nguyen, P.Q., Pointcheval, D. (eds.) PKC 2010. LNCS, vol. 6056, pp. 444–461. Springer, Heidelberg (2010)
20. Gong, J., Qian, H., Zhou, Y.: Fully-secure and practical sanitizable signatures. In: Lai, X., Yung, M., Lin, D. (eds.) Inscrypt 2010. LNCS, vol. 6584, pp. 300–317. Springer, Heidelberg (2011)
21. Lai, J., Ding, X., Wu, Y.: Accountable trapdoor sanitizable signatures. In: Deng, R.H., Feng, T. (eds.) ISPEC 2013. LNCS, vol. 7863, pp. 117–131. Springer, Heidelberg (2013)
22. de Meer, H., Pöhls, H.C., Posegga, J., Samelin, K.: On the relation between redactable and sanitizable signature schemes. In: Jürjens, J., Piessens, F., Bielova, N. (eds.) ESSoS 2014. LNCS, vol. 8364, pp. 113–130. Springer, Heidelberg (2014)
23. Pöhls, H.C., Peters, S., Samelin, K., Posegga, J., de Meer, H.: Malleable signatures for resource constrained platforms. In: Cavallaro, L., Gollmann, D. (eds.) WISTP 2013. LNCS, vol. 7886, pp. 18–33. Springer, Heidelberg (2013)
24. Chang, E.-C., Lim, C.L., Xu, J.: Short redactable signatures using random trees. In: Fischlin, M. (ed.) CT-RSA 2009. LNCS, vol. 5473, pp. 133–147. Springer, Heidelberg (2009)
25. Samelin, K., Pöhls, H.C., Bilzhause, A., Posegga, J., de Meer, H.: Redactable signatures for independent removal of structure and content. In: Ryan, M.D., Smyth, B., Wang, G. (eds.) ISPEC 2012. LNCS, vol. 7232, pp. 17–33. Springer, Heidelberg (2012)

26. Brzuska, C., et al.: Redactable signatures for tree-structured data: definitions and constructions. In: Zhou, J., Yung, M. (eds.) ACNS 2010. LNCS, vol. 6123, pp. 87–104. Springer, Heidelberg (2010)

27. Haber, S., Hatano, Y., Honda, Y., Horne, W.G., Miyazaki, K., Sander, T., Tezoku, S., Yao, D.: Efficient signature schemes supporting redaction, pseudonymization, and data deidentification. In: ASIACCS, pp. 353–362 (2008)

28. Ahn, J.H., Boneh, D., Camenisch, J., Hohenberger, S., Shelat, A., Waters, B.: Computing on authenticated data. ePrint Report 2011/096 (2011)

29. Attrapadung, N., Libert, B., Peters, T.: Computing on authenticated data: new privacy definitions and constructions. In: Wang, X., Sako, K. (eds.) ASIACRYPT 2012. LNCS, vol. 7658, pp. 367–385. Springer, Heidelberg (2012)

30. Attrapadung, N., Libert, B., Peters, T.: Efficient completely context-hiding quotable and linearly homomorphic signatures. In: Kurosawa, K., Hanaoka, G. (eds.) PKC 2013. LNCS, vol. 7778, pp. 386–404. Springer, Heidelberg (2013)

31. Backes, M., Meiser, S., Schröder, D.: Delegatable functional signatures. IACR Cryptology ePrint Archive 2013, 408 (2013)

32. Boneh, D., Freeman, D.M.: Homomorphic signatures for polynomial functions. In: Paterson, K.G. (ed.) EUROCRYPT 2011. LNCS, vol. 6632, pp. 149–168. Springer, Heidelberg (2011)

33. Boyle, E., Goldwasser, S., Ivan, I.: Functional signatures and pseudorandom functions. IACR Cryptology ePrint Archive 2013, 401 (2013)

34. Samelin, K., Pöhls, H.C., Bilzhause, A., Posegga, J., de Meer, H.: On structural signatures for tree data structures. In: Bao, F., Samarati, P., Zhou, J. (eds.) ACNS 2012. LNCS, vol. 7341, pp. 171–187. Springer, Heidelberg (2012)

35. Gottlob, G., Koch, C., Pichler, R.: The complexity of XPath query evaluation. In: Symposium on Principles of Database Systems, PODS, pp. 179–190. ACM, New York (2003)

36. Barić, N., Pfitzmann, B.: Collision-free accumulators and fail-stop signature schemes without trees. In: Fumy, W. (ed.) EUROCRYPT 1997. LNCS, vol. 1233, pp. 480–494. Springer, Heidelberg (1997)

37. Benaloh, J.C., de Mare, M.: One-way accumulators: a decentralized alternative to digital signatures (extended abstract). In: Helleseth, T. (ed.) EUROCRYPT 1993. LNCS, vol. 765, pp. 274–285. Springer, Heidelberg (1994)

38. Goldwasser, S., Micali, S., Rivest, R.L.: A digital signature scheme secure against adaptive chosen-message attacks. SIAM JoC 17, 281–308 (1988)

39. Goldwasser, S., Micali, S.: Probabilistic encryption. J. Comput. Syst. Sci. 28, 270–299 (1984)

40. Lipmaa, H.: Secure accumulators from euclidean rings without trusted setup. In: Bao, F., Samarati, P., Zhou, J. (eds.) ACNS 2012. LNCS, vol. 7341, pp. 224–240. Springer, Heidelberg (2012)

41. Sander, T.: Efficient accumulators without trapdoor extended abstract. In: Varadharajan, V., Mu, Y. (eds.) ICICS 1999. LNCS, vol. 1726, pp. 252–262. Springer, Heidelberg (1999)

42. Camenisch, J., Lysyanskaya, A.: Dynamic accumulators and application to efficient revocation of anonymous credentials. In: Yung, M. (ed.) CRYPTO 2002. LNCS, vol. 2442, pp. 61–76. Springer, Heidelberg (2002)

43. Buldas, A., Laud, P., Lipmaa, H.: Accountable certificate management using undeniable attestations. In: ACM Conference on Computer and Communications Security, pp. 9–17 (2000)

44. Nyberg, K.: Fast accumulated hashing. In: Gollmann, D. (ed.) FSE 1996. LNCS, vol. 1039, pp. 83–87. Springer, Heidelberg (1996)
45. de Meer, H., Liedel, M., Pöhls, H.C., Posegga, J., Samelin, K.: Indistinguishability of one-way accumulators. Technical report MIP-1210, University of Passau (2012)
46. Hirose, S., Kuwakado, H.: Redactable signature scheme for tree-structured data based on merkle tree. In: SECRYPT, pp. 313–320 (2013)
47. Brzuska, C., Pöhls, H.C., Samelin, K.: Non-interactive public accountability for sanitizable signatures. In: De Capitani di Vimercati, S., Mitchell, C. (eds.) EuroPKI 2012. LNCS, vol. 7868, pp. 178–193. Springer, Heidelberg (2013)
48. Brzuska, C., Pöhls, H.C., Samelin, K.: Efficient and perfectly unlinkable sanitizable signatures without group signatures. In: Katsikas, S., Agudo, I. (eds.) EuroPKI 2013. LNCS, vol. 8341, pp. 12–30. Springer, Heidelberg (2014)

Encryption Schemes Secure Against Profiling Adversaries

Sandra Díaz-Santiago$^{(\boxtimes)}$ and Debrup Chakraborty

Department of Computer Science, CINVESTAV IPN,
Av. Instituto Politécnico Nacional No. 2508,
Col. San Pedro Zacatenco, 07360 Mexico, D.F., Mexico
sdiaz@computacion.cs.cinvestav.mx, debrup@cs.cinvestav.mx

Abstract. A profiling adversary is an adversary which aims to classify messages into pre-defined profiles and thus gain useful information regarding the sender or receiver of such messages. User profiling has gained lot of importance today, this activity supports the big business of online advertising at the cost of user privacy. Usual chosen-plaintext secure encryption schemes are capable of securing information from profilers, but these schemes provide more security than required for this purpose. In this paper we study the requirements for an encryption algorithm to be secure only against profilers and finally give a precise notion of security for such schemes. We also present a full protocol for secure (against profiling adversaries) communication, which neither requires a key exchange nor a public key infrastructure. Our protocol guarantees security against non-human profilers and is constructed using CAPTCHAs and secret sharing schemes. The security notions developed in this paper are also further used to analyze an existing scheme meant for providing security against profilers.

Keywords: Data encryption · Profiling adversary · User profiling · CAPTCHA · Secret sharing

1 Introduction

Informally a spam email is an email which is not of interest to the receiver. Everyday almost every one of us finds hundreds of such spam emails waiting in our in-boxes. A spammer (who sends spam emails) generally has a business motive and most spam emails try to advertise a product, a web-page or a service. If the spam emails can be sent in a directed manner, i.e., if a spammer can send a specific advertisement to a user who would be interested in it, then the motive of the spammer would be successful to a large extent. Thus, one of the important objectives of a spammer would be to know the preferences or interests of the users to whom it is sending the un-solicited messages.

Sandra Díaz-Santiago is on academic leave from Escuela Superior de Cómputo (ESCOM-IPN), Av. Juan de Dios Bátiz, Col. Lindavista, México D.F. 07738, México.

© Springer-Verlag Berlin Heidelberg 2014
M.S. Obaidat and J. Filipe (Eds.): ICETE 2012, CCIS 455, pp. 172–191, 2014.
DOI: 10.1007/978-3-662-44791-8_11

In today's connected world we do a lot of communication through emails and it is not un-realistic to assume that a collection of email messages which originate from a specific user U carries information about the preferences and interests of U. Based on this assumption a spammer can collect email information originating from different users and based on these emails try to make a profile of each user (based on their preferences or interests), and later use this profile for directed spamming.

Here we assume that given a message space an adversary aims to map each message in the message space into certain classes of its interest. Using this classification of messages the adversary can try to conclude which user is associated with which class and this is expected to reveal information regarding the profile of a given user. Thus, in the scenario of our interest we consider an adversary that classifies messages into pre-defined classes. Such an adversary would be further called as a profiler.

Other than directed spamming, there may be other motives for user profiling. Currently there has been a paradigm shift in the way products are advertised in the internet. In one of the popular new paradigm of *online behavioral advertising* (OBA) [17], internet advertising companies display advertisements specific to user preferences. This requires profiling the users. To support this big business of internet advertising, innovative techniques for user profiling have also developed. It is known that some internet service providers perform a procedure called *deep packet inspection* on all traffic to detect malware etc., but this technique has been used to generate user profiles from the information contents of the packets received or sent by an user, and this information is later sold to advertising companies [17]. This currently has led to many policy related debates, and it has been asked whether such practices should be legally allowed [12].

In the context of emails, a solution to the problem of profiling attacks would be encrypting the communications so that the contents of the emails are not available to the profiler. Or to make the communications anonymous so that given a message it would not be possible for a profiler to trace the origin of the message. In this paper we ask the following question: What would be the exact security requirements for an encryption scheme which can protect the communication from profilers? Intuitively a cipher obtained from a secure encryption algorithm should not reveal any information regarding the plaintext which was used to produce the cipher. Hence, a secure encryption algorithm should surely resist attacks by profilers. But, as the goal of a profiler is only to classify the messages, it is possible that an encryption algorithm which provides security in a weaker sense would be enough to resist profilers. We explore in this direction and try to fix the appropriate security definition of an encryption scheme which would provide security against profilers.

Using any encryption scheme involves the complicated machinery of key exchange (for symmetric encryption) or a public key infrastructure (for asymmetric encryption). When the goal is just to protect information against profilers the heavy machinery of key exchange or public key infrastructure may be unnecessary. Keeping in mind security against profilers we propose a new protocol which does not require explicit key exchange. To do this we use the notion of CAPTCHAs, which are programs that can distinguish between humans and machines by automated Turing tests which are easy for humans to pass but difficult for any machine. The use of CAPTCHAs makes our protocol secure from non-human profilers, but the protocol is still vulnerable to human adversaries. In the context that we see the activity of profiling, it would be only profitable if a large number of users can be profiled and this goal seems to be infeasible if human profilers are employed for the task.

To our knowledge the only prior work on the issue of securing email communication from profilers have been reported by Golle and Farahat in [6]. In [6] it was pointed out that an encryption scheme secure against profilers can be much weaker than normal encryption algorithms, and thus using a normal encryption algorithm can be an overkill. The solution in [6] hides the semantic of the plaintext by converting an English text into another English text with the help of a key. In their protocol also they do not need explicit key exchange or a public key infrastructure. The key is derived from the email header by using a hash function with a specific property. The hash function they use is a "slow one-way hash function", which was first proposed in [4]. Such hash functions are difficult to compute, i.e., may take a few seconds to get computed and are hard to invert. This high computational cost for the hash function prevents a profiler to derive the key for a large number of messages. Our method is fundamentally different from [6] in its use of CAPTCHAs. Slow hash functions which were proposed long ago have not seen much use, and its suitability is not well tested. But CAPTCHAs are ubiquitous in today's world and had been used successfully in diverse applications. Also, our work presents a theoretical analysis of the problem, and provides the security definitions which to our knowledge is new to the literature.

Golle and Farahat [6] did not present a security analysis of their proposed scheme. We provide a formal security analysis of their scheme and point out the exact assumptions required for the hash function used in their protocol. This analysis uses the security definitions proposed in this work.

The rest of the paper is organized as follows. In Sect. 2 we describe basic concepts related to indistinguishability, CAPTCHA and secret sharing. In Sect. 3 we present a formal definition of a profiling adversary and security against such adversaries. In Sects. 4 and 5 we describe our protocols and argue regarding their security in terms of the security notion given in Sect. 3. In Sect. 6, we revisit the scheme in [6], and give some preliminary arguments regarding its security in accordance with our definitions and security notions. We conclude the paper in Sect. 7 where we discuss about the limitations of our approach and some future directions.

2   Preliminaries

2.1   Notations

The set of all n bit strings would be denoted by $\{0, 1\}^n$. For a string x, $|x|$ will denote the length of x and for a finite set A, $|A|$ would denote the cardinality of A. For a finite set S, $x \xleftarrow{\$} S$ will denote x to be an element selected uniformly at random from S. In what follows, by an adversary we shall mean a probabilistic algorithm which outputs an integer or a bit. $\mathcal{A}(x, y) \Rightarrow b$, will denote the fact that an adversary $\mathcal{A}$ given inputs x, y outputs b. In general an adversary would have other sorts of interactions, maybe with other adversaries and/or algorithms before it outputs, these would be clear from the context. In what follows by $E : \mathcal{K} \times \mathcal{M} \to \mathcal{C}$ would denote an encryption scheme with $\mathcal{K}$, $\mathcal{M}$, $\mathcal{C}$ as the key space, message space and cipher space respectively. For $m \in \mathcal{M}$ and $k \in \mathcal{K}$ we shall usually write $E_k(m)$ instead of $E(k, m)$.

2.2   Indistinguishability in the Presence of an Eavesdropper

Security of encryption schemes is best defined in terms of indistinguishability. Here we consider indistinguishability in presence of an eavesdropping adversary. This security notion, which we call as IND-EAV security, is defined with the help of interaction between two entities called an adversary and a challenger. It considers that an adversary chooses a pair of plaintext messages and then ask for the encryption of those messages to the challenger. The challenger provides the adversary with the encryption of one of the messages chosen by the adversary. The adversary is considered to be successful if it can correctly guess which message of its choice was encrypted. More formally, to define the security of an encryption algorithm $E : \mathcal{K} \times \mathcal{M} \to \mathcal{C}$, we consider the interaction of an adversary $\mathcal{A}$ with a challenger in the experiment below:

Experiment Exp-IND-EAV$^{\mathcal{A}}$
1. The challenger selects K uniformly at random from $\mathcal{K}$.
2. The adversary $\mathcal{A}$ selects two messages $m_0, m_1 \in \mathcal{M}$, such that $|m_0| = |m_1|$.
3. The challenger selects a bit b uniformly at random from $\{0, 1\}$, and returns
   $c \leftarrow E_K(m_b)$ to $\mathcal{A}$.
4. The adversary $\mathcal{A}$ outputs a bit b'.
5. If $b = b'$ output 1 else output 0.

Definition 1. *Let $E : \mathcal{K} \times \mathcal{M} \to \mathcal{C}$ be an encryption scheme. The* IND-EAV *advantage of an adversary $\mathcal{A}$ in breaking E is defined as*

$$\mathbf{Adv}_E^{\text{ind-eav}}(\mathcal{A}) = \Pr[\text{Exp-IND-EAV}^{\mathcal{A}} \Rightarrow 1] - \frac{1}{2}.$$

Moreover, E is (ϵ, t) IND-EAV secure if for all adversaries $\mathcal{A}$ running for time at most t, $\mathbf{Adv}_E^{\text{ind-eav}}(\mathcal{A}) \leq \epsilon$. $\Diamond$

The IND-EAV security as defined above is used only for one time encryption and it is different from the most used security notion for symmetric encryption which is indistinguishability under chosen plaintext attack (IND-CPA). In an IND-CPA attack the adversary is given access to the encryption oracle and thus can consult this oracle before it chooses the messages, and has the option of asking encryption of multiple pairs of messages before it outputs. IND-EAV notion is strictly weaker than the IND-CPA notion of security. All IND-CPA secure encryption schemes are also IND-EAV secure.

A related notion of security is that of semantic security. Informally a symmetric encryption scheme is called semantically secure if an adversary is unable to compute any function on the plaintext given a ciphertext.

Definition 2. *Let $E : \mathcal{K} \times \mathcal{M} \to \mathcal{C}$ be an encryption scheme. E is called (ϵ, t) SEM-EAV secure, if for all functions f and for all adversaries running for time at most t*

$$| \Pr[\mathcal{A}(E_K(x)) \Rightarrow f(x)] - \max_{\mathcal{A}'} \Pr[\mathcal{A}'(.) \Rightarrow f(x)]| \leq \epsilon \qquad (1)$$

where the running time of $\mathcal{A}'$ is polynomially related to t, and x is chosen uniformly at random from $\mathcal{M}$.   ◇

Note, in the above definition, by $\mathcal{A}'(.)$ we mean that the adversary is given no input, i.e., $\mathcal{A}'$ is trying to predict $f(x)$ without seeing $E_K(x)$. And in the second term of Eq. (1) the maximum is taken over all adversaries $\mathcal{A}'$ which runs for time at most $poly(t)$, for some polynomial $poly()$. Thus, if E is SEM-EAV secure then no adversary can do better in predicting $f(x)$ from $E_K(x)$ than an adversary who does so without seeing $E_K(x)$. It is well known that IND-EAV security implies SEM-EAV security (for example see Claim 3.11 in [10]).

2.3   CAPTCHA

A CAPTCHA is a computer program designed to differentiate a human being from a computer. The fundamental ideas for such a program were first proposed in an unpublished paper [11] and then these ideas were formalized in [18], where the name CAPTCHA was first proposed. CAPTCHA stands for *Completely Automated Public Turing test to tell Computers and Humans Apart*. In fact, a CAPTCHA is a test which is easy to pass by a human user but hard to pass by a machine. One of the most common CAPTCHAs are distorted images of short strings. For a human it is generally very easy to recover the original string from the distorted image, but it is difficult for state of the art character recognition algorithms to recover the original string from the distorted image. Other types of CAPTCHAs which depend on problems of speech recognition, object detection, classification etc. have also been developed.

Recently CAPTCHAs have been used in many different scenarios for identification of humans, like in chat rooms, online polls etc. Also they can be used to prevent dictionary attacks on the password based systems [14], and more recently for key establishment [5].

A CAPTCHA is a randomized algorithm G, which given a input string from a set of strings STR produces the CAPTCHA $G(x)$. A CAPTCHA G is called (α, β) secure, if for any human or legitimate solver S

$$\Pr[x \xleftarrow{\$} \text{STR} : S(G(x)) \Rightarrow x] \geq \alpha,$$

and for any efficient machine C

$$\Pr[x \xleftarrow{\$} \text{STR} : C(G(x)) \Rightarrow x] \leq \beta,$$

For a CAPTCHA to be secure it is required that there is a large gap between α and β. In Sect. 4, we will propose an alternative security definition for CAPTCHAs.

2.4 Secret Sharing Schemes

A secret sharing scheme is a method designed to share a secret between a group of participants. These schemes were first proposed by Shamir in 1979 [16]. Although there have been improvements to these kind of schemes, here we will use the basic construction due to Shamir. In a (u, w) threshold secret sharing scheme a secret K is divided into w pieces called *shares*. These w shares are given to w participants. To recover the secret, at least $u \leq w$ of the w shares are required. And it is not possible to recover the secret with less than u shares.

We describe a specific construction proposed by Shamir. To construct a (u, w) secret sharing scheme we need a prime $p \geq w + 1$ and the operations take place in the field $\mathbb{Z}_p$. The procedure for splitting a secret K into w parts is depicted in the algorithm below:

SHARE$_{u,w}^p(K)$
1. Choose w distinct, non-zero elements of $\mathbb{Z}_p$, denote them as x_i, $1 \leq i \leq w$.
2. Choose $u - 1$ elements of $\mathbb{Z}_p$ independently at random. Denote them as $a_1, \ldots, a_{u-1}$.
3. Let, $a(x) = K + \sum_{j=1}^{u-1} a_j x^j \bmod p$, and $y_i = a(x_i)$, $1 \leq i \leq w$.
4. Output $\mathcal{S} = \{(x_1, y_1), \ldots, (x_w, y_w)\}$ as the set of w shares.

The secret K can be easily recovered using any $B \subset \mathcal{S}$ such that $|B| \geq u$, but if $|B| < u$ then K cannot be recovered. To see this, observe that the polynomial used in step 3 to compute the y_is is a $u - 1$ degree polynomial. Thus using u pairs of the type (x_i, y_i) one can generate u linear equations, each of the type $y_i = K + a_1 x_i + \cdots a_{u-1} x_i^{u-1}$. Using these equations the value of K can be found. It can be shown that this set of u equations would always have a unique solution.

3   Profiling Adversaries

Let $\mathcal{M}$ be a message space and $\mathcal{P} = \{1, 2, \ldots, k\}$ be a set of labels for different possible profiles. We assume that each message x in $\mathcal{M}$ can be labeled by a unique $j \in \mathcal{P}$. Thus, there exists a function $f : \mathcal{M} \to \mathcal{P}$, which assigns a label to each message in the message space. In other words, we can assume that the message space can be partitioned into disjoint subsets as $\mathcal{M} = M_1 \cup M_2 \cup \cdots \cup M_k$ and for every $x \in \mathcal{M}$, $f(x) = i$ if and only if $x \in M_i$.

We call f as the profiling function or a classifier. Thus, in this setting we are assuming that each message in the message space $\mathcal{M}$ represents some profile, and messages in $M_i (1 \leq i \leq k)$ correspond to the profile i. The function f is a classifier which given a message can classify it into one of the profiles. We also assume that the function f is efficiently computable for every $x \in \mathcal{M}$, in particular, we assume that for any $x \in \mathcal{M}$, $f(x)$ can be computed in time at most μ, where μ is a constant.

The function f is public, thus given $x \in \mathcal{M}$ any adversary can efficiently compute $f(x)$. We want to define security for an encryption scheme which is secure against profiling adversaries, i.e., we want that when a message from $\mathcal{M}$ is encrypted using the encryption algorithm no efficient adversary would be able to profile it.

3.1   PROF-EAV Security

Here we propose a definition for encryption schemes secure against profiling adversaries.

Definition 3 [PROF-EAV Security]. *Let $\mathcal{M}$ be a message space and $f : \mathcal{M} \to \mathcal{P}$ be a profiling function. Let $E : \mathcal{M} \times \mathcal{K} \to \mathcal{C}$ be an encryption algorithm. We define the advantage of an adversary $\mathcal{A}$ in the PROF-EAV (read profiling under eavesdropping) sense in breaking E as*

$$\mathbf{Adv}_{E,f}^{\text{prof-eav}}(\mathcal{A}) = \Pr[\mathcal{A}(E_K(x)) \Rightarrow f(x)] - \max_{\mathcal{A}'} \Pr[\mathcal{A}'(.) \Rightarrow f(x)],$$

where $K \xleftarrow{\$} \mathcal{K}$, $x \xleftarrow{\$} \mathcal{M}$ and $\mathcal{A}'$ is an adversary whose running time is a polynomial of the running time of $\mathcal{A}$. An encryption algorithm $E : \mathcal{M} \times \mathcal{K} \to \mathcal{C}$ is called (ϵ, t) PROF-EAV secure for a given profiling function f, if for all adversaries $\mathcal{A}$ running in time at most t, $\mathbf{Adv}_{E,f}^{\text{prof-eav}}(\mathcal{A}) \leq \epsilon$. $\diamond$

In the definition above, we want to capture the notion that for a PROF-EAV secure encryption scheme, an adversary $\mathcal{A}$ trying to find the profile of a message seeing its cipher cannot do much better than the best adversary $\mathcal{A}'$, who tries to guess the profile without seeing the ciphertext.

This definition is in accordance with the definition of semantic security as discussed in Sect. 2.2. Recall that an encryption scheme is called semantically secure if no adversary can efficiently compute *any* function of the plaintext given its ciphertext. But in the PROF-EAV definition we are interested only on a specific function f. Thus, PROF-EAV security is strictly weaker than semantic security. Semantic security trivially implies PROF-EAV security but PROF-EAV security does not imply IND-EAV security, we give a concrete example to illustrate this.

Example 1. Let $\mathcal{M} = \{0,1\}^n = M_1 \cup M_2$ be a message space, where

$$M_1 = \{x \in \mathcal{M} : \text{first bit of } x \text{ is } 0\},$$

and $M_2 = \mathcal{M} \setminus M_1$, and f be the profiling function such that $f(x) = i$ iff $x \in M_i$. Let E^{one} be an encryption scheme which uses a one bit key k (chosen uniformly from $\{0,1\}$) and given a message $x \in \mathcal{M}$ it xors k with the first bit of x. It is easy to see that an adversary trying to guess the profile of a message x given $E_k^{\text{one}}(x)$ cannot do better than with probability half, and this success probability can be achieved even without seeing the ciphertext, as here $|M_1| = |M_2|$. Hence E^{one} is PROF-EAV secure, but trivially not secure in the IND-EAV sense.

4 Encryption Protocol Secure Against Profiling Adversaries

In this section we describe a complete protocol which would be secure against profiling adversaries. As mentioned in the introduction here we care about adversaries who are not humans. Our motivation is to prevent communications getting profiled in large scale mechanically. The protocol is not secure from human adversaries, and we do not care much about that as we hope that it would be economically infeasible to employ a human for large scale profiling.

The protocol $\mathbb{P}$ consists of the following entities:

- The message space $\mathcal{M}$, the cipher space $\mathcal{C}$.
- The set of profiles $\mathcal{P}$ and the profiling function f associated with $\mathcal{M}$.
- A set STR which consists of short strings over a specified alphabet.
- An encryption scheme $E : \mathcal{K} \times \mathcal{M} \to \mathcal{C}$.
- A hash function $H : \text{STR} \to \mathcal{K}$.
- A CAPTCHA generator G which takes inputs from STR.

Protocol $\mathbb{P}(x)$
1. $k \xleftarrow{\$} \text{STR}$;
2. $k' \leftarrow G(k)$;
3. $K \leftarrow H(k)$;
4. $c \leftarrow E_K(x)$;
5. **return** (c, k')

Fig. 1. The protocol $\mathbb{P}$.

Given a message $x \in \mathcal{M}$, $\mathbb{P}$ produces a ciphertext as shown in Fig. 1. In the protocol as described in Fig. 1, k, an element of STR is hashed to form the key K and k is also converted into a CAPTCHA and transmitted along with the ciphertext. The only input to $\mathbb{P}$ is the message and the key generation is embedded in the protocol. It resembles the scenario of hybrid encryption [1], which consists of two mechanisms called key encapsulation and data encapsulation where an encrypted version of the key is also transmitted along with the cipher. For a human decryption is easy, as given a ciphertext (c, k') a human user can recover k from k' by solving the CAPTCHA and thus compute $E^{-1}_{H(k)}(c)$ to decipher.

4.1   Security of $\mathbb{P}$

The security of a protocol $\mathbb{P}$ against profilers is defined in the same way as in Definition 3.

Definition 4 [PROF Security]. *The advantage of an adversary attacking protocol $\mathbb{P}$ is defined as*

$$\mathbf{Adv}^{prof}_{\mathbb{P},f}(\mathcal{A}) = \Pr[\mathcal{A}(\mathbb{P}(x)) \Rightarrow f(x)] - \max_{\mathcal{A}'} \Pr[\mathcal{A}'(.) \Rightarrow f(x)],$$

where $x \xleftarrow{\$} \mathcal{M}$ and $\mathcal{A}'$ is an adversary whose running time is a polynomial of the running time of $\mathcal{A}$. Additionally $\mathbb{P}$ is called (ϵ, t) secure in the PROF sense if for all adversaries running in time at most t, $\mathbf{Adv}^{prof}_{\mathbb{P},f}(\mathcal{A}) < \epsilon$.   ◇

The above definition is different from Definition 3 by the fact that it does not mention the key explicitly, as key generation is embedded in the protocol itself. To prove that $\mathbb{P}$ is secure in the PROF sense we need an assumption regarding the CAPTCHA G and the hash function H. We state this next.

Definition 5 [The Hash-Captcha Assumption]. *Let G be a CAPTCHA generator, let r be a number, let $H : \mathsf{STR} \rightarrow \{0,1\}^r$ be a hash function, and let $\mathcal{A}$ be an adversary. We define the advantage of $\mathcal{A}$ in violating the Hash-Captcha assumption as*

$$\mathbf{Adv}^{hc}_{G,H}(\mathcal{A}) = \Pr[x \xleftarrow{\$} \mathsf{STR} : \mathcal{A}(G(x), H(x)) \Rightarrow 1]$$
$$- \Pr[x \xleftarrow{\$} \mathsf{STR}, z \xleftarrow{\$} \{0,1\}^r : \mathcal{A}(G(x), z) \Rightarrow 1].$$

Moreover, (G, H) is called (ϵ, t) HC secure if for all adversaries $\mathcal{A}$ running in time at most t, $\mathbf{Adv}^{hc}_{G,H}(\mathcal{A}) \leq \epsilon$.   ◇

This definition says that the pair formed by a CAPTCHA generator G and a hash function H is secure, if an adversary $\mathcal{A}$ is unable to distinguish between a $(G(x), H(x))$, where x is some string, and $(G(x), z)$, where z is a random string. This security notion of a CAPTCHA inspired by the notion of *indistinguishability* is quite different from the (α, β) security notion as described in Sect. 2.3. Here the adversary has some more information regarding x through the value $H(x)$.

If the adversary can efficiently solve the CAPTCHA G then it can break (G, H) in the HC sense irrespective of the hash function. Given the CAPTCHA is secure, i.e., no efficient adversary can find x from $G(x)$ still an adversary may be able to distinguish $H(x)$ from a string randomly selected from the range of H.

If we consider a keyed family of hash functions $\mathcal{H} = \{H_\ell\}_{\ell \in \mathcal{L}}$, such that for every $\ell \in \mathcal{L}$, $H_\ell : \mathcal{D} \to \mathcal{R}$ for some sets $\mathcal{D}$ and $\mathcal{R}$. Then $\mathcal{H}$ is called an entropy smoothing family if for any efficient adversary it is difficult to distinguish between $(\ell, H_\ell(x))$ and (ℓ, z), where ℓ, x, z are selected uniformly at random from $\mathcal{L}$, $\mathcal{D}$ and $\mathcal{R}$ respectively. An entropy smoothing hash along with a secure captcha can resist HC attacks. Entropy smoothing hashes can be constructed from universal hash functions using the left over hash lemma [8], but the parameter sizes which would be required for such provable guarantees can be prohibitive. We believe that using ad-hoc cryptographic hashes like the ones from the SHA family can provide the same security. In our definition we do not use a keyed family of hash functions, but such a family can be easily used in the protocol $\mathbb{P}$, and in that case the hash key will also be a part of the ciphertext.

With these discussions we are now ready to state the theorem about security of $\mathbb{P}$.

Theorem 1. *Let $\mathbb{P}$ be a protocol as in Fig. 1 and $\mathcal{A}$ is an adversary attacking $\mathbb{P}$ in the PROF sense. Then there exist adversaries $\mathcal{B}$ and $\mathcal{B}'$ such that*

$$\mathbf{Adv}_{\mathbb{P}, f}^{\mathrm{prof}}(\mathcal{A}) \leq \mathbf{Adv}_{G, H}^{\mathrm{hc}}(\mathcal{B}) + \mathbf{Adv}_{E, f}^{\mathrm{prof\text{-}eav}}(\mathcal{B}').$$

And, if $\mathcal{A}$ runs for time t, both $\mathcal{B}$ and $\mathcal{B}'$ runs for time $O(t)$.

Proof. Let $\mathcal{A}$ be an adversary attacking the protocol $\mathbb{P}$ in Fig. 1. We construct an adversary $\mathcal{B}$ attacking the hash-captcha (G, H), using $\mathcal{A}$ as follows.

Adversary $\mathcal{B}(G(k), z)$
1. $x \xleftarrow{\$} \mathcal{M}$;
2. Send $(E_z(x), G(k))$ to $\mathcal{A}$;
3. $\mathcal{A}$ returns j;
4. **if** $f(x) = j$;
5.   **return** 1;
6. **else return** 0;

As $\mathcal{B}$ is an adversary attacking the hash-captcha assumption, hence there are two possibilities regarding the input $(G(k), z)$ of $\mathcal{B}$, z can either be $H(k)$ or a uniform random element in $\mathcal{K}$, and the goal of $\mathcal{B}$ is to distinguish between these two possibilities.

Considering the first possibility that z is $H(k)$, the way the adversary $\mathcal{B}$ is defined, $\mathcal{A}$ gets a valid encryption of the message x (which is a random element in the message space) according to the protocol $\mathbb{P}$. Hence we have

$$\Pr[k \xleftarrow{\$} \mathcal{K} : \mathcal{B}(G(k), H(k)) \Rightarrow 1]$$
$$= \Pr[k \xleftarrow{\$} \mathcal{K}, x \xleftarrow{\$} \mathcal{M} : \mathcal{A}(E_{H(k)}(x), G(k)) \Rightarrow f(x)]$$
$$= \Pr[x \xleftarrow{\$} \mathcal{M} : \mathcal{A}(\mathbb{P}(x)) \Rightarrow f(x)]. \tag{2}$$

Similarly, for the second possibility, i.e., when the input z to $\mathcal{B}$ is an element chosen uniformly at random from $\mathcal{K}$, we have

$$\Pr[k, K \xleftarrow{\$} \mathcal{K} : \mathcal{B}(G(k), K) \Rightarrow 1]$$
$$= \Pr[x \xleftarrow{\$} \mathcal{M} : \mathcal{A}(E_K(x), G(k)) \Rightarrow f(x)]. \tag{3}$$

In Eq. (3), k and K are chosen independently uniformly at random from $\mathcal{K}$. Thus, the adversary $\mathcal{A}$ has as input $E_K(x)$ and $G(k)$, where k is independent of K, thus $G(k)$ carries no information about K. Hence $\mathcal{A}$ cannot do better than some PROF-EAV adversary $\mathcal{B}'$ who has only $E_K(x)$ as its input, and runs for same time as that of $\mathcal{A}$. Thus

$$\Pr[x \xleftarrow{\$} \mathcal{M} : \mathcal{A}(E_K(x), G(k)) \Rightarrow f(x)]$$
$$\leq \Pr[x \xleftarrow{\$} \mathcal{M} : \mathcal{B}'(E_K(x)) \Rightarrow f(x)] \tag{4}$$

From definition of PROF-EAV advantage of $\mathcal{B}'$ we have

$$\Pr[x \xleftarrow{\$} \mathcal{M} : \mathcal{B}'(E_K(x)) \Rightarrow f(x)]$$
$$= \mathbf{Adv}_{E,f}^{\text{prof-eav}}(\mathcal{B}') + \max_{\mathcal{A}'} \Pr[\mathcal{A}'(.) \Rightarrow f(x)] \tag{5}$$

Thus, using Eqs. (3), (4) and (5) we have

$$\Pr[k, K \xleftarrow{\$} \mathcal{K} : \mathcal{B}(G(k), K) \Rightarrow 1]$$
$$\leq \mathbf{Adv}_{E,f}^{\text{prof-eav}}(\mathcal{B}') + \max_{\mathcal{A}'} \Pr[\mathcal{A}'(.) \Rightarrow f(x)] \tag{6}$$

Finally, from Eqs. (2) and (6) and Definitions 5 and 4 we have

$$\mathbf{Adv}_{\mathbb{P},f}^{\text{prof}}(\mathcal{A}) \leq \mathbf{Adv}_{G,H}^{\text{hc}}(\mathcal{B}) + \mathbf{Adv}_{E,f}^{\text{prof-eav}}(\mathcal{B}'),$$

as desired. Also if $\mathcal{A}$ runs for time t, then $\mathcal{B}'$ runs for time t and $\mathcal{B}$ runs for time $t + c$ for some small constant c. $\qquad \square$

Some Remarks about Security of $\mathbb{P}$. We defined the security of the protocol $\mathbb{P}$ only a fixed profiling function f, but note that we can modify the definition for any arbitrary function f which would give us a security definition equivalent to SEM-EAV (discussed in Sect. 2.2). If the encryption algorithm E used within the protocol is SEM-EAV secure then using the same proof we can obtain SEM-EAV security for $\mathbb{P}$.

5   A Practical Instantiation

A very common problem using CAPTCHAs is that sometimes even humans may fail to solve them. As in the protocol $\mathbb{P}$ if a human user fails to solve the CAPTCHA then (s)he will not be able to decipher and there is no way to repeat the test (as is done in normal CAPTCHA usage), hence this stands as a serious weakness of the proposed protocol $\mathbb{P}$. A solution to this problem can be attempted by providing some redundancy in the CAPTCHAs so that a valid user can have more chance in solving the CAPTCHA. As a solution we propose that the initial string k chosen by the protocol is broken into w shares such that with u or more of the shares would be enough to generate k. These w shares are converted into CAPTCHAs and sent along with the ciphertext. To incorporate this idea we changed the initial protocol $\mathbb{P}$ to $\mathbb{P}'$. The protocol $\mathbb{P}'$ is a specific instantiation, thus before we describe the protocol we fix some details of its components, in particular for $\mathbb{P}'$ we would require an encoding mechanism ENCD which we discuss first.

Let $\mathsf{AL} = \{A, B, \ldots, Z\} \cup \{a, b, \ldots, z\} \cup \{0, 1, \ldots, 9\} \cup \{+, /\}$, thus making $|\mathsf{AL}| = 64$. We define an arbitrary (but fixed) bijection $\rho : \mathsf{AL} \to \{0, 1, \ldots, 63\}$, and for any $\sigma \in \mathsf{AL}$ and $n \geq 6$, $\mathsf{bin}_n(\sigma)$ will denote the n bit binary representation of $\rho(\sigma)$. Note that for all $\sigma \in \mathsf{AL}$, at most 6 bits are required to represent $\rho(\sigma)$. If ψ is a binary string, then let $\mathsf{toInt}(\psi)$ be the positive integer corresponding to ψ, similarly for a positive integer $v < 2^n$, $\mathsf{toBin}_n(v)$ denotes the n bit binary representation of v. We fix a positive integer m and let STR be the set of all m character strings over the alphabet AL. Let p be the smallest prime greater than 2^{6m} and let $d = p - 2^{6m}$. Let $\mathsf{ENCD} : \mathsf{STR} \times \{0, 1, ..., d\} \to \mathbb{Z}_p$ be defined as follows

$\mathsf{ENCD}(s, \lambda)$
1. Parse s as $\sigma_0 || \sigma_1 || \ldots || \sigma_m$, where each $\sigma_i \in \mathsf{AL}$;
2. $\psi \leftarrow \mathsf{bin}_6(\sigma_0) || \ldots || \mathsf{bin}_6(\sigma_m)$;
3. $v \leftarrow \mathsf{toInt}(\psi)$;
4. **return** $v + \lambda$;

And let $\mathsf{ENCD}^{-1} : \mathbb{Z}_p \to \mathsf{STR} \times \{0, 1, \ldots, d\}$ be defined as

$\mathsf{ENCD}^{-1}(y)$
1. **if** $y \geq 2^{6m}$,
2. $\lambda \leftarrow y - 2^{6m} + 1$;
3. $y \leftarrow 2^{6m} - 1$;
4. **else** $\lambda \leftarrow 0$;
5. $z \leftarrow \mathsf{toBin}_{6m}(y)$;
6. Parse z as $z_0 || z_1 || \ldots || z_m$, where $|z_i| = 6$;
7. $s \leftarrow \rho^{-1}(\mathsf{toInt}(z_0)) || \ldots || \rho^{-1}(\mathsf{toInt}(z_m))$;
8. **return** (s, λ);

The modified protocol $\mathbb{P}'$ is shown in Fig. 2. It uses the encoding function ENCD and the secret sharing scheme as depicted in Sect. 2.4. For $\mathbb{P}'$ we assume that STR contains all m character strings over the alphabet AL, and p is the smallest prime greater than 2^{6m}, these can be considered the fixed and public parameters for $\mathbb{P}'$. The encoding mechanism is specifically designed to convert a string in STR to an element in $\mathbb{Z}_p$ so that Shamir's secret sharing can be suitably used.

Protocol $\mathbb{P}'(x)$

1. $k \xleftarrow{\$} \mathsf{STR}$;
2. $k' \leftarrow \mathsf{ENCD}(k, 0)$;
3. $\{(x_1, k'_1), \ldots, (x_w, k'_w)\} \leftarrow \mathsf{SHARE}^p_{u,w}(k')$;
4. **for** $i = 1$ **to** w;
5. $(k_i, \lambda_i) \leftarrow \mathsf{ENCD}^{-1}(k'_i)$;
6. $c_i \leftarrow G(k_i)$;
7. **end for**
8. $K \leftarrow H(k)$;
9. $C \leftarrow E_K(x)$;
10 **return** $[C, \{(x_1, c_1, \lambda_1), \ldots, (x_w, c_w, \lambda_w)\}]$

Fig. 2. The protocol $\mathbb{P}'$ which uses a secret-sharing scheme.

To decrypt a cipher produced by $\mathbb{P}'$ a human user must solve at least some u of w CAPTCHAs. Using these u solutions together with x_i, k can be recovered. A specific recommendation for SHARE can be Shamir (2,5)-threshold scheme. Thus the user would have much flexibility on solving the CAPTCHAs.

5.1 Security of $\mathbb{P}'$

The security of $\mathbb{P}'$ can be easily proved in the sense of Definition 4 in a similar way as we prove Theorem 1 if we make a new assumption regarding the CAPTCHA as follows:

Definition 6 [The Hash-MultiCaptcha Assumption]. *Let G be a CAPTCHA generator, let r be a number, let $H : \mathsf{STR} \rightarrow \{0,1\}^r$ be a hash function, and let $\mathcal{A}$ be an adversary. Also, let $x = g(x_1, \ldots x_w)$ be such that if at least u out of w of $x_1, \ldots, x_w$ are known then x can be recovered. We define the advantage of $\mathcal{A}$ in violating the Hash-MultiCaptcha assumption as*

$$\mathbf{Adv}^{\mathrm{hmc}}_{G,H}(\mathcal{A}) = \Pr[\mathcal{A}(G(x_1), \ldots G(x_w), H(x)) \Rightarrow 1]$$

$$- \Pr[z \xleftarrow{\$} \{0,1\}^r : \mathcal{A}(G(x_1), \ldots G(x_w), z) \Rightarrow 1].$$

where $x \xleftarrow{\$} \mathsf{STR}$. Moreover, (G, H) is called (ϵ, t) HMC secure if for all adversaries $\mathcal{A}$ running in time at most t, $\mathbf{Adv}^{\mathrm{hmc}}_{G,H}(\mathcal{A}) \leq \epsilon$. ◇

As in the definition of Hash-Captcha assumption, in this definition if the adversary can efficiently solve at least u of w CAPTCHAs, then it can break (G, H) in the HMC sense irrespective of the hash function. If this assumption is true, then we can show the security of protocol $\mathbb{P}'$ just as we did for protocol $\mathbb{P}$.

A CAPTCHA is an example of a weakly-verifiable puzzle [2], since a legitimate solver S may not be able to verify the correctness of its answer. For this kind of puzzles, it has been proved [7] that if it is difficult for an attacker to solve a weakly-verifiable puzzle P, then trying to solve multiple instances of a puzzle in parallel is harder. Most recently, Jutla found a better bound to show how hard it is for an attacker to solve multiple instances of weakly-verifiable puzzles [9]. The next theorem is based on the main theorem proposed by Jutla, but it has been adapted to CAPTCHAs, which are of our interest in this work.

Theorem 2. *Let G be a CAPTCHA generator which is (α, β) secure. Let $k \in \mathbb{N}$, $\delta = 1 - \beta$ and γ $(0 < \gamma < 1)$ be arbitrary. Let $\mathcal{A}$ be an arbitrary polynomial time adversary, which is given as input k CAPTCHAs $(G(x_1), \ldots, G(x_k))$ and outputs a set X of solutions of the k CAPTCHAs. If $\mathsf{InCorr}(X)$ denotes the number of incorrect solutions in X, then*

$$\Pr[\mathsf{InCorr}(X) < (1 - \gamma)\delta k] < e^{-(1-\gamma)\gamma^2 \delta k/2}$$

This theorem establishes that for any adversary if the probability of failure in solving a CAPTCHA is at least δ, then the probability of failing on less than $(1 - \gamma)\delta k$ out of k puzzles, is at most $e^{-(1-\gamma)\gamma^2 \delta k/2}$.

Based on this fact, it may be possible to show that for any arbitrary adversary $\mathcal{A}$ attacking the HMC assumption, there exists a HC adversary $\mathcal{B}$ such that $\mathbf{Adv}_{G,H}^{\mathrm{hmc}}(\mathcal{A}) < \mathbf{Adv}_{G,H}^{\mathrm{hc}}(\mathcal{B})$. This would imply that the HC assumption implies the HMC assumption. But, for now we are not sure whether such a result holds.

5.2   Discussions

- **About the Encryption Scheme.** In this work we have not said anything about the encryption scheme to be used in the protocol. We only said that we require our encryption scheme to be PROF-EAV secure and any IND-EAV secure encryption scheme can provide such security. Thus most symmetric encryption schemes which are usually in use like CBC mode, counter mode etc. (which provide security in the IND-CPA sense) can be used for the encryption function E in $\mathbb{P}'$. A more efficient scheme which provides security only in the PROF-EAV sense would be much interesting, we would like to explore in this direction.
- **Key Sizes.** Another important thing to consider is that the effective size of a key for the protocol is dictated by the parameter m, i.e., the size of each string in STR. This value cannot be made arbitrarily large as solving big CAPTCHAs for human beings may be tiresome, a usual CAPTCHA length is five to eight characters. If we use eight character strings from the alphabet AL then the effective size of the key space would be 2^{48}. Increasing the alphabet size is also not feasible as we need un-ambiguous printable characters to

make CAPTCHAs. Thus, the key space is not sufficiently large for a modern cryptographic application, but for the application which we have in mind this may be sufficient, as we do not expect that a profiler would be ready to use so much computational resource for profiling a single message.

6   Analyzing the Golle and Farahat's Scheme

As we mentioned in the introduction, a previous work on the issue of securing email communication from profilers was proposed by Golle and Farahat [6]. The basic idea behind their proposal is to hash the header of an email message to generate the key, and further use the key to encrypt the payload of the message. They require that the encryption algorithm should be resistant to profiling attacks. In addition, they assume some properties of the hash function for assuring security of the scheme. In particular they mention that the hash function used for deriving the key should be a *slow one-way hash* function. They argued that the security of the scheme relies on the high computational cost for the hash function and on (some weak) privacy of the encryption scheme. Though it is not clear, why the property of one-wayness of the hash is important in this context. They claimed that though their scheme do not satisfy the semantic security notion, but it would provide adequate security for the application. No proper security analysis of the scheme is done in the paper. In this section we apply the security notions that we previously defined to establish the security of the Golle and Farahat's scheme.

In Fig. 3 we show a slightly different version of Golle and Farahat's scheme. Here instead of using the header to derive the key we are considering a random string (line 1). We assume that $H : \mathsf{STR} \rightarrow \mathcal{K}$, and E an encryption scheme with key space $\mathcal{K}$ and message space $\mathcal{M}$. Now we proceed to analyze it.

6.1   Security of Protocol $\mathbb{S}$

It is to be noted that the hash function H used in $\mathbb{S}$ is public, hence any adversary can derive the key from the ciphertext and hence decrypt the message. The type of security that is expected from the protocol $\mathbb{S}$ is a bit different from that expected from usual encryption schemes. A profiling adversary would be successful if it can profile "many" messages, in particular we can think that for the activity of profiling to be economically profitable an adversary has to profile at least N different messages in a day (where N can be in the order of millions).

The main argument in [6] was to choose such a hash function which is "slow". Suppose the evaluation of one hash requires 5 s, then an adversary would not be able to profile more than 17280 messages in a day. Whereas for a normal user, this "slow"-ness of the hash function does not have a significant effect, as (s)he would need to decrypt far less than say 100 messages in a day.

It is obvious that the security of the scheme $\mathbb{S}$ critically depends on the time an adversary spends to break the scheme. Restricting the running time of the

Protocol $\mathbb{S}(x)$
1. $s \xleftarrow{\$} \mathsf{STR}$;
2. $K \leftarrow H(s)$;
3. $c \leftarrow E_K(x)$;
4. **return** (c, s)

Fig. 3. Protocol proposed by Golle and Farahat to protect email communications.

adversary is always essential in any cryptographic scheme which is not information theoretically secure, for example in all the previous security definitions we talked of (ϵ, t) secure schemes. In the definitions that we would use to argue about the security of $\mathbb{S}$, the running time restriction would be of central importance, hence for convenience we define a time restricted adversary as follows.

Definition 7 [T-**restricted Adversary**]. *A T-restricted adversary is an adversary which runs for time at most T.* $\diamond$

Next we formalize the notion of a "slow hash function".

Definition 8 [T-**slow Hash Function**]. *Let $H : \mathsf{STR} \to \{0,1\}^\ell$ be a hash function. If the time required to compute $H(x)$ for every $x \in \mathsf{STR}$ is at least T then we say that H is a T-slow hash function.* $\diamond$

For $\mathbb{S}$ to be secure, we need the hash function to be "well behaved" in some sense in addition to being slow. The specific property that we would require is that given x, there should be no other feasible way to predict $H(x)$ other than computing the value of $H(x)$. We formalize this notion in the following definition.

Definition 9 [(ϵ, T)-**indistinguishable Hash Function**]. *Let $H : \mathsf{STR} \to \{0,1\}^\ell$ be a T-slow hash function, let $\mathcal{A}$ be a T-restricted adversary, and $y \xleftarrow{\$} \{0,1\}^\ell$. We define the advantage of $\mathcal{A}$ in distinguishing (x, y) from $(x, H(x))$ as*

$$\mathbf{Adv}_H^{\mathrm{ind}}(\mathcal{A}) = \Pr[x \xleftarrow{\$} \mathsf{STR} : \mathcal{A}(x, H(x)) \Rightarrow 1)]$$
$$- \Pr[x \xleftarrow{\$} \mathsf{STR}, y \xleftarrow{\$} \{0,1\}^\ell : \mathcal{A}(x, y) \Rightarrow 1].$$

H is (ϵ, T)-indistinguishable if for all T-restricted adversaries $\mathcal{A}$, $\mathbf{Adv}_H^{\mathrm{ind}}(\mathcal{A}) \leq \epsilon$. $\diamond$

With this we are ready to establish the security of protocol $\mathbb{S}$ in the PROF sense (see Definition 4) as we did with protocols $\mathbb{P}$ and $\mathbb{P}'$.

Theorem 3. *Let $\mathbb{S}$ be a protocol as in Fig. 3. Let us assume that for all $x \in \mathcal{M}$ to compute $E_k(x)$ one requires a constant time t_c, and recall that computing $f(x)$ for every $x \in \mathcal{M}$ requires μ time. If H is $(\epsilon_1, T + t_c + \mu)$ indistinguishable, and E is (ϵ_2, t) PROF-EAV secure, then $\mathbb{S}$ is $(\epsilon_1 + \epsilon_2, T)$ PROF secure, where $T \leq t$.*

Proof. To prove the Theorem we will construct a $(T+t_c+\mu)$ restricted adversary $\mathcal{B}$ which breaks the hash function H in the indistinguishability sense by using a T-restricted adversary $\mathcal{A}$ which attacks $\mathbb{S}$. Subsequently we show that

$$\mathbf{Adv}_{\mathbb{S},f}^{\text{prof}}(\mathcal{A}) \le \mathbf{Adv}_H^{\text{ind}}(\mathcal{B}) + \mathbf{Adv}_{E,f}^{\text{prof-eav}}(\mathcal{B}'),$$

where $\mathcal{B}'$ is a t restricted adversary. This asserts the Theorem.

Let $\mathcal{A}$ be an adversary attacking the protocol $\mathbb{S}$ in Fig. 3. We construct an adversary $\mathcal{B}$ attacking the hash H, using $\mathcal{A}$ as follows.

Adversary $\mathcal{B}(s,k)$

1. $x \xleftarrow{\$} \mathcal{M}$;
2. Send $(E_k(x), s)$ to $\mathcal{A}$;
3. $\mathcal{A}$ returns j;
4. **if** $f(x) = j$;
5.   **return** 1;
6. **else return** 0;

As $\mathcal{B}$ is an adversary attacking the indistinguishability of the hash function, it receives as input a pair (s, k), hence there are two possibilities regarding the input (s, k) of $\mathcal{B}$, k can either be $H(s)$ or a uniform random element in $\{0,1\}^\ell$, and the goal of $\mathcal{B}$ is to distinguish between these two possibilities.

Considering the first possibility that k is $H(s)$, the way the adversary $\mathcal{B}$ is defined, $\mathcal{A}$ gets a valid encryption of the message x (which is a random element in the message space) according to the protocol $\mathbb{S}$. Hence we have

$$\Pr[s \xleftarrow{\$} \text{STR} : \mathcal{B}(s, H(s)) \Rightarrow 1] = \Pr[s \xleftarrow{\$} \text{STR}, x \xleftarrow{\$} \mathcal{M} : \mathcal{A}(E_{H(s)}(x), s) \Rightarrow f(x)]$$

$$= \Pr[x \xleftarrow{\$} \mathcal{M} : \mathcal{A}(\mathbb{S}(x)) \Rightarrow f(x)]. \tag{7}$$

Similarly, for the second possibility, i.e., when the input k to $\mathcal{B}$ is an element chosen uniformly at random from $\{0,1\}^\ell$, we have

$$\Pr[s \xleftarrow{\$} \text{STR}, k \xleftarrow{\$} \{0,1\}^\ell : \mathcal{B}(s,k) \Rightarrow 1] = \Pr[x \xleftarrow{\$} \mathcal{M} : \mathcal{A}(E_k(x), s) \Rightarrow f(x)]. \tag{8}$$

In Eq. (8), s and k are not related at all, since s is chosen independently at random from STR and k is chosen independently uniformly at random from $\{0,1\}^\ell$. Thus, the adversary $\mathcal{A}$ has as input $E_K(x)$ and s, where s is independent of k, thus k cannot be derived from s. Hence $\mathcal{A}$ cannot do better than some PROF-EAV adversary $\mathcal{B}'$ who has only $E_k(x)$ as its input, and runs for same time as that of $\mathcal{A}$, which must be less than T. Thus

$$\Pr[x \xleftarrow{\$} \mathcal{M} : \mathcal{A}(E_k(x), s) \Rightarrow f(x)] \le \Pr[x \xleftarrow{\$} \mathcal{M} : \mathcal{B}'(E_k(x)) \Rightarrow f(x)] \tag{9}$$

From definition of PROF-EAV advantage of $\mathcal{B}'$ we have

$$\Pr[x \xleftarrow{\$} \mathcal{M} : \mathcal{B}'(E_K(x)) \Rightarrow f(x)]$$
$$= \mathbf{Adv}_{E,f}^{\text{prof-eav}}(\mathcal{B}') + \max_{\mathcal{A}'} \Pr[\mathcal{A}'(.) \Rightarrow f(x)], \tag{10}$$

for any t restricted adversary for E. Thus, using Eqs. (8), (9) and (10) we have

$$\Pr[s \xleftarrow{\$} \mathsf{STR}, k \xleftarrow{\$} \{0,1\}^\ell : \mathcal{B}(s, k) \Rightarrow 1]$$
$$\leq \mathbf{Adv}_{E,f}^{\text{prof-eav}}(\mathcal{B}') + \max_{\mathcal{A}'} \Pr[\mathcal{A}'(.) \Rightarrow f(x)] \tag{11}$$

Finally, from Eqs. (7) and (11) and Definitions 4 and 9 we have

$$\mathbf{Adv}_{\mathbb{S},f}^{\text{prof}}(\mathcal{A}) \leq \mathbf{Adv}_H^{\text{ind}}(\mathcal{B}) + \mathbf{Adv}_{E,f}^{\text{prof-eav}}(\mathcal{B}'),$$

as desired.   □

6.2   More Considerations

In a real scenario, a profiler will see a large amount of messages and will try to profile them. The restriction that we want to put on an adversary is that (s)he should not be able to profile more than N^* messages in time less than Γ, where the values of N^* and Γ would be decided based on the application.

If $\mathcal{A}$ be a Γ restricted sequential adversary, and $\mathsf{NProf}_\Gamma^{\mathcal{A}}$ be a random variable denoting the number of messages profiled correctly by $\mathcal{A}$ within time Γ. It is desirable that for all sequential adversaries $\mathcal{A}$, $\Pr[\mathsf{NProf}_\Gamma^{\mathcal{A}} \geq N^*] \leq \delta$, for some small constant δ.

It is easy to see that the following result holds.

Proposition 1. *Let $\mathbb{S}$ be a (ϵ, T) PROF secure scheme, and Γ be a number. Then, for any Γ restricted sequential adversary $\mathcal{A}$*

$$\Pr\left[\mathsf{NProf}_\Gamma^{\mathcal{A}} \geq \frac{\Gamma}{T}\right] \leq \epsilon.$$

Thus, assuming a sequential adversary and adjusting the slowness of the hash function H, one can obtain the desired security objective out of $\mathbb{S}$.

We assume a sequential adversary, which may not be realistic. As an adversary may try to profile several messages in the same time. But, an adversary using more parallelism uses more computation power in terms of amount of hardware used etc. Thus, instead of restricting the adversary on computation time, one can put a restriction on the total *computation cost*, and based on this cost metric it is possible to develop a security model where the restriction on sequential adversaries can be removed.

6.3   Slow Hash Functions

Slow hash functions have been previously used to protect passwords. The main purpose of this kind of hash functions is preventing *off-line* attacks, where a list of password hashes is stolen and the attacker tries to guess the password by testing all possible candidates and verifying if the result matches. If a hash function is slow enough, then guessing a password would be harder, since an attacker must try many candidates and the cost of doing this will be high. Usually a slow one-way hash function can be constructed by iterating cryptographic hashes (such as SHA1) multiple times. There have been some interesting proposals like bcrypt [15] and scrypt [13] which are designed to achieve the slow-ness goal. Moreover, these functions can be tuned to achieve various degrees of slowness as desired. More recently another interesting option to construct slow hash functions appeared which spends computing cycles to solve other computational problems [3]. All these proposals can be suitably used in the context of the protocol $\mathbb{S}$.

7   Concluding Remarks

In this paper we did a theoretical analysis of profiling adversaries and ultimately described a protocol which is secure against profiling adversaries. Our protocol does not require any key exchange or public key infrastructure and uses CAPTCHAs and secret sharing schemes in a novel way. We also applied our definitions and methodologies to analyze security of an existing scheme.

Encryption may not be the only way to protect a user from profilers. As profilers can use many different techniques which cannot be stopped using encryption. For example it is possible to track the web usage of a specific user and profile him/her on that basis. Here (probably) encryption has no role to play, or at least cannot be used in the way we propose in our protocol. Anonymity is probably the correct direction to explore in solving such problems. Also, as user profiling is a big business, and some think that the free content in the web is only possible due to online advertisements, so putting a total end to user profiling may not be desirable. So there have been current attempts to develop systems which would allow targeted advertisements without compromising user security [17]. These issues are not covered in our current work.

Acknowledgements. The authors thank Francisco Rodríguez Henríquez for his comments on an early draft of this paper. Debrup Chakraborty acknowledge the support from CONACYT project 166763.

References

1. Abdalla, M., Bellare, M., Rogaway, P.: The oracle Diffie-Hellman assumptions and an analysis of DHIES. In: Naccache, D. (ed.) CT-RSA 2001. LNCS, vol. 2020, p. 143. Springer, Heidelberg (2001)
2. Canetti, R., Halevi, S., Steiner, M.: Hardness amplification of weakly verifiable puzzles. In: Kilian, J. (ed.) TCC 2005. LNCS, vol. 3378, pp. 17–33. Springer, Heidelberg (2005)
3. Dürmuth, M.: Useful password hashing: how to waste computing cycles with style. In: Zurco, M.E., Beznosov, K., Whalen, T., Longstaff, T. (eds.) NSPW, pp. 31–40. ACM (2013)

4. Dwork, C., Naor, M.: Pricing via processing or combatting junk mail. In: Brickell, E.F. (ed.) CRYPTO 1992. LNCS, vol. 740, pp. 139–147. Springer, Heidelberg (1993)
5. Dziembowski, S.: How to pair with a human. In: Garay, J.A., De Prisco, R. (eds.) SCN 2010. LNCS, vol. 6280, pp. 200–218. Springer, Heidelberg (2010)
6. Golle, P., Farahat, A.: Defending email communication against profiling attacks. In: Atluri, V., Syverson, P.F., di Vimercati, S.D.C. (eds.) WPES, pp. 39–40. ACM (2004)
7. Impagliazzo, R., Jaiswal, R., Kabanets, V.: Chernoff-type direct product theorems. J. Cryptol. 22(1), 75–92 (2009)
8. Impagliazzo, R., Zuckerman, D.: How to recycle random bits. In: FOCS, pp. 248–253. IEEE (1989)
9. Jutla, C.S.: Almost optimal bounds for direct product threshold theorem. In: Micciancio, D. (ed.) TCC 2010. LNCS, vol. 5978, pp. 37–51. Springer, Heidelberg (2010)
10. Katz, J., Lindell, Y.: Introduction to Modern Cryptography. Chapman & Hall/CRC, Boca Raton (2008)
11. Naor, M.: Verification of a human in the loop or identification via the Turing test (1997). http://www.wisdom.weizmann.ac.il/~naor/PAPERS/human.pdf
12. NYT. Congress begins deep packet inspection of internet providers (2009). http://bits.blogs.nytimes.com/2009/04/24/congress-begins-deep-packet-inspection-of-internet-providers/
13. Percival, C.: Stronger key derivation via sequential memory-hard functions. In: BSDCan'09 (2009)
14. Pinkas, B., Sander, T.: Securing passwords against dictionary attacks. In: Atluri, V. (ed.) ACM Conference on Computer and Communications Security, pp. 161–170. ACM (2002)
15. Provos, N., Mazieres, D.: A future-adaptable password scheme. In: Proceedings of 1999 USENIX Annual Technical Conference, pp. 81–92 (1999)
16. Shamir, A.: How to share a secret. Commun. ACM 22(11), 612–613 (1979)
17. Toubiana, V., Narayanan, A., Boneh, D., Nissenbaum, H., Barocas, S.: Privacy preserving targeted advertising. In: Proceedings of Annual Network and Distributed Systems Security Symposium (2010). http://www.isoc.org/isoc/conferences/ndss/10/pdf/05.pdf
18. von Ahn, L., Blum, M., Hopper, N.J., Langford, J.: CAPTCHA: using hard AI problems for security. In: Biham, E. (ed.) EUROCRYPT 2003. LNCS, vol. 2656, pp. 294–311. Springer, Heidelberg (2003)

Large-Scale Traffic Anomaly Detection: Analysis of Real Netflow Datasets

Angelo Spognardi[1], Antonio Villani[2](✉), Domenico Vitali[3],
Luigi Vincenzo Mancini[3], and Roberto Battistoni[3]

[1] Institute of Informatics and Telematics of CNR, Via G. Moruzzi 1,
56124 Pisa, Italy
`a.spognardi@iit.cnr.it`
[2] Dipartimento di Matematica, Università Roma Tre,
Largo San Leonardo Murialdo 1, 00146 Rome, Italy
`villani@mat.uniroma3.it`
[3] Dipartimento di Informatica, Sapienza Università di Roma,
Via Salaria 113, 00198 Rome, Italy
`{lv.mancini,vitali}@di.uniroma1.it, rbattistoni@acm.org`

Abstract. The analysis of large amount of traffic data is the daily routine of Autonomous Systems and ISP operators. The detection of anomalies like denial-of-service (DoS) or distributed denial-of-service (DDoS) is also one of the main issues for critical services and infrastructures. The suitability of metrics coming from the information theory for detecting DoS and DDoS episodes has been widely analyzed in the past. Unfortunately, their effectiveness are often evaluated on synthetic data set, or, in other cases, on old and unrepresentative data set, e.g. the DARPA network dump. This paper presents the evaluation by means of main metrics proposed in the literature of a real and large network flow dataset, collected from an Italian transit tier II Autonomous System (AS) located in Rome. We show how we effectively detected and analyzed several attacks against Italian critical IT services, some of them also publicly announced. We further report the study of others legitimate and malicious activities we found by ex-post analysis.

Keywords: Distributed denial-of-service attacks · Information divergence · Relative Entropy · Network security · Autonomous Systems · Internet security · Attack detection

1 Introduction

Autonomous Systems and Internet Service Providers continually face menaces coming from other networks in order to protect their hosted services. Among

This work has been partially supported by the European Commission Directorate General Home Affairs, under the GAINS project, HOME/2013/CIPS/AG/4000005057, and by the TENACE PRIN Project (n. 20103P34XC) funded by the Italian Ministry of Education, University and Research

© Springer-Verlag Berlin Heidelberg 2014
M.S. Obaidat and J. Filipe (Eds.): ICETE 2012, CCIS 455, pp. 192–208, 2014.
DOI: 10.1007/978-3-662-44791-8_12

the more impairing activities there are denial-of-service (DoS) and *distributed* denial-of-service (DDoS) attacks. The damages of such activities are continuously growing as their ease of actualization, at least when directed against network systems. Among the most critical aspects of DDoS attacks, there are artlessness and simplicity. Many examples of such activities can be found in the past years, as reported by the Cisco security annual report [21]: Operation Payback against payment institutions like PayPal and Mastercard, the attack against MPAA, the attack that targeted Sony for the lawsuit against PS3 hackers, just to cite a few. In general, every Internet Critical Infrastructure or any sensitive economic service can be considered a possible target.

Although the victim can usually mitigate the effect of a (D)DoS, the normal defenses that resides in stub ASes are totally useless: only the intermediate networks can handle such traffic thanks to their high bandwidth pathways, but the end networks, that invests only on as much bandwidth as they might need, have no defenses at all. The main adopted solution consists in blocking the malicious traffic before it reaches the AS where the target is located: that is in one of the intermediate ASes, belonging to the upper tiers of the Internet hierarchy. Hence, the challenge lies in the capacity to distinguish the malicious packets among the aggregated traffic at AS level. This can be done exploiting mechanisms that makes the (D)DoS and other anomalies to *emerge* from the whole traffic flows.

In this work we report how we were able to analyze AS aggregated traffic with information theory based metrics. No conditions are imposed to the packets nature: they can be genuine or bogus, since we collected the normal traffic of a real tier II AS. This work is a result of the research activities lead within the ExtrABIRE Project (Exchanged Traffic Analysis for a Better Internet Resiliency in Europe). We are collecting the traffic that flows through an important national Tier II Autonomous System. In detail, we capture the Netflows of all the traffic exchanged across a transit AS that shares connections within other ISPs in a IXP (Internet eXchange Point). We believe that our network testbed can be considered a general and representative sample of Autonomous System.

Our research starts from this large dataset of netflow entries obtained during several months of the collection phase, where we have recorded meaningful high resources network events and several attacks. All the collected events allow us to evaluate and estimate the effectiveness of previous approaches to (D)DoS attack detection, using just netflow data. One of the most used metrics for network anomaly detection is *Entropy* or *informational divergence*, which involves network dump (like *tcpdump* or old dataset as DARPA-2000 [13]) and imposes high computations and heavy resource effort. Netflow records, instead, are extremely compact and representative, avoiding to maintain any payload packet and making analysis and computation lighter. While several kinds of attacks crafted in the traffic payload are able to circumvent the detection filter, traffic anomalies are still effectively observable. Netflow is therefore recognized as a network monitoring tool: many research papers as well as professional software use this tool as source of data to query network status or get back data log.

Contributions. Starting from the huge and **real** network dataset, in this paper we provide sundry contributions:

- we validate the theoretical research results, applying the metrics taken from the information theory; moreover, we compare the different metrics and evaluate their effectiveness against different network activities (DoS, DDoS and bandwidth intensive communications), in terms of anomaly detection and robustness;
- we propose the use of the above metrics on lightweight dump dataset, which means that no heavy computation or I/O efforts are required. Indeed, our dataset only contains netflow records;
- we describe how we implemented FAN (Fast Network Analyzer), a flexible framework able to analyze the collected traffic, evaluating the above metrics;
- we report the ability to perform (D)DoS detection by the analysis of netflow traffic data. We show how analyzed metrics can be effectively used to detect (D)DoS attacks on upstream provider side. Extensive use of such detection could prevent and mitigate attacks that focus on bandwidth saturation, allowing network operators to use a single network analysis point, like a border router[1] to monitor all physical and virtual networks;
- we compare the different metrics and evaluate their effectiveness against several network activities, both in terms of anomaly detection and robustness.

Organization of this Paper. Section 2 introduces to the main representative works on DoS and DDoS detection; Sect. 3 describes our network environment and surveys on some meaningful recorded malicious event. Section 4 shows our results and Sect. 5 concludes our work, drawing some directions for future research in this topic.

2   Related Works

Detection and mitigation of DoS and DDoS attacks attracted many networking and security researcher. As such, several detection techniques have been proposed in literature to address this problem. In this section we survey some of such techniques. It is worth mentioning that, in this work, we focus on flow-based detection since the analysis of the payload is prohibitive on large-scale networks.

One of the first works that define a comprehensive analysis of DDoS attacks is [14], where Mirkovic et al. define a well formed and complete taxonomy of attacks. In order to distinguish between different type of attacks, according to the several criteria such as Victim Type or Impact on the Victim.

Many results (e.g. [4,16,17]) agree upon the use of Entropy and Relative Entropy (or information divergence) as effective metric for anomaly detection. In [4], the authors use blocks of consecutive packets to compute entropy and frequency-sorted distribution of selected packet attributes. The authors obtained

---

[1] In this paper we refer to a border router as a router that connect two, or more, autonomous systems.

several traces from real network as well as some other synthetic traces that have been used to simulate (D)DoS attacks.

In [16] the authors studied how the use of a fixed-dimension block of packets can take a long time in small organization and impose a cpu-burning process for big bandwidth network edge. Oshima et al. introduce a dynamic threshold evaluation in order to mitigate entropy fluctuations.

Others works ([12,15,18]) improve attack detection using other information theory metrics (like cumulative entropy). *Information divergence* (e.g. Rényi [11] and Kullback Leibler divergence [10]) have proved to be effective metrics for (D)DoS detection. These metrics can improve the anomaly detection providing an earlier response and a low false positive rate [23] (please refer to Sect. 4 for more details).

Information theoretical metrics have proved to be suitable also for distinguishing between (D)DoS attacks and flash-crowds [7,22]. However, in our experiments we do not consider flash-crowds since the events we study in this work, are real attacks. Other detection metrics rely upon time series and statistical measures. In [5] previous measurements are used for forecasting the next ones. If the measured value does not lie within a certain range of the forecasted value, the measurement sample is considered malicious and an anomaly has been detected. In [19] the authors use a statistical test to infer strong correlations among flows. With this technique it is possible to correlate different flows even when these flows do not share common features (e.g. IP addresses).

Common issues of related works is the consistency and the nature of used dataset. Almost all the papers refer to datasets that are historically consolidated (like the DARPA dataset [10,15,16,18]), or that have been collected from restricted and unrepresentative traffic ([4,9]). DARPA data sets are organized by experts based on the DDoS attacking software leading that these attacks have the simplicity of structure and type in spite of the complexity of the real data. Furthermore, as indicated in [6], the methodology used to generate the data in DARPA dataset and the nature of data itself are not appropriate for simulating different, non academic, network environments. For such reason, many works suffer of the limitation of their experiments. Additionally, roughly all the proposed works use synthetic traffic in combination with attack-free network traces ([11,23]). This kind of methodology can limit the research result and lack of generality.

In [2] an analysis of high tech criminal threats to national critical infrastructures can be found. The authors consider some real cases where crackers were involved to disrupt national infrastructures, introducing the "hacktivism" concept to emphasize the new user's role: users *"who carry out politically-motivated hacking and bringing down Government agencies' website"*. The "Operation payback" is actually a proof of this statement. Again, in the case of historically consolidated datasets [16], it is easy to notice that they are too old to represent recent (D)DoS attack under the hacktivist zombie.

3   Network Environment and Experiments Setup

In this section we depict the network environment and the tools developed for the purposes of this study. First, we briefly report the network environment, the position of the netflow collector and some technical and statistical information related to the observable and observed attacks[2]. Second, we recall the metrics based on the Information theory that lead the experiments and, finally, we describe FAN (Fast Network Analyzer), a framework developed to perform on-line and off-line analysis of network flows. FAN extends *nfdump*[3], the mostly used open source tools that collect and process netflow data in Unix OS.

3.1   Monitored Networks and Data Sources

The monitored networks, *AS1* in the following, is an Italian Tier2 *multihomed* Autonomous System. *AS1* relies on two distinct upstream providers and provide Internet connection for other ASes.

All the experiments described in this paper are based on the analysis of real data gathered from such network. In detail, we use the Cisco NetFlow records as data source. Despite previous studies which used synthetic data sets, we use genuine traffic data to evaluate how our considered metrics behave in a real network setting. Moreover, many works about anomaly detection over synthetic data sets report conflicting results. Then, we choose to avoid direct comparisons with results of any synthetic data set, and focused only on our collected material.

AS1 exchange data within an important Internet eXchange Point (IXP) and hosts several publicly reachable services like web and mail servers and also x-DSL connections, managing thousands of unique IP addresses. Table 1 reports some statistics about the average exchanged traffic of the monitored network.

Since our AS is composed by heterogeneous networks and services, we state that it can be considered as a good testing case for our research activity. Furthermore, we claim that it is general enough to represent many other real contexts.

Table 1. Network traffic characterization (IN/OUT).

Time of the day	Flows/s	Packets/s	Mbit/s
00:00AM–11:00AM	377/312	8.8 K/6.4 K	37/44
11:00AM–06:00PM	1.3 K/930	21 K/13 K	113/54
06:00PM–11:59PM	764/575	14 K/ 8 K	80/27

---

[2] With the respect of the Non-Disclosure-Agreement of the ExTrABIRE project, no detailed information about AS (such as AS name or number) nor ISP interconnections will be provided in order to preserve AS and host privacy.

[3] http://sourceforge.net/projects/nfdump/

Netflows Dataset. NetFlow is a Cisco[TM] technology used for gathering IP traffic. Despite the classical packet collector (packet dump), Cisco[TM] NetFlow technology monitors data in Layers 2–4 and determines applications by port numbers, using aggregating the information [20].

The typical configuration to leverage the NetFlow protocol is made of a router with netflow capabilities and a probe ("netflow collector") able to store received data. NetFlow records are sent as a *UDP* stream of bytes.

A netflow-enabled router creates one record with only selected fields from the TCP headers of *each* transiting connection. More precisely, a single netflow record is defined as a *unidirectional* sequence of packets all sharing the 7 values source IP address, destination IP address, source and destination ports (for UDP or TCP, 0 for other protocols), IP protocol, Ingress interface (SNMP ifIndex) and IP Type of Service. Other valuable information associated to the flow, like timestamp, duration, number of packets and transmitted bytes are also recorded. Then, we can consider a single flow as a record that represents the data exchanged between two hosts only in one direction, since it aggregates all the IP packets that composed a single communication session. A netflow-enabled router sends to the probe a single flow as soon as the relative connection expires. This can happen: (1) when TCP connection reaches the end of the byte stream (FIN flag or RST flag); (2) when a flow is idle for a specific timeout; (3) if a connection exceeds long live terms (30 min by default).

The use of NetFlow technology has several advantages with respect to the raw packet sniffing, since using just few information it is able to give a lightweight "picture" of monitored network. Several researchers proposed to use netflow collectors as IDSs (Intrusion Detection Systems), traffic classifiers as well as a specific security tools ([1,3]). Finally, our work is based on real events and we cannot be aware of them in advance, then it is impossible to recover full network traffic information of the attack through a posteriori analysis.

3.2   FAN and Experiments Setup

To perform our experiments, we designed and implemented *FAN*, FAst Netflow analyzer[4]. *FAN* is a framework that allows network administrator to easily setup a secure and lightweight probe for Cisco Netflow. It allows an efficient and simple off-line testing of algorithms and protocols. Furthermore, *FAN* can also be used as on-line probe, to perform a complete real time netflow collection and analysis.

FAN's architecture is composed by several building blocks, according to the separation of concerns pattern: data gathering, storage and logging subsystems. Two innovative components enrich the architecture and allow a flexible and complete management of netflow datasets: the *timeout manager* and the *plugin handler*.

The analyzer is composed by three elements: the *collector*, the *plugin manager* and the *logging system*. The *collector* receives raw netflows and packs them in blocks according to timeouts. Then, each block of netflows is passed to the *plugin*

---

[4] https://github.com/icsecurity/fan

manager, in charge to optimize the sequences of operations for netflows analysis. Both collector and plugin manager reports to the *logging system* that presents the analysis output by each plugin. In the following we detail the two more interesting elements of our framework, the *timeout* and the *plugin managers*.

Timeout Management. Monitor probes generate a new flow under two different conditions: when the peers explicitly terminate the connection according to the protocol, and when a *timeout* expires. Netflow probes use two independent timeouts that expire under different conditions. The *inactive timeout* (θ_i) triggers when the peers do not exchange packets for θ_i seconds and the connection has not been terminated. For each newly exchanged packet, the probe resets θ_i. The *active timeout* is used to break up long-lived flows into several fragments, and triggers each θ_a seconds until two peers exchange packets at a high rate on the same flow. Tuning θ_a parameter can be tricky for network administrators. In fact, long-lived flow fragments can alter the real representation of the data crossing the network. Usually, low active timeout values are used for detection purposes (i.e. high responsiveness), while higher values are typically used for classification tasks (pattern recognition or statistical problems, where there is the need to analyze the flows in the correct order and without segmentation). Flows that span over multiple fragments are managed by *FAN* using the *block timeout* parameter and the *time slot size*: the β_t block of flows contains all the flows exchanged during time slot t, of duration τ (e.g. 60 s). The *block timeout* is used to cache all the netflows of several blocks and to properly aggregate them to fix the effects of the active timeout. The *block timeout* is needed by behavioral-based traffic detection engines (like [8]), since it enables time-coherent analysis. Further, it makes possible ex-post analysis, quality of service evaluations or the implementation of traffic classification algorithms. Since the active timeout value also affects *FAN*'s cache size, it should be set according with the Netflow probe configuration.

Plugins Manager. *FAN* can dynamically load new plugins during its execution, since it exploits the programming interface to the dynamic linking loader, namely *dlopen, dlsym, dlclose* functions. Each plugin is a *shared object* that can be attached on demand, without restarting the processes or recompiling the binaries.

Each plugin requires the implementation of three functions: *so_init, so_process, so_close*. The *so_init* function is executed to allocate resources for each flow block. The *so_process* function performs the core operations for the plugin, while the *so_close* function releases the used resources.

FAN also has a *plugin dependency subsystem* to optimize the plugin execution. Using a configuration file, we can define how the active plugins depend between them. For example, we can enable a list of plugins (e.g. p_1, p_2) and require that their executions depend on the results of others ones (e.g. p_3). The dependency subsystem uses a graph representation to verify consistency constraints and evaluate the order of the plugin executions. In this way, the framework will perform

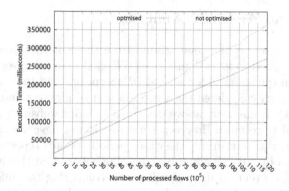

Fig. 1. Effects of the plugins dependency subsystem on the execution time.

the plugins computation in a rational order (e.g. p_3, p_1, p_2). A *so_getResult* function also is provided for intra-plugins communications.

Figure 1 shows the effects of the plugin dependency subsystem optimization in terms of execution time. For example, processing 10 millions of netflow the dependency subsystem saves 80 s of computations (around 25 % of speed improvement), optimizing 6 plugins based on information theory.

3.3 Considered Metrics

To conduct our study, the considered metrics take as input Network flows aggregated into time blocks f^t of a fixed size (e.g. 1 min). With f_i^t as the number of flows having the same IP_i as destination (or source) address in block f^t, we define [10, 11]:

$$Entropy:\ H(f^t) = -\sum_{\forall i} \frac{f_i^t}{f^t} \log_2 \frac{f_i^t}{f^t} \tag{1}$$

$$Kullback\text{-}Leibler:\ KL(f^t \| f^{t-1}) = \sum_{\forall i} \frac{f_i^t}{f^t} \log_2 \frac{\frac{f_i^t}{f^t}}{\frac{f_i^{t-1}}{f^{t-1}}} \tag{2}$$

$$Rényi:\ R_\alpha(f^t \| f^{t-1}) = \frac{1}{\alpha - 1} \log_2 \sum_i \left(\frac{f_i^t}{f^t}\right)^\alpha \left(\frac{f_i^{t-1}}{f^{t-1}}\right)^{1-\alpha} \tag{3}$$

As suggested by [11], for the Rényi divergence, we set the value of α to 5. In order to make a complete and fair comparison between Entropy, Kullback-Leibler and Rényi metrics with the previous research results, we evaluated the metrics considering separately the destination and the source IP fields. Only the Rényi divergence is evaluated on the sole destination IP: in our experiments Rényi on source address exhibited an extremely fuzzy behavior, making it completely unreliable. We refer to H_s, KL_s and H_d, KL_d, R_d as entropy, Kullback Leibler and Rényi, evaluated on source and destination IP, respectively.

4   Attack and Anomaly Analysis

In this section we report the comparison of the three metrics presented in the above section, applied to several anomalies collected in our dataset. Our netflow dataset has been the scenario for several DDoS episodes, in Italy and abroad.

Our experiments considered the whole dataset of netflows and were carried out with the FAN framework, above described (see our website www.extrabire. eu for the complete results). However, since we did not have a complete knowledge of the attacks present during the whole period, we only reported the attacks officially reported by our ISP administrators. We believe that the detailed analysis of the reported events is more significant in comparing the different metrics studied here. The considered anomalies were detected looking for metrics fluctuations that produced "plots peaks". Once such high peak were identified, we conducted a deeper inspection in order to capture the motivations behind the anomaly. This kind of analysis produced several insights about the behaviors and limitations of the metrics, at the same time.

In addition to the anomalies, we chose to analyze another kind of network activity, namely the abnormal traffic generated by scheduled and automated administration activities (like scheduled backups or maintenance procedure) and a streaming session. Those activities can make service outage sensible to users. By observing the relative netflows is possible to identify sudden and relatively short mutations of the traffic pattern, resulting in a deep alteration of the metrics. Even if all of them are able to detect these alterations, we experienced several false positive alerts and false negative. Actually, this condition is really hard to handle, since with genuine data sources, it is hard to know when and how malicious (or meaningful) events can occur.

All the comparison charts we show in this section are composed by all the metric results. However, to ease the readability, the results of Entropy and source IP Kullback Leibler are plotted as multiplied by -1, to mirror the charts w.r.t. the x axis.

4.1 E_1 - DoS Attack

This episode has been studied analyzing the three metrics and has been classified as a DoS attack. In fact, we made a brief statistic to show which IP generated the highest number of flows directed to our network and we found that there was a single *IP* playing a primary role during the attack against one single host server. There were also few other *IP* addresses participating to the attack, with a smaller contribution.

All the metrics correctly detected the malicious activity, as shown by the fluctuations and the spikes of Fig. 2(a). Rényi distribution, indeed, shows the lower peak. The DoS nature of the attack is well described by the downfall of both entropy lines (in the lower part of the plot) around *4:00pm*. This behavior expresses that a small number of source addresses generates the largest amount of connections towards a small set of destinations, namely the typical scenario of a DoS attack. At the same time, *KL* on destination *IP* grows significantly.

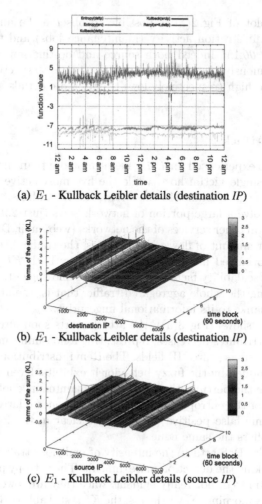

(a) E_1 - Kullback Leibler details (destination IP)

(b) E_1 - Kullback Leibler details (destination IP)

(c) E_1 - Kullback Leibler details (source IP)

Fig. 2. E_1 - Network analysis.

To have a deeper insight of KL behaviors, we graphically report the contribution of every destination IP to the final KL_s and KL_d values. In Fig. 2(b) we report the first ten time-blocks since the beginning of the malicious activity. It is evident how the final value of KL_d is obtained by the contribution of one main component (the victim host 2000), while the contribution of the other hosts is negligible. On the other hand, since during a DoS attack, only few sources generate the largest part of the traffic, each attacking host addresses many flows towards the victim host. Sampling the network traffic we will see that the attacking IPs are the most frequent among the source addresses. This anomaly is perfectly captured by the peaks of Fig. 2(c), that corresponds to the main contributors to the KL_s value.

In the same plot of Fig. 2(a) is possible to observe the anomaly that we introduced as administration activity (maintenance jobs) and that we labeled with E_4: before *7:00AM* indeed both source and destination entropy metrics rise and fall continuously, since they generate maximum (respectively minimum) traffic compared to high (respectively low) traffic. More details will be provided in Sect. 4.5.

4.2 E_2 - DoS Attack

In this episode, we experienced an *IP1* generating more than the 50 % of all the flows toward one single victim host, while the five most active *IP*s was generating 93.8 % of the whole traffic. In this event, the *IP* address targeted by DoS attacks do not involve a large portion of network flows (just 2.9 % of the whole traffic), while several other services of the networks (web, mail, DNS servers etc.) generate the larger amount of flows. Nevertheless, the traffic diversity expressed when the attack occurred has been well detected by both *KL* measures. This aspect represent a scalability factor of this measure and suggests that the attack is detectable among the whole aggregated traffic: that is, the attack "emerges" from the traffic thanks to its informational fingerprint.

As entropy line shows (Fig. 3(a)), the attack starts soon after *1:00PM*. The entropy on both attributes decreases, representing a non-uniform distribution of destination IP as well as source IP fields. The Rényi distribution reveals a small peak, but this is hidden by the fuzzy behavior it exhibits. Even in this case it is possible to observe the perturbations due to the maintenance jobs: rather, their peaks in the case of the entropy are higher than the ones relative to the attack E_2, generating some false positive (as it will be clear in the following). Rényi divergence also suffers the same issue.

In this particular DoS attack, the intensity of malicious traffic is significantly lower than E_1, making the detection more difficult. The entropy peaks associated to the attack are, indeed, not really evident, since they are lower than the false positive of the early morning. Nevertheless, the *KL* is still able to detect the anomaly. Again, the deeper representations of the *KL* contributors at the time of the attack (Figs. 3(b) and (c)) show how this metric correctly reveals the attack and characterizes it as a DoS.

4.3 E_3 - DDoS Attack

In this case we describe a Distributed Denial-of-Services attack, characterized by a large number of attack sources. The network activities indicate that the most active hosts, *IP*1, participates only for the 0.5 % in the traffic flows. This kind of attack is really different from E_1 of Sect. 4.1, where the most active *IP* makes more than half of total flows.

Figure 4(a) reports the metric behavior. As in Sect. 4.1, Rényi distribution seems to generate several peaks associated to a non-attack instances. The most significant example can be found around *6:00PM*. The attack started soon after *10:00PM*: both entropy metrics reveal the event and catch its DDoS nature.

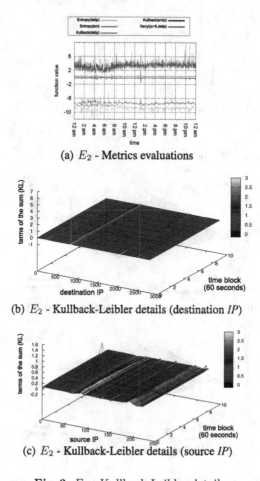

(a) E_2 - Metrics evaluations

(b) E_2 - Kullback-Leibler details (destination IP)

(c) E_2 - Kullback-Leibler details (source IP)

Fig. 3. E_2 - Kullback-Leibler details.

The abrupt growth of source IP entropy line suggests that there was a great amount of diversity in this field. The peak of destination IP entropy represents that there is an anomalous variation in the connected endpoints. Attack dynamic is represented in Fig. 4(b), where the roughness and quickness of the malicious event causes a jump of the KL value. The presence into the traffic flows of several new entities drawn by the DDoS attack induces a continuous variation in the source IP distribution (see Fig. 4) and, then, makes the KL to fluctuate constantly. As opposite to previous cases, the plot shows that the variation of the KL metric is caused by multiple components, that contribute to its final value.

4.4 E_4 - Streaming

We were able to test the entropy metrics when facing with streaming events, in order to shed some light on the resiliency of these metrics to legitimate peaks

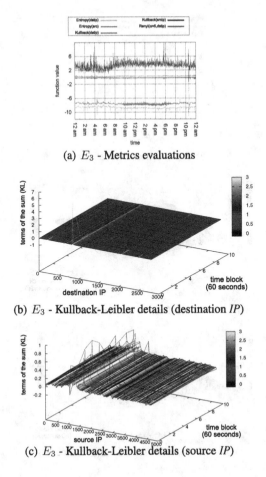

(a) E_3 - Metrics evaluations

(b) E_3 - Kullback-Leibler details (destination IP)

(c) E_3 - Kullback-Leibler details (source IP)

Fig. 4. E_3 - Kullback-Leibler details (source IP).

of traffic. For this purpose, we performed the analysis of the netflows collected during an external event that caused a peak of requests of a specific video streaming, as documented in Fig. 5(a) where we report the number of exchanged bytes during the day of the event. Despite the number of bytes exchanged has grown very rapidly between 10 and 12, both Entropy (Fig. 5(b)) and Kullback-Leibler (Fig. 5(c)) do not exhibit any evident spike. The only noticeable peaks are observable during the early morning hours (between 4–6), similarly to the maintenance jobs of Sect. 4.5.

4.5 E_5 - Maintenance Jobs

In order to explore how entropy metrics are prone to false positive (see Sect. 4.2), we make a deep analysis of "maintenance job" events. These events are common to all networks and consist in high computation or backup activities scheduled

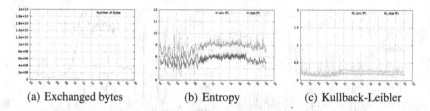

(a) Exchanged bytes   (b) Entropy   (c) Kullback-Leibler

Fig. 5. E_4 - Evaluation of a legitimate peak of network traffic. In this case, even if the absolute value of exchange bytes increases significantly, both the entropy and the Kullback-Leibler do not classify the event as a (D)DoS attack.

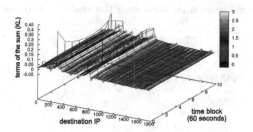

Fig. 6. E_5 - metrics evaluations.

during the early hours of each days, aimed to reduce host workload and service degradation. Figure 6 reports a 3D graph showing how each IP contributes to the final KL value. The component's order of magnitude is clearly smaller than the other KL detailed graphs. KL values, as well as the values of entropy metrics, are sensible to traffic variation. Since the entropy metrics sense destinations (respectively sources) IP address distribution diversity, they notice a lacks of "regular" traffic flows and increase their values. On the opposite, KL values warns distributions divergence, but the low level of traffic activity attenuates the final result, keeping the value of the metric under below suspicious value.

4.6 E_6 - Network Scan

The last episode we report has been revealed during the analysis of two weeks of netflows. During this period we were able to identify a suspicious network activity. Figures 7(a) document that the traffic behavior assumes a regular pattern over the whole period: an increasing activity of traffic during the morning, decreasing in the afternoon, notably reduced in the night and during the week end. By contrast, Fig. 7(b) details the number of exchanged flows: by this point of view, the traffic presents an anomalous traffic pattern, with an high number of flows during the morning of the day 18/11. Figures 8 presents the results of the analysis with the considered metrics. From Fig. 8(a) we ca see how both the Entropy metrics have a periodic trend that follows traffic pattern during all the days, except for the anomaly of the day 18/11. The Rényi, instead, does not exhibit any noticeable fluctuations. Figure 8(b) provides a magnification of

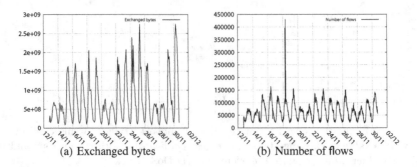

(a) Exchanged bytes   (b) Number of flows

Fig. 7. E_6 - Exchanged traffic during the analyzed two weeks period.

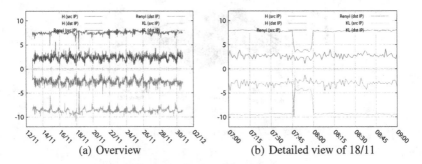

(a) Overview   (b) Detailed view of 18/11

Fig. 8. E_6 - metric evaluations.

the results for the anomaly. Both the *source IP* and *destination IP* Entropy, instead, indicate an unexpected traffic pattern. The Rényi and Kullback Leibler values evaluated on *source IP* do not manifest any peak, but, on the other hand, the same metrics evaluated on *destination IP* reveal the anomaly. Considering the asymmetry of the two divergence based metrics, we can conclude that the anomaly was caused by a single host performing a network scanning against one of the network of our monitored Autonomous System.

5   Conclusions and Future Works

In this paper we report our study of true and genuine netflow dataset to efficiently detect (Distributed) Denial of Services at AS level. Thanks to the huge genuine dataset we collected in the ExTrABIRE project, we were able to compare and evaluate the main metrics based on information theory proposed in the literature Our analysis brought several insights. We report as malicious activity can be detected in aggregated traffic, making the attacks to "emerge" from the whole set of netflows. We pointed out as real attacks have several different ways to be performed, that synthetic dataset used in previous research often miss. We observed that the Kullback-Leibler divergence seems to be the best suited to analyze huge amount of traffic, since it has been able to detect DoS and DDoS activity, maintaining a low level of false positive. Future works will concern the definition of a threshold metric, which correctness could be intuitively but also formally proved.

References

1. Chan, Y.-T.F., Shoniregun, C.A., Akmayeva, G.A..: A netflow based internet-worm detecting system in large network. In: Pichappan, P., Abraham, A. (eds.) Proceedings of Third IEEE International Conference on Digital Information Management (ICDIM), pp. 581–586. IEEE (2008)
2. Choo, K.-K.R.: High tech criminal threats to the national information infrastructure. Inf. Secur. Tech. Rep. **15**, 104–111 (2010)
3. Dübendorfer, T., Wagner, A., Plattner, B.: A framework for real-time worm attack detection and backbone monitoring. In: Proceedings of 1st IEEE International Workshop on Critical Infrastructure Protection (IWCIP 2005) (2005)
4. Feinstein, L., Schnackenberg, D.: Statistical approaches to DDOS attack detection and response. In: Proceedings of the DARPA Information Survivability Conference and Exposition, pp. 303–314 (2003)
5. Hofstede, R., Bartoš, V., Sperotto, A., Pras, A.: Towards real-time intrusion detection for netflow and ipfix. In: Proceedings of the 9th International Conference on Network and Service Management, pp. 1–6. International Federation for Information Processing (2013)
6. Hugh, J.M.: Testing intrusion detection systems: a critique of the 1998 and 1999 DARPA intrusion detection system evaluations as performed by lincoln laboratory. ACM Trans. Inf. Syst. Secur. (TISSEC) **3**, 262–294 (2000)
7. Jung, J., Krishnamurthy, B., Rabinovich, M.: Flash crowds and denial of service attacks: characterization and implications for cdns and web sites. In: Proceedings of the 11th International Conference on World Wide Web, WWW '02, pp. 293–304. ACM, New York (2002)
8. Karagiannis, T., Papagiannaki, K., Faloutsos, M.: Blinc: multilevel traffic classification in the dark. In: Proceedings of the 2005 Conference on Applications, Technologies, Architectures, and Protocols for Computer Communications (SIGCOMM), vol. 35, No.4, pp. 229–240 (2005)
9. Lawniczak, A.T., Di Stefano, B.N., Wu, H.: Detection & study of DDoS attacks via entropy in data network models. In: Proceedings of the Second IEEE International Conference on Computational Intelligence for Security and Defense Applications, CISDA'09, pp. 59–66. IEEE Press, Piscataway (2009)
10. Li, K., Zhou, W., Yu, S.: Effective metric for detecting distributed denial-of-service attacks based on information divergence. IET Commun. **3**(12), 1851–1860 (2009)
11. Li, K., Zhou, W., Yu, S., Dai, B.: Effective DDoS attacks detection using generalized entropy metric. In: Hua, A., Chang, S.-L. (eds.) ICA3PP 2009. LNCS, vol. 5574, pp. 266–280. Springer, Heidelberg (2009)
12. Li, L., Zhou, J., Xiao, N.: DDoS attack detection algorithms based on entropy computing. In: Qing, S., Imai, H., Wang, G. (eds.) ICICS 2007. LNCS, vol. 4861, pp. 452–466. Springer, Heidelberg (2007)
13. Mahoney, M.V., Chan, P.K.: An analysis of the 1999 DARPA/Lincoln laboratory evaluation data for network anomaly detection. In: Vigna, G., Kruegel, C., Jonsson, E. (eds.) RAID 2003. LNCS, vol. 2820, pp. 220–237. Springer, Heidelberg (2003)

14. Mirkovic, J., Reiher, P.: A taxonomy of DDOS attack and DDOS defense mechanisms. SIGCOMM Comput. Commun. Rev. **34**, 39–53 (2004)

15. No, G., Ra, I., An efficient and reliable DDOS attack detection using a fast entropy computation method. In: Proceedings of the 9th International Conference on Communications and Information Technologies, ISCIT'09. pp. 1223–1228. IEEE Press, Piscataway (2009)

16. Oshima, S., Nakashima, T., Sueyoshi, T.: DDoS detection technique using statistical analysis to generate quick response time. In: Proceedings of the 2010 International Conference on Broadband, Wireless Computing, Communication and Applications, BWCCA '10, pp. 672–677. IEEE Computer Society, Washington, DC (2010)

17. Oshima, S., Nakashima, T., Sueyoshi, T.: Early DoS/DDOS detection method using short-term statistics. In: Proceedings of the 2010 International Conference on Complex, Intelligent and Software Intensive Systems, CISIS '10, pp. 168–173. IEEE Computer Society, Washington, DC (2010)

18. Sardana, A., Joshi, R., Kim, T.: Deciding optimal entropic thresholds to calibrate the detection mechanism for variable rate DDOS attacks in ISP domain. In: Proceedings of the 2008 International Conference on Information Security and Assurance (isa 2008), pp. 270–275. IEEE Computer Society, Washington, DC (2008)

19. Silveira, F., Diot, C., Taft, N., Govindan, R.: ASTUTE: detecting a different class of anomalies. In: Proceedings of the ACM SIGCOMM Symposium on Network Architectures and Protocols, August 2010

20. Cisco Systems. Cisco Systems NetFlow Services Export Version 9 (2004). http://tools.ietf.org/html/rfc3954

21. Cisco Systems. Cisco 2011 Annual Security Repor, Highlighting global security threats and trends (2011). http://www.cisco.com/en/US/prod/vpndevc/annual_security_report.html

22. Tao, Y., Yu, S.: Ddos attack detection at local area networks using information theoretical metrics. In: Proceedings of 12th IEEE International Conference on Trust, Security and Privacy in Computing and Communications (TrustCom), pp. 233–240, July 2013

23. Xiang, Y., Li, K., Zhou, W.: Low-rate DDOS attacks detection and traceback by using new information metrics. In: IEEE Transactions on Information Forensics and Security, vol. 99. IEEE Press (2011)

Signal Processing and Multimedia Applications

Image Segmentation Using Diffusion Tracking Algorithm with Patch Oversampling

Lassi Korhonen[✉] and Keijo Ruotsalainen

Department of Electrical Engineering, Mathematics Division, University of Oulu,
P.O. Box 4500, 90014 OULU, Finland
{lassi.korhonen,keijo.ruotsalainen}@ee.oulu.fi

Abstract. An image segmentation process can be considered as a process of solving a pixel clustering problem. This paper represents and combines a new clustering algorithm that we call as a Diffusion Tracking (DT) algorithm and a new clustering based image segmentation algorithm. The DT algorithm is related to classical spectral clustering techniques but overcomes some of their problems which guarantees a better starting point for the image segmentation process. The image segmentation process introduced in this paper joins seamlessly to the DT algorithm but can also be used together with other clustering methods like k-means. The segmentation algorithm is based on oversampling pixels from classified patches and using simple statistical methods for joining the information collected. The experimental results at the end of this paper show clearly that the algorithms proposed suit well also for very demanding segmentation tasks.

Keywords: Clustering · Image segmentation · Diffusion process

1 Introduction

Clustering is one of the most widely used techniques for data mining in many diverse fields such as statistics, computer science and biology. One of the most used applications for clustering algorithms is image segmentation which plays a very important role in the area of computer vision. The best known and still commonly used methods for clustering are k-means (KM) and fuzzy c-means (FCM) which are also used in some quite new image segmentation algorithms [1, 2]. In recent years, the spectral clustering based image segmentation algorithms have risen among the most popular clustering based segmentation methods. There is a large variety of spectral based clustering algorithms available some of which are described in [3,4]. Basically, it is possible to use any of them as a part of image segmentation algorithms, but quite a little attention has paid to the shortcomings of these spectral clustering based segmentation algorithms, even if some of the limitations are quite easy to reveal as shown, for example, in [5]. These limitations affect straightforward also to the performance and accuracy of the image segmentation process.

© Springer-Verlag Berlin Heidelberg 2014
M.S. Obaidat and J. Filipe (Eds.): ICETE 2012, CCIS 455, pp. 211–227, 2014.
DOI: 10.1007/978-3-662-44791-8_13

In this paper, we introduce a novel clustering based image segmentation algorithm that is closely related to but have some significant advantages compared to the classical spectral clustering based methods. The algorithm is based on tracking diffusion processes individually inside each cluster, or we can say inside each image segment, through consecutive multiresolution scales of the diffusion matrix. The nature of the algorithm supports combining segmentation results from different sources reliably. This enables the statistical point of view to the segmentation process and allows precise results also when using quite large regions, patches, around each pixel when collecting the local color and texture information. The paper is organized as follows. First, in Sect. 2, we familiarize ourselves with some existing clustering algorithms, and we will take a closer look at a couple of spectral clustering algorithms that are commonly used as a part of image segmentation algorithms. In Sect. 3, we then introduce a new algorithm for clustering and a new image segmentation algorithm will be represented in Sect. 4. In Sect. 5, the clustering and image segmentation results are reviewed. Finally, some conclusions and suggestions for future work will be provided in Sect. 6.

2   Some Clustering Algorithms

There is a large variety of clustering algorithms available nowadays, and it is not possible to introduce them extensively. The most common algorithms, KM, introduced in 1967 [6], and FCM, introduced in 1973 [7], are both over 40 years old, and a lot of work to enhance them has done also in recent years [8–11]. Of course, many algorithms that are not based on these two have been introduced during these years. One of the newest algorithms is the linear discriminant analysis (LDA) based algorithm presented in [12]. The other interesting one, especially from our point of view, is the localized diffusion folders (LDF) based algorithm presented in [13]. The LDF based algorithm can be counted in to the category of spectral clustering algorithms, and the hierarchical construction of the algorithm has some similarities compared to the algorithm presented in this paper.

As mentioned earlier, the spectral clustering algorithms are commonly used as a part of image segmentation algorithms nowadays, and this is due to their excellent performance when dealing with data sets with complex or unknown shape. The clustering algorithm presented in this paper can also be thought as a spectral clustering algorithm, although the spectral properties of the diffusion matrix do not have to be directly examined. Because of this relationship, we introduce next a couple of classical spectral clustering algorithms that are also used as a baseline when testing the performance of our algorithm later in this paper.

2.1   A Couple of Spectral Clustering Algorithms

The main tools in the spectral clustering algorithms are the variants of graph Laplacian matrices or some relatives to them. One popular choice is the diffusion matrix which is also known as the normalized affinity matrix. This matrix is also the core of the classical Ng-Jordan-Weiss (NJW) algorithm [14] and the Zelnik-Manor-Perona (ZP) algorithm [15]. Next we will take a closer look at these algorithms. Further information about spectral clustering may be found in [3].

We use the notation $A(x, y)$ for the entry of a matrix A in a row x and in a column y through this paper.

Let $X = \{x_i\}_{i=1}^N$, $x_i \in \mathbb{R}^d$, be a set of N data points. The clustering process using the NJW algorithm is done as follows assuming that the number of clusters M is available:

1. Form the weight matrix $K \in \mathbb{R}^{N \times N}$ of the similarity graph $G(V, E)$ where the vertex set $V = \{v_i\}_{i=1}^N$ represents the data set $X = \{x_i\}_{i=1}^N$. Use Gaussian weights: $K(i, j) = e^{-\frac{\|x_i - x_j\|^2}{\sigma^2}}$ where σ^2 is a fixed scaling parameter.
2. Construct the diffusion matrix (i.e. the normalized affinity matrix) $T = D^{-\frac{1}{2}} K D^{\frac{1}{2}}$ where D is a diagonal matrix so that $D(i, i) = \sum_{i=1}^N K(i, j)$.
3. Find the M largest eigenvalues and the corresponding eigenvectors $u_1 \ldots u_M$ of the matrix T. Form the matrix $U \in \mathbb{R}^{N \times M}$ with column vectors u_i.
4. Re-normalize the rows of U to have unit length in the $\| \cdot \|_2$-norm yielding matrix Y.
5. Treat each row of Y as a point in $\mathbb{R}^M$ and cluster via the KM algorithm.
6. Assign the original point x_i to cluster J if and only if the corresponding row i of the matrix Y is assigned to cluster J.

The ZP algorithm has a same kind of structure and is based on the same basic principles as the NJW algorithm. However, there are a couple of major advantages in the ZP algorithm:

- The fixed scaling parameter is replaced with a local scaling parameter so that $K(i, j) = e^{-\frac{\|x_i - x_j\|^2}{\sigma_i \sigma_j}}$ where $\sigma_i = \|x_i - x_n\|$, and x_n is the n:th neighbor of x_i. This modification allows the algorithm to work well also in situations where the data resides in multiple scales.
- The KM step (5) can be ignored.
- The number of clusters can be estimated during the process, so there is no need to know it beforehand.

Both of these algorithms are based on same basic ideas and if the fixed scaling parameter is replaced with local one, their accuracies on clustering are quite the same, and both suffers from same shortcomings. In next sections, we will represent a new algorithm that overcomes some of these shortcomings.

3 Diffusion Tracking Algorithm

The diffusion matrix T tells us how the data points are connected with each other in a small neighborhood. The powers T^t, $t > 1$, describe then the behavior of the diffusion at different time levels t, and how the connections between data points evolve through the time. This process we call as the diffusion process.

We can make a couple of general assumptions concerning the behavior of the diffusion process and clustering. First of all, the spectral clustering algorithms, including the algorithm presented here, are generally based on the assumption that the diffusion moves on faster inside the clusters than between the clusters. Second, if we assume that the diffusion leakage between clusters is relatively small, the diffusion inside the clusters can reach almost the stationary state, i.e. the state when the diffusion process has stabilized inside the cluster.

The classical spectral clustering algorithms (including the ZP algorithm) are based on computing the eigenvectors of the diffusion matrix (normalized affinity matrix) and assigning the data points with help of these eigenvectors. However, these kinds of methods suffer from limitations as presented in [5] where it was shown that if there exist large clusters with high density and small clusters with low density the clustering process may fail totally. This is because the first assumption does not hold. Even if the situation would not be that bad, the accuracy of the clustering process suffers from this shortcoming when handling clusters with different inner geometries. This problem may be partially overcome by tracking diffusion processes through the consecutive scales (time steps) inside each cluster individually, as will be shown.

The clustering algorithm presented here can be separated in following phases:

1. Compute the distances between data points and construct the diffusion matrix T using local scaling or some other suitable scaling method.
2. Construct the multiresolution based on T up to the level needed for the efficient computation of the powers of T.
3. Track the diffusion processes inside clusters using the points and levels provided by the multiresolution construction process.
4. Do the final cluster assignments and repeat the tracking process if needed.

It is remarkable that all these phases are possible to implement by using just basic programming routines without computing, for example, eigenvalues or eigenvectors and without using any specific libraries or functions such as k-means. However, if there is a lot of noise present, the k-means step can be included in the phases 3 and 4.

The phases 2–4 will be explained in more detail in following sections, whereas the phase 1 will not need any further explanations or details, as it is implemented directly in the same manner as explained in Sect. 2.

3.1 Phase 2: Multiresolution Construction

The multiresolution construction is needed for the efficient computation of high powers of the diffusion matrix T so that the time evolution of the matrix can be analyzed. The multiresolution construction used in here was first introduced in [16] and allows a fast, efficient and highly compressed way to describe the dyadic powers T^{2^p}, $p > 0$, of the matrix within a precision needed. The parameter

p indicates the multiresolution level and this time resolution is adequate and suitable for our purpose.

We made previously an assumption that the diffusion process is much faster inside the clusters than between them. This means that the decay of the spectrum of the diffusion matrix constructed from the data inside the cluster is far faster than that of the matrix constructed from all the data. This causes the euclidean distance between the columns of T^{2^p} that belong to a same cluster to approach towards zero, and in some point, the numerical range of T^{2^p} has decreased so that only one column is needed for representing each cluster. We can trace the columns that survived last during the multiresolution construction and use these points as an input to the next phase as starting points for the tracking process.

3.2   Phase 3: Tracking the Diffusion Process

The second assumption gives us a good starting point for choosing the right multiresolution level, or we can say the right moment of time, to stop the diffusion process. The speed of the diffusion process inside each cluster depends on the decay of the spectrum of the diffusion matrix concerning that part of the data set. This means that time needed by the diffusion process to settle down inside each cluster varies, and it would be necessary to have a possibility to choose the stop level of the diffusion process for every cluster individually as mentioned earlier. This can be done in a following way:

Let N_k be an approximate number of data points belonging to a cluster k, $\{s_k\}_{k=1}^M$ a set of indices of the columns tracked, or one can say the starting points, during the diffusion process and $\{q_{(i,k)}\}_{i=1}^{n_k}$ a small set, $n_k \ll N_k$, of column indices of the data points at the neighborhood of s_k (inside cluster k). The set $\{q_{(i,k)}\}$ may be get from the support of columns s_k of the matrix T.

The process is started at level $p = 1$ by calculating the approximation $\tilde{T}^2$ from the multiscale representation constructed in the previous phase, normalizing the columns tracked and storing them to the matrix C_p, $p = 1$:

$$C_p(l,k) = \frac{\tilde{T}^{2^p}(l, s_k)}{\frac{1}{n_k}\sum_{i=1}^{n_k}\tilde{T}^{2^p}(q_{(i,k)}, s_k)\sum_{l=1}^{N}\tilde{T}^{2^p}(l, s_k)} \tag{1}$$

where $l = 1, 2, \ldots, N$ and $k = 1, \ldots, M$.

Next the data points are assigned to clusters at this level by the function

$$g_p(l) = \operatorname*{argmax}_{k=1,2,\ldots,M} C_p(l,k) \tag{2}$$

where $l = 1, 2, \ldots, N$. The decision whether to continue or to stop the diffusion process inside each cluster is made as follows: If

$$R_{(p,k)} = \frac{\dfrac{1}{n_k} \displaystyle\sum_{i=1}^{n_k} \tilde{T}^{2^p}(s_k, q_{(i,k)}) \sum_{l=1}^{N} \mathbf{1}_{g_p(l)=k}}{\displaystyle\sum_{j=1}^{N} \tilde{T}^{2^p}(j, s_k)}, \tag{3}$$

$k = 1, \ldots, M$, is smaller than the chosen threshold r, stop the process inside the cluster k, else continue. In an ideal case, there will not be any leakage between clusters and $R_{(p,k)}$ approaches to 1 when the diffusion moves towards the stationary state. This is obvious because the mean of the points included in the small neighborhood $q_{(i,k)}$ tends towards the mean of all the points inside the support $\mathbf{1}_{g_p(l)=k}$. However, the values above 1 as a threshold for making the decision would be too high if there is a significant leakage present, and, therefore, it would be reasonable to choose $0.8 \leq r \leq 1$.

If all the processes were allowed to continue, we can let the diffusion processes move forward and step to the next level $p = 2$ by computing the approximation $\tilde{T}^4$, updating the neighborhoods and computing the matrix $C_2(l, k)$ using the tracked columns of $\tilde{T}^4$. The cluster assignments and the decision making process will also be made in the same manner as at the previous level but using $\tilde{T}^4$ instead of $\tilde{T}^2$. The tracking process continues in this way through consecutive levels until the level where some of the diffusion processes will not be allowed to continue will be reached.

When the case $R_{(p,k)} < r$ appears, the corresponding column of $C_p(l, k)$ is transferred to the next level by storing it to $C_{p+1}(l, k)$ to the same place and will not be updated by the normalized columns of the diffusion matrix at that or other following levels. The process is continued through the levels until all the individual processes have stopped, and the cluster assignments may then be found in g_{p_F} where p_F indicates the final level.

3.3   Phase 4: Final Cluster Assignments

In some cases, the diffusion tracking process started from the points provided by the multiresolution construction gives results accurate enough for final cluster assignments. However, one can ask, "Why not to run in a loop the tracking algorithm and benefit from the information provided the previous tracking phase?" This is a justifiable question because if we can choose the tracked columns so that the diffusion processes inside the clusters settles down as fast as possible, we could also decrease the amount of leakage between clusters.

Let X_k be the data set of size N_k assigned to the cluster k and T_k the diffusion matrix constructed from this data set. The rate of the connectivity between points x_i and x_j inside a cluster k at level p can be measured with diffusion distance

$$D_{(2^p,k)}^2(i,j) = T_k^{2^p}(i,i) + T_k^{2^p}(j,j) - 2T_k^{2^p}(i,j) \tag{4}$$

as proposed in [17]. Let the diffusion centroid of the cluster k be the point with the minimum mean diffusion distance inside the cluster:

$$c_k = \operatorname*{argmin}_{i=1,2,\dots,N_k} \frac{1}{N_k} \sum_{j=1}^{N_k} D^2_{(2^{p_k},k)}(i,j) \tag{5}$$

where p_k is the level where the diffusion was stopped. The diffusion distance measures the connectivity between points of the data set so it is small if there are a lot of connections, and vice versa. The point c_k is, therefore, the one where from the diffusion process can spread most effectively through the cluster k.

New cluster assignments may then be got after a new tracking process started from the centroids, $s_k = c_k$. In most of the cases, there is not significant change in the cluster assignments after a couple of iterations.

4   Proposed Image Segmentation Algorithm

Image segmentation is one of the most used application for clustering algorithms. The development of these clustering algorithms leads also to better image segmentation algorithms some of which, quite recent ones, are presented in [18–20]. The segmentation algorithm presented here can be applied to any kind of color or grayscale images. The size of the image can be anything up to several megapixels, although the used accuracy have to be adapted to the image size. The segmentation process is based on dividing the image naturally to different areas by the properties of the texture on these areas. Therefore, the image has to be divided into patches. The patches, in this case, overlap each other almost entirely and the pixel assignments to different segment are done by collecting the information from these overlapping patches. This process we call as patch oversampling. The algorithm consists of following sequential phases:

1. Choose the patch size and the way to collect different layers from the image and form a stack from the layers with correct alignment.
2. Extract the non-overlapping patches from the layer stack and form the feature vectors from the patches.
3. Choose the number of segments to be revealed and find out the patches to be tracked using the diffusion tracking algorithm if not provided with some other way.
4. Apply the diffusion tracking clustering algorithm to all the layers individually using the patches provided by the previous phase as starting points.
5. Segment all the layers using the results of the previous phase and align the layers to a stack in the same way they were collected.
6. Compute the mode value of each pixel from the stack and form the segmentation given by these values.
7. Find out the areas, where the segmentation was not clear enough and pass them to next phase if more accurate segmentation is needed. If not, skip the next phase.
8. Go back to phase 1.
9. Perform mode filtering on the image plane to the result image.

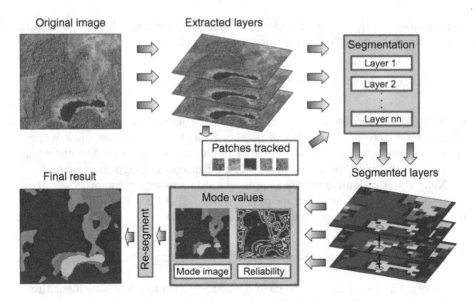

Fig. 1. Image segmentation algorithm, flow chart.

A simplified flowchart representing the segmentation process is shown in Fig. 1. This algorithm is quite simple to implement, and there are some interesting parts in it. One of these, and maybe the most interesting one, is the possibility to track the same patches in different images or layers. In other words, the cluster centroids are the same in all cases. This gives us the possibility to join the segmentation results from different layers if we know the alignment of the layers. The other interesting thing is that we can measure the uncertainty of the segmentation process on the image plane and run the segmentation procedure on these areas again with a finer scale using a smaller patch size. Next we will take a closer look at all the phases presented.

4.1 Phase 1: Collecting the Layers

We call the different pixel alignment choices as layers in this context. Let us consider a case we have an image of size $N \times M$. The different layers from the image can be collected by selecting all or a restricted number of the sub images of size $N - n \times M - m$ from the original image. For example, if we choose $n = 1$ and $m = 1$, it is possible to collect four different sub images from the original one; the top, most left pixel $(1, 1)$ in the sub image can be chosen from a pixel set $(1, 1)$, $(1, 2)$, $(2, 1)$ and $(2, 2)$ in the original image. One crucial issue, which affects strongly on the way to choose the layers, is the size of the patch used for the texture description. The larger the patch size, the more possible layers we have so that the non-overlapping patches inside the layers are all different. In case of the patch size 3×3 pixels, for example, we have 9 possible different layers so that there are not any similar patches inside the different layers.

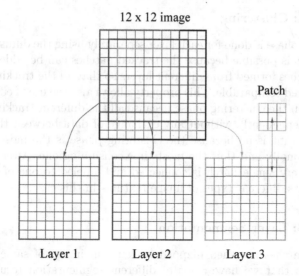

Fig. 2. Layer selection with patch size 3×3 and original image size 12×12.

Of course, it is not necessary, or even possible, to collect all the layers when the patch size grows. One possible way to choose layers from all possible choices in case of patch size 3×3 and image size 12×12 is presented in Fig. 2. The layers are then stacked so that the correct alignment remains.

4.2   Phase 2: Forming the Feature Vectors

All the non-overlapping square patches are then extracted from each layer separately and a description of every patch is stored in a feature vector. The description is constructed in a following simple way. First all pixels are sorted according to the value of each pixel in a single color component and stored to a vector. This sorting process is done for every component separately. Next all of these vectors are concatenated so that the resulting vector is of size $3n^2$ in case of a RGB-image and a patch size $n \times n$.

4.3   Phase 3: Choosing the Patches to Be Tracked

One very important thing on ensuring the proper working of the diffusion tracking algorithm used for clustering is the choice of the starting points for the diffusion processes inside each cluster, or we can say inside each image segment in this case. When segmenting an image, a natural way to choose these starting points or patches is to manually select patches from the areas to be treated as different segments. This is possible because the tracking algorithm allows the patches tracked to be fixed. Of course, it is possible to search these patches automatically as explained previously in Sect. 3. In that case, only the number of different segments and the set of layers, where from to search the patches, have to be given to the algorithm.

4.4   Phase 4: Clustering

The clustering phase is done for each layer separately using the diffusion tracking algorithm. This is possible because the tracked patches can be added to each of the sets of patches formed from different layers so that all the tracking processes can be considered comparable. This property allows also the use of efficient parallel computing in the clustering phase because all the different tracking processes can be ran independently without any exchange of data between them. This is quite an important issue because the clustering phase is the most demanding one computationally and thus the most time-consuming one. After the clustering process, every single patch is connected and labeled to one of the clusters which represents different types of image textures in this case.

4.5   Phase 5: Layer Segmentation

The labeled patches are then mapped back to an image of same size as the original one so that we have a set of different segmentation results, one per every layer, from that image. These different segmented layers are stacked so that the alignment of the layers corresponds the original alignment.

4.6   Phase 6: Joining the Results

The segmented layer stack gives us a lot of possibilities to choose the final label of each pixel in the result image. A straightforward and reasonable way to approach this problem is to use the statistical point of view. There are a lot of propositions for the label of each pixel, so why not to choose the one which has the most of votes. This idea is very easy to implement just by choosing the mode value from the set of labels of each pixel. This solution has proven to be very reliable and stable also in experimental tests. Because of the different alignment of the layers, there will be a narrow border area around the image where the number of labels is smaller than elsewhere and, therefore, the reliability suffers a bit on that area.

4.7   Phase 7: Measuring the Reliability of the Segmentation

As presented earlier, a set of different labels is attached to every single pixel. The reliability of the segmentation result of each pixel is then revealed simply by examining the distribution of the labels, pixel by pixel. If the number of votes for the mode value at each pixel clearly outnumbers the other values, the chosen label can be considered reliable and the segmentation of that pixel final. In other case, the pixel examined is tagged as uncertain one and may need further processing and re-segmentation. Choosing the threshold between uncertain and certain labeling is a tradeoff between more accurate results and more computing time. The experimental tests have shown that a good choice as a threshold could be as high as 75 % of all votes for the won label.

4.8   Phase 8: Loop

If more accurate results were needed, the areas to be re-segmented are then passed to the phase 1 where the patch size is scaled downwards compared to the previous round. The patches tracked are also scaled down and kept as a starting points for the next round clustering process.

4.9   Phase 9: Smoothing

After the accuracy wanted is achieved, the remaining phase is to smooth the image. This may be necessary due to the single separate pixels or small pixel groups on the re-segmented areas. The filtering method proposed here is related to the median filtering on the image plane, but instead of using the median value of the pixel neighborhood, the mode value is used.

4.10   Using Other Clustering Methods

The proposed image segmentation algorithm suits especially well together with the DT algorithm. However, it is possible to use also other clustering methods as a part of the segmentation process presented. The interface between the clustering method used and the segmentation algorithm can be done using the KM algorithm with one iteration using the cluster centroids provided by the user or the clustering method as starting points. The number of iterations have to be limited to one because the centroids of the clusters must not move. They have to be the same between different layers. Because of this interface, clustering methods that uses the KM algorithm when forming the final cluster assignments work together with this image segmentation algorithm.

5   Experimental Results

The performance of the clustering algorithm presented in this paper was tested together with the ZP algorithm based segmentation algorithm using an aerial image as a data source. The ZP algorithm outperforms usually the classical NJW algorithm and therefore the results achieved with classical NJW are omitted. However, when clustering some of the data sets extracted from the image, the ZP algorithm provided by authors of [15] failed totally. Therefore, the performance of our algorithm is compared also with the NJW algorithm enhanced with local scaling. Neither ZP nor NJW algorithm supports directly the image segmentation procedure presented here, so the final segmentation results using these clustering methods could not be provided this time.

5.1   Aerial Image Segmentation

The image segmentation algorithm presented in this paper is based on clustering patches collected from an image. In this experiment, two color aerial images

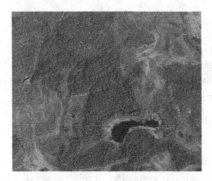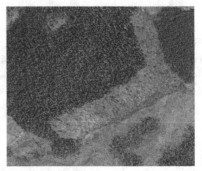

Fig. 3. Original aerial images.

are used as a source of data to be clustered and as an example cases for the segmentation algorithm. Figure 3 represents the aerial images to be segmented. The images are RGB images of size 750×900 pixels (height × width) and are acquired from the National Land Survey of Finland (2010). Only a slight contrast enhancement has been done for both of the images before the segmentation process. The main goal of the segmentation process is to reveal the areas of different terrain types such as lakes, forests of different densities and bogs using the information provided by rectangular patches extracted from the image. The number of different terrain types is chosen to be five in both of the cases. This choice is reasonable when looking at the images: There is a clearly visible water area, woodless bog areas and the forest areas can be divided quite clearly to three types with different densities in the image on the left side, whereas there are four different types of forest areas and a woodless bog area in the image on the right side.

To provide some proof of the good performance in the clustering accuracy of the proposed method, our algorithm is compared with the ZP algorithm and also with the NJW algorithm with local scaling because the ZP algorithm failed totally in some tests as can be noticed in following results. The comparison was done by segmenting a single layer extracted from the aerial image on the left side in Fig. 3. Figure 4 shows the results using three different patch sizes. The patch sizes are chosen so that visible differences can be noticed. In addition to the segmentation results, there are also the embeddings via the first three eigenvectors of the diffusion matrix presented, and these embeddings show even more clearly the differences between algorithms. The dark red color represents water areas, light blue woodless areas, green sparse forest areas, orange forest areas with medium density and dark blue dense forests.

All the algorithms perform quite well when using the patch size 44×44 and the reason for that is clearly seen on embeddings via the eigenvectors. The five different clusters are all well separated, and this guarantees the good performance also for the spectral clustering algorithms like NJW and ZP.

Changing the patch size a little bit smaller to size 40×40 makes the clustering problem much more difficult. Both the NJW and ZP algorithm fail to reveal the

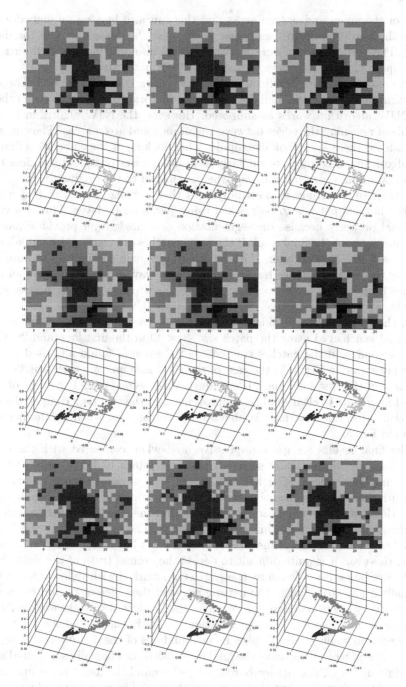

Fig. 4. Rows 1, 3, 5: segmentation results with patch sizes 44×44, 40×40 and 33×33. From left: NJW, ZP, and our algorithm. Rows 2, 4, 6: the results embedded via the first three eigenvectors of the diffusion matrix.

edges of the green and orange areas and this can also be seen on embeddings where the border between these areas go through the densest part of the data cloud. The performance of our algorithm suffers also a little bit, but the result is still quite close to the one achieved with larger patch size.

The most interesting results are found when using patch size 33×33. The ZP algorithm fails totally while mixing the green and orange areas with each other. The NJW algorithm works as supposed. However, the NJW algorithm is not capable of revealing the edges between the orange and green areas. The clusters it founds for these areas look like dipoles when looking at the embedding figure. Our algorithm succeeds quite similarly as in other cases presented and does the segmentation in a very natural way when compared to the original image.

It is quite surprising to see from Fig. 4 that our algorithm can find quite well the natural patches to be tracked using just a single layer. This is a very beneficial property because the segmentation of a single layer provides quite a good hunch about the final result if the same patches are tracked through all the layers, as it can be seen later. However, there are some possibilities to improve the way to find the patches tracked. One simple way is just to combine all the patches from several layers together and try to search the starting points from that set.

In the case of the left side image in Fig. 3, the final segmentation result presented is achieved using the patch size 40×40 in the first loop and 20×20 in the second, and the patches tracked are the same as found and used in the single layer case in Fig. 4. In the case of the right side image, patch size 35×35 was used in the first loop and 21×21 during the second one. The effect of the second loop is quite clear, and the improvement in the accuracy compared with the result after the first loop is obvious, as can be seen when comparing the results in Fig. 5.

The final results are quite impressive, and when compared with the original images or the manually segmented images shown in Fig. 5, only a slight errors may be noticed. The left side image was obviously more difficult to segment, thus there is one obvious error on surroundings of the small lake, where there can be seen a clear open area around the lake in the original image, but the segmentation algorithm fails to reveal it. The second one can be found in the bottom center part of the image where the wet bog is segmented as a dense forest. However, it is quite difficult to decide the ground truth of the right class for the wet bog areas. Therefore, these areas are marked with yellow color in the manually segmented image. The natural edges of the different terrain types are found as they are in real and, for example, the borders of the lake are nearly as accurate as they can be. The segmentation results in the case of the right side image contain some small mistakes in surroundings of the dense forest nose, as can be noticed when comparing the final result with the manually segmented and the original image. The orange border stripes around the forest areas may also be thought as mistakes, but that is not so obvious. The percentage of similarly segmented pixels between the manual and automatic segmentation in the more difficult case was 80.1 % and in the easier case, 89.5 %. The accurate manual

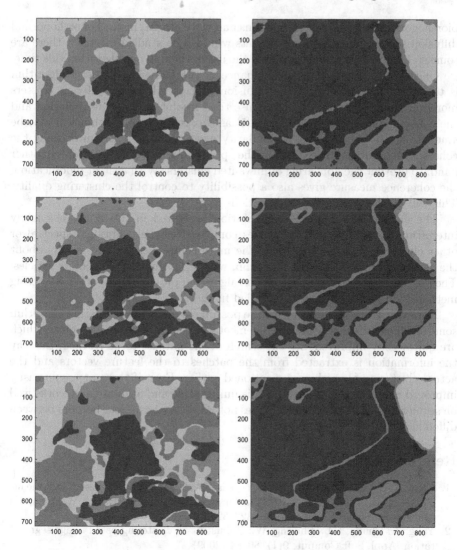

Fig. 5. First row: segmentation results after the first loop. Second row: the final segmentation results. Third row: segmentation results with manual segmentation.

segmentation in these kind of cases is an impossible task, so the importance of these values can be questioned.

6   Discussion and Conclusions

The results of our algorithm are really promising, although there are a lot of possibilities to develop it still. One main target to develop is the construction of the multiresolution which is not optimized for clustering at all and may produce, in some cases, bad starting points for the tracking algorithm. The use of biorthogonal diffusion scaling functions and wavelets [21] instead of orthonormal diffusion scaling functions and wavelets will also be studied carefully; there are some stability issues which prevented the use of them in our algorithm this time.

One way to improve the performance of the Diffusion Tracking algorithm is to prevent the leakage of the diffusion processes between different clusters more efficiently. The use of more dense time resolution with interpolation and the coherence measure presented in [5] as a part of our algorithm will also be studied like the use of different similarity measures also. The aim of using the coherence measure is to try find out the optimal number of clusters and, in other hand, to prevent the appearing of unwanted clusters. With a slight modification, the coherence measure gives also a possibility to control the clustering quality. This will be shown in future publications.

The algorithm for image segmentation presented in this study has many interesting advantages and properties compared to the traditional spectral or other clustering based algorithms. The more comprehensive test results about the accuracy of the clustering algorithm will be presented in upcoming articles. The possibility to use the segmentation algorithm proposed with other clustering methods will also be tested and studied further.

However, a lot of improvements are possible to make to the existing algorithm some of which are already under implementation phase. The crucial points, which are quite easily improved, are the search of the patches to be tracked, the way the information is extracted from the patches to the feature vectors and the actual clustering algorithm as mentioned earlier. Even if there are some easily improved things in our algorithm, it is quite stable and accurate and works well on segmenting color images which does not necessary have clear borders between different segments.

References

1. Chen, T.W., Chen, Y.L., Chien, S.Y.: Fast image segmentation based on k-means clustering with histograms in HSV color space. In: 2008 IEEE 10th Workshop on Multimedia Signal Processing, pp. 322–325 (2008)
2. Yang, Z., Chung, F.L., Shitong, W.: Robust fuzzy clustering-based image segmentation. Appl. Soft Comput. 9(1), 80–84 (2009)
3. Luxburg, U.: A tutorial on spectral clustering. Stat. Comput. 17, 395–416 (2007)
4. Filippone, M., Camastra, F., Masulli, F., Rovetta, S.: A survey of kernel and spectral methods for clustering. Pattern Recogn. 41, 176–190 (2008)
5. Nadler, B., Galun, M.: Fundamental limitations of spectral clustering. In: Schölkopf, B., Platt, J., Hoffman, T. (eds.) Advances in Neural Information Processing Systems, vol. 19, pp. 1017–1024. MIT Press, Cambridge (2007)
6. Macqueen, J.B.: Some methods of classification and analysis of multivariate observations. In: Proceedings of the Fifth Berkeley Symposium on Mathematical Statistics and Probability. pp. 281–297 (1967)
7. Dunn, J.C.: A fuzzy relative of the ISODATA process and its use in detecting compact well-separated clusters. J. Cybern. 3(3), 32–57 (1973)
8. Chitta, R., Murty, M.N.: Two-level k-means clustering algorithm for k-τ relationship establishment and linear-time classification. Pattern Recogn. 43(3), 796–804 (2010)

9. Liu, Q., Zhang, B., Sun, H., Guan, Y., Zhao, L.: A novel k-means clustering algorithm based on positive examples and careful seeding. In: 2010 International Conference on Computational and Information Sciences (ICCIS), pp. 767–770 (2010)

10. Yu, F., Xu, H., Wang, L., Zhou, X.: An improved automatic FCM clustering algorithm. In: 2010 2nd International Workshop on Database Technology and Applications (DBTA), pp. 1–4, November 2010

11. Vintr, T., Pastorek, L., Vintrova, V., Rezankova, H.: Batch FCM with volume prototypes for clustering high-dimensional datasets with large number of clusters. In: 2011 Third World Congress on Nature and Biologically Inspired Computing (NaBIC), pp. 427–432 (2011)

12. Li, C.H., Kuo, B.C., Lin, C.T.: LDA-based clustering algorithm and its application to an unsupervised feature extraction. IEEE Trans. Fuzzy Syst. **19**(1), 152–163 (2011)

13. David, G., Averbuch, A.: Hierarchical data organization, clustering and denoising via localized diffusion folders. Appl. Comput. Harmon. Anal. **33**(1), 1–23 (2012)

14. Ng, A.Y., Jordan, M.I., Weiss, Y.: On spectral clustering analysis and an algorithm. In: Advances in Neural Information Processing Systems, pp. 849–856. MIT Press (2001)

15. Zelnik-manor, L., Perona, P.: Self-tuning spectral clustering. In: Advances in Neural Information Processing Systems, vol. 17, pp. 1601–1608. MIT Press (2004)

16. Coifman, R.R., Maggioni, M.: Diffusion wavelets. Appl. Comput. Harmon. Anal. **21**(1), 53–94 (2006)

17. Coifman, R.R., Lafon, S.: Diffusion maps. Appl. Comput. Harmon. Anal. **21**(1), 5–30 (2006)

18. Tziakos, I., Theoharatos, C., Laskaris, N.A., Economou, G.: Color image segmentation using Laplacian eigenmaps. J. Electron. Imaging **18**(2), 023004 (2009)

19. Tung, F., Wong, A., Clausi, D.A.: Enabling scalable spectral clustering for image segmentation. Pattern Recogn. **43**(12), 4069–4076 (2010)

20. Liu, H., Jiao, L., Zhao, F.: Non-local spatial spectral clustering for image segmentation. Neurocomputing **74**(1–3), 461–471 (2010)

21. Maggioni, M., Bremer, J.C., Coifman, R.R., Szlam, A.D.: Biorthogonal diffusion wavelets for multiscale representations on manifolds and graphs. In: Wavelets XI - Proceedings of SPIE, vol. 5914, p. 59141M. SPIE (2005)

Cloud-Based Automatic Video Editing Using Keywords

Abdelkader Outtagarts[✉], Sylvain Squedin, and Olivier Martinot

Alcatel-Lucent Bell Labs, Route de Villejust, 91620 Nozay, France
{abdelkader.outtagarts,sylvain.squedin,
olivier.martinot}@alcatel-lucent.com

Abstract. In this paper we propose a cloud-based video editing application designated to manage abundance of video using automatic video editing and summarization algorithms. Our approach uses text processing, statistic analysis and information retrieval techniques to analyze audio transcripts of video corpus. A model approach of mashup based on keywords is proposed. A video editing testbed has been designed and implemented. Finally the video editor engine is deployed on Openstack cloud computing platform which deliver a massively scalable cloud operating system.

Keywords: Automatic video editing · Cloud computing · Mashups · Speech2text · Annotation · Reasoning · Collaboration · Web 2.0

1 Introduction

Video editing is the process of selecting segments from a set of raw videos and chaining them by adding piece of audio, effects and transition in order to create a new video or mashup. Most available video editing tools are time-consuming and require specific knowledge. There is therefore, an increasing demand for simple, user-friendly online video editing tools. Online video editing tools can afford less costly and more accessible processes that can be completed anytime, anywhere. In this context, this paper presents a new tool to facilitate the creation and handling of video content. What our video editor wants to enable is a keyword-based automatic video editing deployed in the cloud with a previewing web client. Videos are coming from video sharing platforms, directly from the webcam, uploaded video files by users or captured from camera network. They can be composed and viewed on the fly. Those compositions, called video mashups can be shared and modified collaboratively, and their privacy easily is managed. This video editor is also a research testbed for studying automatic video editing and summarization based on text and statistical data and metadata. The paper is organised as follows. In Sect. 2, we present the video editing model. The video editing testbed is detailed in Sect. 3. We'll present the current status of our research in Sect. 4. The model and algorithms validation methods are described in Sect. 5. Conclusions are drawn in Sect. 6.

Automated video editing and summarization have gained momentum in recent years. Many algorithms such as shot detection are developed to extract representative key-frames from video. The majority of authors use video analysis or signal processing

© Springer-Verlag Berlin Heidelberg 2014

M.S. Obaidat and J. Filipe (Eds.): ICETE 2012, CCIS 455, pp. 228–241, 2014.
DOI: 10.1007/978-3-662-44791-8_14

in order to perform automatic video composition (mashup). Among the authors, Hua and Zhang [1, 2] develop an approach for extracting temporal structure and determining the importance of a video segment in order to facilitate the selection of highlight segments. They also extract temporal structure, beats and tempos from the incidental music. In order to create more professional-looking results, the selected highlight segments satisfy a set of editing rules and are matched to the content of the incidental music. The strategy of [1] is to parse the video sequence into hierarchical structures consisting of scenes, shots, and sub-shots. For music, they segment it into clips by strong beats, and for each clip, tempo is estimated, which indicates the speed of the music sub-clips. In their system, the video segment selection is also based the work proposed by Ma et al. [3], Hua and Zhang [1] refine the method by adding an "attention fusion" function, which generates improved results. Müller et al. [4] present Odessa framework, which automates the preparation of footage during composition and the editing process. Real-time audio analysis extracts music feature vectors, which are mapped to editing parameters of a video montage engine. The engine can be controlled through high-level editing parameters, such as looping speed or cutting rate. The authors apply a reverse editing of a video. The original video is analysed and re-organised in terms of individual scenes, groups, and shots. Odessa implements methods such as audio beat tracking or music similarity analysis to operate in real-time. Takemae et al. [5, 6] propose an automatic video editing system using stereo-based head tracking in multiparty conversations for conveying the contents of the conversations to the viewers. Their system can automatically detect participants' head 3D position and orientation during a conversation. Based on the detection results, the author's system selects the shot of the participant that most participants' heads are facing. This approach exploits participants gaze behaviour to select the most effective shots of participants. Mudhwuchutyula et al. [7] propose an automatic mechanism for XML based video metadata editing, in tandem with video editing operations. An implementation framework for editing metadata in accordance with the video editing operations is demonstrated. The video metadata editing mechanism has been implemented in the context of Digital Video Album (DVA) system for editing metadata in accordance with presentation/summarization operations performed on video. Foote et al. [8] have presented a music video creation system that can automatically select and align video segments to music. Authors have analyzed both audio and video sequences in order to automatically create music videos for a given sound track.

As a conclusion of the state of the art, existing video editing solutions are time consuming. To facilitate video edition, many authors have worked in automatic video editing and summarization. The most algorithms developed to extract representative key-frames from video are based on video and/or audio analysis. These solutions require significant processing especially when it must deal with hundreds or thousands of videos.

2   Model

A video mashup is a combination of video and audio sequences, effects and transitions. The manual video editing is recommended when a user is working with a small number of media. When the number of media increases, it is necessary to help users by managing automatically the abundance of media. In the example of mashup shown in Fig. 1, a video mashup consists of a set of video clips, transitions, titles... The videos are trimed to select only the interested segments or clips to build a small movie or a video mashup. After the trims, the selected clip will correspond to a time Δtk as shown in Fig. 1. The position (start attribute) of the video clip in the mashup and attribute values (length, trimstart, trimend, metadata positions in the mashup,...) are stored in a database using XML format.

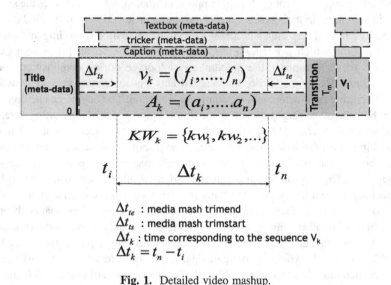

Δt_{te} : media mash trimend
Δt_{ts} : media mash trimstart
Δt_{k} : time corresponding to the sequence V_k
$\Delta t_{k} = t_n - t_i$

Fig. 1. Detailed video mashup.

A video is a sequence of video frames captured by a webcam, phones or other devices during a certain time. A video v_k containing (n-i) frames during the time $t_i < t < t_n$, is given by (Fig. 1):

$$v_k = (f_i, \ldots, f_n) \tag{1}$$

The corresponding audio sequence contained in the video is represented by:

$$A_k = (a_i, \ldots, a_n) \tag{2}$$

A_k is an audio sequence containing (n-i) number of audio frames.
Between the times t_i and t_n, the extracted keywords from the corresponding audio of video file is given by the following expression:

$$vKW_k = \{vKW_1, vKW_2, \ldots\} \tag{3}$$

vKW_k is the keyword list extracted during between t_i and t_n of the video V_k.
The video V_k can be represented with both video frames, audio frames and metadata (keywords).

$$V_k = \begin{bmatrix} (f_i, \ldots, f_n) \\ (a_i, \ldots, a_n) \\ \{Kw_1, Kw_2, \ldots\} \end{bmatrix} \tag{4}$$

A video transition is the visual movements as one picture or video clip inserted between two video sequences. It is the way in which video sequences/shots are joined together. Preferably, a transition must be related to the context of the created mashup video. We can represent a transition with a matrix containing a suite of video frames and keywords/tags which describes the transition.

$$T_m = \begin{bmatrix} (f_{n+1}, \ldots, f_{n+m}) \\ \{tkw_1, tkw_2, \ldots\} \end{bmatrix} \tag{5}$$

Where T_m is a transition and tkwi keywords/tags corresponding to the transition T_m.

A Mashup M is basically represented by a sequence of non-overlapping sequences from a multiple video:

$$M = \sum_{j=0}^{j=x} V_j \tag{6}$$

x is the number of video sequences. Transitions can be added between video sequences to join them.

A mashup when encoded become a video and identified by a suite of frames of images, audios and keywords.

$$M = \begin{bmatrix} \sum_j f_i \\ \sum_j a_j \\ \{kw_1, kw_2, \ldots\} \end{bmatrix} \tag{7}$$

The challenges in this work is how, from one or more keywords, we can automatically selecting segments/sequences/shots from a set of raw videos and chaining them by adding transition in order to create a new video or mashup.

Automatic video editing helps to manage the abundance of the media by proposing mashups for users. As showed in Fig. 2, the feedback of users is necessary to validate the mashups.

We consider two possible users feedbacks which can be introduced in the automatic video editing algorithms:

Implicit: This user feedback is characterized by the number of times the video is viewed as well as modifications done in the proposed mashup.

Explicit: Here the user gives his opinion directly or delete the proposed mashup. These parameters can be added to the model in order to automatically taking into account the user feedback by using machine learning algorithms.

Video mashups

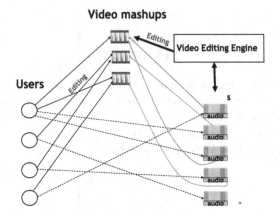

Fig. 2. Video mashups.

3   Video Editing Testbed

3.1   Description

The video editor testbed platform allows online cloud-based collaborative video edition. This testbed is composed on six main components: a web-based video editing application, import multimedia, mashup browser and media manager, a database, an XML2Video converter and an automatic video editor engine:

- **Video Editing Application:** It is a web-based video editor flash applet which has not need pre-installation of editing software in client's devices. It allows online video editing or video mashup creation and annotation. Using the video editing application user has possibilities to modify videos using function such as: drag and drop media, trim, cut, adding audio, image, effects and transitions... All the mashups and text data are stored in Mysql database using XML format. The XML descriptor contains metadata such as: trim start/end attributes of videos and audios, videos and mashups length, the beginning and the end of a title, a caption, a textbox ...
- **Mashup Browser:** This function allows displaying the private and public video mashup, the contributors for each mashup, links to edit the composition and to export the composition into the streaming server.
- **Mysql Database:** Two types of data are stored in the video editor testbed database: Critical data and statistical data. The critical data include: users, the media used to create compositions and compositions created by users. The statistical data are collected and processed to perform automatic annotation of the media. This data include: specific changes to a composition for each edition, How a user edits in compositions, metadata added by users and the data associated with imported videos.
- **Import Multimedia Features:**
  - Import from Tivizio: Using REST APIs, a user can collect videos from Tivizio, an enterprise video sharing platform.

- Webcam Video Recorder: this function allows user to record a pitch in order to create a video mashup using other media and metadata.
- Import from camera network: using Camera Search Engine component, a user navigate in camera network to collect images which are imported into the video editing application using REST APIs in order to be part of a video composition.
- Upload file from the device: from PC or Android OS devices, a user is able to upload media with standard format.

- **XML2Video Converter:** this component allows converting XML descriptor of a video composition generated by the video editing application component into a file video format. This feature allows also exporting the video to Tivizio or Youtube.
- **Automatic Video Editor Engine:** this function allows for instance, automatic video edition based on keyword and rule.
- **Video Editing Testbed APIs:** REST APIs are provided for uploading videos, setting/getting metadata and composing mashup using keyword.

3.2 Data and Algorithm

Our algorithm of automatic video editing is based on keywords extracted from audio file of the video and other parameters of the media. A media can be a video, an image, an audio file or a mashup. As described in Table 1 which shows the media table, the main attribute of a media used the automatic video editing algorithm are:

- The type.
- The Meta data.
- The mashup descriptor.
- The media viewed counter.

When uploaded in the video editing testbed, the video frames and audio file are extracted and stored the multimedia database. Other data are stored in MySql database in the media containing attributes described in Table 1.

Two types of data are stored in the database:

a-Critical Data
The first type of data is required to operate the video editing testbed:

- Users.
- The media used to create compositions.
- Compositions created by users.

b-Statistical
The second type of data stored in the database is linked to the use of the video editor. This data is used to compile statistics. Indeed, it is expected in this research project using all data collected to create an engine for implicit automatic annotation of videos. This is roughly able to understand "who publishes what and how":

- Specific changes to a composition for each edition.
- How user edits compositions.

Table 1. Media table description.

Media	
m_id	Media id
u_user	Username
m_type	Video, image, audio, mash
m_label	Media name
m_metadata	Keywords metadata Ex: <speech2keywords begin = '00.00.16' end = '00.01.15' keywords = 'service provider | quality service | right combination | irrational |'> </speech2keywords>
m_duration_seconds	Duration
m_ source_url	Media url
m_date	Creation date
m_xml_string	Mashup XML descriptor
m_last_update	Update the date
m_view_count	Viewed counter
m_fps	Number of frame per seconds
m_audio	url of the audio file

– Metadata added by users.
– The data associated with imported videos.

4 Current Status of Our Research

The post-production video editing requires significant processing, when we have to analyze a large number of media, hundreds or thousands of videos, audios and images. That is why we propose a solution based only on text data and metadata. These data and metadata are obtained in three ways:

– Classical video annotation by users.
– Implicit annotation video by inheritance of the text data added by users during the compositions. This annotation approach is described below.
– Extracting the text from the audio: speach2keyword during the media upload process.

The annotations collected by each media are analyzed using text processing and statistical algorithms for improving the media description. The automatic video algorithms use these text data in order to generate an XML descriptor as an output of video composition. An example of the XML mashup descriptor is given in Fig. 3. Each segment of a clip is represented as a link to the original one, which maintains associated data in the case of being deleted or moved, as well as some more descriptions. The transitions and effects are either a link with descriptions and media links.

```
< descriptor >
<mashup width="320" height="240" id="c8ddafe1233b29125e4f69be8123f763"
                    label="XML descriptor example>
    <clip type="video" id="5eef274620a55a78b6c90a845cfcf307" begin="100"
end="200"
            label=http://www.youtube.com/watch?v=HlxIWmA4pMk" length="100"
            description= " Shot description .... " />
    < clip type="video" id="jgjg274620a55a78b6c90a845dfhf67" begin="0"
end="100"
            label=http://www.youtube.com/watch?v=_uI_4kJCy9E" length="100"
            description= " Shot description .... " />
    <media group="video" type="video" id="5eef274620a55a78b6c90a845cfcf307"
            label="http://www.youtube.com/watch?v=HlxIWmA4pMk"
            source=" http://www.youtube.com/watch?v=HlxIWmA4pMk"
            fps="10" duration="1000"
            description= " General description .... " />
    <media group="video" type="video" id=" jgjg274620a55a78b6c90a845dfhf67 "
            label="http://www.youtube.com/watch?v=_uI_4kJCy9E"
            source=" http://www.youtube.com/watch?v=_uI_4kJCy9E"
            fps="10" duration="800"
            description= " General description .... " />
</ mashup>
</descriptor >
```

Fig. 3. Example of XML mashup descriptor.

Figure 4 shows the global architecture of the video editing testbed. On this figure main component are detailed in this paper such as:

- Speech2keyword generator,
- Implicit Video Annotations and,
- keyword-based video editing.

4.1 Speech2keyword Generator

Speech-to-text engine like Nuance speech recognition engine, Sphinx or other are really efficient for a limited of vocabulary, but can be less efficient when voice or accent is not trained by the system. Currently we obtain 50–80 % quality for the text transcription. In some cases we do not need the full text transcription but only an idea of

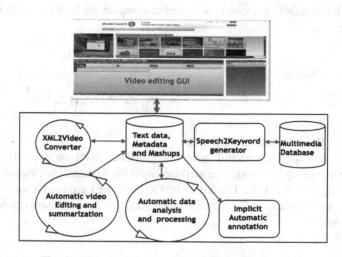

Fig. 4. Global architecture of the video editing testbed.

the concepts and subjects addressed by the speaker. The idea is to reduce errors of the Speech-to-text engine with the Speech2keyword generator, that is able to extract the keywords in a time-based manner from the speech transcription in real-time. Next steps are to apply semantic algorithms to improve the consolidation/disambiguation of extracted keywords and reduce the errors.

The current implementation includes ASR (Automatic Speech Recognition) of Nuance [9] and semantically methods to extract keywords (Fig. 5).

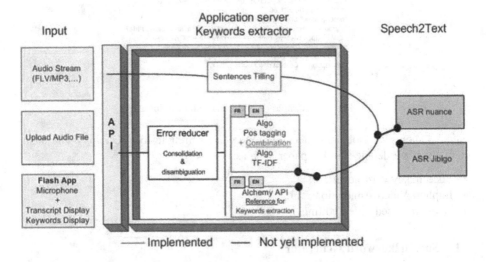

Fig. 5. Speech2keyword generator.

The quality of the speech to text is key element in the keyword extractor and when the voice or accent is not trained by the system. The result of the transcription success is about 50–80 % depending on audio file input.

The cosine similarity computation is used to compare the both extracted keywords is given by:

$$similarity = \cos(\theta) = \frac{A.B}{\|A\|\|B\|} = \frac{\sum_{i=1}^{n} A_i \times B_i}{\sqrt{\sum_{i=1}^{n}(A_i)^2} \times \sqrt{\sum_{i=1}^{n}(B_i)^2}} \qquad (8)$$

Where A and B are vectors of attributes.

To show the speech2keyword generator efficiency with an example, we have converted a text to mp3 file and have used the audio file to extract the transcription and keyword using alchemy APIs. To convert text to mp3, we have used a web-based free access tools text2speech.org (http://www.text2speech.org/). The following parameters have been used:

Voice type: American Male 1
Volume scale: 5
The original text is:

Video editing is the process of selecting segments from a set of raw videos and chaining them by adding piece of audio, effects and transition in order to create a new video or mashup. Most available video editing tools are time-consuming and require specific knowledge. There is therefore, an increasing demand for simple, user-friendly online video editing tools. Online video editing tools can afford less costly and more accessible processes that can be completed anytime, anywhere.

The transcription using speech2keyword generator of the generated audio file by text2speech.org is given below:

<metadata>
<session id = "11">
<stream id = "mp3 text2speech">
<audio>
<speech2keywords begin = "00.00.00" end = "00.00.15" sentences = "Video editing just the process of selecting segments from a set of wrong videos and shaving them by having piece of audio effects and transitions in order to create a video on the sharp most Available video editing tools are time consuming and require specific knowledge there is therefore an increasing demand for simple user friendly online video editing tools online video"
</speech2keywords>
</audio>
</stream>
</session>
</metadata>

As can be seen, there some difference between the audio transcriptions and the original text. Table 2 compares the keywords extracted from original text with the keywords extracted by speech2keyword generator using Alchemy algorithm. More than 60 % of keywords are identical allowing us to confirm that the quality of the transcript is acceptable. This result is very interesting for automatic video editing to quickly edit a mashup when a user is dealing with a large number of videos.

4.2 Implicit Video Annotations

The proposed approach allows, implicitly, annotation of videos. A user when composing the video adds textual data such in titles, captions, textboxes and tickers in order to enrich his video mashup. A video mashup is composed by video clips. These videos are trimmed by the user to select only the interested segments or clips to build his small movie or a video mashup. Figure 5 shows an example of implicit annotation of a video inherited from mashup user annotations. Text processing and statistics analysis will be performed in the future work in order to obtain a better description of each video shots or segments.

Table 2. Comparing original text with speech2keyword generator.

Original text using http://www.alchemyapi.com/api/demo.html	Speech2keyword generator using Alchemy
Video editing tools	Video editing
Online video editing	Video editing tools
Most available video	User-friendly
User-friendly online video	Online video
New video	Available video
Raw videos	Wrong videos
Specific knowledge	Audio effects
Chaining	Specific knowledge
Time-consuming	Time-consuming
	Online
	Accessible processes
	Tools
	Anywhere

4.3   Keyword-Based Automatic Video Editing

In our research, the video compositions are based on text data added by users directly of implicitly and meta-data extracted by media analyzers (speech2keyword generator). The text data will be continually processed using text processing and statistical algorithms in order to better describing shot, sequences or all media file. For instance, the video composition allows automatic video composition by keyword (Fig. 6). First a user or an application performs an HTTP request with a "keyword", a user and the name of the rule as parameters (1). The keyword is processed (2) and a search request is sent to the database (3). Using rules, the automatic video editor (4) compose an XML descriptor which chain different video shots matching with the keyword. Audio file can be added in the video composition if the keyword matches with auto description. The XML descriptor of the composition is stored in the database (5). An end user can perform the following function using the web based video editing application: play the composition (6 and 7), modify the video composition (8) and render the composition by converting the XML descriptor on video format.

5   Model and Algorithm Validations

The video editing testbed has been built for studying and testing automatic video editing based on text data. To experiment the automatic video editing algorithms, we will use a video dataset with multiple semantic concepts in using video. We propose two methods to experimentally validating models and algorithms of automatic video editing: Mashup validation by users and comparison of the mashups to one or more reference mashups (depending on the context). For the first methods, the algorithms

```
<metadata>
    <annotations>
        <annotation>
            <type>textboxeffect</type>
            <text>The buffalo before the attacks of lions</text>
            <start>51</start>
            <duration>9.1</duration>
        </annotation>
        <annotation>
            <type>textboxeffect</type>
            <text>A clan of lions attacking a buffalo</text>
            <start>142</start>
            <duration>71</duration>
        </annotation>
            <type>titletheme</type>
            <text>Wild animals</text>
            <start>0</start>
            <duration>5</duration>
        </annotation>
    </annotations>
    <mashlabel>WildAnimals</mashlabel>
    <othermedia>
        <label>Lions Hunt Buffalo.flv</label>
        <label>Rhinoceros attacking tour bus.flv</label>
    </othermedia>
</metadata>
```

Fig. 6. Implicit media annotation.

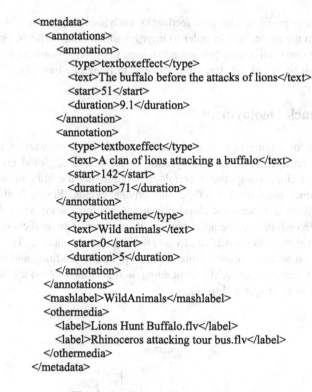

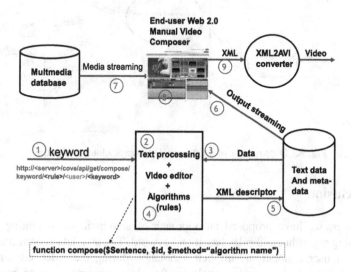

Fig. 7. Automatic video editing engine.

will use the user profiles. The user feedbacks analysis information will be processed and injected in the algorithms in order to improve future compositions. For the second, representative users will create reference mashups in different domains or subjects. The algorithms will be tested the mashup compared to reference mashups.

6   OpenStack Deployment

The video editor engine is deployed on Openstack [10], software which deliver a massively scalable cloud operating system. OpenStack is a global collaboration of developers and cloud computing technologists producing the ubiquitous open source cloud computing platform for public and private clouds. Figure 7 shows on of a deployed perform in Openstack cloud computing platform using several instances of automatic video editing engine and volumes. First a user or an application performs an HTTP request with a "keywords" and video desired duration, a user. The keywords are searched first on cache database before requesting the video editing and summarization engine which generate an XML containing a description of video sequences list matching which the request (Fig. 8).

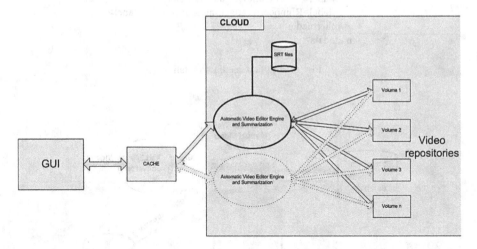

Fig. 8. Deployment of COVE on Openstack cloud computing.

7   Conclusion

In this paper, we have proposed an approach of automatic video editing which is derived using algorithm and rules based on keyword. The text data is collected in three ways: direct user annotations, implicit annotation during the video edition and by extracting keywords from video analysis. For the future we plan to create more complex models and algorithms of video composition to allow composing video from a sentence.

References

1. Hua, X.-S., Zhang, H.-J.: Automatic Home Video Editing. Signals and Communication Technology, pp. 353–386. Springer, Boston (2009)
2. Hua, X.-S., Zhang, H.-J.: AVE - automated home video editing. In: ACM MM (2003)
3. Ma, Y.F., Lu, L., Zhang, H.J., Li, M.J.: A user attention model for video summarization. In: ACM MM, pp. 533–542 (2002)
4. Müller Arisona, S., Müller, P., Schubiger-Banz, S., Specht, M.: Computer-assisted content editing techniques for live multimedia performance. In: Adams, R., Gibson, S., Müller Arisona, S. (eds.) Transdisciplinary Digital Art. Sound, Vision and the New Screen. Communications in Computer and Information Science, vol. 7, pp. 199–212. Springer, Heidelberg (2008)
5. Takemae, Y., Otsuka, K., Yamato, J.: Automatic video editing system using stereo-based head tracking for multiparty conversation. In: CHI 2005, pp. 1817–1820 (2005)
6. Takemae, Y., Otsuka, K., Yamato, J.: Development of automatic video editing system based on stereo-based head tracking for multiparty conversations. IEEE (2005)
7. Mudhwuchutyula, C.L., Kankunhalli, M.S., Mulhem, P.: Content based editing of semantic video metadata. In: IEEE International Conference on Multimedia and Expo (2004)
8. Foote, J., Cooper, M., Girgensohn, A.: Creating music videos using automatic media analysis. In: ACM MM (2002)
9. Beaufays, F., Sankar, A., Williams, S., Weintraub, M.: Learning name pronunciations in automatic speech recognition systems. In: Proceedings of the 15th IEEE International Conference on Tools with Artificial Intelligence (2003)
10. Openstack: Open source software for building private and public clouds

Controlling a Wheelchair Through Head Movement Through Artificial Vision and Using Speech Recognition

Ricardo Fuentes Covarrubias[1(✉)],
Andrés Gerardo Fuentes Covarrubias[1], Cristina Conde Vilda[2],
Isaac Martin de Diego[2], and Enrique Cabello[2]

[1] Facultad de Ingeniería Mecánica y Eléctrica, Universidad de Colima,
C.P. 28440 Coquimatlán, Colima, Mexico
{fuentesr, fuentesg}@ucol.mx
[2] Escuela Técnica Superior de Ingeniería Informática, Universidad Rey Juan
Carlos (URJC), Tulipán s/n, C.P. 62490 Mostoles, Madrid, Spain
{cristina.conde, isaac.martin, enrique.cabello}@urjc.es

Abstract. The Purpose of this project is the control of motion and direction in real time of a wheel chair, using machine vision algorithms. The main goal of this project is signal acquisition from the video camera and collision sensors for post processing in the C# algorithms and later obtaining motor control in the traction mechanism of the wheelchair. The C# algorithm has several tasks. The first is to obtain the real time image from web cam and later processing for the identification of the direction of movement of the human face. The second is to calculate the speed of the movement for generation of the PWM output for motor movement. This information output uses the RS232C driver with a microcontroller card attached to a motor control box in the wheel chair mechanism. The final task is to obtain the collision sensor status for security implementation, all in real time. The main reason for development of an implementation of this solution is the use of open source software tools for a more stable platform in the base system due to the characteristics of the end use of the system. The end user of the system will be a quadriplegic.

Keywords: Biometry · Machine vision · Automatic recognition

1 Introduction

While standard wheelchairs are used primarily by those who have the strength to move and handle them, electric wheelchairs are designed for those who cannot: people with excessive body weight, poor health, weakness of the upper limbs and who have been living with disability for a long time [1].

Unfortunately, conventional EW's (Electric Wheelchair) are not always satisfactory to compensate for motor disabilities: people with physical coordination and dexterity, cerebral spasticity, tetraplegia/paraplegia, tremors, spasms or head injury cannot use an EW and are prescribed a standard wheelchair whose mobility is provided by an

© Springer-Verlag Berlin Heidelberg 2014
M.S. Obaidat and J. Filipe (Eds.): ICETE 2012, CCIS 455, pp. 242–254, 2014.
DOI: 10.1007/978-3-662-44791-8_15

auxiliary person. In this case, robotics and mechatronics could be relevant for developing an EW with some degree of autonomy.

Wheelchairs may be considered as autonomous mobile robots; they are equipped with motors, sensors, electronic circuits, processing units and interfaces for communication with the user. In particular, the latter category has led to significant progress: the voice, blinking, eye movement or even thought [2] can control a robotic wheelchair.

It is important to know the disability problem with respect to patient anatomy in order to choose the best wheelchair that allows him to lead his life as normally as possible and it is therefore desirable to know the different types of wheelchairs and basic parts to follow the proper use and maintenance. In this paper we consider only the electric wheelchair because the focus is on patients with critical mobility problems. So the basic parts of an electric wheelchair are: the chassis, which is the frame on which are mounted the other pieces that make up the chair. The material is often steel although there are some aluminum models.

This project integrates a solution aimed at controlling an electric wheelchair by moving the face, using artificial vision techniques and voice command. This article mainly describes the vision module, and details its more representative components.

This project was motivated by a quadriplegic child who lives in an orphanage and also has cerebral palsy which raises the level of complexity of the problem, so the solution makes it necessary to consider the user's problem that the solution is focused on implementing.

In initial tests it was found that, although the young user of the system has very noticeable problems with speaking, he recognizes words, which makes it easier to implement a control for a powered wheelchair with identification of the direction of the movement of the head. Further, a secondary control by voice command is provided, so that an attendant can control the wheelchair in case the user loses control of it and as a third control, the joystick which the wheelchair comes from the factory.

Furthermore, it will provide the wheelchair with an array of sensors to detect objects with which to collide.

It should be noted that it minimizes the problem of electrical power because the power is separated, the chair motors are powered by two batteries, and the circuitry and the computer running the software also have their own power supply.

2   State of the Art

There are some similar projects related to this project:

Tracking and measuring drivers' eyes published by David Tock and Ian Craw, describing a system of support for driving an automobile by means of the movement of the eyes.

Tracking moving heads–processed by Larry S. Shapiro, Michael Brady, and Andrew Zisserman. This work describes the design of computational algorithms to detect movement of the head using three-dimensional analysis of images.

Control of visually guided behaviors by Jana Kosecka, Ruzena Bajcsy, and Max Mintz. This includes/understands the design of a scheme of guidance for a robot from adjustments of infrared sensors that detect the shift of position of objects that comprise a scene and is analyzed based on the systems analysis of real world coordinates.

Active exploration of dynamic and static scenes written by David W. Murray, Ian D. Reid, Kevin J. Bradshaw, Phillip F. McLauchlan, Paul M. Sharkey, and Stuart M. Fairley. This describes a technique to recover in real time the trajectories of sprites which move on a plane in a scene. The detection of movement and its segmentation are made in each scene in real time, having compared the changes of scenes.

Magic Environment by Luis Figueiredo, Tiago Nunes, Filipe Caetano. With the developed application of environment control, the authors intend to provide the user with a simple and configurable tool according to his or her needs, involving low cost hardware that enables the control of any infrared device or any electric device connected to a radio frequency receiver. A function can be associated with each button in order to control an infrared device, an electric device, or both. The only thing that an eye gaze user will have to do is select the communication picture button whose function he or she intends to activate.

3   Methodology Used

3.1   System Description

The system is formed of hardware and software elements. The objective is to allow the user to control the wheelchair through visual information (face movements to indicate the next required movement), audio information (an audible order to indicate the next movement). Also, the wheelchair will detect front and rear obstacles and hardware and software elements are intrinsically and mutually connected. This section will summarizes these elements that will be described in detail in Sect. 4. (Consult Figs. 1 and 2).

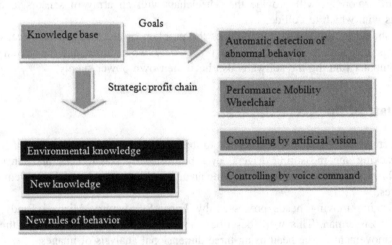

Fig. 1. General view of the system.

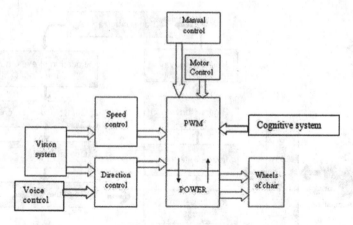

Fig. 2. Schematic view.

3.2   The Analysis and Recognition of the Face Image

The comprehensive structure of the proposed system and interaction with control software is illustrated in Fig. 1. The scene is analyzed and the face of the person is located; the person must be at a maximum distance of 20 cm from the camera with out physical contact with the device. It is located at a reference point called the centroid, which refers to the center between the eyebrows as the calculation of the distance between the eyes, nose, and mouth. In this last place the next waypoint marked as a detector is the mouth. Once located, the mouth is the comparison point between the previous and the current image identifying the movements and changes, as these are defined as optical flow, which indicate the direction towards which such movements are made: left, right, up, or down that will translate into motor commands sent to the wheelchair.

We use a webcam as the image acquisition device and the image quality is shown in Fig. 3 in a test pattern routine.

The image is captured by a webcam and sent to the capture buffer. The image is filtered and binarized, cleaned or the noise removed, and later sweeps the scene to locate the face. Once the face is located, it draws a box to locate the eyes, nose and mouth with a calculation to be described in another section to generate a centroid point which will be between the eyes. This is important because it allows us to detect the mouth in the analysis of the last two frames of the image to identify the sense in which we generate the displacement of the mouth in the optic flow module which will be sent to the cognitive module, which is responsible for storing data blocks related to the optical flow. These are sent to the command converter module which sends a command to the power module and this will activate the motor, thereby achieving wheelchair travel forward, to the left, right or backward. This is shown in Fig. 4.

3.3   Data Processing

Data processing in the vision system can be played from two perspectives [3] (Michael Seul, Lawrence O'Gorman, Michael J. Sammon, 2000):

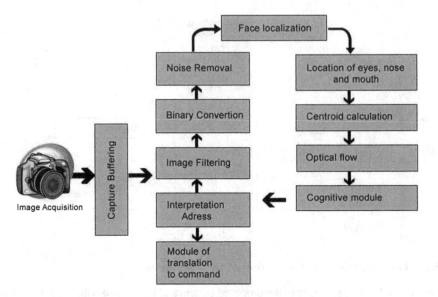

Fig. 3. Main scheme of vision system.

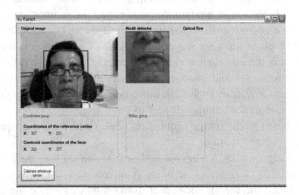

Fig. 4. Locating the face image.

1. Alterations in pixels of data on a global scale (individual)
2. Operations based in multiple locations (vicinity)

The generation of the pixels in a new image will be a function of either the value of each individual pixel location or the values of the pixels in the vicinity of a given pixel, as shown in Fig. 5.

This figure shows the individuality of a pixel which shows the representation of this in a picture. We can also see that the pixel vicinity can be 4 or 9 depending on use. Vicinity increases the number of neighbors [8].

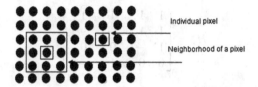

Fig. 5. Functions of point and vicinity.

3.4   Individual Operations (Convolution)

Individual operations involve the generation of a new modified image pixel value in a single location based on a global rule applied to each location of the original image. The process involves having the pixel value at a given location in the image, modifying it by a linear operation or movement, and placing the new pixel value in the corresponding location of the new image. The process is repeated for each and every one of the locations of the pixels in the original image.

One of the algorithms used in this project is the Haar transform, the simplest of the wavelet transforms. This transform cross-multiplies a function against the Haar wavelet with various shifts and stretches, in the same way that the Fourier transform cross-multiplies a function against a sine wave with two phases and many stretches [9].

The Haar transform is derived from the Haar matrix. An example of a 4 × 4 Haar transformation matrix is shown in Fig. 6.

$$H_4 = \frac{1}{\sqrt{4}} \begin{bmatrix} 1 & 1 & 1 & 1 \\ 1 & 1 & -1 & -1 \\ \sqrt{2} & -\sqrt{2} & 0 & 0 \\ 0 & 0 & \sqrt{2} & -\sqrt{2} \end{bmatrix} \tag{1}$$

Fig. 6. The Haar transform.

The Haar transform can be thought of as a sampling process in which rows of the transformation matrix act as samples of finer and finer resolution.

Haar matrix

The 2 × 2 Haar matrix that is associated with the Haar wavelet is

$$H_2 = \begin{bmatrix} 1 & 1 \\ 1 & -1 \end{bmatrix}. \tag{2}$$

Using the discrete wavelet transform, one can transform any sequence $(a_0, a_1, \ldots, a_{2n}, a_{2n+1})$ of even length into a sequesnce of two-component vectors $((a_0, a_1), \ldots, (a_{2n}, a_{2n+1}))$. If one right-multiplies each vector with the matrix H2, one gets the result $((s_0, d_0), \ldots, (s_n, d_n))$ of one stage of the fast Haar-wavelet transform. Usually one separates the sequences s and d and continues with transforming the sequence s.

If one has a sequence of length in a multiple of four, one can build blocks of 4 elements and transform them in a similar manner with the 4 × 4 Haar matrix

$$H_4 = \begin{bmatrix} 1 & 1 & 1 & 1 \\ 1 & 1 & -1 & -1 \\ 1 & -1 & 0 & 0 \\ 0 & 0 & 1 & -1 \end{bmatrix}, \tag{3}$$

which combines two stages of the fast Haar-wavelet transform.

Compare with a Walsh matrix, which is a non-localized 1/–1 matrix.

4 Optical Flow

Optical flow is the pattern of apparent motion of objects, surfaces, and edges in a visual scene caused by the relative motion between an observer (an eye or a camera) and the scene [4, 5]. The concept of optical flow was first studied in the 1940s and recently published by American psychologist James J. Gibson [6] as part of his theory of affordance. Optical flow techniques such as motion detection, object segmentation, time-to-collision, and focus of expansion calculations, motion compensated encoding, and stereo disparity measurement utilize this motion of the objects surfaces, and edges [7, 8].

4.1 Lucas Kanade Algorithm

The Lucas-Kanade method [9] assumes that the displacement of the image contents between two nearby instants (frames) is small and approximately constant within a vicinity of the point p under consideration. Thus the optical flow equation can be assumed to hold for all pixels within a window cantered at p. namely, the local image flow (velocity) vector (Vx, Vy) must satisfy

$$\begin{aligned} Ix(q1)Vx + Iy(q1)Vy &= -It(q1) \\ Ix(q2)Vx + Iy(q2)Vy &= -It(q2) \\ &\vdots \\ Ix(qn)Vx + Iy(qn)Vy &= -It(qn) \end{aligned} \tag{4}$$

where q1, q2,.., qn are the pixels inside the window, and Ix(qi), Iy(qi), It(qi) are the partial derivatives of the image I with respect to position x, y and time t, evaluated at the point qi and at the current time.

These equations can be written in matrix form Av = b, where

$$A = \begin{bmatrix} I_x(q_1) & I_y(q_1) \\ I_x(q_2) & I_y(q_2) \\ \vdots & \vdots \\ I_x(q_n) & I_y(q_n) \end{bmatrix}, \quad v = \begin{bmatrix} V_x \\ V_y \end{bmatrix}, \quad \text{and} \quad b = \begin{bmatrix} -I_t(q_1) \\ -I_t(q_2) \\ \vdots \\ -I_t(q_n) \end{bmatrix} \tag{5}$$

This system has more equations than unknowns and thus it is usually over-determined. The Lucas-Kanade method obtains a compromise solution by the least squares principle. Namely, it solves the 2×2 system

ATAv = ATb or

v = (ATA) − 1ATb

where AT is the transpose of matrix A. That is, it computes

$$\begin{bmatrix} V_x \\ V_y \end{bmatrix} = \begin{bmatrix} \sum_i I_x(q_i)^2 & \sum_i I_x(q_i)I_y(q_i) \\ \sum_i I_x(q_i)I_y(q_i) & \sum_i I_y(q_i)^2 \end{bmatrix}^{-1} \begin{bmatrix} -\sum_i I_x(q_i)I_t(q_i) \\ -\sum_i I_y(q_i)I_t(q_i) \end{bmatrix} \tag{6}$$

with the sums running from i = 1 to n.

The matrix ATA is often called the structure tensor of the image at the point p.

4.2 Canny Algorithm

This method was further refined by J. Canny in 1986 into what is now commonly called the Canny edge detector [10]. One of the differences between the Canny algorithm and the simpler, Laplace-based algorithm is that in the Cannny algorithm, the first derivatives are computed in x and y and then combined into four directional derivatives. The points where these directional derivatives are local maxima are then candidates for assembling into edges [9, 11].

Canny assumed a step edge subject to white Gaussian noise. The edge detector was assumed to be a convolution filter f which would smooth the noise and locate the edge. The problem is to identify the one filter that optimizes the three edge-detection criteria [8].

An edge in an image may point in a variety of directions, so the Canny algorithm uses four filters to detect horizontal, vertical and diagonal edges in the blurred image. The edge detection operator (Roberts, Prewitt, Sobel for example) returns a value for the first derivative in the horizontal direction (Gy) and the vertical direction (Gx). From this, the edge gradient and direction can be determined:

$$G = \sqrt{G_x^2 + G_y^2}$$

$$\Theta = \arctan\left(\frac{G_y}{G_x}\right) \tag{7}$$

The edge direction angle is rounded to one of four angles representing vertical, horizontal and the two diagonals (0, 45, 90 and 135 degrees for example).

5 Experimental Results

5.1 Image Processing

The system source code was developed in C # using open source tools of OpenCV. The main algorithms involve:

(1) Acquisition of the image using a Webcam.
(2) Conversion to grayscale.
(3) Binarization and filtering.
(4) Face Detection algorithm by HAAR.
(5) Calculation of centroid to locate points of interest: eyebrows, nose and mouth.
(6) Location of mouth.
(7) Identification of the movements of the face.
(8) Application of Optical Flow algorithm Lukas Kanade [12].
(9) Data Conversion motor direction commands to the wheelchair.

5.2   Stage Control

This project aims to develop computer algorithms to provide a sliding unit for quadriplegic people as a guide, by interpreting the movement of the face, finding the mouth, eyes, and nose using artificial vision techniques. It also includes the control stage engine displacement unit which interacts with a computer and in turn with humans in real time as shown in Fig. 7.

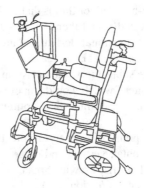

Fig. 7. Integrated system.

The system includes a software-hardware interface which enables or disables the drivers of the wheelchair, interacting with the cognitive module which makes decisions to guide the wheelchair to the place directed by the real-time system.

This system includes the vision module, software-hardware interface, and the control system. It includes the manufacture of a joystick for manual control of the wheelchair and the extended control that includes control of the wheelchair using movements locating the head position of the face.

The proposed project includes the modules shown in Fig. 8 below:

5.3   Artificial Vision System

This module contains the vision algorithms for real-time biometric control which will allow indication of the direction of travel of the wheelchair from the identification of the position of the face. Generated algorithms have been mounted in an embedded

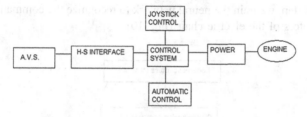

Fig. 8. Block diagram of control system.

system that contains a camera that sends sequences of frames that are processed in real time. Through its analysis, it sends a movement command to the wheelchair control module.

In principle, the system would define the direction of travel of the vehicle from the analysis of facial movement by placement of the user's mouth, as shown in Fig. 9a and b.

We performed a test for facial movements with duration of 50 min which consumed 41 % of the battery from the computer, the battery drain of the wheelchair was an available unit having three recharges ten days before the test, having a cumulative usage time of 4 h average use.

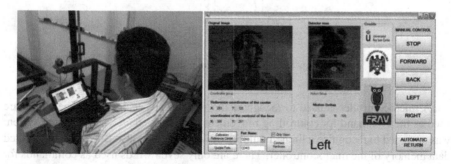

Fig. 9. (a) Integrated system, (b) Identifying the direction of the face.

The conclusions of the test are that the errors identified were presented when the user's head movement passed through the center or point calibration, this may cause the system to move the gauge from benchmark or detection centroid.

One way to solve this problem would be to place a neck support for the user of the chair towards it, keeping his head always located at the focus of the camera.

5.4   Voice Control

We create a knowledge base with reference standards, or phonemes storing commands for the electric chair control such as: forward, backward, left, right and stop.

In the next step, we train the neural network to recognize the commands in order to control the motors of the electric chair (Fig. 10).

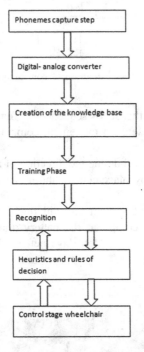

Fig. 10. Automatic recognition voice.

A microcontroller is used to recognize the word in a speech signal. The words are used as the command for controlling movement of a wheelchair. Therefore, the system was designed to recognize a limited number of words. This is also caused by the limited data memory of the microcontroller. There are only seven words used as commands for controlling movement of the wheelchair. They are stop, forward, backward, left, right, up, and down which is used to stop the wheelchair, to move it forward, backward, to turn it left, to turn it right, to increase the speed of the wheelchair, and to decrease the speed respectively.

The microcontroller where the speech recognition was implemented was on a HM2007 voice recognition chip.

Two approaches were implemented to perform the speech recognition. The first approach is Linear Predictive Coding (LPC) and Euclidean Squared Distance (ESD). LPC is used as the feature extraction method and ESD is used as the recognition method. This approach is based on the pattern recognition approach. The second approach applied in this system is Hidden Markov Model (HMM), which is one of the speech recognition approaches that is classified as the statistical pattern recognition. HMM is used as the recognition method.

6   Cognitive Module

The scope of the proposal includes a set of sensors which interact with the machine vision system to detect environmental conditions that allow the integrated device to provide a level of security.

Cognitive applications and human interfaces of the system and the application of cognitive skills are needed to develop awareness of the environmental situation monitored. Cognitive capabilities of the system will allow both the differential capacity, supervised and unsupervised (though always validated by a human operator), to learn from experience. Figure 11 presents a high-level architecture of the proposed system.

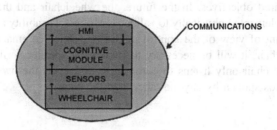

Fig. 11. Architecture of the cognitive module

The system will integrate an automatic "cognitive" to ensure a high level of security through the following capabilities in real time:

– Detection and evaluation of the environment surrounding the wheelchair.
– Intrusion detection (people, animals or moving objects) in the security area of the wheelchair.
– The detection of dangerous situations for the driver of the wheelchair, such as end of the road, dangerous edges, and objects prone to collision with the wheelchair.
– Automatic reports of the situation when the right set of people use predefined procedures based on a previously assigned risk level.

The proposal includes the development of a model for profiling risks that can be used to recognize abnormal behavior, as well as the means to identify the source of the security alert, tracking and back-tracking capabilities to establish the abnormal pattern, decision support mechanisms to establish an action plan, as well as the means to report to the operator and to distribute the information to the appropriate security personnel.

7   Conclusions

This paper proposes an application of a control device for driving the movement of disabled person using computer vision techniques in real time and using control techniques of speech recognition.

Having had the opportunity to break into two of the disciplines of artificial intelligence features such as computer vision and natural language processing, has given us the opportunity to be of use in linking intelligent control applications although the application has been focused on the control of an electric wheelchair.

The proposed robotic wheelchair controller assists the disabled patients or the elderly to reach the desired location targets with comfort and freedom from collision.

Driving voice-command guidance has been thoroughly tested on different proto-types and by different users, with highly satisfactory results and with only a short period of training required. The alternatives of guidance by head movements have also been tested on a wheelchair prototype, and although the results are rather satisfactory, at the present time tests are still being carried out in order to make both the commanding and training simpler.

Finally, based on various validations, the proposed robotic wheelchair controller achieves the desired objectives. In the future, the wheelchair and the proposed controller can be implemented physically to validate the clinical usability and performance.

From the point of view of the control module by voice command, for full functionality of the chair, it will be necessary to implement speaker verification systems. Thus, the control chair only listens to commands spoken by the owner of the chair, rejecting the words spoken by anyone other than the chair.

References

1. Koontz, A., Pearlman, J., Impink, B., Cooper, R., Wilkinson, M.: Wheelchairs (Chapter 8). In: Cooper, R.A., Ohnabe, H., Hobson, D. (eds.) An Introduction to Rehabilitation Engineering, pp. 129–155. Taylor & Francis, Boca Raton (2006)
2. Schneider, E., Bartl, K., Bardins, S., Dera, T., Boening, G., Brandt, T.: Eye movement driven head-mounted camera: it looks where the eyes look. In: Proceedings of the IEEE International Conference on Systems, Man and Cybernetics, Hawaii, USA, pp. 2437–2442 (2005)
3. Seul, M., O'Gorman, L., Sammon, M.J.: Practical Algorithms for Image Analysis. Cambridge University Press, Cambridge (2000)
4. Aires, K.R.T., Santana, A.M., Medeiros, A.A.D.: Optical flow using color information. In: SAC'08. ACM, New York (2008). ISBN 978-1-59593-753-7
5. John, D: Phenotypic versus Genotypic approaches to face recognition. The Computer Laboratory, University of Cambridge (1998)
6. Istance, H., Štěpánková, O., Bates, R.: Communication, environment and mobility control by Gaze. Prague. In: Istance, H., Štěpánková, O., Bates, R. (eds.) Proceedings of COGAIN 2008, September 2008. ISBN 978-80-01-04151-2
7. Burkhardt, H., Neumann, B. (eds.): ECCV 1998. LNCS, vol. 1407. Springer, Heidelberg (1998)
8. Parker, J.R.: Algorithms for Image Processing and Computer Vision. Wiley Publishing Inc, New York (2011)
9. Bradsky, G., Kabler, A.: Learning OpenCV. O'Reilly, Sebastopol (2008)
10. Pajarez Martinsanz, G., De la Cruz Garcia J.M.: Vision por Computador. Alfaomega Ra-Ma (2002)
11. Jain, R., Kasturi, R., Schunck, B.G.: Machine Vision. Mc Graw Hill, New York (1995)
12. Fleet, D.J., Weiss, Y.: Optical flow estimation. In: Paragios, N., Chen, Y., Faugeras, O. (eds.) Handbook of Mathematical Models in Computer Vision. Springer, New York (2006). ISBN 0387263713

Wireless Information Networks and Systems

Assessment of Multimedia Services QoS/QoE over LTE Networks

Gerardo Gómez[1]([envelope]), Esther de Torres[1], Javier Lorca[2], Raquel García[2], Quiliano Pérez[2], and Estefanía Arias[2]

[1] Communications Engineering Department,
University of Malaga, 29071 Malaga, Spain
{ggomez,etm}@ic.uma.es
[2] Telefonica I+D, 28006 Madrid, Spain
{jlh,rgp,qpt,eac}@tid.es
http://www.springer.com/lncs

Abstract. The evaluation of the Quality of Experience (QoE) for data services over wireless technologies is currently a hot topic. In this paper we present service performance evaluation method that is able to estimate both the Quality of Service (QoS) and QoE for different data services over cellular networks. This method is based on specific performance indicators that are evaluated at each layer of the terminal's protocol stack following a bottom-up process from the physical layer up to the application layer. Then, specific utility functions for each data service are used to map QoS into QoE in terms of Mean Opinion Score (MOS). Three different data services (web, YouTube and voice over IP) have been evaluated over a typical LTE network scenario. Performance results show that the MOS is largely affected by the radio level performance (error rate, throughput and delay), so proper protocols' configuration critical to achieve a desired service quality.

Keywords: Quality of Experience · MOS · Performance evaluation · Quality of Service

1 Introduction

Next generation mobile communication systems will support diverse types of services across different types of wired/wireless access technologies. The end-to-end Quality of Service (QoS) provision in such a heterogeneous scenario is one of the main topics in networks research nowadays.

The estimation of the service performance and Quality of Experience (QoE) perceived by the user plays a very important role in wireless networks, as it can be a very valuable input for network design, dimensioning, planning, optimization, configuration or upgrade. However, the assessment of the QoE requires analyzing the performance of the whole network (from user equipment to application server or remote user equipment), which includes the following aspects:

© Springer-Verlag Berlin Heidelberg 2014
M.S. Obaidat and J. Filipe (Eds.): ICETE 2012, CCIS 455, pp. 257–272, 2014.
DOI: 10.1007/978-3-662-44791-8_16

individual performance figures for each network element, interfaces and inter-actions between them, protocols behavior, and how the end-user perception is affected by network-related degradations. In addition, the end-user reacts in a different manner to degradations for different services, e.g., the end-user percep-tion is highly affected by the end-to-end delay in conversational services whereas it has a lower impact on background services such as files transfer.

A common issue from network operators' viewpoint is the process of assess-ing and managing the QoS of their new services as well as evaluating the quality experienced by the end user. Traditionally, network metrics like accessibility, retainability and quality were sufficient to evaluate the user experience for voice services. However, for data services, the correlation between network perfor-mance indicators and application performance indicators is not so straightfor-ward due to the following reasons: firstly, data systems have several protocol layers; and secondly, radio data bearers are typically shared among different ser-vices and applications. In these conditions, data service performance assessment is usually performed through active terminal monitoring over real networks. Obviously, if the operator wants to collect statistics on a reasonable number of terminals, applications and locations, this process is very expensive and time consuming.

In some cases, the service and/or specific network to be evaluated are not available or cannot be tested and configured easily. In other cases, the service or specific network is available, but it is needed to estimate their performance under specific configurations, scenarios or network conditions that cannot be easily reproduced. Additionally, the performance subjectively perceived by the end user, i.e. in terms of Mean Opinion Score (MOS), cannot be directly obtained based on network performance metrics. This is due to the behavior of different protocols and mechanisms along the network elements and their protocol stack, as well as the complex translation of QoS metrics to QoE perceived by the user, which is very service dependent. Typically, the QoE has been measured by performing subjective tests to a wide set of users in order to know their satisfaction degree through a MOS indicator, which can range from 1 (bad) to 5 (excellent); this type of methods is obviously costly and time-consuming for both the subscribers and the operator.

A particular application of this type of solution (i.e. mapping network into application performance indicators and MOS) for determining the quality of experience for on-line gaming traffic is described in [1], with the peculiarity of using a modeling unit to map game and transport level measurements into MOS values. However, this work is only applicable to online-gaming services as the model is just based on game and transport parameters, with no possibility of using performance indicators from lower layers (e.g. radio protocols in a 3G cellular network like MAC, RLC or PDCP). This means that the network element in charge of monitoring the game and transport performance parameters must have access to the application and transport levels.

Other works have focused on the design and/or configuration of lower lay-ers to optimize upper layers' performance [2–4], propose new radio resource management techniques which are adaptive to the QoS or QoE [5] or focus on particular algorithms to enhance objective quality evaluation of a specific service like voice [6]. However, none of the previous works provides a method to easily evaluate the application layer performance or the QoE for different packet data services over any network configuration.

In this paper we present an end-to-end evaluation method that is able to assess the QoS and QoE for different multimedia applications like video, voice over IP (VoIP) and web-browsing. The proposed framework provides a set of performance indicators like throughput, delay, and loss rate at different points of the whole protocol stack. This approach may be used for different purposes like e.g. estimation of the QoE for new data services over a specific wireless network (this process can help on the design and optimization of new services in order to improve the QoE). In addition, it provides a good understanding of how the application performance is affected by the end-to-end network behavior and a way to find the most critical layer in the protocol stack without the need of real networks monitoring.

The remainder of this paper is organized as follows. The proposed methodology to evaluate the QoS and QoE associated to any data service is described in Sect. 2. Section 3 presents a set of performance results for three different data services (web browsing, video YouTube and Skype-based VoIP) under different network and terminal configurations. Finally, some concluding comments are given in Sect. 4.

2   Quality Evaluation Methodology

Packet data services performance and end-user's experience can be characterized considering the cumulative performance degradation along the different network elements and protocol stacks plus the effect of the subjectivity and the perception of the end-user. Generally, such performance is assessed through indicators that are very service dependant, such as response time in web browsing or average throughput when downloading a file.

We propose a new methodology for estimating the QoS and QoE perceived by the user for different packet data services over wireless networks. The proposed methodology is based on network and protocol models, service-related parameters and utility functions that map QoS objective metrics into the subjective experienced quality as perceived by the end-user. Such approach allows easily predicting the performance of different services under specific wireless environments (GPRS, UMTS, LTE, etc.) without the need of running, capturing and analyzing the traffic generated from a real scenario. However, the models can be optionally fed from radio and network performance indicators obtained from different sources: (a) Network Operation and Support Subsystem (OSS), (b) real measurements obtained at the network or the terminal side (if available), or (c) simulation results. The method herein described is based on theoretical models, including the impact of the:

- network elements along the end-to-end path (e.g. user equipment, base station, gateways, server, etc.), protocols and interfaces;
- particular service under analysis, including aspects like content sizes (e.g. in a web browsing service: web page text size, number of embedded objects, object sizes), protocols and signaling, and specific application performance indicators (APIs);
- end-user perception, which includes how the subjective experienced quality is affected by APIs (e.g. initial delay, total response time) and perception (e.g. resolution).

2.1   Quality of Service Evaluation

The model herein proposed offers a methodology of analysis and evaluation of the QoS based on layers. Each layer is modeled and evaluated based on a set of performance indicators. The goal of the proposed methodology is to provide a performance indicator for different services based on the network performance indicators as well as on their own service parameters. The simulations focus on a hypothetical user which experiences a given set of MAC-level radio access performance parameters, from which the model is able to derive application-level QoS indicators after modeling all the intermediate layers. For the topic at hand, a general LTE network architecture has been considered (see Fig. 1). In the proposed methodology each layer is modeled and evaluated based on a set of performance indicators. Note that depending on the particular layer, the scope of each performance indicator may include the end-to-end network (for application, transport and network layers) or just the radio interface (for radio specific layers).

The modeling methodology follows a bottom-up approach, from the physical up to the application layer, taking into account the effects with a higher impact on the overall QoS. Therefore, layer i (L_i) provides a set of performance indicators to the layer above ($i + 1$), and successively, up to the application layer (see Fig. 1).

Without loss of generality, the following performance indicators are considered as the most relevant and are provided at each protocol layer:

- Transmission rate (R_{Li}): defines the amount of data correctly transferred at layer i in a given time (in bits per second). The transmission rate will vary at each layer due to different factors, such as protocol headers, packet loss rate, number of retransmissions, etc.
- Delay (D_{Li}): represents the average time (in seconds) that a data unit (at layer i) takes to be transported from peer to peer. The delay is a very important indicator for real-time services and also for those services that use reliable and congestion-aware protocols like Transmission Control Protocol (TCP).
- Loss rate (P_{Li}): represents the loss rate of data units at layer i. This loss rate may be due to errors at the radio interface or data losses at network queues. In general, the impact of data losses can be minimized by applying correction techniques and/or retransmissions at different levels. However, a high loss rate will produce a large number of retransmissions, which reduces the effective information transmission rate.

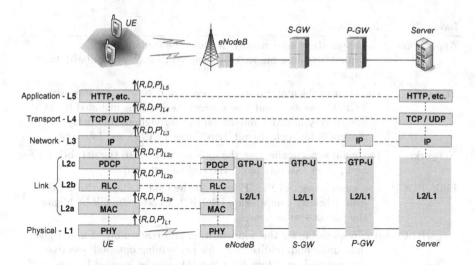

Fig. 1. Scenario and protocol stack under analysis.

The final model is composed of a set of deterministic equations starting from the RLC level up to the application level, where performance indicators at layer i are analytically derived as a function of the performance indicators at layer i-1. The specific equations that model each layer along the protocol stack is out of the scope of this paper, although further details can be found in a previous work from one of the authors [7] and a brief summary of the main aspects affecting the QoS at each layer is described in Table 1.

In this paper we use PHY/MAC link level simulations associated to a LTE network to obtain MAC level performance results under specific configuration (as described in Sect. 3). Such results at the MAC layer are then mapped into performance results at each layer above up to the application layer. Anyhow, MAC layer results from simulations could be replaced by network operator statistics generally available at their OSS database.

2.2 Quality of Experience Evaluation

The final goal of this end-to-end model is to evaluate the application level QoS, which will be later mapped into QoE (in terms of MOS value), as shown in Fig. 2. This last process is proposed to be performed by means of utility functions associated to each particular service. The goal of the utility functions is to map objective measurements (in terms of QoS) into subjective metrics (in terms of QoE perceived by the user).

This mapping process shall consider the specific characteristics of each data service:

– **Web Browsing:** the most important objective parameter to estimate the MOS in a web browsing session is the service response time D_{L5}. The utility

Table 1. Summary of the main aspects affecting the QoS.

Layer		Impact on QoS
Application		The application layer mainly includes the signaling or request/response messages associated to each particular data service
Transport		The most problematic transport protocol over wireless networks is TCP. Congestion and flow control mechanisms included by TCP have a very negative impact on the throughput and delay, especially for high Round Trip Times (RTTs) and loss rate
Network		The main aspects affecting the QoS are related to the network RTT and packet loss rate along the end-to-end path
Link	PDCP	The main impact of PDCP layer on the QoS is due to the use of robust header compression (ROHC), whose gain will be higher as the packet size decreases
	RLC	It is responsible for the segmentation and reassembly of upper layer data units and, additionally, for performing optional selective retransmissions. Thus, the error rate can be lowered by means of retransmissions at the expense of decreasing the throughput and increasing the average delay and jitter
	MAC	The MAC layer at the access node allocates channels to users on a subframe basis; that is, for each new subframe, the system assigns available physical channels to users according to a scheduling policy
Physical		Defines the physical channels structure through which the information will be transported

function that estimates the MOS as a function of D_{L5} (in seconds) is given by [8]:

$$MOS = 5 - \frac{578}{1 + \left(11.77 + \frac{22.61}{D_{L5}}\right)^2} \tag{1}$$

- **Video YouTube:** among the various works devoted to estimate the MOS for video services [9–11], the analysis presented by [9] provides a utility function for HTTP video streaming as a function of three application performance metrics: initial buffering time T_{init} (time elapsed until certain buffer occupancy threshold has been reached so the playback can start, measured in seconds), mean rebuffering time T_{rebuf} (average duration of a rebuffering event, measured in seconds) and re-buffering frequency f_{rebuf} (frequency of interruption events during the playback, measured in s^{-1}). The final MOS expression is given by:

$$MOS = 4.23 - 0.0672 T_{init} - 0.742 f_{rebuf} - 0.106 T_{rebuf} \tag{2}$$

Note that these application layer metrics (T_{init}, T_{rebuf}, f_{rebuf}) can be estimated (at the receiver) from performance indicators at lower layers (like the

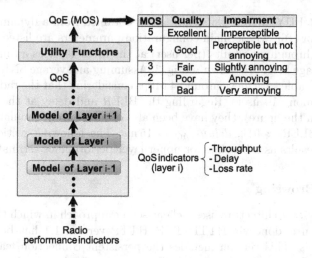

Fig. 2. Bottom-up approach to evaluate the QoE.

TCP throughput) provided by the end-to-end model (described in Sect. 2.1) as well as other configuration parameters like video coding rate or buffer size at the receiver.

– **Skype-Based VoIP:** in this case the MOS formula just maps the result given by an intermediate model into normalized MOS values. This intermediate model, known as the *E-model*, is specified in ITU-T G.107 [12] and it provides a numerical estimation $R \in [0, 100]$ of the voice quality from a set of network impairment factors related with the Signal to Noise Ratio (SNR) of the transmission channel, delay, distortions introduced by the coding/decoding algorithms, packet losses, etc. [13] provides a simplification of the E-model, particularizing it for VoIP communications, where the voice quality R is: $R = 94.2 - 0.024 \cdot d - 0.11 \cdot (d - 177.3) \cdot H(d - 177.3) - I_{e-eff} + A$ being d the end-to-end delay in milliseconds, I_{e-eff} the effective equipment impairment factor, $H(x)$ the unit step function, and A the correcting factor, which takes into account the environment where the communication takes place. Besides, ITU-T G.113 [14] provides a formula to translate the R value into MOS:

$$MOS = 1 + 0.035 \cdot R + R \cdot (R - 60) \cdot (100 - R) \cdot 7 \cdot 10^{-6} \qquad (3)$$

The impairment factors, in turn, depend on the specific codec used for the VoIP communication; the values of these factors for a number of codecs are tabulated in ITU-T G.113 [14] and its amendment 1 [15].

3 Performance Results

In this section, a set of performance figures are shown for web browsing, video YouTube and Skype-based VoIP over a LTE cellular network. Radio performance indicators (at PHY/MAC layers) have been obtained from a dynamic link level LTE simulator [16], whose main configuration parameters are listed in Table 2.

Average throughput results (per user) at the MAC layer as a function of the received average SNR are shown in Fig. 3. Assuming an average SNR of 20 dB, a user would be able to achieve around 4 Mbps considering that the radio resources are shared among 10 users. Regarding the BLER and delay at the MAC layer (not shown in the figure), they have been also obtained from simulations, whose values are: BLER $\approx$ 5 %, $delay_{MAC} \approx$ 15 ms. The following sections will use MAC layer results as a baseline for upper layer performance estimation.

3.1 Web Browsing

The Web service architecture uses a client-server approach in which the exchange of information is done via HTTP/TCP. HTTP version 1.1 has been assumed in the analysis. This version includes the persistent connection feature, which makes it possible to reuse the same TCP connection for downloading subsequent objects. The pipelining feature have been also assumed, thus allowing a number of object requests to be sent without waiting for the reception of the previous object. Figure 4 shows a performance analysis at each protocol layer of the web browsing service, starting from the MAC layer results described in previous section. A web page consisting of 100 kB text and 15 secondary objects whose individual average size is 20 kB has been considered (400 kB page size). It is assumed that all the objects and text are located in the same web server, so that all the data transfers will run on top of the same TCP connection. Regarding TCP configuration, the following settings have been used: maximum segment size MSS = 1460 bytes, initial congestion window W_{init} = 1 segment, advertised window from the receiver AWND = 32 kB, number of ACKs per transmitted segment b = 1, and SYN timeout T_s = 3 s. Results shown in Fig. 4 provide a detailed analysis of the performance achieved at each protocol layer (in terms of throughput, delay and loss rate). Let us analyze the performance in a bottom-up approach, starting from the MAC layer (obtained from simulations) up to the application:

- MAC error rate can be lowered by means of RLC level retransmissions (ARQ protocol). The graph shows the results for two different values of the maximum number of RLC retransmissions (N_{rtx}): 1 and 8. Results show that higher N_{rtx} values make it possible to reduce the error rate at the expense of decreasing the effective throughput and increasing the delay at RLC layer. However, when TCP is used at transport layer, it is highly recommended to decrease the error rate at lower layers so that end-to-end retransmissions are avoided.
- PDCP layer does not apply header compression in this scenario, so its impact on the performance indicators only comes from the PDCP header overhead.
- At the IP layer, the delay from the base station to the web server is assumed to be 5 ms whereas the packet loss rate is negligible compared to the radio interface (the main focus of the analysis is given to the impact of the radio interface on upper layers).

Table 2. PHY/MAC configuration parameters.

Parameter	Value
Carrier frequency	2 GHz
System bandwidth	20 MHz
Duplexing scheme	FDD
Resource block (RB) BW	180 KHz
Subcarriers per RB	12
Sub-frame duration	1 ms
Antenna configuration	1-layer MIMO 2x2
Precoding	LTE 4-words codebook
Power delay profile	Extended pedestrian A channel
UE speed	4 km/h
Channel estimation	Zero-Forcing
MIMO Detection	MMSE
Target BLER	10 %
Control channel overhead	From 1 to 3 OFDM symbols
Modulation / coding rate	16 CQI table (4bits)
Coding scheme	Turbo codes + SOVA
CQI &PMI delay	1 ms
CQI reporting period	1 ms
HARQ model	Incremental Redundancy + Chase Combining
Number of stop and wait processes	8
Scheduling method	Proportional Fair
Averaging window size	500 ms
Number of users	10
Source model	Full buffer

- TCP behavior is very sensitive to IP loss rate, as its congestion control protocol tries to adapt the instantaneous transmission rate to the network characteristics in order to provide reliability, i.e. loss rate zero. In that sense, if IP loss rate is minimized at the radio interface by means of a higher number of local retransmissions (e.g. $N_{rtx} = 8$), TCP will be able to achieve higher average sending rates; additionally, in that situation, average TCP delay is also reduced as the number of end-to-end TCP retransmissions is decreased.
- At application layer, HTTP delay results represent the complete click-to-download time of the whole web page, including: DNS query, TCP connection establishment, text and secondary objects request and download.

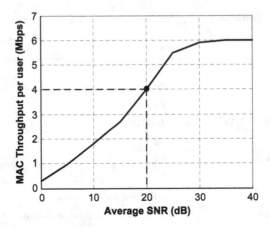

Fig. 3. Average throughput at the MAC layer vs SNR.

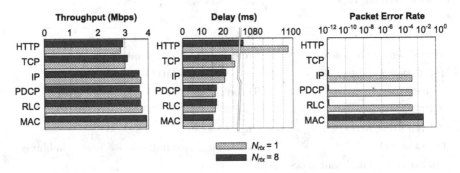

Fig. 4. Performance evaluation at each protocol layer (web browsing).

From previous analysis, it is important to highlight the impact of the loss rate on TCP performance. For that reason, the reliability of lower layers is an issue when the radio conditions are poor.

The results associated to the web page downloading time (D_{L5}) and MOS, computed from (1), for different MAC error rate values are shown in Fig. 5. Three different RLC configurations have been evaluated: Unacknowledged Mode (UM), which does not perform any retransmissions, and Acknowledged Mode (AM) with 1 and 8 as maximum number of retransmissions (N_{rtx}). As shown, the difference between RLC transmission modes increases for higher error rates, being AM with $N_{rtx} = 8$ the best performing configuration since it provides a MOS > 4 (Good) up to 20 % of MAC error rate.

Figure 6 shows the MOS results for different network RTTs and different number of secondary objects in the web page. Firstly, long RTTs lead to a worse TCP performance (in terms of throughput) as a consequence of its inherent congestion control mechanisms based on a transmission window (both during slow start and steady state phases). Such throughput reduction has a direct impact on

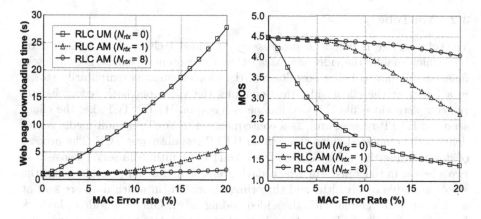

Fig. 5. Web page downloading time (left) and MOS (right).

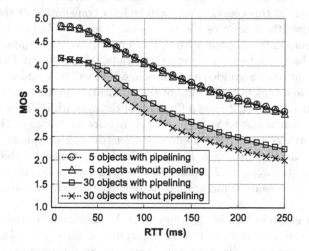

Fig. 6. MOS (web browsing) for different RTT.

the web page downloading time and MOS. Secondly, a higher number of objects in the web page (assuming equal sizes) leads to longer downloading times. This behavior may be enhanced by using pipelining feature, which provides higher gains as the number of objects is increased. Pipelining can be achieved to different extents depending on how the request-sending is scheduled on the client's browser. In the figure, a totally pipelined scenario is assumed, i.e. all the object requests are sent in parallel. If a lower number of parallel requests is configured at the browser, the results would be located between both curves (shadowed area in the graph). If we compare the results between 5 and 30 secondary objects (i.e. 200 kB and 700 kB including the text), it can be concluded that much shorter RTTs are required to keep the same MOS (e.g. 110 ms and 40 ms, respectively to achieve good performance: MOS = 4).

3.2 YouTube

YouTube service is based on progressive download technique, as explained by
[17], which enables the video playback before the content download is completely
finished. As data is being downloaded, the video content is temporarily stored
in a buffer at the client side, thus enabling the video playback before having
the complete video file. This technique is based on HTTP/TCP, i.e. the client
sends an HTTP request and, as a consequence, the YouTube multimedia server
delivers the requested video through an HTTP response over TCP. The process
of downloading the video content from YouTube multimedia server consists of
two phases: initial burst (in which data are sent as fast as possible using the
whole available bandwidth) and throttling algorithm (in which data are sent at
a constant rate related with the video coding rate). Once the video playback
has started (which implies that the buffer has certain data to be consumed), if a
network congestion episode takes place, the data that are not able to be delivered
(from the server) at this constant rate will be later transmitted at the maximum
available bandwidth as soon as the congestion is alleviated. This circumstance
could trigger a rebuffering event if the client buffer runs out of data. In this case
the video playback will be paused until the data buffer is restored. Otherwise, the
rebuffering event will be avoided and the congestion will be seamlessly elapsed to
the user. Figure 7 depicts the results of the application performance metrics for
YouTube (defined in Sect. 2.2) as a function of the network RTT for a particular
RLC transmission mode (AM with $N_{rtx} = 8$ retransmissions). The following
application settings have been used: video length = 250 s, client data buffer
necessary to start the playback $B_{full} = 32$ s, buffer threshold that triggers a
rebuffering event $B_{empty} = 2$ s, and video coding rate of 512 kbps. Regarding
TCP settings, the same configuration as defined for web browsing have been
considered.

The upper graph in Fig. 7 (left) represents the achievable average TCP goodput [18] for the specified TCP configuration, network RTT and loss rate
($\approx 2 \cdot 10^{-12}$ as shown in Fig. 4 for web browsing). So if the average TCP goodput is higher than the video coding rate (512 kbps), then no rebuffering events
will take place. As the RTT is increased, the TCP goodput is decreased until it
becomes lower than the video coding rate at certain RTT value; from this RTT
value and above, the parameters related to the rebuffering events (T_{rebuf} and
f_{rebuf}) are higher than zero (as shown in the lower graph). The initial buffering
time (T_{init}) is also increased for higher RTTs since lower TCP goodput values lead to longer delays to reach the minimum buffer occupancy (B_{full}). The
rebuffering time (T_{rebuf}) has the same behavior, although it is null as long as
TCP goodput is above the video coding rate (i.e. no rebufferings occur). Besides,
it can be seen that $T_{rebuf} < T_{init}$ for the same RTT value due to the following
reasons: (1) the amount of data needed to be filled (B_{full}) for the computation of T_{init} is greater than the amount of data ($B_{full} - B_{empty}$) required for
the computation T_{rebuf}; and (2) the computation of T_{init} assumes that TCP
data transfer start with a slow start phase whereas the computation of T_{rebuf}

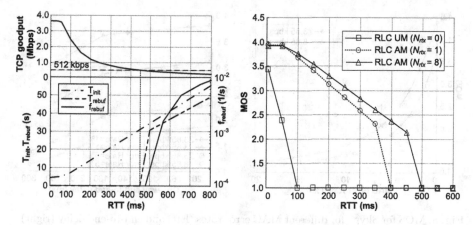

Fig. 7. Application Performance Metrics (left) and MOS results (right) for YouTube as a function of RTT (RLC AM, $N_{rtx}=8$).

considers the TCP steady state to be reached (being the TCP goodput higher in this second phase).

Figure 7 (right) shows the MOS results, from (2), for different RTTs and RLC transmission modes. As mentioned above, for low RTT values (which achieve TCP goodput values higher than the video coding rate), the initial buffering time is the only metric affecting the MOS (the higher the Tinit, the lower the MOS). When the rebuffering events start to take effect over the MOS, its value is rapidly decreased, since interruptions over the playback are annoying for the users. As shown in the results, MOS value could be improved by selecting a proper RLC transmission mode: MOS values are higher for RLC AM mode than for UM mode. It can also be seen that the minimum RTT value that triggers rebuffering events is higher when the AM mode is selected, and even further for a larger number of RLC retransmissions.

3.3   Skype

In this section, the performance of a Voice over IP (VoIP) service using Skype is analyzed. Skype usually relies on UDP as transport layer, unless the UDP communication is unfeasible, in which case Skype would fall back to TCP. We will focus on the usual Skype behavior over UDP. This section is focused on the E2E communication (i.e. between two Skype clients). The codec used by the software has a big impact on the service performance, being SILK the codec currently supported for E2E communications (since version 4.0). This codec has a set of coding rates from 6 kbps to 40 kbps. Due to the low data rates that a VoIP flow usually needs, throughput requirements at the network side are not usually an issue for Skype service. Instead, the network performance indicators mostly affecting the service quality are: loss rate and end-to-end delay.

The following MOS results have been obtained, from (3), for medium and low voice coding rates, considering an A factor value according to a cellular

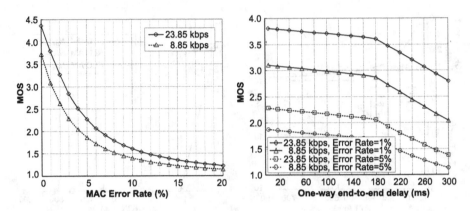

Fig. 8. MOS for Skype for different MAC error rates (left) and end-to-end delay (right).

communication inside a building (see Sect. 2.2). The impairment factor associated to this scenario has been obtained from ITU-T G.113 [14] for the selected voice codecs. Taking into account the characteristics of the VoIP traffic, a Robust Header Compression (RoHC) mechanism has been applied at the PDCP layer. In addition, the RLC UM mode has been selected in order to minimize the end-to-end delay, which is the application layer metric that mostly affects the MOS.

Figure 8 (left) shows the MOS results (for different voice coding rates) as a function of the MAC error rate at the radio interface. As the RLC UM mode has been assumed in this case, potential data errors have a very negative impact on the voice quality. Concretely, fair quality (MOS > 3) is achieved for MAC error rate below 2.5 % (for 23.85 kbps) and 1 % (for 8.85 kbps). In order to solve this problem, stricter target BLER values are recommended to be configured at the physical layer so that more robust coding schemes are applied.

Figure 8 (right) shows the MOS results as a function of the end-to-end UDP delay, which has a lower impact on the MOS (for the range of typical delay values) than the error rate. Furthermore, it can be observed that when using default MAC error rate results (5 %), MOS results are always poor (i.e. below 3) even for negligible end-to-end delays. If 1 % error rate is considered at the MAC layer, maximum end-to-end delays that makes it possible to obtain a fair quality are around 100 ms (for 8.85 kbps) and 270 ms (for 23.85 kbps).

4   Conclusions

This paper presents a QoS and QoE performance evaluation method for data services over cellular networks. In particular, a bottom-up performance analysis have been proposed for evaluating the application layer metrics whereas a set of service-specific utility functions have been used to estimate the MOS for web browsing, video YouTube and VoIP-based on Skype. The methodology here proposed makes it possible to identify the sources of performance degradation along different elements and protocols in addition to the end-users' experienced quality. Additionally, this approach provides the following advantages: (1) it makes it possible to predict the QoE when measurements in real network are not available; (2) it is applicable to any service and wireless network, simply by providing appropriate models; (3) services and networks under analysis do not necessarily require being up and running.

Performance results show that the MOS associated to a particular data service is largely affected by the radio level performance (error rate, throughput and delay), so proper protocols' configuration is a key issue to maximize the QoE. Performance results for web browsing show the great impact of the network loss rate on TCP performance, thus a proper configuration at the radio protocols is a key to improve the QoE; additionally, the network RTT is also a critical performance indicator, which subtracts ≈ 1 point from the MOS scale with each additional 100 ms. In the case of YouTube, results are very dependent on the video coding rate and network metrics (RTT and loss rate); our performance estimations show that fair quality (MOS > 3) can be obtained for RTTs below 200 ms when an RLC AM is configured. Finally, Skype results show the great influence of the voice coding rate and error rate on the MOS as the RLC UM is usually configured for VoIP. End-to-end delay also plays an important role in Skype performance, whose maximum admissible value depends on the coding rate and error rate in the network (as an example, a maximum delay of 100 ms is admissible for 8.85 kbps and 1 % MAC error rate).

Acknowledgements. This work has been partially supported by the Spanish Government and FEDER under project TEC2010-18451 and by the University of Malaga.

References

1. Gustafsson, J., Heikkila, G., Sandberg, P.: Method of determining Quality of Service for on-line gaming in a network. Patent Application, Publication number: US 2010/0273558 A1 (2010)
2. Luo, H., Ci, S., Wu, D., Wu, J., Tang, H.: Quality-driven cross-layer optimized video delivery over LTE. IEEE Commun. Mag. **48**(2), 102–109 (2010). doi:10.1109/MCOM.2010.5402671
3. De May, O., Schumacher, L., Dubois, X.: Optimum number of RLC retransmissions for best TCP performance in UTRAN. In: IEEE 16th International Symposium on Personal, Indoor and Mobile Radio Communications (PIMRC), pp.1545–1549 (2005). doi:10.1109/PIMRC.2005.1651703
4. Lassila, P., Kuusela, P.: Performance of TCP on low-bandwidth wireless links with delay spikes. Eur. Trans. Telecommun. **19**, 653–667 (2008). doi:10.1002/ett.1207
5. Piamrat, K., Singh, K.D., Ksentini, A., Viho, C., Bonnin, J.M.: QoE-aware scheduling for video-streaming in high speed downlink packet access. In: IEEE Wireless Communications and Networking Conference (WCNC) (2010). doi:10.1109/WCNC.2010.5506102
6. Lee, W., Lee, M., McGowan, J.: Enhancing objective evaluation of speech quality algorithm: current efforts, limitations and future directions. Eur. Trans. Telecommun. **20**, 594–603 (2009). doi:10.1002/ett.1334

7. Gómez, G., Poncela González, J., Aguayo-Torres, M.C., Entrambasaguas Muoz, J.T.: QoS modeling for end-to-end performance evaluation over networks with wireless access. EURASIP J. Wirel. Commun. Netw. **2010**, 17 (2010). doi:10.1155/2010/831707. Article ID 831707
8. Ameigeiras, P., Ramos-Munoz, J.J., Navarro-Ortiz, J., Mogensen, P., Lopez-Soler, J.M.: QoE oriented cross-layer design of a resource allocation algorithm in beyond 3G systems. Comput. Commun. **33**(5), 571–582 (2010). doi:10.1016/j.comcom.2009.10.016
9. Mok, R.K.P., Chan, E.W.W., Chang, R.K.C.: Measuring the Quality of Experience of HTTP video streaming. In: 12th IFIP/IEEE International Symposium on Integrated Network Management (IFIP/IEEE IM) (2011)
10. Porter, T., Peng, X.: An objective approach to measuring video playback quality in lossy networks using TCP. IEEE Commun. Lett. **15**(1), 76–78 (2011). doi:10.1109/LCOMM.2010.110310.101642
11. Ketykó, I., Moor, K., Pessemier, T., Verdejo, A., Vanhecke, K., Joseph, W., Martens, L., Marez, L.: QoE measurements of mobile YouTube video streaming. In: 3rd Workshop on Mobile Video Delivery (MoViD10) (2010). doi:10.1145/1878022.1878030
12. ITU-T recommendation G.107: The E-model, a computational model for use in transmission planning (2009)
13. Cole, R.G., Rosenbluth, J.H.: Voice over IP performance monitoring. ACM SIG-COMM Comput. Commun. Rev. **31**(2), 9–24 (2001). doi:10.1145/505666.505669
14. ITU-T recommendation G.113: General recommendations on the transmission quality for an entire international telephone connection (2007)
15. ITU-T amendment 1 for recommendation G.113: Amendment 1: revised appendix IV provisional planning values for the wideband equipment impairment factor and the wideband packet loss robustness factor (2009)
16. Gómez, G., Morales-Jiménez, D., Sánchez-Sánchez, J.J., Entrambasaguas, J.T.: A next generation wireless simulator based on MIMO-OFDM: LTE case study. EURASIP J. Wirel. Commun. Netw. **2010**, 1–15 (2010). doi:10.1155/2010/161642
17. Gill, P., Arlitt, M., Li, Z., Mahanti, A.: YouTube traffic characterization: a view from the edge. In: 7th ACM SIGCOMM Conference on Internet measurement (2007). doi:10.1145/1298306.1298310
18. Padhye, J., Firoiu, V., Towsley, D., Kurose, J.: Modeling TCP throughput: a simple model and its empirical validation. ACM SIGCOMM Comput. Commun. Rev. **28**(4), 303–314 (1998)

Using TETRA Technology for Improving
a Decentralized Positioning System
for Trains and Trams

Roberto Carballedo(✉), Pablo Fernández, Unai Hernández Jayo,
and Asier Perallos

Deusto Institute of Technology, University of Deusto,
Av. Universidades, 24, Bilbao, Spain
{roberto.carballedo,pablo.fernandez,
unai.hernandez,perallos}@deusto.es
http://www.deusto.es

Abstract. Today virtually all of our vehicles have GPS devices that provide highly accurate positioning. This type of positioning system has also come to public transportation such as trains and trams. These positioning systems represent a cost effective solution for railway companies operating in not evolved regions. The problem in these cases is that the routes of these trains pass through areas where coverage to calculate the position, or to send that position to the control center, is not sufficient. This paper focuses on the problem of the lack of coverage for the wireless transmission of positioning information. It discusses the feasibility of incorporating TETRA radio technology to increase the reliability of communications systems based on commonly mobile technologies (GPRS/3G). The main objective is to analyze the performance of TETRA technology for transmitting positioning information on a rail system. In the analysis, this technology is compared to alternatives based on GPRS and 3G.

Keywords: Wireless communications · Terrestrial trunked radio · Train positioning system · Railway industry

1 Introduction

Since the traffic police, through signs, and even the traffic lights, the regulation and management of vehicle traffic was conducted centrally. In all areas of transport, control centers are still responsible for managing the signaling elements. These control centers are still the cornerstone for the management and regulation of traffic. But in recent years, some intelligence has been transferred to vehicles. This is due to the evolution of wireless communication technologies in the last 20 years. This has caused vehicles to take a greater role in traffic regulation. This new vehicle management paradigm is called intelligent transportation systems [11]. One of the most important tasks that should incorporate ITS systems is the positioning of the vehicles. This is because the basis of the regulation of traffic and autonomous movement is based on the location occupied by each vehicle at all times. This paper presents the work in the railway sector to design and implement a train positioning system that is autonomous and

© Springer-Verlag Berlin Heidelberg 2014
M.S. Obaidat and J. Filipe (Eds.): ICETE 2012, CCIS 455, pp. 273–283, 2014.
DOI: 10.1007/978-3-662-44791-8_17

decentralized. With this new positioning system trains know their exact position at all times, and are able to transmit wirelessly to other trains and the control center. The paper has two aspects of great relevance. On one hand the autonomous positioning system, and secondly the communications architecture that enables a train to transmit its position using wireless technologies.

Train positioning systems are a key element to ensure the safety of the rail system. Most positioning systems are based on electronic devices that are installed on the tracks. These positioning systems are very robust and reliable, but when they stop working, security levels are significantly reduced. In these situations the position of trains is done manually by live-voice communication between drivers and control centers. For this reason, in recent years, there have been many initiatives to develop backup positioning systems, in which the train becomes the protagonist [1, 6]. These positioning systems calculate the position of the trains by means of different position sources: GPS, MEMS gyroscope, maps, ATP, odometer, etc. Once the position is calculated, it is sent to the control center using a wireless communications network, usually GPRS or 3G. The main limitations of these systems are the coverage of mobile communications (tunnels, overgrown or isolated areas, etc.), and the cost of the communications (usually communications network belongs to a private operator). To tackle this limitation, this paper presents the results of tests performed with a train positioning system in order to improve reliability. The tests were focused on evaluating the improvement achieved by incorporating the TETRA as a backup channel in situations where there is no GPRS/3G coverage.

The paper is organized in 5 sections: Sect. 2 details the potential of TETRA technology for transmitting position information in the railways. Section 3 explains the underlying details of the positioning system and communications architecture to send the position from the trains to the control center. Section 4 shows the results of the tests; and finally, the paper concludes with Sect. 5 which details the conclusions and future lines of work.

2 Terrestrial Trunked RAdio for Data Transmission

TETRA (TErrestrial Trunked RAdio) is the communications standard, defined in 1999 by the European Telecommunications Standards Institute, for a generation of digital radio products. The main characteristics of TETRA are:

- It is an open standard air interface so it provides real interoperability with other communication systems.
- High spectrum efficiency with short bandwidth that allows creating private workgroups of users and high quality of services, for example at voice communications.
- It can be used on all frequencies below 1000 MHz frequency bands for Private Mobile Radio (PMR) and public safety applications are assigned on a national basis.
- In the railway context it offers encrypted and high-quality communications in noisy environments and whatever the signal conditions, providing up to 28 Kbps bit rate.
- It is a mature technology with several suppliers of terminals.

At the beginning, TETRA was deployed to satisfy the needs of the Private Mobile Radio (PMR), Public Access Mobile Radio (PAMR), Land Mobile Radio (LMR) and the public applications for security and protection corps, guard coast, fire-fighter's services and ambulances. But later developments at the standard allowed Package Data Optimized (PDO) transmission mode and Short Data Services (SDS) that is comparable with the Short Data Message (SMS) of GSM.

Package Data Optimized is used by modern systems to transmit voice message, electronic mail, data interchange, and so on. In this regard, Enhanced-PDO known as DAWS (Digital Advanced Wireless Services) provides a 2Mbps bit rate to be used in combination with UMTS in high mobility scenarios as Railroad Digital Networks [10].

Short Data Services are transmitted over the control channel in a point-to-point or point-to-multipoint format without any reception acknowledgement. Two message formats are available:

- Status messages that only with 16 bits can represent 65,535 messages
- User messages that use a variable package size from 16 to 2,047 bits.

In Railroad Networks basic TETRA Short Data Service for polling and transmitting GPS position in Location Information Protocol (LIP) format can be easily used with a high reliability in different scenarios because SDS messages can be send between subscribers, between subscriber and dispatcher and subscriber and fixed host in the network. Moreover, SDS messages can be sending to individual subscribers or broadcasted on a number of base stations to all subscribers using that base station.

In the railroad applications TETRA works in PDO or SDS modes. These systems are connection oriented so the mobile node installed in the train requires first a connection to a specific Base Station to start the data transmission. As the train is a moving node, fast handover techniques are needed to maintain the node connected to the network. This process produces a delay in the communication that can break down the link and cause the failure of the data transmission [7]. Moreover, railway networks may also suffer from the following problems caused by the handover applied techniques:

- Handover to a wrong cell, which has the same main control channel frequency as a neighbour cell. The Mobile Station (MS) then loses all sensible neighbours as it gets information on neighbours to the "wrong" cell.
- Cell dragging by an MS, where frequency reuse is reduced by interference of the transmitting MS with others that would otherwise be out of range.

3   Positioning System Architecture

Our positioning system [3] is organized conceptually into two functional blocks: (1) the positioning system itself, and (2) communications system. The positioning system is responsible for calculating the position, while the communications system sends the position from the train to the control center. Then the particularities of each are described.

3.1   Positioning System

Train positioning system is primary based on GPS data. This system is able to generate train positioning information applying a logical approximation algorithm for matching railway lines and GPS coordinates [4]. To generate the most accurate positioning information, this system uses railway lines lengths (in kilometres) and traffic signals positions. Based on this information, the data extracted from the hardware (GPS, MEMS gyroscope, maps, ATP and odometer) and positioning algorithms, this system translates the train position to kilometric points. A kilometric point is a metric used by the railway company to tabulate the lines where its trains circulate.

Nowadays, GPS is a good and low cost positioning solution because of its reliability in railway environments [2]. But due to GPS inherent error (multipath, ionospheric propagation…), GPS only based systems have not enough accuracy. The reason is that besides the position of trains, it is also necessary to know the exact track each train takes. This is especially complex because the GPS positioning accuracy is around three meters, and the tracks are separated by less than 2 m. Therefore, in order to detect the exact track, 5 different position information sources area are used:

- *GPS Coordinates*. It provides absolute position data. The GPS chip is in the on board hardware. The development of the positioning system has been based on standards. Therefore, in the future, it would be possible to migrate to or integrate another navigation satellite system like Galileo.
- *MEMS Gyroscope*. It provides angular speed. It is also integrated in the on board hardware.
- *Maps*. They are organized as in [4, 8–10] with coordinates information. Combining maps information with gyroscope data, it is possible to identify the exact track. All the maps are stored in the internal memory of the positioning systems.
- *Automatic Train Protection (ATP) Data*. They are an additional part of signaling systems. There are different kinds of ATPs, but all of them need beacons located in the infrastructure. These beacons provide a unique ID and are used to correct possible gyroscope-based track detection mistakes. Relation between tracks and beacon ID is also stored in the memory of the positioning system.
- *Odometer*. It provides relative position data. It is a covered distance register. It has an accumulative error due to wheels wearing away and wheels slide. But it is very useful when there is no GPS coverage. In fact, for tracks without GPS coverage, only distance and speed data are used to determine the exact position of the trains.

3.2   Communications Architecture

Today, with the development of wireless communication technologies, it is possible to exchange information in the form of "data" between trains and applications deployed on the control centers. It is very common to deploy multiple communications devices on trains for the exchange of information with the control centre applications. These devices are usually dedicated to a specific task or application. On the other hand, by the fact of incorporating their own communication hardware, each application (on-board and terrestrial) must manage all issues related to media access, control, flow control and error handling coverage in mobile communications.

This approach to information exchange has a number of drawbacks or difficulties:

- High deployment cost, since each application has its own communications hardware.
- Communications hardware underutilization, since it is unusual for an application to transmit information continuously.
- Applications complexity, since they have to manage the main issues of wireless communication management.

The communications architecture proposes in our system is based on an evolution of a wireless communications architecture which allows a full-duplex transmission of information between trains and the control center [5]. This architecture has been implemented and deployed on a router manufactured by Hirschmann which meets the specifications of the railways. In addition to the router, the communication system integrates two GPRS/3G modems and a WiFi radio interface.

Each train rides two communication systems (one at each end of the train) that operate according to a master-slave scheme. The master system manages communications with the control center, and the slave monitors its behaviour. If an abnormality is detected, the slave takes the role of the master.

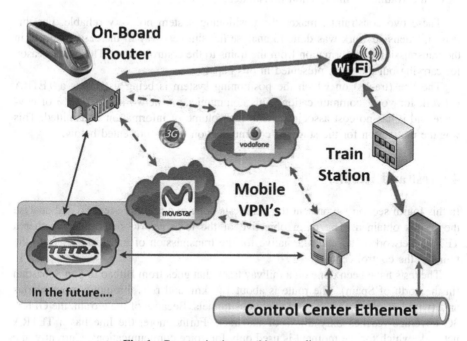

Fig. 1. Communications architecture diagram.

The communications system is programmed to switch between the two communication technologies (mobile or WiFi) based on a number of parameters, such as: priority, volume of information, coverage and communication cost. On one hand, WiFi technology is used for transmitting large volumes of information, such as logs of operation or CCTV images. Furthermore mobile technology is used for transmitting information of small size and high priority, such as the position of trains.

Figure 1 shows the communications architecture of the positioning system. As can be seen, the trains are connected to the control center via two GPRS/3G links (each with a different phone operator, to ensure maximum coverage and robustness) and a WiFi link (which is only active in the stations). All subnets (GPRS/3G and WiFi) are integrated into the Ethernet network of the control center by means of firewalls, ensuring the security of the information transmitted from the trains. Finally, the figure also illustrates the future integration of the TETRA network in the communications architecture.

Currently the communication system is operational, but mobile technology has the following limitations:

- There is only 80 % of coverage. This is because the railway line which is using the communications system goes through mountainous areas, with lots of vegetation, and also there are many tunnels.
- The transmission of information via the mobile network has a cost, which depends on the volume of information transmitted.

These two constraints, makes the positioning system not very reliable. For this reason, extensive work was done to analyse the simplest way to increase coverage in the transmission of information from the trains to the control center. This is the reason for carrying out the work presented in this paper.

The line (tracks) on which the positioning system is being used, has a TETRA network for voice communication. This communication network has 100 % of coverage and it has no cost associated with the volume of information transmitted. This was the motivation for the study of communication delays presented below.

4 Test and Results

In this fourth section we present the field tests done in a real life scenario and analyse the results obtained. The main objective of the tests was to determine whether a TETRA network is a valid alternative for the transmission of the positions from the trains to the control center.

The tests have been done on a railway track that goes from Bilbao to San Sebastian (in the north of Spain). The route is about 140 km. and runs through a mountainous area (with lots of vegetation) and numerous tunnels. Because of the terrain, the GPRS/3G coverage reaches only 80 % of the track. Furthermore, the line has a TETRA network, which for the moment is used only for voice communications. Currently, the communications architecture of the positioning system is based primarily on GPRS/3G communications. So, all the tests have been focused on comparing the performance of the current solution (GPRS/3G) with a new solution that integrates the transmission of the position through a TETRA network. To make this comparison three different scenarios have been defined, as detailed below:

In the first scenario (which corresponds to the current version of the positioning system), the position is transmitted via GPRS/3G technology. To establish communication, the mobile phone provider has defined a virtual private network (VPN) in its communications network. This VPN is integrated with the Ethernet network of the control center. Thus, train positions are transmitted securely from the trains to the control center (Fig. 2).

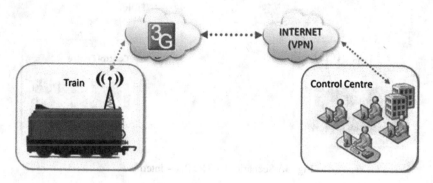

Fig. 2. Scenario 1 - 3G to Internet.

In the second scenario, both the train and the control center are equipped with a TETRA radio. Thus, all communications are made through the TETRA network, without the intervention of other networks. This second scenario analyses the performance of the communications between two TETRA radios. The main objective of this test scenario is to improve the positioning system in the future. In order to increase safety levels, the trains running on the same section, could exchange their positions. Thus, each train would know the location of nearby trains (like radar) (Fig. 3).

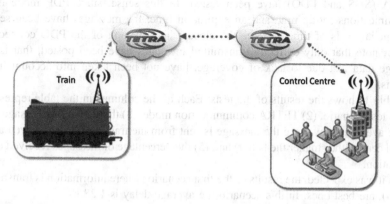

Fig. 3. Scenario 2 - TETRA to TETRA.

The third scenario is the one to be implemented in the final solution. A TETRA radio will be installed on the train. This radio transmits the position to the TETRA network. And finally, the position will reach the control center through a VPN that integrates the TETRA network and Ethernet network of the control center. Note the TETRA radios mentioned in the second and third scenarios are dedicated exclusively for the transmission of the position (Fig. 4).

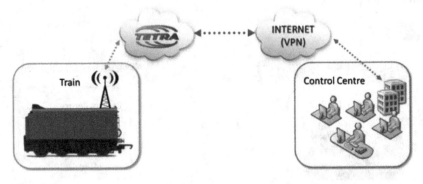

Fig. 4. Scenario 3 - TETRA - Internet.

With the three scenarios, several tests batteries have been developed. The tests have consisted of sending position messages between a train and the control center. The messages have a size of 572 bytes and their content describes the train itself, the position where the train is located and the quality (source) of the position. During testing, the time it takes to get messages from the train to the control center has been measured. To ensure that the time was correct, both the train positioning system as the control center have been synchronized using NTP client. All transmissions have been made through TCP sockets; so that the messages were received in the same order they were sent. To cover all the possibilities, the two modes of data transmission that offers TETRA (SDS and PDO) have been tested. In this sense, since PDP mode has a communications set-up time and an expiration time, the messages have been sent at different intervals of time to force the closure and opening of the PDO connection. Finally, note that only correctly transmitted messages have been posted, that is, the message data lost due to lack of coverage, have not been taken into account in the analysis.

Table 1 shows the results of the tests. Each of the columns in the table represents: (1) the test scenario, (2) TETRA communication mode, (3) the size of the message sent, (4) the average delay since the message is sent from the train until it is received at the control center (the smaller the better) and (5) the percentage of messages received at the destination.

As it was expected, the results of the first scenario (where information is transmitted via 3G), are best ones. In this scenario the average delay is 1.28 s.

Although this delay is the best, the problem of this scenario is that 20 % of messages are lost due to lack of coverage.

Table 1. Tests results.

Scenario	Mode	Msg. Size (bytes)	Received %	Delay (seconds)
Scenario 1 (3G --> VPN)	---	572	80,12%	1,279
Scenario 2 (Tetra --> Tetra)	PDP	572	99,75%	4,851
Scenario 2 (Tetra --> Tetra)	SDS	572	99,80%	4,040
Scenario 3 (Tetra --> VPN)	PDP	572	99,87%	3,510
Scenario 3 (Tetra --> VPN)	SDS	572	99,68%	4,090

In relation to the results obtained in the scenarios 2 and 3, which are those that use TETRA for transmitting position information; as can be observed the delays are between 3 and 5 s. The best results of TETRA technology are achieved in scenario 3 (using PDO). Furthermore, the worst results are obtained in stage 2 (also with PDO). Another important issue is the fact that in scenarios 2 and 3, no messages are lost. This is because the TETRA network has coverage of 100 %.

Although the delay of TETRA is 3 times the delay of GPRS/3G, this technology is still valid for our positioning system. The justifications for this statement are:

- The average speed of the trains using our positioning system is about 85 km/h. This implies that in 3 s, the train could move about 70 m.
- The most critical areas with regard to safety are the stations. The stations are usually located near urban centers. In these areas there is mobile phone coverage and so, GPRS/3G transmission can be used.

In conclusion, TETRA technology provides acceptable results despite having a delay higher than GPRS/3G. The main advantage of TETRA technology is that 100 % of messages sent, arrive at the destination. Therefore, these tests confirm that adding to our communications architecture, the possibility of transmitting information through a TETRA network, will make it more robust. Accordingly, this will increase the reliability of the positioning system proposed.

5 Conclusions and Future Work

This paper presents the results of the tests performed to increase the reliability of a train positioning system. The train positioning system tested uses different sources of information to calculate the position of the train: GPS, MEMS gyroscope, maps, ATP and odometer. After calculating the position, it is sent to the control center using a wireless communications architecture based on GPRS/3G. Due to the nature of the railway line, the coverage of the communications architecture only reaches 80 %. This implies that the positioning system is not very reliable. The railway line in which the positioning system is deployed has a TETRA communications network that is used for voice communications. The TETRA network has 100 % coverage. This network could be a good alternative for areas where there is no GPRS/3G coverage, but currently there are no studies to confirm this hypothesis.

The aim of the work done has been to confirm whether the TETRA network is a valid alternative to improve the reliability of the positioning system. For this, a series of tests were done. The tests have been focused on measuring the delay in sending the position from the trains to central control. It has also been counted the number of messages sent successfully.

The results of the tests confirmed the initial hypothesis. Therefore, TETRA technology is a good alternative to increase the coverage of the communications architecture.

In the future, efforts will focus on the integration of the TETRA network in the current communication system and the evolution of the communications architecture. To do this, we must modify both the hardware and software of the communications architecture. On the one hand, we must connect two new TETRA stations to the router that manages the communications between the train and the control center. On the other hand, we must define a scheme for selecting the right communications technology (GPRS/3G or TETRA) according to the existing coverage.

Another area of work will improve communication performance. The communications architecture is based on synchronous communications (using TCP sockets). This causes an overload both the process and the information transmitted. For that reason, we are currently redesigning communications to support asynchronous communication and other communication protocols that reduce the amount of information transmitted.

Acknowledgements. This work would not have been possible without the collaboration of EuskoTren (which is a railway company operating in the north of Spain), and without funding from the industry department of the Basque Government.

References

1. Bai-Gen, C., Yi, A., Guan-Wei, S., Jiang, L., Jian, W.: Application simulation research of Gaussian particle filtering in train integrated position system. In: Prof of IEEE International Conference on Service Operations, Logistics, and Informatics (SOLI), Beijing, China, pp. 527–531 (2011). ISBN: 978-1-4577-0573-1
2. Bertran, E., Delgado-Penin, J.A.: On the use of GPS receivers in railway environments. IEEE Trans. Veh. Technol. **53**(5), 1452–1460 (2004)
3. Carballedo, R., Salaberria, I., Perallos, A., Odriozola, I., Gutierrez, U.: A backup system based on a decentralized positioning system for managing the railway traffic in emergency situations. In: Proceedings of 13th International IEEE Conference on Intelligent Transportation Systems - On the Way to Intelligent Sustainable Mobility (ITSC), Madeira Island, Portugal, pp. 285–290 (2010). ISBN: 978-1-4244-7658-9
4. Guan-Wei, S., Bai-Gen, C., Jian, W., Jiang, L.: Research of train control system special database and position matching algorithm. In: Proceedings of the IEEE Intelligent Vehicles Symposium, Xian, China, pp. 1039–1044 (2009)
5. Gutiérrez,U., Salaberria, I., Perallos, A., Carballedo, R.: Towards a broadband communications manager to regulate 'train-to-earth' communications. In: Proceedings of the 15th IEEE Mediterranean Electrotechnical Conference (MELECON), Valletta, Malta, pp. 1600–1605 (2010). ISBN: 978-1-4244-5794-6

6. Jiang, L., Bai-Gen, C., Tao, T., Jian, W.: A CKF based GNSS/INS train integrated positioning method. In: Proceedings of International Conference on Mechatronics and Automation (ICMA), Xi'an, China, pp. 1686–1689 (2010). ISBN: 978-1-4244-5140-1

7. Palit, S.K., Bickerstaff, S., Langmaid, C.: Design of wireless communication sensing networks for tunnels, trains and building. Int. J. Smart Sens. Intell. Syst. 2(1), 118–134 (2009)

8. Saab, S.S.: A map mathing approach for train positioning part I: development and analysis. IEEE Trans. Veh. Technol. 49(2), 467–475 (2000)

9. Saab, S.S.: A map mathing approach for train positioning part II: application and experimentation. IEEE Trans. Veh. Technol. 49(2), 467–475 (2000)

10. Wenlong, X., Haige, X., Hongjie, Y.: TETRA protocol interfaces features and potential applications in railway. In: Proceedings of the IEEE Region 10 Conference on Computers, Communications, Control and Power Engineering (TENCON), Beijing, China, pp. 1086–1088 (2002). ISBN: 0-7803-7490-8

11. Papadimitratos, P., et al.: Vehicular communication systems: enabling technologies, applications, and future outlook on intelligent transportation. IEEE Commun. Mag. 47 (11), 84–95 (2009)

Knowledge Acquisition System based on JSON Schema for Electrophysiological Actuation

Nuno M.C. da Costa$^{(\boxtimes)}$, Tiago Araujo, Neuza Nunes, and Hugo Gamboa

CEFITEC, Departamento de Fsica, FCT,
Universidade Nova de Lisboa, Lisbon, Portugal
`nm.costa@campus.fct.unl.pt, taraujo87@gmail.com,`
`nnunes@plux.info`

Abstract. Data stored and transferred through the Internet increases every day. The problem with these data begins with the lack of structure, making information disperse, uncorrelated, non-transparent and difficult to access and share. The World Wide Web Consortium (W3C), proposed a solution for this problem, Semantic Web, promoting semantic structured data, like ontologies, enabling machines to perform more work involved in finding, combining, and acting upon information on the web. Using this to our advantage we created a Knowledge Acquisition System, written in JavaScript using JavaScript Object Notation (JSON) as the data structure and JSON Schema to define that structure, enabling new ways of acquiring and storing knowledge semantically structured. A novel Human Computer Interaction framework was developed based on this knowledge system, providing a Electrophysiological Actuation Mechanism. We tested this mechanism by controlling an electrostimulator.

Keywords: Knowledge Acquisition System · Human computer interaction · Ontology · Schema Language · Electrophysiological actuation mechanism · Electrostimulation · Multi-purpose software

1 Introduction

The easiness of access, storage, transmission of data and the exponential proliferation of internet users enclose new complexities: authentication; scalable configuration management; security; huge masses of high dimensional and often weakly structured data (the main problem addressed in this project). Structuring data pursued by Semantic Web leaves many opportunities open because there is always room for improving and to develop more adequate languages. Methods and approaches to solve the problem emerged from research in Human-Computer Interaction (HCI) [1], Information Retrieval (IR), Knowledge Discovery in Databases and Data Mining (KDD) [2]. These methods assist end users to identify, extract, visualize and understand useful information from data.

The establishment of ontologies is one of the methods to solve the problem, possible with Semantic Web, holding much promise in manipulating information in ways that are useful and meaningful to the human user. Ontologies are

© Springer-Verlag Berlin Heidelberg 2014
M.S. Obaidat and J. Filipe (Eds.): ICETE 2012, CCIS 455, pp. 284–302, 2014.
DOI: 10.1007/978-3-662-44791-8_18

collections of information with specific taxonomies and inference rules to define relations between terms. A taxonomy defines classes of objects and relations among them, and inference rules provide advanced ways of relating information by deduction. Classes, subclasses and relations among entities are a very powerful tool for Web use. We can express a large number of relations among entities by assigning properties to classes and allowing subclasses to inherit such properties. The structure and semantics provided by ontologies make it easier for an entrepreneur to provide a service, making its use completely transparent. Ontologies can enhance the functioning of the Web in many ways, like relating information on a Web page to the associated knowledge structures and inference rules, thus creating robust and clean applications [3].

Mechanisms to specify ontologies have spring in the late years, the Schema Language is one of them. Given the fact that Xtensible Markup Language (XML) allows users to add arbitrary structure to their documents, but lacks in describing the structures, Schema was developed as a notation for defining a set of XML trees [4]. From this concept, a set of specifications were established to create a Schema for JavaScript Object Notation (JSON), a self descriptive language for data storage and transmission, enabling the description of the data structure. A useful Schema notation must have some specific properties: identify most of the syntactic requirements that the documents in the user domain follow; allow efficient parsing; be readable to the user; concede limited transformations corresponding to the insertion of defaults; be modular and extensible to support evolving classes [5]. This language aids in the creation of structured data and automated tools to present the data in a human readable form, making easier the extraction and visualization of useful information from data. Therefore, in this field of structuring data, Schema largely supersedes Document type Definitions (DTDs) for markup language.

Using this mechanism for structuring the data a Human Computer Interaction was created with an innovative Knowledge Acquisition System to control the actuation of a Biosignals Acquisition System. One of the purposes, and as a practical example, is to control an electrostimulator enabling the user to create their own protocols, pursuing a non-specific software for Electrostimulation.

This field of medicine is known variously as Electrical Muscle Stimulation or Electromyostimulation (EMS), Neuromuscular Electrical Stimulation (NMES) and Functional Electrical Stimulation (FES) electromyostimulation, consisting in nerve manipulation through electrical pulses aiming muscular contraction or sensory response for distinct applications [6]. Nowadays, the applications can be divided in two main areas:

- **Electrotherapy:** Rehabilitation [7]; Spinal cord injury, stroke, sensory deficits, and neurological disorders (with Neural prostheses) [8]; Urinary incontinence [9]; Transcranial Electrical Stimulation (TES) as a method to elicit electronarcosis, electrosleep and electroanalgesia (for pain relief) [10,11]; Treatment of lower limbs venous insufficiency related symptoms in pregnant women [12]; electrostimulation of the acoustic nerve profoundly deaf patients

can, in the best cases, reach almost complete speech understanding without lip reading [13]; and many others.
- **Physical conditioning:** fitness; active recovery; optimizing physical performance by improvement of maximum strength of a muscle (muscular tonus) in less time [14–16].

Although Electrical Stimulation or Electrostimulation (ES) may hold much promise there are many technical challenges that need to be surpassed. Commercial software solutions for electrostimulators grow every day, but these are often limited by a variety of factors including cost, source code inaccessibility, hardware compatibility, and more [17,18]. Consequently, a strong tradition in scientific research is to write custom software routines. While superb for the specific tasks at hand, these custom solutions rarely offer the flexibility and extensibility needed for them to be transferable across platforms, hardware configurations, and experimental paradigms without significant modifications. Therefore, in present time, is needed software/hardware solutions providing a device with a multi-purpose platform (sport, therapy or investigation) and a dynamic software, which enables the user to create their own protocols [19,20]. To contribute in solving this necessity, we created a WEB based Human Computer Interaction (HCI) that allows the user to employ the software in different types of ES applications, pursuing a non-specific software.

This paper presents our work, a novel Knowledge Acquisition System based on JSON Schema with the specific focus on creating user interfaces to configure biosignals acquisition devices, and with this information control the actuation of that device. Ultimately, the software will pursue usability and acceptability, because ease of use affects the users performance and their satisfaction, while acceptably affects whether the product is used or not [21]. Our proposal defines Application Programming Interfaces (APIs) and low-level infrastructures to create a system for Electrophysiological Actuation, where the acquisition and actuation parameters are acquired from the user. At the core of this system is a JSON Schema enabling validation (data integrity), interaction (UI generation - forms and code) and documentation.

The next section describes the components of the Human Computer Interaction: data structure, used to construct the Knowledge Acquisition System; Configuration, methods provided to the user to compile electrical impulses in a session (configuration generated from the KAS); Control, the section of the software that actuates the sessions in the device.

2   Human Computer Interaction

The HCI is integrated in a WEB based software for biosignals acquisition and processing from PLUX - Wireless Biosignals, S.A., enabling the control of a generic device. In this way, actuation, acquisition and processing is possible in a closed-loop cycle [22].

Our main purpose is to provide the end user the liberty to create and sequentially compile electrical impulses. This enables the user to create actuation sessions for electrical devices. In our test to demonstrate the HCI feasibility, we wanted the user to configure an electrostimulator and design sessions to test different types of Electrostimulation protocols. With these purposes in mind we developed the KAS from the data structure and construct mechanisms to meet the HCI objectives. Through the next sections the core of the HCI (data structure) and the final product (HCI Interface) is depicted.

2.1 Data Structure

Chosing the data structure was the first step to build the KAS and from it the HCI. We chose JSON because it's a simple, lightweight and human readable text-data structure for information exchange. The approach for information exchange is simpler than XML, by the less verbose structure of the notation. Interpreting JSON is native in some languages with the existence of several support libraries that make JSON a platform independent language [23]. JSON structure is composed of name/value pairs separated by comma, curly brackets holds objects and square brackets holds arrays. Values can be numbers, strings, booleans, arrays, objects and null. In the example below is an object containing information of an address and phone number:

```
{"address":{
    "streetAddress": "21 2nd Street",
    "city":"New York"
 },
 "phoneNumber":
 [{
    "type":"home",
    "number":"212 555-1234"
 }]
}
```

Considering these features, JSON was selected as the data structure of this work, and is defined by JSON Schema.

A JSON Schema is a Media Type (standard draft of options) that specifies a JSON-based format to define the structure of JSON data, providing a contract (set of rules) required in a given application, and how to interact with the contract. Accordingly, JSON Schema specifies requirements for JSON properties and other property attributes with the following intentions:

– Validation (data integrity);
– Documentation;
– Interaction (UI generation - forms and code);
– Hyperlink Navigation.

JSON Schema is also a JSON with a compact implementation and can be used on the client and server. Specifications are organized in two parts [24]:

- **Core Schema Specification:** primary concerned with describing a JSON structure and specifying valid elements in the structure.
- **Hyper Schema Specification:** define elements in a structure that can be interpreted as hyperlinks, in others JSON documents and elements of interaction (This allows user agents to be able to successfully navigate JSON documents based on their Schemas).

Below is an example of a JSON Schema defining the structure for the JSON example showed before:

```
{"type":"object",
 "required":false,
 "properties":{
    "address": {
       "type":"object",
       "required":true,
       "properties":{
         "city": {
             "type":"string",
             "required":true
         },
         "streetAddress": {
             "type":"string",
             "required":true
         }
       }
    },
    "phoneNumber": {
        "type":"array",
        "required":false,
        "items":{
            "type":"object",
            "required":false,
            "properties":{
                "number": {
                   "type":"string",
                   "required":false
                },
                "type": {
                   "type":"string",
                   "required":false
                }
            }
        }
}}}}
```

As shown in the diagram, Fig. 1, JSON Schema allows the definition of ontologies and will be in the core of the program, enabling: **interaction**, Schema serves as blueprint to architect the necessary forms, with or without Graphical User Interfaces (GUI), and define the other editors for the Knowledge Acquisition System; **documentation**, APIs and low-level software infrastructures in JavaScript enable the transformation of the information acquired from the user in a JSON data structure defined by the Schemas, then the data (JSONs and Schemas) is stored in the server and retrieved to the client (JavaScript) through websockets (full-duplex communications channels over a single TCP connection); **validation**, JSON data can be imputed directly in a raw editor (an editor to acquire knowledge) by the end user. Nevertheless, the data is only stored if the structure agrees with the Schema.

With these structures the KAS becomes a powerful system: robust; error - free; with human readable data structures making visualization and extraction of information easier. From this powerful system we develop an interaction with the users to meet our objectives.

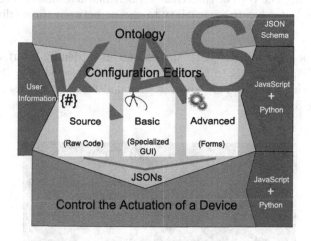

Fig. 1. Generic diagram showing the flow of information.

2.2   HCI Interface

In Biomedicine, the configuration of a device should only be performed by clinical experts, where they can adapt sessions to each patient. Overly complicated user interfaces and large, bulky designs can deter users from operate the device on a day to day basis. For example, home health care devices should have sessions previously programmed restricting the patient to only start or stop a session prepared for him, in this way the patient is not allowed to configure or change any parameter in the software.

Therefore, to economize time, simplify interfaces, automate the device actuation and separate our tool for experts and non-experts the software was divided in Configuration and Control. Configuration, where clinical experts can configure a device with sessions for each channel, and Control, where the user just need to choose the device and session previously configured (for patients use, only one device should be configured with the appropriate session), connect to the device, then if connected start the session. If for some reason, the session should not stop automatically (before the stop time is reached), the user can stop the session. Basically, as shown in Fig. 2, to control we need to configure the electrostimulator, and create temporal sessions, i.e. sequence of impulse modes, for each channel of that device. Consequently, the configuration is hierarchically structured in device, mode and session. In the control we only need to choose the device and connect to it, if connected chose the session to setup the hardware, then start the session. The stop can be manual or automatic (end of the session). This mechanism makes the control very simple.

Configuration. The core of the KAS is a Schema, and in the section Configuration the end user has the possibility to choose between three editors (like in Fig. 1):

– Basic Editor (Specialized GUI): simple and user-friendly interface with the minimum required fields to fill. The information is saved in a JSON format defined by the Schema. This editor is intended for the basic users. It can be seen in Fig. 3.

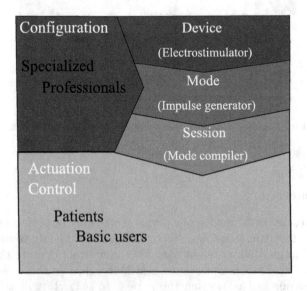

Fig. 2. Generic diagram of the HCI Interface.

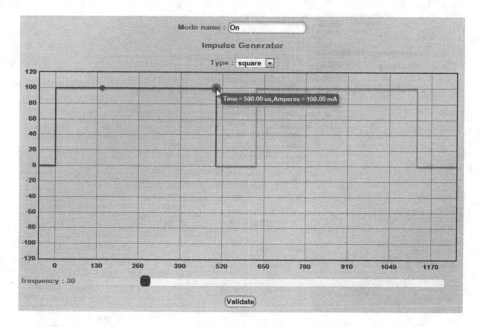

Fig. 3. Basic Editor. Configuration of the mode "On" for the electrostimulator.

- Advanced Editor: a form generated automatically from the Schema specifications, with the possibility of edition in GUI. Information is also saved in JSON format defined by the Schema. The most profitable editor because it shows directly how the information will be saved in the JSON. This way, users understand the architecture of the data. Figures 4 and 7 have the configuration of a device and a session, respectively, in the Advanced Editor.
- Source Editor: an editor to upload or create JSONs, where the user writes the JSON (like the JSONs exported in Fig. 5 or copy and paste the JSON in the editor. JSONs are valid and can be saved if they agree with JSON Schema, if not, reports with errors are generated. This Editor is intended for users with more knowledge of the data structure, or for the ones that just want to copy and paste information or upload.

Configuration is divided in three sections - Device, Mode and Session. In each one we can use the distinct editors to provide the required information to configure a certain device. Below we illustrate examples for the three sections by using the configuration of an electrostimulator.

Device. In the case of an electrostimulator, some specific options need to be satisfied. The specifications for the potentials and limits of ES is dependent of the application and the electrostimulator. The requisites of the electrostimulator we used for this project, are:

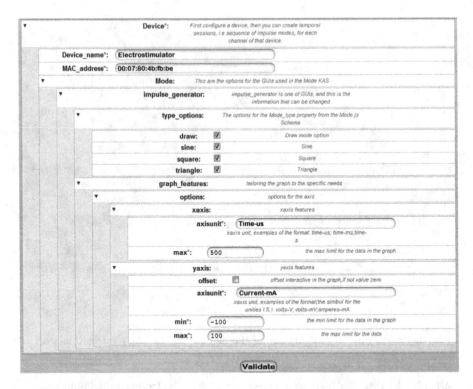

Fig. 4. Advanced Editor. Device Configuration for the electrostimulator used to test the software.

– MAC Address:
  00:07:80:4b:fb:be
– Pulse amplitude:
  0–100 mA (1 mA step)
– Pulse Width:
  0–500 µs (5 µs step)
– Pulse frequency:
  1–200 Hz (1 Hz step)
– Number of channels:
  2
– Number of modes:
  4
– Waveform type:
  Rectangular, triangular, sinusoidal, customized waveform (constant potential with no offset)

In this way, Fig. 4 represents the Device Configuration with the above requirements: device name, MAC Address and restrictions for the impulse generator in the Mode. The restrictions are for the type of impulse and graph options.

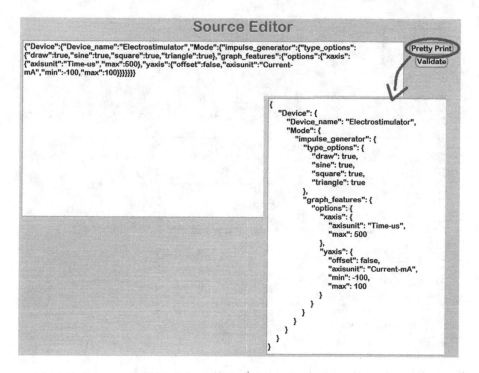

Fig. 5. Source Editor. Device Configuration.

In the graph options the user has the possibility to define: axis value and unit in the format "value-unit" (with unit in the international unit system), like in the example, the axis unit for xaxis is "Time-us" representing time in microseconds; data limits, max for the xaxis is 500 μs and for the yaxis max is 100 mA and min −100 mA; the offset, active or not.

Mode. After the specification of the device requisites the user can project a new mode for a specific device. The mode permits four types of impulse configuration: square, rectangular pulse that can be changed within the data limits; sine, sin pulse that can be changed within the data limits; triangle, triangular pulse that can be changed within the data limits; draw, a novel and innovative impulse generator. The user is also able to choose the frequency (impulse per second) by moving a slider.

In the three default types square, sine and triangle, the user have to click and pull the interactive points: square have two interactive points that can be moved along x an y axis within the data limits; sine also have two, one for the amplitude and other for the period; triangle have four with two points that just move along the x axis. Examples of the three types are shown in Fig. 6, each row represents an example of the respective impulse after moving the interactive

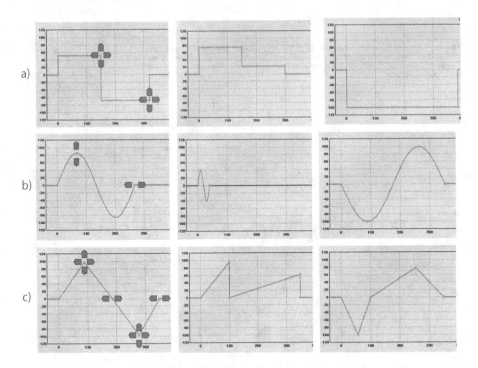

Fig. 6. Example of the default impulses with the restrictions specified in the Device Configuration: a) square, b) sine and c) triangle. The arrows mark the direction in which the interactive points can be moved. In each row are presented examples of the respective impulse after moving the interactive points.

points. These types allow the end user to create a lot of different impulses, but to be able of creating any type we had to devise a new form of impulse generation, the draw method.

In this new type, the user has the possibility to draw an impulse within the data limits, from this draw we retrieve 100 points that will be processed by an algorithm. The idea behind this algorithm it is to search within the 100 points that seem connected to each other, then propose a series of simple equations to describe the links. The best are selected, tweaked, and again tested against the data. Next, the algorithm repeats the cycle over and over, until it finds equations that have a good probability of modulate the data. Then, by choosing one of the equations, the user can see a graph with 100 points based in the equation and compare it to the drawing. If it fits the user objectives, save the equation, if not, the user can tweak the equation manually, and see the effects, or just save the 100 points from the draw. This algorithm will have large benefits when finished, because it provides a mechanism of storing the draw data mathematically structured, in this way, the user will have the possibility of re-editing the data by changing some parameters in the stored equations. So, instead of just providing

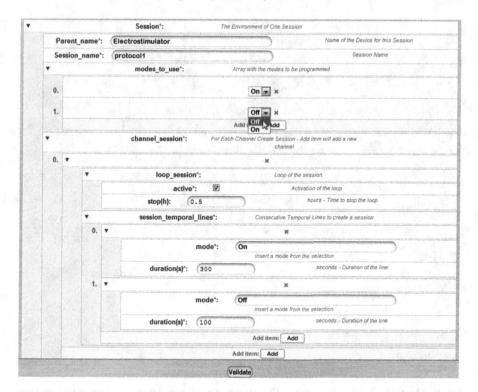

Fig. 7. Advanced Editor. Configuration of one channel session with the modes "On" and "Off".

a draw method to create impulses, an equation method is also available, with great relevance by simplifying the impulse generation when the impulse can be described by an equation and only few parameters need to be changed.

This algorithm is still in the initial stage and is based in the work of Schmidt and Lipson, the Eureqa, a highly praised symbolic regression program [25].

In Fig. 3 is possible to view an example of how a mode can be configured within the data limits for x axis 0–500 μs and for y axis −100–100 mA. The figure shows the creation of "On" mode for the electrostimulator, a rectangular pulse with 500 μs, amplitude 100 mA, and 20 Hz of pulse frequency, i.e. 20 pulses per second.

Session. The user can create a new session for a specific device. A session is a sequence of modes, and each channel of a device can have one session programmed. A device has a maximum number of programmable modes, but they can be repeated infinitely. This mechanism is very important to program stimulation protocols, automating the control. In our electrostimulator two channels can be programmed with four modes: first we define the modes that will be used,

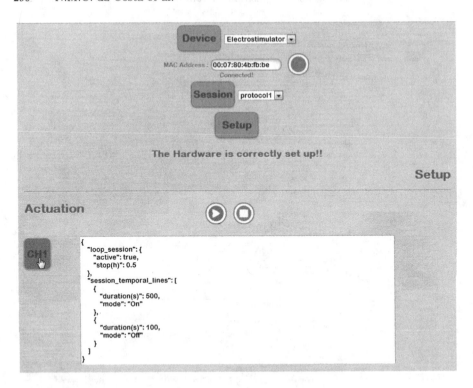

Fig. 8. Control environment using the electrostimulator defined in the configuration and session "protocol1".

then we add channel sessions. In each channel session we have to define if the session has loop, then we need to sequentially compile the modes. Figure 7 shows an example of session configuration. Primarily, the definition of the modes that will be used, four is the maximum that the hardware can memorize. Afterwards, the creation of a session for the channels required, in this case, only one channel is programmed with two modes: On, 300 s activated and, Off, during 100 s (Off is a pulse with 500 µs and amplitude 0 mA). This sequence is repeated during half an hour by activating the loop for that specific session.

Additionally, we remark that each configuration presented is not static, input new fields, re-edit or delete is fast and simple due to the hierarchical Knowledge Acquisition System implemented for the HCI. This Hierarchy was possible due to the JSON Schema, a very important mechanism to optimize and adapt quickly the software (especially the configuration). In appendix you can visualize the configuration environment (Figs. 9 and 10).

Control. Control, division for actuation and acquisition of biosignals. In here, the user first needs to choose the device, in our case the electrostimulator, and the session to program. When the device is ready, start/stop of the session is feasible. In the course of the session is possible to acquire real time biosignals and synchronize them with the session. Also, note that in the background, an API (Application Programming Interface) makes the bridge between the software and the hardware, parsing the high level programming language to machine language enabling the control of the hardware. Trough this API we set up the hardware with the necessary for the protocols of stimulation, and start/stop the session.

Figure 8 presents the Control environment, divided in Setup and Actuation. In the Setup the user picks one of the devices configured, connects using the MAC address defined in the Device Configuration, then chooses the session to program in the Hardware. If the hardware is correctly set up, start/stop and information of the session for each channel are available within the Actuation.

The control area will have many device sessions templates. Therefore, a quick approach by the user will enable the simple selection of a pre-defined session and start the actuation immediately.

3 Conclusions

A strong tradition in neurophysiology research (including electrostimulation) is to write custom software routines. These software are specific and rarely offer the flexibility and extensibility needed for them to be transferable across platforms, hardware configurations, and experimental paradigms without significant modifications. Also, most of the times these software have confuse, large and bulky interfaces that can deter users from using the software.

For these reasons, this project envisions a software with powerful capabilities. The most important parts are the infrastructures that conduct the flow of information between the Schema, the editors, the GUIs and finally the process of saving in JSON data. After the APIs and low-level infrastructures are programmed is easy and fast to create information editors with other Schemas, develop configuration interfaces for that editors and allow the engineering of new human computer interactions. This explains the impressive usability of this knowledge acquisition system. For this reason, is important to refute that the main mechanisms behind this software are JSON, the human-readable data structure, and JSON Schema that defines the structure of JSON, allowing interaction (creation of forms with specialized GUIs), documentation and validation, producing an error-free, semantically structured and human-readable knowledge acquisition system, contributing to the HCI system robustness.

We provide mechanisms to configure and control a device. Configuration, where clinical professionals can configure a device with sessions for each channel trough the compilation of electric impulses. Control, where the user just needs to choose the device and session (set up the device) then simply start/stop the session prepared in the configuration; the sequence of configuration (Device, Mode, Sessions), that supplies the user with a structured configuration; the tools in Mode, enabling the end user to shape the impulses at is own desire, and with the draw, plus equation algorithm, implemented the user will be able to produce any kind of impulse and store information mathematically structured; the compilation of modes in Session allowing the creation of temporal sessions for the actuation of an electrostimulator, i.e. permits to program stimulation protocols. Thus, creating a dynamic, flexible way of automate the actuation of stimuli.

Depending on the stakeholder the combination Configuration-Control will change. Configuration will be enabled, disabled or will have different levels of restrictions. In the Control area different devices and sessions will be programmed by default for a fast approach by the user (setup the device then start/stop the session). Ideally, the various envisioned users should be consulted on whether they would be interested to use such a software package and, if so, under what restrictions. Interviews or questionnaires will be suitable instruments for this. We hope this could be the foundation for building a business model and further develop ideas on how to penetrate the market.

We also provide a tool to generate dynamic configurations, that are fast and simple to re-edited. Therefore, if for example the configurations described in this article are not optimized to configure a specific electrostimulator we can easily optimized them.

This software, above all, pursues usability, for this reason, in future stages of the project, the following tasks will be conducted: user studies, extended unit tests, usability tests, and usability expert evaluation. Also, the draw algorithm, to sketch any type of wave then modulate it with mathematical formulas, needs to be further developed to make the software even more dynamic and extensible.

With this powerful tool we provide a user-friendly software solution with a multi-purpose platform for sport, therapy and research.

Acknowledgements. I thank the co-authors for helping when was needed.

Appendix

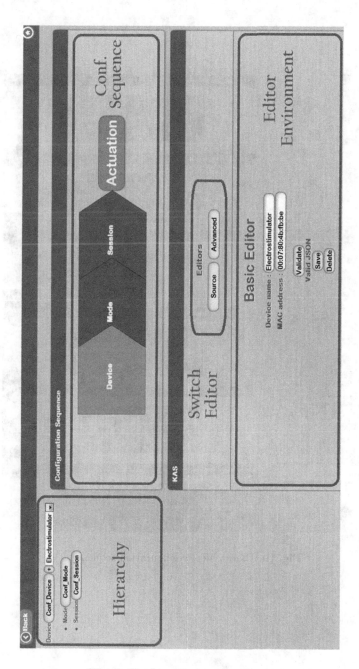

Fig. 9. Configuration environment.

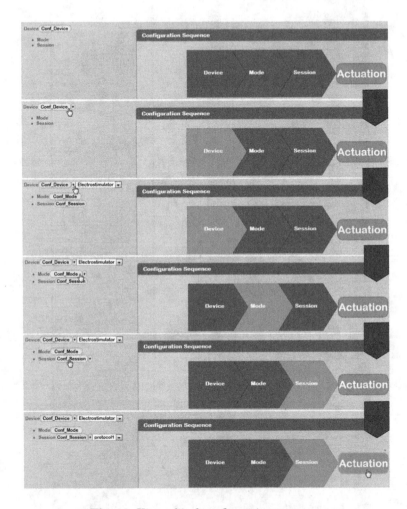

Fig. 10. Hierarchical configuration sequence.

References

1. Prabhu, P.: Handbook of Human-Computer Interaction. North Holland, Amsterdam (1997)
2. Fayyad, U., Piatetsky-Shapiro, G., Smyth, P.: The kDD process for extracting useful knowledge from volumes of data. Commun. ACM **39**, 27–34 (1996)
3. Berners-Lee, T., Hendler, J., Lassila, O.: The semantic web. Sci. Am. Mag. **284**(5), 34–43 (2001)
4. Thompson, H., et al.: XML schema. W3C working draft, May 2001 (2000)
5. Klarlund, N., Møller, A., Schwartzbach, M.: DSD: a schema language for xml. In: Proceedings of the Third Workshop on Formal Methods in Software Practice, pp. 101–111. ACM (2000)
6. Malmivuo, J., Plonsey, R.: Bioelectromagnetism, vol. 34. Peter Peregrinus Ltd, London (1996)
7. von Lewinski, F., Hofer, S., Kaus, J., Merboldt, K., Rothkegel, H., Schweizer, R., Liebetanz, D., Frahm, J., Paulus, W.: Efficacy of EMG-triggered electrical arm stimulation in chronic hemiparetic stroke patients. Restor. Neurol. Neurosci. **27**, 189–197 (2009)
8. Cogan, S.: Neural stimulation and recording electrodes. Ann. Rev. Biomed. Eng. **10**, 275–309 (2008)
9. Perrigot, M., Pichon, B., Peskine, A., Vassilev, K.: Électrostimulation et rééducation périnéale de lincontinence urinaire et des troubles mictionnels non neurologiques. Annales de réadaptation et de médecine physique **51**, 479–490 (2008). Elsevier
10. Lebedev, V., Malygin, A., Kovalevski, A., Rychkova, S., Sisoev, V., Kropotov, S., Krupitski, E., Gerasimova, L., Glukhov, D., Kozlowski, G.: Devices for noninvasive transcranial electrostimulation of the brain endorphinergic system: application for improvement of human psycho-physiological status. Artif. organs **26**, 248–251 (2002)
11. Mayor, D., Micozzi, M.: Energy medicine east and west: a natural history of qi (paperback). Recherche **67**, 02 (2011)
12. Le Tohic, A., Bastian, H., Pujo, M., Beslot, P., Mollard, R., Madelenat, P.: Effets de l'électrostimulation par veinoplus® sur les troubles circulatoires des membres inférieurs chez la femme enceinte. étude préliminaire. Gynécologie Obstétrique & Fertilité **37**, 18–24 (2009)
13. Motz, H., Rattay, F.: A study of the application of the Hodgkin-Huxley and the Frankenhaeuser-Huxley model for electrostimulation of the acoustic nerve. Neuroscience **18**, 699–712 (1986)
14. Siff, M.: Applications of electrostimulation in physical conditioning: a review. J. Strength Cond. Res. **4**, 20 (1990)
15. Marqueste, T., Messan, F., Hug, F., Laurin, J., Dousset, E., Grelot, L., Decherchi, P.: Effect of repetitive biphasic muscle electrostimulation training on vertical jump performances in female volleyball players. Int. J. Sport Health Sci. **8**, 50–55 (2010)
16. Brocherie, F., Babault, N., Cometti, G., Maffiuletti, N., Chatard, J.: Electrostimulation training effects on the physical performance of ice hockey players. Med. Sci. Sports Exerc. **37**, 455 (2005)
17. Breen, P., Corley, G., O'Keeffe, D., Conway, C., ÓLaighin, G.: A programmable and portable NMES device for drop foot correction and blood flow assist applications. Med. Eng. Phys. **31**, 400–408 (2009)

18. Keller, T., Popovic, M., Pappas, I., Müller, P.: Transcutaneous functional electrical stimulator compex motion. Artif. Organs **26**, 219–223 (2002)
19. Suter, B.A., O'Connor, T., Iyer, V., Petreanu, L.T., Hooks, B.M., Kiritani, T., Svoboda, K., Shepherd, G.M.G.: Ephus: multipurpose data acquisition software for neuroscience experiments. Front. Neural Circ. **4**, 100 (2010)
20. Prochazka, A., Gauthier, M., Wieler, M., Kenwell, Z.: The bionic glove: an electrical stimulator garment that provides controlled grasp and hand opening in quadriplegia. Arch. Phys. Med. Rehabil. **78**, 608–614 (1997)
21. Holzinger, A., Leitner, H.: Lessons from real-life usability engineering in hospital: from software usability to total workplace usability. In: Holzinger, A., Weidmann, K.-H. (eds.) Empowering Software Quality: How Can Usability Engineering Reach these Goals, pp. 153–160. Austrian Computer Society, Vienna (2005)
22. Broderick, B., Breen, P., ÓLaighin, G.: Electronic stimulators for surface neural prosthesis. J. Autom. Control **18**, 25–33 (2008)
23. Crockford, D.: The application/json media type for javascript object notation (JSON) (2006)
24. Zyp, K.: A JSON media type for describing the structure and meaning of JSON documents (2011)
25. Stoutemyer, D.: Can the Eureqa symbolic regression program, computer algebra and numerical analysis help each other? Arxiv preprint arXiv:1203.1023 (2012)

Author Index